Trade Unions and the Coming of Democracy in Africa

Edited by Jon Kraus

palgrave
macmillan

First published in 2007 by
PALGRAVE MACMILLAN™
175 Fifth Avenue, New York, N.Y. 10010 and
Houndmills, Basingstoke, Hampshire, England RG21 6XS.
Companies and representatives throughout the world.

PALGRAVE MACMILLAN is the global academic imprint of the Palgrave
Macmillan division of St. Martin's Press, LLC, and of Palgrave Macmillan Ltd.
Macmillan® is a registered trademark in the United States, United Kingdom, and other
countries. Palgrave is a registered trademark in the European Union and other countries.

ISBN-13: 978-0-230-60061-4
ISBN-10: 0-230-60061-1

Library of Congress Cataloging-in-Publication Data is available from the Library of
Congress.

A catalogue record of the book is available from the British Library.

Design by Scribe Inc.

First edition: December 2007

10 9 8 7 6 5 4 3 2 1

Printed in the United States of America.

Contents

Illustrations

Preface

This study was animated by the strikes and demonstrations that broke out all over Africa in 1989–91 and after, as workers and unions overwhelmed the barriers of authoritarian rule and repression to present demands for workers' rights and democratic political life. Trade unions had done this intermittently in individual African countries from the 1960s to the 1980s. But never had they done so in such numbers, in so many African countries, and with such a dramatic effect on the birth or the rebirth of democracy in public life. It was, observers felt, a genuinely glorious time for Africa, which had been visited with profound economic malaise and depressions in the 1980s as well as burdened with the mean dead hands of authoritarian rulers, the brutal and the less brutal alike. Such authoritarian rule, justified in various tortured ways by actors inside and outside Africa, stifled an incredible vibrancy in African public life by a wide range of social groups, a vibrancy that has existed at many times in countless African countries.

While large numbers of scholars have researched ethnic groups, women's groups, students, market women, and many local social groups, remarkably few African and Africanist scholars have studied trade union movements in the 1990s and 2000s. The number is fewer, for instance, than in the 1960s and 1970s, perhaps because the Marxist and non-Marxist Left was far more vigorous at that time in academic life. I have still been surprised by the low levels of attention by scholars to the parts played by trade unions and workers in the struggles for democracy.

When I cast about for scholars working on trade union movements in Africa, I was happy to find those who have joined me in this effort. No less than three of them had recently completed PhD theses on labor movements in African countries. Geoff Bergen wrote on Senegal, Gretchen Bauer on Namibia, and Emmanuel Akwetey on Zambia and Ghana. Robert Charlick, who had worked extensively on democratization and civil society in Niger and in French-speaking Africa, undertook to write on Niger unions. Richard Saunders was working with the Zimbabwe union movement as well as other civics in Zimbabwe when I met him by chance at a conference in Canada. I had (unknowingly) reviewed for publication his PhD thesis on communications in Zimbabwe a year earlier. William Freund, a well-known specialist on African labor and South Africa in particular, consented to contribute a South African chapter. The chapter written on Nigeria's vibrant trade union movement was ultimately unsuitable for the book and had to be dropped, but my introduction and conclusion include information on Nigeria's labor movement in order to include it among our sample.

First and foremost I have to thank this handful of scholars in joining me in this enterprise and then persisting when I allowed the project to lapse as I became absorbed in two other research/writing obligations. When I returned to complete this project after several years, all of my contributors, without angry words or reproach, which would have been entirely justified, graciously revised their chapters, sometimes substantially. Their scholarly research adds greatly to our knowledge of trade union movements in democratization and made it possible for me to develop some generalizations in the conclusion. I am deeply indebted to them.

I thank all those who have read this manuscript in whole or in part and provided me with critical guidance and ways of improving it. Those who provided a critical reading of the introduction some years ago include Richard Sandbrook of the University of Toronto; Bob Charlick of Cleveland State; Nick van de Walle, then at Michigan State; James Hurtgen, a colleague at SUNY/Fredonia; and Roger Southall, then a journal editor in South Africa, who gave me important ideas for streamlining and cutting. I elicited readings of the conclusion from Bob Charlick at Cleveland State, Richard Sandbrook at the University of Toronto, and Richard Saunders, at York University. The latter two made detailed comments regarding areas that could be improved, for which I am deeply appreciative. Roger Southall read the entire manuscript and made valuable suggestions for changes.

I am indebted intellectually to the small community of those who, over the years, have devoted their efforts to the study of trade unions in Africa and elsewhere and the debates on trade unions and democratization. With some I have exchanged ideas at conferences and notable colloquia on trade union movements and strikes. My immense debts to them are indicated by the reference lists in my chapters. I have communicated with some of them on and off over the years, exchanging information and drafts of writings. These include Peter Waterman, Tayo Fashoyin, Richard Sandbrook, Richard Jeffries, Jeff Crisp, and Joseph Scalfani, among others. Scholars shared information through a now- vanished Internet labor list in the early and mid-1990s. And in the 1980s we benefited from Peter Waterman's creation, writing, and distribution of the *Newsletter of International Labor Studies* from the Institute of Social Studies in The Hague, which kept our minds focused.

I could not have produced this work on Ghanaian and other unions without the cooperation, interest, and tolerance of several generations of Ghanaian trade union- ists and a smaller number of Nigerian union leaders. The Ghanaian trade unionists understood that my interest in their unions was genuine. Many met with me year after year, enduring my many questions and frequent requests for various internal union documents and reports. They often permitted me to pursue highly intrusive questions about union history, affairs, and conflicts, and they were usually very frank in response. They have trusted me to use their verbal information and internal doc- uments in a worthy way, a trust I hope that I have fulfilled. It is an indication of the open, democratic spirit of Ghana's unions that only a couple of the seventeen national unions regarded their affairs as private and not to be shared with researchers and the public.

I wish to thank the following individuals within Ghana's Trade Union Congress (TUC), its national federation: Benjamin Bentum, its secretary-general, or SG in Ghanaian parlance, during 1966–72 for opening wide the union files; Augustus K. Yankey, a brave and unassuming SG during the hard, intimidating years of 1983–92, when authoritarian rule was resisted, and who became a friend who shared his knowledge with me readily; Christian Appiah-Agyei, SG during 1993–2000; and Kojo Adu-Amankwah, SG since 2000, who readily made documents about the TUC's internal life available to me. Jonathan O. Abidi, Yankey's personal assistant over many years, was a valuable source about the internal dynamics of intra-union relationships. Ben Yinsob, Adu-Amankwah's administrative assistant, frequently extended himself to assist me in securing information not easily accessible. He also frankly discussed the quality of union-state relations. Dennis Vorwamor, a deputy SG during 1992–98, was also helpful. K. Mbia, the longtime doyen of the TUC's Administrative Department, had a deep knowledge of the movement and was often helpful and genial. Most recently, the deputy SG for Operations, Kofi Asamoah, was extremely helpful regarding TUC linkages with its Regional and District Labor committees, and J. Y. N. Atopoly, deputy SG for Administration, also shared his knowledge.

Jonathan Tetteh, who was the sole man in the Research Department in the 1970s, was always friendly, thoughtful, and helpful. I also want to thank the many others in various TUC offices over the years who have assisted my research.

I extend my special thanks to Peter Arthiabah posthumously. I first met Peter in 1973, when he worked for the Public Service Workers Union (PSWU). He was immediately helpful and became a constant correspondent and provider of documents via mail for many years. Peter was a man totally engaged with the union movement. He understood the need for the TUC—for which he worked in the 1980s and 1990s—to maintain relations with other social groups in Ghana, for which he was the main link. Ali Ibrahim, an old acquaintance, was a deputy secretary-general in the Organization of African Trade Union Unity, headquartered in Accra in the mid-1980s. He provided important information on the attempted takeover of the Ghana union movement by Jerry Rawlings and the Provisional National Defense Council (PNDC) in 1982–83.

Within the Industrial and Commercial Union (ICU), long Ghana's largest union, I have benefited from years of support from many of its leaders. In the early 1970s Patrick Kumady and Benjamin Bartimeus shared documents and information regarding their years under the Nkrumah regime, when they served as ICU leaders. Ben Edjah, general secretary (GS) during 1972–82, willingly agreed to be interviewed and shared ICU documents, even by mail when I could not get back to Ghana. L.K.K. Ocloo, the dynamic ICU GS in 1983–91 during the turbulent PNDC years, who was forced to flee into exile, provided useful information. Even more forthcoming and helpful were Abraham Koomson, a deputy GS, and Joseph Haywood Dadie, acting GS during a time of ICU crisis in 1991–92.

The ICU has had its problems, but Napoleon Kpow, its GS since 1992, has been exceptionally open in sharing documents and information about the ICU's internal life and its disputes with the TUC. He has shared documents and information on repeated visits. F. Kofi Davoh, who led another breakaway within the ICU in the 2000s, which has since rejoined the TUC, readily met with me to discuss the dynamics of ICU life. I have talked to many others within the ICU over the years, in Accra and Tema, to whom I owe thanks. I have also received essential assistance from union office personnel who have found and assembled documents and files for me while managing other duties. The always busy Eric Atrow, personal assistant to general secretary Kpow, deserves my special thanks.

Abraham Koomson became a friend, and he has continued to teach me about trade union life and the dynamics of Tema union life as head of the now independent Textile, Leather, and Garment Workers Union (TLGWU) and the new Ghana Federation of Labor he created.

I am likewise grateful to Richard Baiden, the dynamic GS of the Maritime and Dockworkers Union (MDU) during the 1966–82 era, who enjoyed the great confidence of his members in Tema and Takoradi. But he fell afoul of the PNDC regime after he became TUC SG and once again (as during 1961–66) had to go into exile. I owe enormous thanks to Baiden's successor, Seth Abloso, who has long since become a friend, who was GS for the period 1983–88. I learned a great deal from him about the dynamics of union-state conflicts during Rawlings's PNDC government and about political life in the 1990s. Several succeeding MDU GSs have been extremely forthcoming, including Kofi Asamoah, now TUC deputy SG, and the current MDU GS, K. O. Afrieye, who recently shared candidly his knowledge of the dynamics of intra-TUC leadership struggles between 1988 and 2004.

In 1972 I met I. K. Osei-Mensah, then general secretary, GS, of the General Transport, Petroleum, and Chemical Workers Union (GTPCWU), and he graciously shared information about the union. I was surprised, upon returning a year later, to find A. K. Yankey in the GS's chair. Supported by internal union documents, he explained that the union executive committee had found financial irregularities on the part of its GS and therefore changed the leadership. This proved to be an early lesson for me in how Ghanaian unions maintain leadership accountability. Yankey went on to become the TUC SG and, with others, to bring the TUC out from under the heavy hand of PNDC-attempted domination and intimidation during 1983–92. Yankey's successor as GTPCWU's GS was Napoleon Amoah, who served from 1983 through the mid-1990s. He was a highly competent and strong leader, who shared information about GTPCWU's conflicts with the PNDC government in the 1980s and early 1990s. The next two GSs in succession, J. N. Y. Atopoly, now deputy TUC SG for Administration, and E. A. Mensah, have also generously shared information.

I also appreciate the assistance I received from successive officials in the PSWU starting with Peter Arthiabah in the 1970s. They are: Korang Opare-Ababio, GS in the 1980s and early 1990s; E. T. Ofori, a deputy GS; and A. T. K. Okine, the current GS. I am also grateful to John Brimpong, national chairman, and Robert Coles, GS of the Mine Workers Union, for interviews and assistance. In the large General Agricultural Workers Union (GAWU), former GSs Kweku Haligah and Samuel Asante provided interviews and union documents. In recent years GAWU deputy GS, Kingsley Ofei-Nkansah, has been a friendly source of information about union thinking. In the 1970s Charles Attah of the Construction and Building Workers Union made available information on the union as has, more recently, P. M. K. Quainoo, a deputy GS.

I am also grateful to officials in the Teachers & Educational Workers Union, Local Government Workers Union, Communications Workers Union, Timbers and Woodworkers Union, Public Utility Workers Union, and Private Transport Workers Union for providing information through interviews over the years.

Within the ranks of labor, but outside of the TUC, successive leaders in the very large Ghana National Association of Teachers (GNAT) have provided me with information on GNAT's activities and GNAT-government relations. I have had a long relationship with its leaders in the 1970s and 1980s, Tom Bediako and Nana-Henne Ababio, respectively. Nana was also a mid-career university student of mine in the United States and remains a good friend. Their successor in the 1990s, Paul Osei-Mensah, was always especially generous in meeting with me and providing detailed documentation about ongoing pay and other disputes with the governments.

I am also deeply indebted to the Labor Department in Accra, which since the 1980s has made available to me some of its files on contemporary and historical areas of trade unions. The detailed reporting on labor by district labor officers has created an important and indispensable historical record of union activities and union-government interactions. In particular, I am very grateful to the successive chief labor officers who have enabled me to conduct research there, including E. Aseidu-Nyarko, Patrick Obeng-Fosu, Alex Gyebi, and Mr. Appenteng.

A number of other Ghanaians have become good friends, and they are remarkably knowledgeable about the Ghanaian union movement and Ghanaian politics generally. One is Yaw Graham, a student radical and then a leftist labor and political organizer in industrial Tema in the 1980s, who has also written on labor. After a brief visit with Ghana's penal facilities in the 1980s and a period in exile, Yaw returned to Ghana in the early 1990s to start Ghana's best newspaper, the then-weekly *Public Agenda*, the only paper with decent coverage of labor. Now head of the most influential policy think tank in Ghana, Third World Network, Yaw has often given me insight into Ghana's political dynamics through his intimate knowledge of Ghanaian political life.

A second is Akoto Ampah, a former student radical who is exceptionally knowledgeable about Ghana's union movement and the ideological and policy choices of leadership. He generously takes time from his busy schedule as a lawyer for the hectored and harassed of Ghana to discuss politics and trade unions with me.

I am perhaps most deeply indebted to Kwesi Pratt, a good friend and the perpetual agitator of the Ghanaian Left who found himself repeatedly in jail for his resistance to the PNDC in the 1980s and early 1990s, as did Graham and Ampah. I first introduced myself to Kwesi in 1991, as he was organizing the first meeting of a revived (if still illegal) Nkrumahist party. Within days he took me to a meeting of some of the leaders of the recently organized political opposition. Since that time Kwesi has extended to me enormous time, his warm friendship, his great knowledge of Ghanaian politics, and extraordinary efforts to assist me, not least through introducing me to his unparalleled network of friends from all sides of the political spectrum. I have been quite blessed by my acquaintance with these three leftist Ghanaians, who persist in their fundamental antagonism to inequality.

I also thank my friend Kwame Ninsin, a professor in the Political Science Department of the University of Ghana, who has repeatedly shared his radical intelligence and abundant knowledge about politics in Ghana, as has my longtime friend and excellent analyst of Ghanaian political life, Cyril Daddieh of Miami University of Ohio.

I am deeply grateful to my youthful, engaging, and highly attractive and political wife, Wilma, the object of my considerable affections and desires, who has always supported me in my time-consuming research and writing endeavors. She has exercised substantial tolerance for my abundance of Ghanaian materials.

I greatly appreciate the extensive and exacting labors of the copy editor who worked with me on this manuscript, Dale Rohrbaugh.

Ultimately, this book was written in solidarity with, and as witness to, the insistent demands of many African trade unions and workers in all these countries for a voice and for democratic representation, for a right to participate in processes and choices that affect their lives.

Abbreviations

Ghana

AFRC—Armed Forces Revolutionary Council government 1979
CDRs—Committees for Defense of the Revolution
CPP—Convention People's Party, 1949–66
CSA—Civil Servants Association
DCL(s)—District Council(s) of Labor
EOSBs—end of service benefits
GRNA—Ghana Registered Nurses Association
GNAT—Ghana National Association of Teachers
HIPC—Highly Indebted Poor Countries
ICU—Industrial and Commercial Workers Union
IMF—International Monetary Fund
KNRG—Kwame Nkrumah Revolutionary Guards
MDU—Maritime and Dockworkers Union
NDC—National Democratic Congress party, 1992–
NDM—New Democratic Movement
NPP—New Patriotic Party, 1992–
NUGS—National Union of Ghanaian Students
PDCs—People's Defense Committees
PP—Progress Party, 1968–72
PNP—People's National Party, 1979–81
PNDC—Provisional National Defense Council, 1982–92
PSWU—Public Service Workers Union
SMC—Supreme Military Council government, 1971–79
TUC—Trade Union Congress
WDCs—Workers Defense Committees

International and Other

HDI—Human Development Index
HIPC—Highly Indebted Poor Countries
ICFTU—International Confederation of Free Trade Union
ILO—International Labor Organization
IMF—International Monetary Fund
NLC—Nigerian Labor Congress
OATUU—Organization of African Trade Union Unity
SAPs—structural adjustment programs

Namibia

CBO—community based organization
CDM—Consolidated Diamond Mines
COD—Congress of Democrats
DTA—Democratic Turnhalle Alliance
EIU—Economist Intelligence Unit
EPZ—export processing zone
JCF—Joint Coordinating Forum
LaRRI—Labour Resource and Research Institute
MP—member of parliament
MUN—Mineworkers Union of Namibia
NAFAU—Namibia Food and Allied Union
NAFTU—Namibian Federation of Trade Unions
NANGOF—Namibia Nongovernmental Organization Forum
NANTU—Namibia National Teachers Union
NAPWU—Namibia Public Workers Union
NAWU—Namibia Workers Union
NCSTU—Namibian Christian Social Trade Unions
NGO—nongovernmental organization
NPSM—Namibia People's Social Movement
NUNW—National Union of Namibian Workers
PSUN—Public Service Union of Namibia
SWAPO—South West African People's Organisation
TUCNA—Trade Union Congress of Namibia
WOSC—Workers Steering Committee

Niger

ACET—*Alliance crédible aux exigences des travailleurs*
ANDP—*Alliance nigérienne pour la démocratie et le progrès*
CDS—*Convention démocratique et sociale*
CDTN—*Confédération démocratique des travailleurs du Niger*
CNT—*Confédération nigérienne des travailleurs*
MNSD-NASSARA—*Mouvement national pour la société de développement*
PNDS—*Parti nigérien pour la démocratie et le socialisme*
PPN-RDA—*Parti progressiste nigérien-Rassemblement démocratique africaine*
RDP-JAMA'A—*Rassemblement pour la démocratie et le progrès*
SNEN—*Syndicat national des enseignants du Niger*
SNECS—*Syndicat national des enseignants et chercheurs du supérieur*
UGTN—*Union général des travailleurs du Niger*
UNTN—*Union nationale des travailleurs du Niger*
USTN—*Union des syndicats des travailleurs du Niger*

Senegal

CNTS—*Confédération national des travailleurs du Sénégal*
CSA—*Confédération des syndicats autonomes*
PDS—*Parti démocratique sénégalais*
PIT—*Parti de l'indépendance et du travail*
PS—*Parti socialiste*
SUDES—*Syndicat unique et démocratique des enseignants sénégalais*
UDEN—*Union démocratique des enseignants sénégalais*
UNSAS—*Union des syndicats autonomes du Sénégal*
UPS—*Union progressiste sénégalais* (later, PS)
UTLS—*Union des travailleurs libres du Sénégal*

South Africa

ANC—African National Congress
COSATU—Congress of South African Trade Unions
CUSU—Council of South African Unions
FOSATU—Federation of South African Trade Unions
GEAR—Growth, Employment, and Redistribution policy
LRA—Labour Relations [Amendment] Act
NEDLAC—National Economic Development and Labour Council
NUM—National Union of Mineworkers
PAC—Pan-Africanist Congress
SACTU—South African Congress of Trade Unions
SACP—South African Communist Party
UDF—United Democratic Front

Zambia

CSUZ—Civil Servants Union of Zambia
FFTUZ—Federation of Free Trade Unions of Zambia
MUZ—Mineworkers Union of Zambia
MMP—Movement for Multiparty Democracy
UNIP—United Nationalist Independence Party
ZCTU—Zambian Congress of Trade Unions
ZNCB—Zambian National Commercial Bank
ZNUT—Zambia National Union of Teachers
ZUFIAW—Zambia Union of Financial Institutions and Allied Workers

Zimbabwe

ICA—Industrial Conciliation Act of 1934
ILO—International Labor Organization
LRA—Labor Relations Act
MDC—Movement for Democratic Change

NCA—National Constitutional Assembly
NECF—National Economic Consultative Forum
TNF—Tripartite Negotiating Forum
PVO Act—Private Voluntary Organizations Act
ZANU and ZANU-PF—Zimbabwe African National Union and ZANU-Patriotic
    Front
ZAPU—Zimbabwe African People's Union
ZCTU—Zimbabwe Congress of Trade Unions
ZFTU—Zimbabwe Federation of Trade Unions

CHAPTER 1

Trade Unions in Africa's Democratic Renewal and Transitions: An Introduction

Jon Kraus

Workers are demanding effective and democratic organizations, whether in government or in the unions. People are actively discussing political, economic and social issues. The sleeping giant is beginning to wake up in Zimbabwe. . . . We have given too much power to the state; now we are watching helplessly while it runs out of control with our jobs and our lives. In 1980 we gave the state power to redistribute the wealth in Zimbabwe, but some misused that power to distribute jobs and opportunities to their own friends and family. . . . We need independent watchdogs and checks on central state power. One of those watchdogs is the trade union movement.

Gibson Sibanda
President of the Zimbabwe Congress of Trade Unions
May Day, 1991

Observers watched with fascination the outbreaks of protests, demonstrations, and demands for political liberalization and democracy in Africa in 1989–91. Discussions immediately sought to identify the crucial sources for this unprecedented upsurge in democratic sentiment and protests. Africa's political landscape was decorated with decaying one-party systems, personal autocracies, and military regimes. This book had its origins in the observation that workers and trade unions were often among the earliest and most energetic demonstrators in the African countries experiencing democratic protests (Kraus 1995).

Workers or trade unions have been one of the most crucial groups demanding and forcing authoritarian regimes to liberalize political life in a wide range of countries. In Benin, unions brought the bankrupt government to a halt in 1989 in a long and widespread series of strikes by teachers and civil servants. The Zambian Congress of Trade Unions (ZCTU) consistently fought Kaunda government economic policies in the 1980s and asserted its autonomy. In 1990–91 it was the most important force in the creation of the Movement for Multiparty Democracy (MMD). The ZCTU leader defeated Kaunda in the presidential elections. In Mali, Niger, Côte d'Ivoire, Congo, Algeria (1988–89), and Central African Republic (CAR), union and worker protests were central to the emergence of political liberalization and democracy. In South Africa, the unions in the Congress of South African Trade Unions (COSATU) became the dominant organizational basis for continuing the protests against apartheid rule after the state of emergency edict in June 1986 and the arrest of civic and political leaders at all levels (Marx 1992, 199–219).

In Nigeria, the unions in the Nigerian Labor Congress (NLC) were major engines of protest against authoritarian rule and structural adjustment policies in 1988–89 (Fashoyin 1990a) and, despite divisions, against General I. B. Babangida's cancellation of the June 1993 elections and his successsor's, Abacha's, military tyranny. Despite severe government countermeasures, the NLC remained a foe of the Abacha military regime until its demise. In Namibia, trade unions also played an important mobilizing role in the final years of the independence struggle.

That the workers and trade unions were important in launching, sustaining, and sometimes shaping the democratization process is not a widespread perception in studies of democratization in Africa. But trade unions had, in many instances and countries, acted since 1960 to overthrow some governments through intensive protests and to weaken other governments through sustained strikes. They also demanded political autonomy for their unions. Explicitly or implicitly this raised a persistent demand for democratic and civic space for the exercise of trade union (and democratic) rights. *Structurally*, unions in some African countries have appeared to constitute a force for the development of political liberties and democratic practices. This was true even where internal democracy within the unions was imperfect, but it was not true where all union leaders were government appointees, for example, in Tanzania and Côte d'Ivoire. With great frequency in recent years, African union movements, even some previously linked politically to ruling parties, challenged the right of authoritarian regimes to impose their economic policies, especially structural adjustment policies. This was so in Congo, Niger, Mali, Ghana, Zambia, and elsewhere. Such challenges to specific policies then escalated to a denial of the right of these regimes to rule and to a demand for democratic institutions where their voices could be heard.

This book explores the impact of African trade unions on the democratization process in Africa, a process that is proceeding strongly in some countries, is lagging in others, and has failed in still others. This introduction does several things. First, it sets forth clearly the central questions the authors have collectively addressed, each in his or her own way. Second, it attempts to offer some analytical distinctions regarding democracy and how one can pose questions regarding the democratization process. Third, it draws attention to existing theory and analytical approaches regarding the sources of political liberalization and democratization and the role of trade unions.

It is difficult to develop generalizations regarding the relative impact of trade unions on democratization in Africa based on case studies of seven or eight countries out of almost fifty. One of the limitations of this work is that relatively few scholars have focused their attention on the impact of unions even after the protean roles of those unions in the democratization process became visible. The countries for which we have studies are Ghana, South Africa, Namibia, Zimbabwe, Zambia, Senegal, and Niger. In the conclusion I will draw heavily on Nigeria, too. They constitute a reasonable representation of countries in terms of certain variables:

- countries within Anglophone and Francophone Africa, with their distinctive colonial inheritances that affected trade union structures;
- countries with relatively large wage-labor forces (for Africa) as a percent of the total labor force, such as South Africa, Zambia, Zimbabwe, and Ghana, and those with smaller and newer ones, such as Namibia and Niger;
- countries with relatively large (in absolute number) trade union movements, as in South Africa and Ghana (and Nigeria), and those with much smaller movements;
- countries in which unions have developed in alliance with recent national liberation movements, as in South Africa and Namibia, or under their relative domination initially, as in Namibia and Zimbabwe, and those with older independent union movements, as in Zambia and Ghana; and
- countries where organized labor has frequently engaged in militant strikes, such as Zambia, Senegal, South Africa, and Ghana, and those where there is a low tradition of militant union protest, as in Zimbabwe, Niger, and Namibia.

Our case studies include countries in which the struggles for political liberalization and democratization have been quite different. In three countries—Ghana, Niger, and Zambia—there was a struggle to move from a clearly authoritarian African government to multiparty democracy. In two countries—South Africa and Namibia—African and other subject peoples struggled mightily over many years to claim the democratic rights enjoyed by a white minority and to destroy rigid racial and class barriers to progress. In two other countries—Senegal and Zimbabwe—formal democratic institutions and elections existed. The liberalization and democratization processes in the 1990s and 2000s did, at least initially, involve highly significant expansions in actual political freedoms, significant reductions in the hegemonic claims of dominant party regimes, and much more significant electoral competition.

Central Questions

Contributors to this volume were asked to respond to three sets of questions. *First*, did the trade unions or workers in the African country they studied play an important, moderate, or minor role in the political struggles that led to political liberalization and democratic transitions? Did the unions play a direct role—by strikes, protests, open political demands—or only an indirect one?

Second, what was the importance of economic and political conditions in animating increased worker and trade union protests or demands for political liberties?

Third, what roles have trade unions played in the newly democratized political systems, and have they been supporters or opponents, beneficiaries or victims, of the new political systems and political economies? What are the implications of economic conditions for trade union–state relations under democratic regimes? Newly democratic governments in Africa are being compelled by international financial institutions (IFIs) and Western aid donors to pursue market policies and also "flexible" labor policies in implementing structural adjustment programs (SAPs) (Standing 1991; Wohlmuth and Messner 1996). Have labor movements' opposition to SAPs brought them into conflict with the new democracies? Has democracy enabled the unions to become more involved in political processes or more independent in mobilizing their members in behalf of their interests? Have union activities strengthened democratic institutions?

Not all of the case studies respond equally to all of the issues raised. Bergen's Senegal chapter focuses on the democratization process. It argues that the impact of trade unions has been exceptionally important in Senegal over a long time period, in terms of their implicit threat and Senegal's leaders' perception of their threat. The Zambian chapter examines all three questions and the post-transition phase in which Zambian unions are assessed in terms of their continuing role in keeping the government accountable through mobilizing protests and strikes. Saunders' study of Zimbabwe, which has had a one-party dominant regime, focuses on the extended effort of the union movement to mobilize widespread support among many civic groups to keep the government accountable in the face of falling living standards and regime corruption. He examines how union efforts certainly forced open the system and, with a labor-mobilized party in 1999, generated the first hotly contested elections since independence. But with a violent militarized regime smashing democratic liberties again, a successful transition has not occurred.

Debates about Democracy and Democratic Transitions

I am interested in assessing the role and impact of workers and trade unions in the passage from authoritarian rule to the restoration of basic civil liberties (freedom of speech, freedom of the press, rights to organize parties and unions), referred to as *political liberalization*. I am also interested in the introduction of new democratic procedures (elections) and institutions—*a democratic transition*. Such transitions could be substantially democratic, blocked, or flawed, or they could fail (Bratton and van de Walle 1997, 118–20). I am also concerned with how trade unions are able to use the new political liberties and what role they play in the new democratic arenas. It is important to *democratic consolidation* if large associational groups find that democratic institutions are compatible with their ability to pursue their interests.

Trade unions may and often do play very different roles in the political processes that lead to political liberalization, democratic transitions, and the later democratic consolidation, if it occurs.

(a) Trade unions may play much more important roles in the political liberalization and democratic transitions than in democratic consolidation, which occurs over a longer period of time and in which explicitly political actors and institutions may be more important.

(b) The extent of direct union participation is more likely in the liberalization and, to a lesser degree, transition stages because the blunt nature of trade union interventions (strikes, protests, popular pressures, participation in parties) are more likely to come into play in opposing an authoritarian regime than in participation in ongoing political institutions (Barchiesi 1996; Bermeo 1997; Valenzuela 1989).

(c) Trade unions' enthusiasm for political liberalization and democratization may not extend to support for existing democratic institutions if they are excluded from participation or their activities are frustrated or repressed, which has occurred in Western, Latin American, and African democracies.

One definition of democracy is a political regime that possesses three conditions: free and extensive competition among individuals and organized groups in regular elections for the holding of governmental office at all levels; high levels of political participation among citizens in the selection of leaders and policies, by means of regular elections, with no social groups excluded; and a full enjoyment of political and civil liberties (speech, press, association) in order to ensure that political participation and competition are open to all (Diamond, Linz, and Lipset 1988, xvi).

This definition is largely a procedural one, regarding basic procedures by which power is contested, and most political analysts favor it (Bratton and van de Walle 1997, 10–13; Burton, Gunther, and Higley 1992, 1). But these are manifestly inadequate procedural criteria for defining democracy as we generally understand it. The practice of representative democracy involves not only the competitive selection of leaders and parties but also some participation or voice, however indirect, in the selection of policies and passage and implementation of legislation. This latter area which is so crucial to the quality of democratic polities has been ignored by scholars when defining democracy. The idea of whether or not varying social groups have access to (not influence in) policy arenas can be considered in terms of procedures (not outcomes) as readily as can levels of electoral competitiveness, participation, and political liberties. Indeed, theories of pluralist democracy depict the struggle for power and representation as one which occurs between groups in society and takes place in the electoral, legislative, bureaucratic, and other arenas (Truman 1971, chapters 2, 4, and 9 on access). Pluralist theories argue that democracy requires that no groups are entirely excluded from the political bargaining process and that policy is the result of such bargaining. But political scientists have not sought to calculate levels of access by diverse groups to the lawmaking and implementation arenas of public life.

Other scholars depart sharply from the narrow procedural definition of democracy cited by Diamond, Linz, and Lipsitz. Rueschemeyer, Stephens, and Stephens add to the basic procedural conditions the "responsibility of the state apparatus to the elected parliament" (1992), an accountability procedure and an acknowledgment of the representation of people's voices or claims upon government. Ruth Berins Collier defines democracy in terms of three components: "liberal constitutional rule, . . . in which government leaders and state actors" are constrained from arbitrary action by the rule of law, enforced by an independent judiciary; free and competitive elections, with basic civil liberties and open contestation; and "a legislative assembly that is popularly elected and has substantial autonomy from the executive power" (1999, 24).

Charles Tilly has developed a more complex idea of democracy, and democratization, which responds to many of our criticisms. "Democratization means increases in the breadth and equality of relations between governmental agents and members of the government's subject population, in binding consultation of a government's subject population with respect to governmental personnel, resources, and policy, and in protection of that population (especially minorities . . .) from arbitrary action by government agents" (2004, 14–15). Tilly acknowledges that actually existing democracies only come to approximate the fulfillment of these qualities. He specifies a range of causal mechanisms which, occurring historically, work to reduce "categorical inequalities from public politics," over time helping to create more equality of access, to integrate trust networks in political life, and to increase the "breadth, equality, enforcement, and security of mutual obligations" between governments and citizens (16–20). He assesses democratization in terms of these mechanisms.

Tilly's concepts also encompass, in different terms, the concerns of analysts who have used the concept of civil society in explaining the essential bases for democratization. They have argued that there must be vigorous, autonomous societal groups, one of whose roles is to offset the power of the state and represent the interests of their members within the polity. Crucial aspects of state-society (governor-governed) relationships in a democracy require the existence of these groups—for example, churches, unions, business associations—their ability to develop material and organizational bases, and their role in articulating the collective interests of their groups. In addition, analysts have been deeply concerned with the extent to which state activities are transparent, accountable, and responsive to societal interests. These ideas reinforce the notion that access to policy-making arenas is a crucial quality of democracy.

Many groups in African and other societies consider it a measure of democracy's existence whether or not they can at least make their voices and claims heard in the public (press) or policy arenas, such as through meetings with ministers, a National Assembly, or an existing consultative committee. The last thirty years have been ones in which such IFIs as the International Monetary Fund (IMF) and the World Bank, and Western aid donors have become central players in many African political systems. They have incredible policy leverage as providers of indispensable capital and foreign exchange. Policy initiation and implementation interventions by these external groups have been regular and ongoing, and they have come to be regarded as normal by African governments.

Until the mid-1990s, the procedures for adopting and implementing SAP policies have been secretive (until sprung on the public) and have excluded virtually all major social groups—including business and labor— from access to arenas where the policies were determined and their implementation considered. The IFIs and Western donors have laid down in SAPs, as conditions for receiving aid, the major macroeconomic policies these countries have had to pursue, in such domains as devaluation, government spending, deficit levels, interest rates, deregulation, ending price controls, privatizing state industries, trade liberalization, and ending barriers to multinational corporations. As SAPs met rising levels of public and political resistance, the World Bank made attempts in the late 1990s to make their policies more widely known to groups in African societies. But this is largely public relations and an attempt to resocialize politicians and intellectuals away from economic nationalism, not consultation.

These SAPs have deeply affected African economies and living standards, as most groups in African politics are well aware. There are sharply varying judgments regarding the utility and impact of stabilization and SAPs imposed by the IFIs (Green 1993; Killick 1995a; van de Walle 2001; World Bank 1994). Also, it is important to note that these SAPs came in response to major crises in African economies; the SAPs did not cause such crises. Nonetheless, even if some SAP policies were economically imperative, there is enormous evidence that the SAPs have often been unsuccessful in their "adjustment" goals and have had a sharp contractionary impact in African economies. They have created major debt crises for domestic industries through massive devaluations; constricted lending to local business; severely hurt the living standards of many urban workers and consumers; required major layoffs of workers; and compelled states to constrict the range and spheres of their economic activity in an undiscriminating fashion (Broad 1988; Campbell and Loxley 1989; Ghai 1991; Gibbon 1993; Helleiner 1990; Killick 1995a, 1995b; Kraus 1991; Mahon 1999; Mosley, Harrigan, and Toye 1991; Stiglitz, chapters 2 and 3).

The debt and economic crises of the 1980s and 1990s have meant that many African governments have lost much control over their own domestic economic policies to the IFIs and Western aid donors as they exchanged aid for policy compliance. African reliance on this aid reduced the responsiveness of governments to important domestic constituencies, which is one reason why policies were determined in secret. Hence, in Africa the significance of democracy for public policy is probably dubious, as is the quality of democracy. Moreover, the neoliberal economic policies the IFIs and most Western countries urge have speeded globalization in commerce, production, and capital markets, with some devastating impacts upon workers, even as some other workers benefited (Bloch 1991; Coote 1996; Greider 1997; Kapstein 1996; Kraus 1996; Rodrik 1997). The impact of neoliberal economic policy advocacies and impacts has been to weaken labor standards and to institute "flexible labor" supply policies. This has involved deregulation in the domain of labor and trade union laws and safeguards; creation of "export zones" where unions may not organize, or do so only with difficulty; and attacks on unions (International Confederation of Free Trade Unions, 1996, 1997, 2003, 2006; Kapstein 1996; Standing 1991).

Meanwhile the IMF, the World Bank, and the United States and other Western donors have worked energetically in policy and ideological terms to strengthen market ideologies and weaken the idea that states should play a role in regulating market failures (World Bank 1983, 1987). That is, these international institutions and countries have wanted to systematically alter the thinking of political and socioeconomic elites regarding public policies, normally by promises of money and scarce resources to policy and government elites and important academics.

In addition, most analysts of democracy have failed to specify very closely what constitutes "high levels of participation among citizens in the selection of leaders and policies." There are vast inequalities among people in developing countries—in literacy, access to information and sophistication, social position and prestige, and organizing skills and resources. And these inequalities powerfully influence which interests come to have organized expression in political life and are regarded as important. Huber, Rueschemeyer, and Stephens argue that formal (procedural) democracy is crucial because it tends to be more than formal. It offers the many in society the chances for a voice in real decisions, which creates the possibility for changes in the distribution of societal power (1997, 323–424).

However, Huber, Rueschemeyer, and Stephens note that current efforts to consolidate formal democracy in Latin America and Eastern Europe are moving away from the tendency for democracy to ensure full participation and equality in access, as is true in Africa (1997, 325). Major factors obstructing full participation include:

- most social movements that articulate the interests of the lower and working classes have been weak;
- political parties have generally failed to establish linkages to subordinate classes or articulated their interests;
- subordinate classes are linked to the system, if at all, by clientele-oriented networks, which exchange support for individual favors; and
- power has been so centralized in the executive branch that there is little room for groups to exercise influence or to participate beyond the act of voting (333–34).

For formal democracy to be more substantive requires that social, economic, organizational, and political power are not tightly concentrated and civil liberties are not constrained. These permit subordinate class to organize for power.

Many analysts have been interested in the positive impact of international actors and events upon democracy (Bratton and van de Walle 1997). Huber, Rueschemeyer, and Stephens discuss the impact that international financial institutions (and presumably Western aid donor countries) can have in reducing democratic possibilities, depressing citizen participation, and constraining policy debate, when they condition aid on the adoption of neoliberal economic policies that are outside the domestic debate. Indeed, in a number of African countries the IMF and the World Bank managed to have appointed as finance ministers Africans employed by them.

Those who are concerned with the shortcomings of democratic practices criticize students who prefer procedural definitions of democracy. Some analysts prefer substantive definitions of democracy, which evaluate a regime according to whether the system works well (outcomes) for most of the people. The manifestly corrupt, manipulative, and unaccountable qualities of some democracies in Africa and elsewhere—where competitive elections have occurred and there are civil liberties—create skepticism regarding the meaningfulness of procedural definitions. The prevalence of practices favoring political clientele, state patronage, authoritarian and high-deference cultures, as well as weak institutions of accountability, have been widespread (Diamond 1988, 1995).

Beckman (1989) raised the question "Whose Democracy? Bourgeois versus Popular Democracy" to discuss the debate on the value of formal democracy among Nigeria's political Left in the late 1980s. The ethnic divisions and manipulations, exceptional elite corruption, pervasive clientele-oriented practices, low responsiveness to popular needs, and elite self-enrichment in the Second Republic (1979–83) had soured many Nigerians on democracy. Conditions seem, if anything, worse under the 3rd Republic (1999–present). Military manipulation of the transition to democracy in the late 1980s, including General Babangida's decision to permit only two parties and the corruption of the process, created massive dismay among Nigerian democrats (Diamond 1995; Lewis 1996). Some Nigerian radicals believed in an alliance with authoritarian rule as a route to equality and power (Beckman 1989, 88–93).

Subordinate classes are much less likely than more powerful classes and groups to be able to organize in behalf of their interests or have their voices heard. This clearly influences views on the legitimacy of democratic regimes by leaders of these classes. On a variety of occasions the trade union movements in democratic regimes in Africa, for example, in Nigeria and Ghana, have had their interests ignored or their union organizations attacked—or both—at the hands of democratic regimes, as is common in Africa today (ICFTU 1996–2006). They have then proceeded to (briefly) greet with enthusiasm and a bestowal of legitimacy authoritarian military leaders who seized power. They initially sought an alliance with new military regimes as a way of safeguarding their organizational power and the interests of their members. But many radicals and union leaders in African countries have come to value highly a renewal of civil and political liberties as a basis for protecting their own ability to organize and the rights of subordinate class groups (Beckman 1995; Kraus interviews in Ghana 1991, 1993, 1996, 2004).

Nonetheless, the inability of trade unions in countries like Ghana, Nigeria, Zambia, and Zimbabwe to have their voices heard, to protect their organizational autonomy, or to prevent vast erosions in real wages has at times made them sometimes extremely skeptical of the advantages of democracy. This reflects the inadequacy of procedural criteria and the ongoing tension between the promise of democracy as conveyed by procedural ideals and the realities of pervasive economic, class, and organizational inequalities, as indicated by the substance of democratic life.

Theory Regarding Sources of Democratic Transitions and Democracy

This critical discussion of existing theory is animated by the belief that the current approaches tend to privilege contingent over structural explanations and to obscure the key role of such collective social groups as trade unions in the democratization process.

There is substantial consensus that no single factor or cause, necessary and sufficient, explains why political liberalization and democratization have occurred in so many countries since 1970. They arise from a combination of factors (Shin 1994,

150–51). After studying many cases of democratization in southern Europe and Latin America, O'Donnell and Schmitter conclude that they would not develop a theory of democratic transitions because it would have to focus on the extreme uncertainty in transitions where "there are insufficient structural or behavioral parameters to guide and predict the outcome" (3). Huntington has developed a long list of proximate causes of some of the democratizations in the "Third Wave" since 1974 (1986, 31–108). He concludes that general factors create conditions favorable to democratization; they do not, however, make it necessary (106).

Tilly is most emphatic in arguing that "we should . . . expect to discover not one but multiple paths to democracy. . . . Prevailing circumstances for democratization vary significantly from era to era and region to region as a function of previous histories, international environment, . . . models of political organization, and predominant models of social relations" (2003, 9).

Authors have looked at distinctive types of explanations: structural or contingent ones; domestic versus international causes; elite or mass actors as the key agents in political liberalization and democratization; and economic or political factors. The debate over whether the key actors are elites or mass groups is most germane to our interest.

Much pre-1970 theorizing about the causes of democracy tended to posit the crucial importance of long-term *structural factors*, such as high levels of economic development and incomes, a general modernization of society which creates diverse associational groups, and the development of a strong bourgeoisie or, as some argue, a middle class. The wide range of countries at various levels of development that have had a democratic transition (for the moment) has clearly induced most theorists to abandon the idea that broad underlying structural changes in economies and society are prerequisites for democratic transitions. Analysts also note the remoteness of structural factors from the apparent dynamics of political transitions. However, Bratton and van de Walle argue that while analysts prefer contingent-type explanations for political transitions, which allow for substantial agency by key elites and groups, most observers still argue that structural characteristics are necessary for democratic consolidation (1997, 47). This refers to the long-term acceptance of democratic institutions, procedures, and norms (Mainwaring et al. 1992). The emphasis by many observers upon the need for strong civil associations for democracy suggests one should not ignore structural social forces.

Using cross-national data and comparative historical studies, Rueschemeyer, Stephens, and Stephens have argued that a strong, long-term link exists between capitalism and democracy. They maintain that the interplay of three clusters of power—namely, class power, state power, and transnational sources of power—is crucial to explain the development, and demise, of democracy. The three factors combine and interact in ways that explain different sequences of democratic development and failure (1992, 1–27, 40–75, 269–81). Capitalist development spawns new social classes—the bourgeoisie, the middle class, and the proletarian working class—that grow in size, resources, and organizational capabilities as they struggle for power with a ruling class and the state. The struggle is for equal political rights and status and access to arenas of public power. The strengthening of the structure and autonomy of the state is necessary. Its autonomy permits it to avoid being the instrument of a single class and to become an arena for power. Transnational structures (e.g., powerful states, multinationals) have important interactions with states and social classes within them.

Rueschemeyer et al. further argue, based on their historical studies, that "those who have only to gain from democracy will be its most reliable promoters and defenders, those who have the most to lose will resist it and will be tempted to roll it back when the occasion presents itself" (1992, 57). In contrast to many liberal and Marxist scholars, they deny that the bourgeoisie and urban middle classes are the most important agencies of democracy. "Capitalists and the parties they primarily supported rarely if ever pressed for the full introduction of democracy" (271). Changes in the balance of class power were central to the process of democratization. Capitalist development—which brings into being and generally strengthens the bourgeoisie, the middle class, and the working class—"is related to democracy through changes in the balance of class power" (272). *The organized working class was found to be the key actor in the generation of full democracy in most countries, though often in cooperation with other parties; it could not by itself bring democracy into being.* Other scholars have disagreed, noting the important roles of liberal bourgeois and middle-class dominant parties in instituting democracy in various countries (Collier 1999; Ertman 1998).

Bratton and van de Walle note the arguments for contingency-type explanations, which focus on the choices and behavior of individuals and, to a lesser extent, of groups (1997, 24–26). They include a wide variety of analytical approaches; most attempt to explain behavior on the basis of motives and preferences of self-interested actors, which interact with those of other actors and groups (see Bates 1994, 17–23). Appreciation for the contingent quality of change responds to observations of the swiftly changing events and positions of actors and groups in periods of democratic transition. Bratton and van de Walle argue that "contingency theorists find little evidence that processes of transition are shaped by preexisting macroeconomic conditions and class interests, or even by inherited political institutions. Instead, individual behavior hinges on subjective perceptions of the actions of others and calculations of the potential risks and benefits of aligning with political incumbents or opposition movements" (1997, 24). But the behavior of important groups in democratic transitions, including trade unions, seems to correspond often to class interests, macroeconomic conditions, and inherited political institutions, *that is, structural conditions.*

Disagreement exists over whether the sources of democratization are international or domestic. Some have argued that the collapse of communist regimes in Eastern Europe or the pressure of Western aid donors stimulated democratization in Africa (Shin 1994, 151–53). Such arguments often depend upon the coincidence in the timing of these events, not evidence that those events themselves animated the actors or groups (Bratton and van de Walle 1997, 29–30).

The debate over internal vs. external factors ignores that the different actors involved in the liberalization and democratization processes often acted under the impetus of *different causes.* These included trade unions and organized workers as well as university students, who were on the leading edge of protests in most African states; the urban crowd; the intelligentsia and professionals; political opposition leaders; and political incumbents. I would argue that organized workers and students had low levels of information from abroad (except Francophone students), the middle-class intelligentsia and professionals had somewhat more information, and the opposition and incumbent leaders undoubtedly had the most information. But, it was organized workers, students, and the urban crowd in most African states that precipitated the political protests and democratization.

Most studies have argued that democratization originated within domestic political systems. O'Donnell and Schmitter draw upon the thirteen country studies in their survey and conclude that apart from Italy's defeat in World War II, "the reasons for launching a transition can be found predominantly in domestic, internal factors" (1986, 18). They note ideological constraints at the international level, some misfortunes in war (Cyprus, Argentina, Portugal's colonial wars), and the bad consequences of international economic declines. But, they cannot find an international factor that alone can compel an authoritarian regime to start political liberalization. They also argue persuasively that democratic transition "involves . . . a crucial component of mobilization and organization of large numbers of individuals, thereby attenuating the role of external factors" (18).

Bratton and van de Walle similarly argue powerfully in behalf of causes within the domestic political system. They also make one of the few attempts to systematically test for the potential impact of international events or factors as sources of democratization. They found that political diffusion was highly related to political protests among countries with similar colonial backgrounds: that is, the impact of early protests in French-speaking west and central African states upon nearby states. The presence of democratizing states nearby seems to have affected the *timing* of protests, as some late democratizing states began transitions only when nearly surrounded by other political reformers (1997, 134–38). Bratton and van de Walle found another strong association between international actors and protests: countries that had initiated large numbers of stabilization and SAP agreements with the IMF and the World Bank experienced high levels of protests (133–34). They treat this as an economic factor.

The financial aid and political support that international and Western trade unions and a few governments gave to some African trade unions probably added to those unions' organizational capabilities and, crucially, ideologically reinforced union demands for organizational autonomy. These helped the unions and workers later initiate protests (Southall 1995).

There is a fundamental distinction in the literature regarding the relative importance of the role of elites and of mass groups in precipitating political liberalization and democratization. That distinction is extremely relevant in assessing trade union roles. Collier observes that this is part of an older debate over the role of the working class in democratic change and the emergence of liberal democracy (1999, 1). Was democracy as it emerged in the nineteenth and twentieth centuries part of an assertion to power from below, in which previously excluded and subordinate groups demanded the right to equal political participation in national life? This was the era in which industrialization developed in the United States and Europe; an industrial working class was created; and trade unions, often suppressed, demanded not only economic rights but also political rights where they were excluded from any, or an equal, place in political life, as was true in much of western Europe. Both Marxists and pluralists perceived class actors and groups as instrumental in the emergence of a more-participatory and less-restrictive kind of democracy.

Or did democracy emerge "from above," where the power of already rising groups of prosperous peasant farmers or urban capitalists demanded access to political power and policies that fit their needs? One could argue that the recent wave of democratization in southern Europe, Latin America, Asia, and Africa has sometimes involved "re-democratization" rather than an original winning of civil liberties and universal franchise. However, given the antagonism to unions and workers during Latin America's industrial surge under authoritarian rule in the 1960s–90s, and under the newly industrializing Asian regimes, the political legitimacy of workers and unions was not accepted. They were regarded as dangers, while industrial/financial elite often had complicit access to public power under military regimes.

The current debate has been among the many analysts who have conceived of democratization as a result of elite strategies and transactions in weakened authoritarian regimes and a few who have seen democracy emerging from the collective action of subordinate social classes and actors. The "elites" in elite explanations are not normally assessed in class terms; rather, these elites seem to be socially anomalous, denuded of class character despite their preference for and embrace of capitalist ideas, institutions, and alliances.

We use the term working class here to depict a wide group of wage workers—industrial, commercial, white-collar clerks, skilled workers—who tend, despite many divisions, to share some common aspirations and grievances (Collier 1999, 14–15). Conceptually, the working class expresses itself and assumes significance in the organized and common actions of these workers, usually acting through an organization, a trade union, or a union-influenced party. There are many divisions in African countries among unskilled (and uneducated), semi-skilled, and skilled workers, blue collar and white-collar, and even teachers. But their common experience in recent years of deeply depressed standards of living *and* exclusion of their voices from participation in the policies that affect their lives has often brought diverse members of the working class to act with solidarity in their common demands.

Trade unions in Africa include not only members of the working class but also large numbers of lower civil servants, commercial workers, and others who regard themselves as workers. The term is clearly not confined to industrial workers. On several occasions workers have demonstrated and gone on strike in large numbers in actions neither initiated nor supported by the major unions or federations in a country, for example, the massive protests in Algeria in 1990 and the protests in Côte d'Ivoire in 1990–91. But even these workers tended to carry out their protests through the collective agency of the local unions and workplaces in which they were organized, not as formless mobs.

Collier frames her discussion of actors in democratization as those with explicit democratic agendas. But one can readily conceive of circumstances where strikes and protests by trade unions in Africa, and elsewhere, have unleashed a path to democratization without democracy being the main initial purpose of their collective actions. However, most of the studies in this book observe that unions did in fact self-consciously demand democratization because of the old regime's failures and because they realized that their ability to organize and act freely, and to have a voice in public policy, required basic freedoms and a democratic society.

Among elite theorists, O'Donnell and Schmitter devote a major emphasis to elite activities and pacts "because they largely determine whether or not an opening [to liberalization] will occur at all and because they set important parameters on the extent of possible liberalization and eventual democratization" (1986, 5). But other analysts have looked at some of the same cases and have perceived that, whatever the elite decisions, they were propelled by and were a response to the actions of mass groups and their protests, for example, in Peru, Argentina, and Spain (Bermeo 1997; Collier and Mahoney 1997). Actually, O'Donnell and Schmitter take into account mass forces but believe that elites are more important in the democratic transitions. In apparent contradiction, O'Donnell separately notes that in Latin American cases, elite pacts were rarely important in transitions. This is because they can occur only where the development of mass-based popular groups is low, which was not the case in Latin America in the 1960s through the 1980s, or where these forces are represented in strong political parties (these had been outlawed) (O'Donnell 1986, 12–14).

Bratton and van de Walle observe that the distinction between liberalization and democratization is important because "the prevailing view in the literature is that political liberalization launches regime transition—that is, an incumbent elite driven by divisions within its own ranks initiates concessions to its opponents" (1997, 159). But they document that in Africa the impetus for political reform originated in the incumbent elite in only a minority of cases. "More commonly African transitions began with popular protest," with groups composed of popular classes, which compelled incumbent rulers and other elites to initiate political democratization (159).

Clearly, there is an important debate over who were the initiating actors in democratization. Part of the difference certainly rests in whose behavior (elites or collective class actors) we focus upon in our explanations. It also involves the explicitness or distance in time between incidents of mass protest—signaling withdrawal of consent or an active attempt to remove leaders—and the decision of rulers to concede to a renewal of liberties. There is also an often-unstated debate regarding who the *most crucial actors* are in the democratic transitions or, better stated, in the different phases of the transitions. *Most analysts appear to focus on the phase where the new democratic procedures and institutions are being crafted and founding elections are being held.*

For our purposes, however, it is useful to distinguish between several phases. *The pre-transition phase* studies which groups or actors have been important in *creating political space* in civil society by claiming or demanding political rights and space. *The political liberalization phase* involves the restoration of political liberties and may start the democratization process, often after assaults against the old authoritarian regimes. *The democratization phase* involves the crafting of new procedures and institutions, constitutionmaking, organizing political parties, running in elections, and the exercise of the new democratic institutions.

Many students of democratic transitions emphasize that elites play the most important role (see Diamond 1993). Shin summarizes a wide range of recent scholarship and concludes that democratic transitions are seen "as a product of strategic interactions and arrangements among political elites." Scholarship tends to focus on "the role that political leaders or strategic elites have played or should play" (1994, 139). He cites Juan Linz and Huntington as supporters of this idea. Karl and Schmitter specifically argue that "stable democracies" have seldom if ever occurred as an outcome of reformist transitions where popular groups mobilize support and "impose a compromised outcome without resorting to violence" (cited in Shin 1994, 161). Shin, indeed, is emphatic that "strategic elites have been a key factor in bringing about a majority of democratic transitions in the present wave. . . . [Thus] the literature does not consider the commitment of the mass public to democracy as an absolute requirement for democratic transitions. Indeed, it suggests that democracy can be created even when a majority of the citizenry does not demand it" (153–54).

This astonishing statement argues that democracies are created without sectors of the mass public, that is, collective actors, wrenching power from the grasp of autocrats and upper class elites. Shin and others suggest explicitly that autocrats surrender their political power willingly, without being compelled to do so. Historical evidence runs counter to this. This thesis implies the beneficence of autocrats and dominant class actors.

Some analysts conceive that individual leaders decide to democratize after consultation with a few close lieutenants, in a range of elite explanations (see critique in Osaghae 1995). This is how Herbst explains why and how Rawlings in Ghana permitted political liberalization and democratization to proceed (first phase), though Herbst notes that he does not know why Rawlings acted. And Herbst gives no consideration to the social and political pressures that existed in Ghana (1994, 184–85). Joseph argues that autocrats have apparently "converted" to democratic procedures and rights after they had lost other options or might have lost most of what they had possessed. He cites DeKlerk of South Africa, Vieira of Guinea-Bissau, Kerekou of Benin, and Kaunda of Zambia as apparent converts (1997, 374). But Joseph does not discuss what caused their "conversions." In three of the four cases we know that the leader was forced to act because of high levels of domestic turmoil and popular protest, which he could not suppress: Kerekou in Benin and Kaunda in Zambia literally had no choice, and DeKlerk had almost exhausted his choices. Bates suggests that professional and political elites, acting on rational choice calculations, were the key actors in political liberalization in Africa (1994, 19–25).

Among those focusing on elite behavior, O'Donnell and Schmitter are most explicit about the role of mass groups and why they believe that their role is limited. As noted, they found in their sample of cases from southern Europe and Latin America that *the initiation of the political liberalization* came from fissures within the incumbent regime (1986, 48–49). However, others disagree, using some of the same cases as well as African examples (Bermeo 1997; Bratton and van de Walle 1997; Collier and Mahoney 1997; Kraus 1995).

In a second stage, say O'Donnell and Schmitter, an explosive mobilization of civil society occurs in a repressive and depoliticized environment. Suddenly there bursts into existence a cascade of social and political protest by a wide range of social groups, including the press, intellectuals, trade unions, teachers, students, professionals—what they call "the resurrection of civil society" (1986, 48–50). The catalyst for this social eruption, they suggest, comes from the actions of "exemplary individuals" rather than groups, who test regime limits (49). In Africa, this enormous outburst of social and political activity was contagious and expressed long pent-up grievances and discontent among many groups (*Africa Demos* 1990–94; Baylies and Szeftel 1992; Bratton and van de Walle 1992; Fashoyin 1990a; Heilbron 1993). These protests bond together many diverse groups in social movements of opposition, whose combined efforts are required to unseat the old regime (Waterman 1983a).

But, argue O'Donnell and Schmitter, "the greatest challenge to the transitional regime is likely to come from the new or revived identities and capacity for collective action of the working class and low-ranking, often unionized, employees" (1986, 52). This sector is the one where "liberalization is extended most hesitantly and least irreversibly." Frequently, union rights have been suppressed, and the government has been aligned with private employers. Such social and political mobilization occurs in countries where prior mobilizations and organizational networks may be either strong or weak. This was also true in Africa, but protests did not occur where civil society was very weak (Bratton and van de Walle 1977, 147).

A striking quality of this explosion of protest by a resurrected civil society, according to O'Donnell and Schmitter but not others, is that "regardless of its intensity and of the background from which it emerges, this popular upsurge is always ephemeral" (1986, 55). Bratton and van de Walle argue that this has generally been the case in Africa as well, though it was more clearly this outburst of protest that was central in delivering *both* political liberalization and the onset of political democratization (1997, 102–3). Reasons for the brevity of protest include regime repression and selective cooptation, protest "fatigue," emergence of internal conflicts within protest groups, willingness to compromise for new policies, and initiation of reforms (O'Donnell and Schmitter 1986, 56–57).

The chief consequence of this social and political explosion of activity is to accelerate the democratic transition and extend it beyond where it would otherwise have reached, in terms of civil liberties and the inauguration of democratic processes (O'Donnell and Schmitter 1986; Valenzuela 1989). Once transitional political reforms start, party leaders tend to take the initiatives in constitutional conventions, party formation, elections, and legislation. The central role which explicitly political activities now play in democratic transitions involves certain elites, it is argued, with political skills. This has probably led to so much focus on elites.

In contrast to the elite-centered analytical perspectives, class-based theorists of democratization, historically and in the late twentieth century, have alternative perspectives. Those theorists who perceive a class basis for democratization in some countries give attention to the role of the masses or collective class actors in explaining why democratic transitions occur and take the patterns that they do (Collier and Mahoney 1997; Ruesechemeyer et al. 1992). There is a substantial older literature which documents how African trade union collective protest activity led to the delegitimation and, sometimes, the removal of authoritarian or corrupt regimes (Chikhi 1991; Crisp 1984; Fashoyin 1990a; Friedman 1987; Kraus 1979; Muase 1989; Otobo and Omole 1987; Peace 1979; Sandbrook 1977, 1981; Seidman 1994).

Rueschemeyer et al. offer a powerful argument and evidence that capitalist development led to democratization (1992). Capitalist development brought into being new social classes, which further created class-based organizations and parties that struggled for access to power, rights, and resources, expanding participation in the political arena. Their historical examples indicate that this was hardly a straightforward process. Variables other than the balance of class power are involved. In contrast to prior theorists such as Barrington Moore (1966), whose study on the origins of democracy theorized that "no bourgeoisie, no democracy," Rueschemeyer et al. argue that the organized working class was the major actor in the full development of democracy virtually everywhere. The struggles of trade union movements and labor-based parties for full political and economic rights for workers altered the class balance of power in the nineteenth and twentieth centuries and ushered into being more full and open democratic processes, often with the cooperation of other parties. Other analysts, however, have contested the historical cases of Rueschemeyer et al. in terms of the centrality of working-class movements and parties relative to others. Nonetheless, the Rueschemeyer et al. study has been exceptionally important in reemphasizing for students of working-class movements the general historical evidence of the roles of the working class and trade unions in democratization.

One hastens to add that if unions and working-class parties could not usher in democracy on their own in Europe in the heyday of industrialization, it is even less likely that trade unions and union-supported parties can do this in Africa, where little industrialization has occurred and the size of both the working class and the trade unions are still quite small. However, the political enfeeblement and delegitimation of most traditional political authority structures (though not ethnic identities) in most African states means that the struggle for power and policy in the national political arenas are largely among modern social classes, groups, and institutions. This increases the salience of even small trade union movements. Collier observes that union movements were not always "the most consequential sources of pro-democratic pressure. . . . Other groups also engaged in protests, including . . . human rights groups, nationalist groups, and urban social movements" (1999, 110). These social movements also mobilized larger working class groups in poor urban neighborhoods. As will be seen in our individual country studies, trade unions in strike and protest activities in Africa were often allied with or helped to animate and lead protest activities by a wide range of student, church, teacher, professional, civic, artisanal, and popular urban groups. This was true in Zimbabwe, Zambia, Nigeria, South Africa, Senegal, and Ghana.

Recent critiques of elite-centered approaches have sought to add "collective actors to [explanations of] collective outcomes" and have focused strongly on the significance of trade unions and their protests for democratization. Collier and Mahoney argue, first, that the hegemony of an elite perspective in the discourse on transitions simply fails to take into account major actors and dynamics of the process. It is limited by its focus on leadership, specific decisions, and the crafting of new institutions, which privileges the role of individual actors (1997, 286). It ignores the larger social and political forces that have compelled the elites to act. Second, Collier and Mahoney note that as it delineates actors in terms of their strategic role in the transition process or negotiations, "it has tended to be state-centric, thus subordinating social actors" (286). By conceiving that mass protests have done no more than change somewhat the strategic environment in which elites negotiate a transition, Collier and Mahoney maintain that elite analysis understates in theory and depiction the role and impact of mass-based opposition and labor protest specifically. They detail a significant number of instances in southern Europe and Latin America where organized labor protests and strikes animated a democratization process in which labor played a major role.

Collier has explicitly posited the tension between theories that privilege the role of elites in democratization and those that sustain the role of collective class actors (1999, 1–32). She disagrees with Rueschemeyer et al. on the centrality of the role of organized labor and labor parties in the democratization in western Europe in the nineteenth and early twentieth centuries. But she argues that they understate organized labor's crucial role in late twentieth-century democratization in Europe and in Latin America. Collier and Mahoney and Collier (1999) elaborate on several nonelite patterns of democratization that detail the crucial roles union movements as collective actors have played, both in regimes where the incumbent authoritarian has no transition plans and where an authoritarian regime begins a limited liberalization. In both models they demonstrate that labor has played a crucial role in destabilizing the autocracy, creating space for political liberalization, triggering a political transition, and expanding the arena for political contestation (see next section).

In Africa also, mass protests by collective actors—trade unions especially—were the most important factor in initiating political liberalization and democratization. Of forty regimes that experienced political liberalization, twenty-eight of them, or 70 percent, were in conjunction with *mass protests*, a significant association (Bratton and van de Walle 1997, 185). Bratton and van de Walle observe that "mass political demonstrations were always accompanied by reform; there was no country in Africa in which protest occurred where incumbent elites failed to make at least a token political opening" (185). Political liberalization was a continuing process. In those cases where incumbent leaders did initiate political reforms, "they were usually able to control the reform process; generally they opened up only so far as they felt they had to and then they froze the reform process" (185). Hence, mass protests were necessary, if not sufficient, conditions for democratic transitions on the whole. Moreover, the number of trade unions, business associations (which did not protest), and press publications were positively and strongly correlated with the frequency of political protest (148). Bratton and van de Walle found that of the four variables that best account for political protest in African countries in 1985–92, political competition in civil society, measured by the number of trade unions allowed under the old regime, was the most important factor (1997, 150).

There is also some debate regarding the relative impact of *economic and political factors* in political liberalization and democratization. Most observers of African and Latin American democratization processes tend to argue that the ouster of the authoritarian regimes was *precipitated by severe economic protests* and consequent popular protests (Baylies and Szeftel 1992; Bratton 1994a; Chikhi 1991; Collier and Mahoney 1997; Heilbron 1993; Kraus 1995).

Haggard and Kaufman argue that "in Argentina, Bolivia, Peru, Uruguay, and the Philippines, democratic transitions occurred in the context of severe economic difficulties that contributed to opposition movements." Despite repression, "the political conflicts unleashed by economic crises substantially reduced [rulers'] capacity to achieve these objectives" or to influence the terms of the transition (1995, 45). The protests were precipitated by the popular sectors, which had devastating real income losses during the economic crises of the late 1970s and the 1980s. Haggard and Kaufman distinguish between strikes aimed at economic demands and broader political mobilization and demonstrations against the regime, invariably led by unions. They note that "it is misleading to ignore the political content of economic strike activity [and] would be wrong to overlook the profound economic grievances that motivated political protest" (64). Strike action and popular protest forced the beginning of transitions in Latin American countries and "broke serious logjams in elite negotiations over political reform" (64–65).

Bratton and van de Walle tend to depreciate the significance of economic factors as precipitants of the protests that generated democratization in Africa. They argue that economic factors are compelling "only if and when they are embedded within a political approach." A key political factor they later cite is weak political legitimacy, which, unfortunately, is usually deduced from protest behavior (1997, 36, 134)! They note that economic crises in Africa have been ongoing for several decades without major democratization movements, that protests have often been more in response to government [economic] policies than to economic conditions, and that economic causes cannot explain the how and when of transitions (36–37). But if mass protests were animated by economic conditions or policies, that would explain part of the "how." Actually, there is no doubt that economic conditions in Africa as a whole worsened decade after decade: while per capita economic growth rose by 1.4 percent in sub-Saharan Africa in the 1960s and declined to 0.2 percent in the 1970s, it fell to a negative 2.4 percent in the 1980s (Kraus 1995, p. A68).

Bratton and van de Walle found no systematic relationship between the rate of economic growth in 1980–89 and the extent of political protest, which they measured by *number of instances* of protest during 1985–95, rather than extent and severity of protests (1997, 131, 287). They did, however, find a highly significant association between frequency of IMF and World Bank agreements during 1980–89 and frequency of protest (133). Bratton and van de Walle argue that the mere frequency of negotiations and accords tended to make governments appear weak in the eyes of their people and therefore to lose legitimacy (133–34).

But observers of protest in many African and Latin American countries have documented the outbreak of protests in direct response to specific policy measures, often imposed by the IMF and the World Bank. These involved devaluations, hence higher prices, removal of key subsidies, and reductions in government budgets. These worsened already harsh economic conditions and brought to a climax existing levels of discontent, for example, in Nigeria, Niger, Côte d'Ivoire, Benin, Ghana, Zambia, Congo, and Gabon. I have sought to examine the levels of political protest during 1989–91, which included numbers of instances and rough estimates of the extent of protests (using *West Africa* and *Africa Research Bulletin*). In Table 1.1 protest data for some thirty-six African countries are matched with changes in economic growth during 1986–90 (*Africa Recovery* September 1991, 28–29). Several countries engaged in civil war, which clearly determined economic outcomes, and a number of small islands were excluded. Table 1.1 shows that countries with the highest average GDP growth were not likely to have political protests. Those with the lowest levels of

Table 1.1 Levels of Political Protests, 1989–91

Average annual real GDP growth 1986–90	N	Protest levels in African countries		
		High	Medium	Low
Low (1%–negative)	7	71% (5)	14% (1)	14% (1)
Medium (1–3%)	12	25% (3)	8% (1)	67% (8)
High (3% plus)	17	12% (2)	18% (3)	70% (12)

growth were most likely to have high levels of political protests (Algeria, Benin, Côte d'Ivoire, Gabon, and Zambia).

To conclude, procedural definitions of democracy that exclude the question of access to political arenas, as most do, are inadequate. Exclusionary practices of major social groups are widespread in democracies. Contingent factors in democratization, while important, draw attention away from structural forces in societies—for example, major economic changes and collective actors—which are invariably factors in democratization struggles. Elite analytical perspectives tend to focus on factional intrigues and institutional transitions rather than the social and political forces making these necessary. The slighting of economic factors in animating Africa's democratic changes privileges the role of elites over collective class actors—labor, social movements—who protested and rebelled against disastrous policies and conditions, as well as corruption, and brought down autocracy. The significance of collective actors in the democratic transition process is usually unexamined but receives attention in this book.

Theory Regarding Trade Unions in Democratic Transitions

It is interesting to note that most theory involves the role of unions only in the early stages of democratization, especially in the ouster of the old regime and early jousting for power. There is little current theorizing on unions in Africa—or elsewhere—as a crucial group within civil society that creates democratic political space under authoritarian regimes—despite recent discussions on civil society (Beckman and Jega 1995; Harbeson, Rothchild, and Chazan 1994). Unions that struggle to maintain their institutional autonomy and demand representation of their interests in dictatorial societies court repression but also raise the costs of authoritarianism. They signal to other groups and individuals that successful protest is possible. They broaden the arenas where liberties can be exercised. Trade unions are enormously important in terms of their interest in the accountability of government (on economic policy, for example) and in their frequent conflicts with authoritarian regimes. These conflicts occur because of the unions' interests, relatively large size, and dependence upon legal rights for assertions of autonomy, collective bargaining, and collective protest.

Huge numbers of small associational groups exist in both rural and urban Africa that are linked to a local and ethnically delimited public. Many have little importance for democratization. They function well under either authoritarian or democratic regimes, are too small to exert any leverage upon governments except in intermittent disturbances, and are not "political" (Osaghae 1995). That is, generally, many groups in "civil society . . . [are] largely indifferent to the affairs of the civic public realm over which the state presides" (cited in Osaghae 1995, 194). They have little knowledge of government operations; individuals regard their interactions with the state as not subject to moral scruples. In contrast, the trade unions in Zambia (under Kaunda), in Ghana and Nigeria (under the military regimes in the 1970s to the 1990s), in Tunisia (since independence), and in Zimbabwe (under Mugabe) all struggled to assert their autonomy and interests and to hold governments accountable, which led to repeated conflicts with the regimes.

There is also relatively little theorizing regarding the roles unions have played in the second, or transition, state of democratization—party formation, elections, formation of governments, and early policy making. Despite the relatively small size of organized formal sector workers, some union movements from countries with both small and large trade union movements have played significant roles during the later stages of the transition. Examples of this include in South Africa, with a large union movement; in Zimbabwe and Zambia, with medium-size union movements; and in Benin, Niger, and Mali, with small unions. And unions in almost all the countries have sought early involvement in shaping public policies regarding labor legislation, economic policy, and responses to SAP policies. Most chapters in this volume discuss the role of unions during the later stages of the transitions and under democratic rule.

Surprisingly, Collier and Mahoney confine their pioneer theorizing to the initial stages of democratization, not the later stage. "We see this [later] stage as a closing end-game, necessarily dominated by elites establishing rules for the actual transfer of power and designing the institutions of new democracies" (1997, 287). Clearly trade unions are often less politically active during this stage. Barchiesi argues severely— and with exaggeration, I think—that African trade unions have not played much of a role because of weak organizations and co-opted leadership, except "as a social movement . . . in accelerating the crisis, if not always the collapse, of authoritarian governments, and in putting democratization firmly on the political agenda" (1996, 352).

Many writers agree that trade unions play a central role in the mobilization of opposition against authoritarian regimes, as has occurred from Poland to Peru to South Africa (Barchiesi 1996; Bermeo 1997; Collier and Mahoney 1997; Marx 1992). This is because trade unions have a greater capacity for extensive mobilization of protest than almost any other social group at critical times, given their existing network of unions and branches. These can potentially be mobilized for protests, demonstrations, and strikes, with initiatives taken either by national or local leaders who have the closest links to the rank and file. A union's mass base tends to have some key common interests, and it may have developed a conscious identity on the basis of its lived labor and protest experiences (Crisp 1984; Waterman 1983, part IV). Unlike any other social group, unions are comprised of members who are strategically located to disrupt the economy—and often government as well—and, hence, challenge the operations of the incumbent regime directly.

Samuel Valenzuela has undertaken the most systematic effort to explain the various types of roles that trade union movements play in democratic transitions, one very much within the elite perspective of democratization (1989). Labor can play a major role both through formal or informal pacts with other groups and by participation in the major outbreak of strikes and demonstrations. Valenzuela tends to accept O'Donnell and Schmitter's concern that excessive labor mobilization may lead to "hard-liners" winning in inter-regime struggles. This can lead to a renewal of repression and an end to the democratic transition—though this seems to occur rarely. Valenzuela argues that extremely high levels of protests may help push the regime toward liberalization if it is followed by some restraint in labor demands. He is concerned with some major qualities of labor movements and four major variables that structure the relationship of labor to democratization in order to develop hypotheses regarding *how labor protest can be contained in order not to threaten the democratic transition*. Valenzuela seems to *assume* that the labor protests will be powerful enough to ensure a democratic transition. The complexity of production processes means that capital and the state cannot just wholly repress labor and unions, he notes.

Regimes have used two major alternative *labor control strategies* to prevent unions from developing too much independent power or allying themselves with, or being used as a resource by, a political opposition. The first is the *corporatist strategy*, which involves incorporating the trade unions within the regime's constellation of interests by granting some benefits to the unions in exchange for state limits on trade union behavior. This strategy involves state creation or support of trade unions. It captures or contains unions by means of restrictive legislation, state-mandated finances and required membership, intervention to co-opt or select union leadership, and state monitoring and repression of dissident labor behavior.

A *market strategy* is most frequently an exclusionist one, where labor is outside the regime's coalition of support. It seeks to expose labor to "market" forces (employers, labor markets) and to minimize the ability of unions to counter these forces with its collective mobilization of support. The strategy employs restrictive legislation, which narrows the scope of legal union prerogatives (including strike and bargaining rights), decentralizes bargaining to weaken union leverage, restricts political activism, and permits heavy punishment of unions.

Valenzuela argues that four major variables structure the relationship of the union movement to democratization. First, the stronger the union movement, the more likely it will be able to control or tactically restrain protests, once they have weakened the old regime and started the democratization process. A responsible labor movement will then have to be consulted by those implementing the transition. Second, Valenzuela hypothesizes that the more centralized or united the labor movement is, the more easily national leaders can moderate intense levels of protest and negotiate a role for labor in the system. Third, Valenzuela develops hypotheses regarding the relationship between prior levels of regime harshness or mildness toward unions, as well as open or closed rights to participate in the political system, and democratic transitions. He hypothesizes that the harsher the regime toward unions, and the more closed the political system, the less likely unions can overcome their deep grievances and accept the compromises involved in democracy (1989, 457–61). Fourth, Valenzuela argues that the speedier the transition (old regime collapse) and the more intimate labor's linkage to the new government, the less likely a successful transition will occur (463–66).

Valenzuela's sophisticated approach poses some problems. First, he *assumes* that the central problem of labor in democratic transitions has to do with constraining the levels of protests and strikes in order to prevent a regression to authoritarian rule. This further assumes that democratization *begins* with divisions within the regime between hard-liners and (more democratic) "soft-liners." The level of protest in Latin American and southern European countries may have been sufficient to launch democratization, but in Africa one problem in failures in democratic transitions has been *insufficient levels* of labor and popular protest on a sustained basis. More frequently, in countries where there was too little protest, or it was not sustained and well organized, African leaders resisted protest and either limited the transition or rejected it entirely after initial reforms (Bratton and van de Walle 1997, 185).

Second, Valenzuela's stress on the need for moderation in the protests and strikes of trade unions and leftist parties in order for a democratic transition to occur is open to dispute, though it has also been argued by Huntington, O'Donnell and Schmitter, and others (Bermeo 1997, 305–6). Their evidence is drawn from the historical experiences of labor in nineteenth- and early twentieth-century Europe or the military overthrow of democratic regimes faced with high levels of leftist protests (Brazil 1964, Argentina and Chile 1972–73)—a dynamic different from democratization. However, recent studies by Bermeo on Portugal and Spain argue that moderation in protests and strikes by popular groups is not necessary in order for democratic transitions to occur. She also notes that strikes levels did not moderate but generally increased during the democratic transitions in Brazil, Chile, South Korea, Peru, and the Philippines. Collier and Mahoney similarly reject the argument on the necessity of moderation. Drawing on five recent cases, they argue instead that persistent protests and strikes have tended to keep the transition moving forward and broadened the arenas of democratization. Adler and Webster note that continuing labor protests occurred during, and were important to, the democratic transition in South Africa. Indeed, in many of these countries the persistence of popular protests and strikes helped push the negotiations on democratization to a successful conclusion, for example, in Ghana in 1978–79.

The argument regarding the need for moderation in protests among popular organizations does not seem relevant to African societies. The militaries have intervened in bourgeois-dominated societies in Latin America in which popular group protests have been held to threaten the interests of indigenous and foreign capital and others with strong institutional interests. However, apart from South Africa, Zimbabwe, and Kenya—all ex-settler colonies—and Nigeria, local capitalist classes are poorly developed in Africa.

There are substantial tensions in theory and practice between Valenzuela's thesis that centralized union leadership and control facilitate a democratic transition and (a) the need for high levels of rank and file, and local union leader, involvement in protests and strikes; (b) the idea that a high level of citizen involvement in associational life is crucial for democratic consolidation and offsetting state power; and (c) the idea that trade unions, as (often) representative, democratic organizations, instill democratic norms and the ideas of rights in workers. These are not Valenzuela's interests.

My key concern here is whether there is a relationship between *internal union democracy and the preferences of trade unionists for political democracy.* Michel's iron law of oligarchy suggests that it is difficult for Left parties and trade unions to have internal democracy, given the huge disparity in resources and information between members and leaders. And there is evidence that internal union democracy is not prevalent in many African countries (Beckman and Jega 1995, 178–79; Bratton 1994b; Sandbrook 1975, chapters 3 and 4). However, it is clearly important in some countries, including Ghana, Nigeria, South Africa, Senegal (some unions), Zambia, and Zimbabwe. Governments in Africa's newly independent countries in the 1960s and 1970s sought by repression and corporatist measures to eliminate trade union freedoms and control union leaders, which also meant reducing internal union democracy (Berg and Butler 1964; Crisp 1978; Kraus 1995). This also occurred under radical regimes that had professed support for union power (Kraus 1988).

When trade unions have been actively involved in pro-democratic protests, they have been expressing the overwhelming discontent of the rank and file, whether in Niger, Senegal, Zambia, Ghana, or South Africa (Bergen 1994; Marx 1992; Sandbrook 1975, 1977, 1981). It is clear that a major genesis of the power behind the rise of South Africa trade unions in COSATU rested with the democracy behind the shop steward movement. In Ghana, union leaders have pushed hardest to represent the interests and needs of the rank and file when the rank and file have had the power to protest and offset the pressure of the state upon union leaders (Crisp 1978; Jeffries 1978; Kraus 1979). Where unions are controlled by the state, protest from below may break out, even in spectacular form, as it did in Algeria in 1988–89 (Chikhi 1991). It has clearly been the persistent impulse of regimes to attempt to impose or co-opt union leaders in order to prevent them from representing or being responsive to the interests of rank and file.

Almost no one studies *the tension in the choices of independent unions on whether to launch strong oppositional protests or to accept state pressures for compromised decisions on wages and circumscribed union rights. High opposition protest* risks abolition of the unions, arrests of union leaders, and/or loss of insecure legal rights or political favor. *Compromise under state coercion* risks gains that are often ephemeral or far less than satisfactory to leaders and union members, who are then often angry with the leaders. It probably means acceptance of some government management of union choices and limits on unions' ability to mobilize pressures. It may mean leaders have been bought off by the state. Both tendencies—to protest, to compromise—exist within union movements (Beckman 1995). *The relevant question is, what factors shift the balance within the unions from acceptance of compromises to protest?* The frequency with which this tension exists means one should not easily generalize about leadership domination of rank and file and co-optation by the state. *I hypothesize that, other things being equal, the greater a union's autonomy, the more likely the unions will mount oppositional protests, because greater internal democracy in such unions will generate pressure on leaders.* I explore this in the conclusion.

Valenzuela hypothesizes a strong relationship between union strength and an important role for unions in the transition. This includes participating in negotiations with political elites and business regarding economic policies, some immediate economic demands, and altering labor regulations. He argues that strong unions are better able to exercise restraint after mobilization and that consensual class relations buttress democracy. However, union strength can easily flow from an inversion of Valenzuela's reasoning: constant union pressures and strike threats and an inability to contain rank-and-file protests without favorable policy outcomes. It is difficult to discuss the relative size and strength of unions in Africa. There are limited reliable figures for the *size of wage labor forces* in African countries, and only slightly better data are available for *trade union membership and density* and *strikes* (ILO 1997, 235–37). Based on a small sample of African countries and census data from the early 1980s, the World Bank estimated that some countries (e.g., CAR, Niger, Togo) had wage labor at under 10 percent of the labor force; a large number (Ghana, Cameroon, Malawi, and Nigeria—at 19.5 percent) had around 14–20 percent; and one (Zambia) had more than 50 percent (1995, 148). Trade union strength and activism are found in countries with low, medium, and high levels of urbanization, for example, from Zambia, Senegal, and Congo to South Africa.

In Africa there is no clear relationship between countries with relatively large-size trade union movements and union density (membership as a percentage of nonagricultural labor) and significant roles in democratic transitions. Small as well as large union movements played significant roles in democratization. But it seems probable that union size and strength are related to the persistence of democracy.

Another crucial factor in union strength is the history of union autonomy from the state. Levels of trade union autonomy in Africa are historically related to whether the countries have had relatively liberal or democratic regimes, or at least intermittently had such regimes during which union independence could be reasserted (Kraus 1995, pp. A10–12).

Valenzuela mentions that linkages with political parties strengthen trade union influence in the transition process (1989, 463–66). Reuschmeyer, Stephens, and Stephens note that trade unions have historically been significant in democratization when they were part of a broader coalition of forces, which can include parties or social movements or groups. In African countries it is significant that, *with a few exceptions, trade unions have had little or no linkages to political parties, except in one-party states*. In the conclusion I examine whether or not independent trade unions that are linked with political parties are more likely than others to play a large and more extensive role in democratization in Africa.

Collier and Mahoney theorize the importance of labor movements in democratization by counterposing two alternative models of labor's role to the widely supported "elite" model, in which labor's role is seen as ephemeral or negative. In their alternative models of how transitions proceed they are primarily concerned with the genesis of the transition. In what is called the *elite model* the decision to launch liberalization comes from a conflict *within* the regime, among its elites. "Ephemeral" popular class protests and strikes erupt, as civil society reinvents itself (O'Donnell and Schmitter). The elites proceed to rewrite the constitution, form parties, hold elections, and carry out the transition.

Collier and Mahoney use their alternative models to explain the pattern of transition in five key recent cases (1997, 286–87). In the *Destabilization/Extrication model*, the incumbent regime has had no liberalization project in mind, no intention of departing from power. In this model, which purports to explain the transitions in

Spain (1977), Peru (1980), and Argentina (1983), the regime is compelled to adopt a transition as a means of "forced retreat" in the face of sustained collective, popular protests. Trade union movement plays a central role in these. The protests destabilize the regime and trigger the transition; the continuous, non-"ephemeral" quality of the strikes and protests strengthens the challenges to the rulers. In both models, "collective action secured the legalization of labor-affiliated parties, which otherwise might have fallen victim to elite negotiations" (287).

In the *Transition Game model*, the incumbent authoritarian regime does have a limited, highly gradualist transition project in place in order to legitimate its rule. It has thus opened political space a bit and seeks to co-opt various political actors and parties. The rise of high levels of collective protests, as in Uruguay (1984) and Brazil (1985), derails and aborts the existing transition plan and compels the incumbents to open up the system more quickly than they intended. The incumbent loses control over the transition in terms of rules, timing, and constitutional arrangements. Labor protests play a large role in derailing the narrow incumbent project, recasting it and keeping it moving rapidly.

In a later study Collier adds a third nonelite model, which she calls "parallel tracks." Here there is an explicit transitional project and timetable, but the labor movement's actions still open more political space; labor leads the initial democratic opposition, and its collective protests enforce the democratic project and expand genuine political contestation, as, for example, in Chile (Collier 1999, 110–19).

The Collier and Mahoney models are limited in how much of the transition process they cover. But they counterpose the elite-centered model explanations in which the actions of collective actors (unions, social movements, among others) become part of our understanding of why democratic transitions occur. Other factors in the transition that can alter as a result of protests include changes in (a) which parties—for example, popular class parties—are permitted to participate in electoral politics; (b) the rules of the transition and occupants of the organizations managing the transition;(c) the rules governing trade unions and labor markets; and (d) post-transition access to decision-making arenas.

Last, what does theory suggest is trade union support for democratic consolidation when new democratic governments impose stringent SAPs?

Clearly, trade, price, and regulatory liberalization, privatization of state enterprises, state and private sector layoffs, state spending constraints, and the pursuit of market labor control strategies tend to erode worker incomes, reduce union membership and revenues, and weaken union rights and bargaining leverage (Bloch 1991; Fashoyin 1990b; Graham 1995; Kapstein 1996; Standing 1991; World Bank 1995). These policies and their consequences involve significant shifts in the role of labor unions in potential coalitions and also critical policy and political tensions between the government and unions. They reduce the probability that parties, which might solicit the support of the popular classes, will do so and, in many countries, entails repression of union rights (Haggard and Kaufman 1995, chapter 6; Huber, Rueschemeyer, and Stephens 1997; IFCTU 1997–2005; Thomas 1995).

Case Studies on Unions and Democratization

The country studies in this book analyze the key questions and issues that I have raised. Robert Charlick explains why the small trade union movement in Niger, politically subordinated for years, played an extremely important role in Niger's transition and what role it played in the new democracy. He argues that both government and civil society are weak, and, consequently, slight changes in power (fiscal crises) can lead to major changes in officeholders and state capacities. Charlick notes that Niger's unions played a huge role in the national conference that regulated the transition. But under the new regime and its SAP policies, its influence ebbed rapidly. Charlick explains how the divisions within the unions—ethnic/regional, public vs. private sectors—weakened them in the face of a hostile democratic government and new military rulers.

Akwetey's and my chapter on Zambia explains how the qualities of the labor movement—growing autonomy and democratic leadership—and regime economic policies led labor to organize an opposition political party to oust the one-party state in 1990. The Zambian Congress of Trade Unions' (ZCTU's) support for this party, coupled with the fact that Zambia's new president was the prior head of that organization, severely constrained ZCTU's early willingness to strongly oppose the new government's SAP policies. Our chapter explores whether unions will continue to support a democratic government when they lose organizational influence, members, and worker incomes. The impact of depressed economic conditions and democratic pressures from union rank and file pushed ZCTU unions, and ZCTU itself, to reassert their autonomy and to struggle militantly for union/worker interests and their right to be heard on policy matters. Zambian unions continue to support democratic institutions despite suffering economic losses and harsh treatment from the democratic governments since 1990.

Richard Saunders's study of the Zimbabwe Congress of Trade Unions (ZCTU) situates the unions' struggles for rights in the context of a dominant party state. Facing a corporatist labor control strategy, Saunders explains the economic (SAP), political, and social contexts in which an increasingly democratic ZCTU claimed its independence and demanded a voice in public policies. Absent an opposition political party, can activist civic groups and unions working together obtain civil liberties, associational freedoms, and democratic rights? The ZCTU and many civics did this, under that organization's leadership, by mobilizing insistent strikes and protests, demanding democracy, and organizing a new opposition party in 1999. ZCTU militancy initially widened and reclaimed democratic space while voicing popular class policy claims. A democratic transition under way in the 1990s and 2000s has been aborted as a fully mobilized opposition party, spearheaded by the ZCTU, posed too strong a challenge to President Mugabe's government. It has resorted to a militarized police state and ruinous populist policies in defense of its power.

Geoff Bergen argues that in Senegal's dominant party system the trade unions have "indisputably been key arbiters of political change" and fuller democratization. Bergen shows how the union movement in Senegal has included a large labor federation (CNTS), affiliated with the dominant party, and a number of independent unions, linked to several of Senegal's small radical parties. Bergen explores how the education and skill levels tend to orient workers into support of more corporatist vs. more democratic unions. He demonstrates how the dominant party's attempts to capture the independent unions, and the efforts of the radical parties to generate union protests to destabilize the regime, generated a dynamic of democratic change. The periodic outbreak of politicized labor protests and regime efforts to deflect and weaken these has led, Bergen argues, to a move from single-party rule to the increasingly democratic system of the 1990s. It led finally to a democratic transition with the election of the opposition party to the presidency in 2000.

William Freund assesses the contributions of South Africa's trade unions to democratization from political economy and historical perspectives. The creation of a massively inegalitarian economy and society and its labor control system over non-whites raised for workers and unions the imperative of how to democratize the labor market and gain citizenship rights. Freund links the transformation of South Africa's economy in the 1960s and 1970s to new levels of protest and a reluctant legal recognition of unions. Freund explains the nature of this new labor movement, its independence, and the crucial role it came to play in the internal rebellion of the 1980s. In the context of South Africa's historical democratization, Freund explores the nature of COSATU's relationship to the African National Congress (ANC) and to the Communist Party and COSATU's role in the political transition. The South African case poses sharply the problems of unions in alliance with a ruling liberation party in an era of neoliberal growth strategies. The capitalist class of an ethnic/racial minority must be soothed while the unions seek policy influence and improved lives for their members.

Gretchen Bauer examines whether the trade union movement in Namibia, with its small (1.5 million) population and one-party dominant regime, can become autonomous and contribute to democratic consolidation. The South West African People's Organisation (SWAPO) government is the outcome of a hegemonic liberation movement. It helped establish the unions in Namibia and imposed its control over the largest of three union centers. Namibia is an ex-settler colony with great inequalities, in which a nationalist SWAPO claims to speak for African workers. Bauer explores the central tensions in union-state relations, noting the ability of dominant nationalist regimes to co-opt leaders and constrain union initiatives. But Bauer also demonstrates how the unions have articulated worker/union interests and sought to develop their autonomy by making common cause with other civil associations.

My chapter on Ghana argues that the trade union movement, one of Africa's largest, has consistently sought since the 1950s to develop its capacities and autonomy. Because of its leadership's largely democratic norms and the loss of its autonomy under Nkrumah (1959–66), the Trade Union Congress (TUC) has tended to support democratic regimes. But the attempt of the bourgeois leadership in the 1969–72 democracy to cripple the unions made union leaders willing to support a military regime that restored its rights (1972–78). During the 1970s and 1980s the unions contributed to Ghana's democratic ethos and space through their insistent efforts to assert their own autonomy, union rights, policy claims, and public democratic norms. Persistent efforts to control or coerce union leaders meant that the democratic expression of the unions involved the working out of struggles between state and unions as well as unions and their rank and file. The major assault upon democracy and the unions came under Rawlings's Provisional National Defense Committee (PNDC) regime. I assess how and why the unions came to reassert their autonomy and wage and policy claims, to value democratic rights, to create space for dissent, and to contribute to democratization. The union experience under Ghana's democracy since 1993 illustrates the tensions between democratic promises and capitalist adjustment policies.

In general, the chapters in this volume raise most of the central questions regarding the various ways trade unions have contributed to democratization and offer some data against which we can examine contemporary theory. In the conclusion I draw upon the chapters and some other examples to examine how Africa's trade unions have contributed to democratization thus far. I also explore whether the experiences of democratic life in this era of neoliberal economics and endless SAPs have undermined trade unions—indirectly or directly—by repression, made them more active in civic and political life, or soured them on democracy.

References

Adler, Glenn, and Eddie Webster. 1995. Challenging transition theory: The labor movement, radical reform, and transition to democracy in South Africa. *Politics and Society* 23 (March): 75–106.

Africa Demos. 1990–94. Various issues. Carter Center, Emory University.

Africa Recovery. 1991. New York. September.

Barchiesi, Franco. 1996. The social construction of labor in the struggle for democracy: The case of post-independence Nigeria. *Review of African Political Economy* 23 (September): 349–69.

Bates, Robert. 1994. The impulse to reform. In *Economic change and political liberalization in sub-Saharan Africa*, ed. Jennifer Widner, 13–28. Baltimore: Johns Hopkins University Press.

Baylies, Carolyn, and Morris Szeftel. 1992. The fall and rise of Multi-party politics in Zambia. *Review of African Political Economy* 54 (July): 75–91.

Beckman, Bjorn. 1989. Whose democracy? Bourgeois versus popular democracy. *Review of African Political Economy* 45–46:84–97.

———. 1995. The politics of labor and adjustment: The experience of the Nigeria Labor Congress. In *Between Liberalization and Oppression*, ed. Thandika Mkandawire and Adebayo Olukoshi, 281–323. Dakar: Codesria.

Beckman, Bjorn, and Attahiru Jega. 1995. Scholars and democratic politics in Nigeria. *African Review of Political Economy* 22 (June): 167–81.

Berg, Elliot, and Jeffrey Butler. 1964. Trade unions. In *Political parties and national integration in tropical Africa*, ed. James S. Coleman and Carl Rosberg, Jr., 340–81. Berkeley: University of California Press.

Bergen, Geoffrey. 1994. Unions in Senegal. 2 vols. PhD diss. Ann Arbor: U.M.I. Dissertation Services.

Bermeo, Nancy. 1997. Myths of moderation: Confrontation and conflict during democratic transitions. *Comparative Politics* 29 (April): 305–21.

Bloch, Peter. 1991. Public sector pay, employment, and performance in the context of structural adjustment. In *Democratization and structural adjustment in Africa in the*

1990's, ed. Lual Deng, Markus Kostner, Crawford Young, 142–49. Madison: University of Wisconsin Press, African Studies Program.

Bratton, Michael. 1994a. Economic crisis and political realignment in Zambia. In *Economic change and political liberalization in sub-Saharan Africa*, ed. J. Widner, 101–28. Baltimore: Johns Hopkins University Press.

———. 1994b. Micro democracy? The merger of the farmer unions in Zimbabwe. *African Studies Review* 37 (April): 9–37.

Bratton, Michael, and Nicholas van de Walle. 1992. Toward governance in Africa: Popular demands and state responses. In *Governance and politics in Africa*, ed. Goran Hyden and Michael Bratton, 27–56. Boulder, CO: Lynne Rienner.

———. 1997. *Democratic experiments in Africa*. New York: Cambridge University Press.

Broad, Robin. 1988. *Unequal alliance: The World Bank, IMF and Philippines*. Berkeley: University of California Press.

Burton, Michael, Rirchard Gunter, and John Higley. 1992. Introduction: Elite transformations and democratic regimes. In *Elites and democratic consolidation in Latin America and southern Europe*, ed. John Higley and Richard Gunter, 1–37. New York: Cambridge University Press.

Campbell, Bonnie, and John Loxley, eds. 1989. *Structural adjustment in Africa*. New York: St. Martin's Press.

Chikhi, Said. 1991. *Algeria: From mass rebellion in October 1988 to workers' social protest*. Current African Issues Series, no. 13. Uppsala, Sweden: Nordiska Afrikainstitutet.

Collier, David, and R. B. Collier. 1991. *Shaping the political arena: Critical conjunctures, the labor movement, and regime dynamics in Latin America*. Princeton, NJ: Princeton University Press.

Collier, Ruth Berins. 1999. *Paths toward democracy: The working class and elites in western Europe and South America*. Cambridge: Cambridge University Press.

Collier, Ruth Berins, and James Mahoney. 1997. Adding collective actors to collective outcomes: Labor and recent democratization in South America and southern Europe. *Comparative Politics* 29 (April): 285–303.

Coote, Belinda. 1996. *The trade trap*. New ed. Oxford: Oxfam.

Crisp, Jeffrey. 1978. The laboring poor, trade unions, and political change in Ghana. *Manpower and unemployment research* 11 (2): 93–100.

———. 1984. *The story of an African working class*. London: Zed.

Diamond, Larry. 1988. Introduction: Roots of failure, seeds of hope. In *Africa*. Vol. 2 of *Democracy in developing countries*, ed. L. Diamond, J. Linz, and S. M. Lipset, 1–32. Boulder, CO: Lynne Rienner.

———. 1993. The globalization of democracy. In *Global transformation and the third world*, ed. Robert Slater, Barry Schutz, and Steven Dorr. Boulder, CO: Lynne Rienner.

———. 1995. Nigeria: The uncivic society and the descent into praetorianism. In *Politics in developing countries*, ed. Larry Diamond, Juan Linz, and Seymour M. Lipset, 417–91. 2nd ed. Boulder, CO: Lynne Rienner.

Diamond, Larry, Juan Linz, and S. M. Lipset. 1988. Preface to *Africa*. Vol. 2 of *Democracy in developing countries*, ed. Larry Diamond, Juan Linz, and S. M. Lipset, ix–xxvii. Boulder, CO: Lynne Rienner Publishers.

Ertman, Thomas. 1998. Democracy and dictatorship in interwar Europe revisited. *World Politics* 50 (April): 475–505.

Fashoyin, Tayo. 1990a. Nigerian labor and the military: Towards exclusion? *Labour, Capital and Society* 23 (April): 12–37.

———. 1990b. Economic recession and employment security in Nigeria in the 1980s. *International Labor Review* 129 (5): 649–53.

Friedman, Steven. 1987. *Building tomorrow today: African workers in trade unions 1970–1984.* Johannesburg: Raven Press.

Ghai, Dharam, ed. 1991. *The IMF and the south: The social impact of crisis and adjustment.* London: Zed.

Gibbon, Peter, ed. 1993. *Social change and economic reform in Africa.* Uppsala, Sweden: Nordiska Afrikainstitutet.

Graham, Yao. 1995. World Bank gives ultimatum: Sack workers or no loans. *Public Agenda* 1 (March 10): l, 6.

Green, Reginald H. 1993. The IMF and the World Bank in Africa: How much learning? In *Hemmed in,* ed. Thomas Callaghy and John Ravenhill, 54–89. New York: Columbia University Press.

Greider, William. 1997. *One world, ready or not: The manic logic of global capitalism.* New York: Simon and Schuster.

Haggard, Stephen, and Robert Kaufman. 1995. *The political economy of democratic transitions.* Princeton, NJ: Princeton University Press.

Harbeson, John, Donald Rothchild, and Naomi Chazan, eds. 1994. *Civil society and the state in Africa.* Boulder, CO: Lynne Rienner.

Heilbron, John. 1993. Social origins of national conferences in Benin and Togo. *Journal of Modern African Studies* 31 (June): 277–300.

Helleiner, G. K. 1990. Conventional foolishness and overall ignorance. *Canadian Journal of Development Studies* 10 (1): 107–20.

Herbst, Jeffrey 1994. The dilemmas of explaining political upheaval. In *Economic change and political liberalization in sub-Saharan Africa,* ed. J. Widner, 182–98. Baltimore: Johns Hopkins University Press.

Huber, Evelyne, Dietrich Rueschemeyer, and John Stephens. 1997. The paradoxes of contemporary democracy. *Comparative Politics* 29 (April): 323–41.

Huntington, Samuel. 1991. *The third wave: Democratization in the late twentieth century.* Norman: University of Oklahoma Press.

International Confederation of Free Trade Unions. 1994–2006. *Annual survey of violations of trade union rights.* Brussels: International Confederation of Free Trade Unions.

International Labour Office. 1997. *Industrial relations, democracy, and social stability, world labour report, 1997–98.* Geneva: International Labour Office.

Jeffries, Richard. 1975. Populist tendencies in the Ghanaian trade union movement. In *The development of an African working class,* ed. Richard Sandbrook and Robin Cohen, 261–80. Toronto: University of Toronto Press.

———.1978. *Class, power, and ideology in Ghana: The railway men of Sekondi.* Cambridge: Cambridge University Press.

Joseph, Richard. 1997. Democracy in Africa after 1989. *Comparative Politics* 29 (April): 363–82.

Kapstein, Ethan. 1996. Workers and the world economy. *Foreign Affairs* 75 (May/June): 16–37.

Killick, Tony. 1995a. *IMF programmes in developing countries: Design and impact.* London: Routledge.

———. 1995b. Structural adjustment and poverty alleviation: An interpretive survey. *Development and Change* 16 (2): 305–31.

Kraus, Jon. 1979. Strikes and labor power in Ghana. *Development and Change* 10 (April): 259–86.

———. 1988. The political economy of trade union-state relations in radical and populist regimes in Africa. In *Labour and trade unions in Asia and Africa,* ed. Roger Southall, 171–210. New York: St. Martin's Press.

———. 1991. The political economy of stabilization and structural adjustment in Ghana. In *Ghana: The political economy of reform*, ed. Donald Rothchild, 85–100. Boulder, CO: Lynne Rienner.

———. 1995. Trade unions and democratization in Africa. In *Africa contemporary record, 1989–90*, ed. Marion Doro, A53–A72. New York: Africana.

———. 1996. The impact of structural adjustment upon employment and trade unions in Ghana and Nigeria. In *African development perspectives yearbook, 1994–95*. Vol. 4. Ed. Karl Wohlmuth and Frank Messner, 169–91. Hamburg: Lit Verlag; New Brunswick: Transaction.

Lewis, Peter. 1996. From prebendalism to predation: The political economy of decline in Nigeria. *Journal of Modern African Studies* 34 (March): 79–103.

Mahon, James. 1999. Economic crisis in Latin America: Global contagion, local pain. *Current History* 98 (March): 105–10.

Mainwaring, Scott, Guillermo O'Donell, and Samuel Valenzuela, eds. 1992. *Issues in democratic consolidation*. South Bend, IN: University of Notre Dame Press.

Marx, Anthony 1992. *Lessons of Struggle: South African Internal Opposition, 1960-1990*. New York: Oxford University Press.

Moore, Barrington. 1966. *The social origins of dictatorship and democracy*. Boston: Beacon Press.

Mosley, Paul, Jane Harrigan, and John Toye. 1991. *Aid and power: The World Bank and policy-based lending*. Vol. I Analysis, II Case Studies. New York: Routledge.

Muase, Charles K. 1989. *Syndicalisme et democratie en Afrique noire: l'experience du Burkina Faso (1936–1988)*. Paris: Editions Karthala.

O'Donnell, Guillermo. 1986. Introduction to the Latin American cases. In *Transitions from authoritarian rule, III: Latin America*, ed. Guillermo O'Donnell, Philippe Schmitter, and Laurence Whitehead, 3–18. Baltimore: Johns Hopkins University Press.

O'Donnell, Guillermo, and Philippe Schmitter. 1986. *Transitions from authoritarian rule: Tentative conclusions about uncertain democracies*. Baltimore: Johns Hopkins University Press.

Osaghae, Eghosa. 1995. The study of political transitions in Africa. *Review of African Political Economy* 22 (June): 183–97.

Otobo, Dafe, and M. Omole, eds. 1987. *Readings in Nigerian industrial relations*. Lagos: Malthouse Press.

Peace, Adrian. 1979. *Choice, class and conflict*. Atlantic Highlands, NJ: Humanities Press.

Przeworski, Adam, and Fernando Limongi. 1997. Modernization: Theories and facts. *World Politics* 49 (January): 155–83.

Rodrik, Dani. 1997. *Has globalization gone too far?* Washington, DC: Institute for International Economics.

Rueschemeyer, Dietrich, Evelyne Stephens, and John Stephens. 1992. *Capitalist development and democracy*. Chicago: University of Chicago Press.

Sandbrook, Richard. 1975. *Proletarians and African capitalism: The Kenyan case, 1960–1972*. Cambridge: Cambridge University Press.

———. 1977. The political potential of African urban workers. *Canadian Journal of African Studies* 11:411–33.

———. 1981. Worker consciousness and populist protest in tropical Africa. In *Research in the sociology of work*, ed. Richard Simpson and I. H. Simpson, 1–36. Greenwich, CT: Jai Press.

Seidman, Gay. 1994. *Manufacturing militance: Workers' movements in Brazil and South Africa, 1970–1985*. Berkeley: University of California Press.

Shin, Doh Shul. 1994. On the third wave of democratization: A synthesis and evaluation of recent theory and research. *World Politics* 47 (October): 135–70.

Southall, Roger. 1988. Introduction to *Labor and unions in Africa and Asia*, ed. Roger Southall, 1–31. New York: St. Martin's Press.

———. 1995. *Imperialism or solidarity? International labor and South African trade unions.* Cape Town: University of Cape Town Press.

Standing, Guy. 1991. Structural adjustment and labour market policies towards structural adjustment. In *Toward social adjustment*, ed. Guy Standing and Victor Tokman, 5–51. Geneva: International Labour Office.

Stiglitz, Joseph. 2002. *Globalization and its discontents.* New York: W. W. Norton.

Thomas, Henk. 1995. The erosion of trade unions. In *Globalization and third world trade unions*, ed. Thomas Henk, 3–27. London: Zed.

Tilly, Charles. 2004. *Contention and democracy in Europe, 1650–2000.* Cambridge: Cambridge University Press.

Truman, David. 1971. *The governmental process.* 2nd ed. New York: Knopf.

Valenzuela, J. Samuel. 1989. Labor movements in transitions to democracy. *Comparative Politics* 21 (July): 445–71.

Van de Walle, Nicholas. 2001. *African economies and the politics of permanent crisis.* New York: Cambridge University Press.

Waterman, Peter. 1983. *Aristocrats and plebians in African trade unions?* The Hague: Peter Waterman.

———. 1993. Social-movement unionism. *Review* 16 (Summer): 245–78.

World Bank. 1983. *World development report 1983.* Washington, DC: World Bank.

———. 1987. *World development report 1987.* Washington, DC: World Bank.

———. 1994. *Adjustment in Africa: Reform, results.* Washington, DC: World Bank.

———. 1995. *World development report 1995: Workers in an integrating world.* Washington, DC: World Bank.

CHAPTER 2

Labor, Democracy, and Development in Senegal

Geoffrey Bergen*

S enegal is a bit of a conundrum for students of both democracy and organized labor. Senegal is the anomalous African country that lapsed only briefly into one-party politics during the post-independence period. Following the elimi-nation of opposition parties through a familiar combination of co-optation and sup-pression in the late 1960s, by the mid-1970s the regime of President Leopold Senghor had once again legalized political contestation on the part of a limited num-ber of opposition parties. In 1981, Senghor's successor, Abdou Diouf, decreed unlimited rights of party formation and contestation.

Throughout this time and until its defeat in the presidential elections of 2000 and legislative elections of 2001, the ruling *Parti socialiste* clung jealously to its control of both the presidency and the national assembly. It did so largely through its ability to distribute patronage in exchange for votes, earning Senegal the just designation of "pseudo" or "quasi" democracy. Nonetheless, there is an undeniable progression of Senegal's political opening, from Senghor's highly delimited *ouverture* of the mid-1970s, through the complete party competition of the 1980s, followed by significant electoral reforms and an opening of high government positions to opposition party figures in the 1990s, and finally the victory of Abdoulaye Wade in 2000. There has been evolution within the system. But what accounts for it?

The puzzle is that while trade unions in Senegal have indisputably been key arbiters of political change, by any standard of accounting of organizational power they are weak associations, their collective force frittered away in internal divisions and disputes. Their claims on the state's protection were destroyed by the hammer blows of harsh economic reforms from the 1980s onward. Despite the long and

*Note: The views expressed in this essay are those of the author, based on dissertation research in Senegal, and do not necessarily reflect those of the World Bank.

proud pedigree of labor militancy in Senegal, dating to the famous railway workers' strike of 1947–48, by the 1980s, Senegal's labor force had been successfully divided into a number of union organizations typically as absorbed with battles for primacy among themselves as they were with mounting challenges to the prerogatives of employers or the power of the ruling party. From the mid-1980s onward, unions also seemed helpless as key worker protections within Senegalese labor law were eradicated or diluted. Yet it is precisely trade unions that—I will contend—repeatedly provided the momentum for political change in Senegal, and continued to do so into the 1990s.

Unions in Senegal: An Overview

In 1990 the formal sector of Senegal's economy contained roughly 180,000 workers (including temporary workers),[1] about 70,000 of whom belonged to some trade union. Of this number, about 50,000 belonged to the *Confédération nationale des travailleurs du Sénégal* (CNTS), while 20,000 or so belonged to one of nearly a dozen "autonomous" unions, which at the time were loosely organized within two federations.[2] As a legacy of the French labor law that had been inserted wholesale into Senegal in the 1950s, each of these union groupings competed for members within different workplaces. Secondary school teachers—traditionally the most militant of labor groups—had a choice of three unions, and most other types of workers had a choice of at least two. In workplaces dominated by the government-affiliated CNTS (the case in most industrial occupations), the union organization was typically divided among rival *tendances,* or *"clans,"* identified with one or another claimant to top position within the union. Needless to say, these divisions tended to dilute the striking power of the unions.

This fissiparous tendency had long defined the condition of worker organization in Senegal. At root, it was connected to the extremely divergent sociological, ideological, and workplace interests of a complex labor force—which labor legislation helped only to guide into an organizational motley.

The "blue-collar" labor force of workers in industry, transport, and menial service occupations consisted mostly of workers with low levels of education—many being illiterate—while the "white-collar" workforce of teachers, technicians, and public sector employees typically had postsecondary education, and frequently higher. These differences corresponded to vastly divergent preferences for the form and content of worker organization. For the most part, the less-educated workers in the industrial and service sectors favored patronage-style organizations of the sort familiar to Senegal's countryside; these served as the ruling party's mechanism for holding on to power. This orientation lent itself to the form of unionism presented by the CNTS, which would best be described as a patronage structure deriving its resources from the grander patronage mechanisms of the state. While Senegal's Labor Code provides a formal framework for union structure, elections, and administration, the typical practice within the CNTS is for informal and personal relations to prevail.

Better capable of self-organization, white-collar workers preferred more combative organizations that catered to their professional interests. As a rule, they preferred not to see their interests diluted in the context of broad "lowest-common-denominator" union programs of the type offered by the CNTS—hence their innate preference for independent unionism.[3] Just as these educated professionals tended to prefer smaller unions with a more focused agenda to represent their workplace demands, they equally tended to choose one or another of Senegal's numerous opposition parties to represent their political beliefs. While it is true that a large number of white-collar workers remained loyal to the ruling *Parti socialiste*, it is also the case that these workers formed the bedrock membership of most opposition parties. These parties, for reasons of their own, saw the opportunity to control the leadership of unions of this sort as an extremely important weapon in their political arsenals. Having only limited electoral appeal (the exception being the *Parti Démocratique Sénégalais* [PDS] of Abdoulaye Wade), Senegal's small, mostly Marxist, parties saw unions as the battering ram that would force open the portals of national power, and events were to prove them right.

Thus, the two autonomous union groupings (as of 1990) reflected an underlying split in the party affiliations of union leadership. One of these labor federations, known as the *Confédération des syndicats autonomes* (CSA), consisted of four unions, three of which were associated with the Leninist *Parti de l'indépendance et du travail* (PIT). The other labor federation, the *Union des syndicats autonomes du Sénégal* (UNSAS), contained five unions, four of whose leaders were connected with political parties in a nine-party coalition, *Conférence nationale des chef de parties de l'opposition* (CONACPO), led by Abdoulaye Wade, long the most prominent of Senegal's antigovernment politicians. The lack of cooperation between the CSA and UNSAS union federations reflected a prior falling out between their respective party allies, the PIT and the CONACPO group. When, as in December 1990, one of these groupings went on strike (the UNSAS federation), the other did not support the strike, and the large CNTS remained entirely passive.

That there were inherent divisions within Senegal's labor formations was not lost on national political authorities, who from about 1970 onward pursued a deliberate policy of dividing labor against itself. At the same time, it has equally been the goal of the political opponents of the state to bring as many workers as possible together in combative labor organizations. That they succeeded—if only partially, briefly, and at roughly ten-year intervals (1968–69, 1979–80, and 1989–90)—provides a key explanation for Senegal's progression from single-party rule to increasingly liberal democratic structures.

The following account explores the reasons for the oscillations of Senegal's labor force, and how the labor force has affected national political institutions. Within Senegal, a protean mechanism exists whereby the state, threatened by the mounting combativeness of union-party coalitions, undertakes the alteration of political institutions in ways designed to play upon the natural divisions in the labor movement and thereby break apart the threat. Following a period of relative calm, unions and their party allies adapt to the new institutional nexus in ways that allow them to create a renewed threat to power. Two major factors have converged at regular intervals to bring workers back into relative cohesion: economic distress and political oppression. The emergence of widespread economic deterioration gives workers of vastly different backgrounds the incentive to form tentative alliances around common themes of economic justice and job security. Political oppression gives opposition political organizations incentives to assail power through non-electoral means, which in Senegal has meant their all-out efforts to gain control over unions.

The story of political change in Senegal has been one of institutional adjustment by the state in the face of threats from union coalitions. This has been followed by negative economic effects resulting from these very institutions, as well as by a halt to the momentum of political change. This has driven political opposition to renewed militancy. A threatened government responds with further institutional change that quells the most recent menace, and the cycle begins anew.

Unions and Politics in the 1970s

Worker organizations have existed in Senegal since the nineteenth century, and by the 1940s a tradition of labor militancy against the French colonial administration and *patronat* was already well established. The end of World War II was accompanied by a sudden growth of the labor force as France belatedly invested in the economic growth of its African colonies. This was coupled with successive expansions of political rights, including rights of union formation and activism (the Overseas Labor Code of 1952 extended French labor law, with some modification, to the colonies), and the arrival on the African scene of union organizers from the great French labor federations, especially the French Communist Party–affiliated *Confédération générale du travail*. The result was an increasingly well-organized, militant union movement with organic ties to the various political parties that were also forming at the time. Successive waves of strikes in key economic sectors brought the colonial economies of Senegal and the other territories of French West Africa to a standstill, and they proved perhaps the most significant challenge to French authority in the late colonial period. The strikes also proved to be a central preoccupation of the dominant political formation, the *Bloc démocratique sénégalais*, led by Léopold Senghor, who never was able to win complete control over the unions.

Central to Senghor's approach to unions—indeed, to political opposition—in the 1960s was his conviction (with reasonable cause) that labor militancy resulted from the machinations of political parties entrenched in the unions. Over the course of the 1960s, the Senghor administration experimented with several formulas for keeping its political opponents away from union affairs. As the decade proceeded, with each successive approach failing as a means of labor control, the regime's general political policy took on an increasingly authoritarian demeanor.

Unity of all legally constituted political forces had, by 1966, become the regime's obsession. Its overriding concern was to eliminate all operating capacity of the remaining radical political elements that had plagued it since the late independence era (largely through their infiltration of labor). On June 13, 1966, following secret negotiations, the leadership of the one remaining legal opposition party, the *Parti du rassemblement Africain-Sénégal* (PRA-Senegal), and the ruling *Union progressiste sénégalaise* (UPS) signed an agreement on unification. A key element of the agreement was "unification at the base," which meant a merger into the ruling party–sponsored *Union nationale des travailleurs sénégalais* (UNTS) of the several independent unions that continued to exist—and which harbored large numbers of members from disenfranchised radical parties among its leading militants. See Table 2.1 for union links to parties.

Beneath the surface of labor placidity in the mid-1960s was swelling worker discontent over the serious erosion of purchasing power since the previous wage increases in 1960–61. It was most visibly apparent in the lower ranks of union leadership, which consisted, for the most part, of relatively young skilled employees with at least a primary education and some additional technical training; here and there, one could find an energetic autodidact impatiently closeted in the stifling atmosphere of pro-government unionism. By 1965, with nepotism and corruption proliferating in a number of visible ways in both the ruling party and its affiliated union, with prices for vital consumer goods rising at a rapid rate, and with the government unwilling to budge on its wage freeze, these shop-floor union representatives were beginning to express rebellious anger.

Into this tinderbox the Senghor regime let drop a lighted match when it so enthusiastically brought about the unification of political and union forces. Capable and disgruntled young men who were occupying mid-level union leadership positions had, for the most part, been supporters of Senghor and the UPS. Now, with the unification of the UNTS and independent unions, the Left opposition union cadres were let loose among them. The effect was explosive.

In late May 1968 leftist leaders propelled the UNTS into supporting a student strike at the University of Dakar, an act that opened a floodgate of urban discontent resulting from declining living standards. Although the workers joined into the several days of riots and general mayhem that followed in a largely spontaneous and unorganized way, Senghor clearly considered the event a turning point in the political fortunes of his regime. The events of 1968 (which were followed by rising labor militancy into 1969) provided Senghor with much food for thought. They brought him to initiate both political and economic changes that would have significant consequences for Senegal's future development. Constitutional reforms launched in 1970 increased Senghor's personal power as president, while his concomitant economic plan launched a period of heavy state penetration of production and services.

In the immediate aftermath of the May–June 1968 strike, Doudou Ngom, hitherto the secretary-general of the UNTS who had been cast into a marginal role by the far more vigorous radical leaders, announced the formation of a new labor central, the *Confédération nationale des travailleurs du Sénégal*, or CNTS. The new union would be a "national union central . . . capable of playing its role beside the Party and the Government in the battle against underdevelopment and for the maintenance of an authentic democracy."[4]

Henceforth, workers would be allowed to voice their complaints through "responsible participation." Senghor set forth the principles of *participation responsable* at the 7th UPS Congress in December 1969. First, the CNTS would be an integral part of the UPS. Second, adherence to a CNTS affiliate union would be required of any worker who was a UPS member; any worker who joined some party would have to join the UPS. Third, the CNTS would be admitted into all the organs of the ruling party and of the state: there would thus be at least one, and usually more, CNTS representatives in the UPS National Council and Political Bureau. Fourth, and last, within the state, the CNTS was to constitute an "eighth region" (that is, in addition to its seven geographically defined administrative regions), entitling it to 10 percent of the seats in the National Assembly, two positions within the government, and a like proportion of seats in municipal and regional governing bodies.

The CNTS "system" became the mechanism through which the UPS exercised its ability to name union leaders to its liking. Union elections did continue to occur regularly, yet they were widely considered to be rigged in favor of the ruling party's choices. Through the CNTS even the lowest layer of union leaders, the *délégués du personnel* (shop stewards), might hope for some sinecure and the access to patronage resources that would provide. Individual workers were meant to know that through their membership in some CNTS affiliate they might expect the state's implicit backing in any employment dispute.

Thus the system rapidly came to rest on rewarding loyalty rather than efficacy among the worker representatives. What complicated matters was that competing pretenders to some position of union leadership would come to receive support from one or another faction within the ruling party itself. This rapidly poisoned the internal atmosphere of the CNTS. By the mid-1970s, virtually all professional unions of any significance were absorbed in battles among union *tendances*, which spread upward and outward through the CNTS member federations and into the top circles of union leadership—a feature of the CNTS that continues to the present day. Throughout CNTS's existence, its principle attribute has been instability. Beginning in the 1970s, while the CNTS presented a largely placid exterior appearance, its interior roiled with factional battles over union power.[5] Within the CNTS, a key aspect of such factionalism has been its focus on the qualities of persons rather than any ideology they might represent, although there was inevitably a thin veneer of ideology in disputes over the virtues of absolute loyalty to the state. CNTS's other vital, and ever-present, attribute has been the virtually total abandonment of the traditional union functions of protest and collective bargaining. Under the Senegalese variant of the Labor Code that has descended throughout French-speaking Africa from the *Code du travail* of 1952, an elaborate system of negotiations is supposed to see serious bargaining taking place at several levels: from national-level discussion of the minimum wage to plant-level negotiations over conditions of work and worker privileges. There were periodic increases in the minimum wage in these years, but the largest, occurring in 1974, came as a gesture from Senghor (at a time when he had just sanctioned opposition party formation, leading him to worry about the loyalty of workers) in the absence of bargaining with the CNTS. Although isolated CNTS affiliate unions and federations of unions, for the most part, organized and led protests, the CNTS has operated as one among other patron-client structures that had been established by the state for purposes of political control.

The CNTS was created to separate politically supportive or neutral workers from the covert opposition; what happened in fact was the creation of a union structure that was most amenable to the largely illiterate and highly insecure mass of private-sector workers. The *fonctionnaire* unionists—teachers at the secondary level and higher, health workers, technicians, and others—remained isolated in the old UNTS. By 1973 their union was driven out of legal existence by a government that had adopted an unprecedented aggressiveness in dealing with its foes. Rather than join the CNTS, which many of these workers could not stomach, they retreated to

Table 2.1 Trade Unions and Political Party Relationships in Senegal

Political parties	Trade Unions: affiliated or linked	Changes in linkages/roles
Parti socialiste (PS)/Socialist Party, ruling party 1960–2000. Previously Union progressiste sénégalais (UPS).	Confédération national des travailleurs du Sénégal (CNTS)/National Workers Federation of Senegal. Dominant union federation, largely controlled by ruling PS. Previously called UNTS.	Although aligned w/ PS, some unions would occasionally join anti-PS unions in major strikes. CNTS leader in 1980's achieved some autonomy by threatening to join protests w/ anti-PS.
Parti démocratique sénégalais/Senegalese Democratic Party (PDS), opposition party until it won 2000 elections.	Union des travailleurs libres du Sénégal (UTLS)/Free Workers Union of Senegal, organized by Wade's PDS in 1976. Confédération des syndicats autonomes du Sénégal (UNSAS)/ Federation of Autonomous Unions of Senegal. Loose alliance of nine unions, 4 of whose leaders were linked to CONACPO, alliance of party headed by PDS.	
Parti de l'indépendence et du travail/Independence & Labor Party (PIT), Leninist, small. After split, called PAI-Senegal.	Confédération des syndicates autonomes (CSA)/Federation of Autonomous Unions. Three of four members unions were linked closely to PIT.	During 1980s heads of pro-PIT unions aligned tactically w/ CNTS to strengthen their position.
	Autonomous unions, not part of any federations but part of intermittent alliances w/ other unions & federations: *Sole Democratic Union of Senegalese Teachers (SUDES) 1977–__. Split in 1987, leaving SUDES (pro-PIT) and *Democratic Teachers Union of Senegal (UDEN, pro-LD). *SUTSAS: autonomous health workers union. *SUTELEC, one of national electrical company unions.	Led massive teachers strike, 1980.

amicales, or "worker clubs," which enjoyed none of the legal rights and protections accorded unions. The de facto unattractiveness of the CNTS to middle-class workers would permanently affect the workings of the CNTS. Gone forever was the potential for rallying together private and public sector workers to force the state to its knees. Henceforth, the social basis of the majoritarian union would contribute to its evolution on the model of rural clan politics.[6]

These changes were accompanied by the simultaneous elimination of opposition to the regime, which had taken up residence within what remained of autonomous unions. A series of laws followed in quick succession, effectively making it impossible to launch a legal strike.[7] The UNTS lingered on until March 1973, when the government officially destroyed it under the 1965 law against seditious organizations.

Much of Senegal's subsequent political and union history stems from the period of state-union conflict around 1970. Virtually all the top leaders of radical opposition parties were present in the battles between unions and the government in this period. And the strikes of 1968 are viewed (through rose-tinted glasses) as the model for labor unity that remains the goal of all union formations. That the unity that actually occurred in 1968 was spurious and ephemeral, at best, is beside the point entirely.

Autonomous unions, though suppressed for the time being, would reemerge later in the 1970s, formed around isolated occupational groupings. Contrary to all expectations, their time in the wilderness would serve to reinforce their organic strengths. The pattern of independent unionism that was to emanate from this period would be the secretive, disciplined, and cell-like organizations that formed along lines suggested by the Leninist readings of their leaders. Both the nature of these unions and the mutual dependence formed at this time among them and the clandestine, outlawed parties would affect the character of the autonomous unions and their Marxist party allies right up to the 1990s.

Democratization and the Unions

At some point in 1973 Senghor decided he would permit Abdoulaye Wade to form an opposition party, the *Parti Démocratique Sénégalais* (PDS), which received official recognition on August 8, 1974. On the surface of things, it did not appear that unions had any influence upon Senghor's decision. Yet Donal B. Cruise O'Brien, writing at that time, makes a compelling case that fear of a comeback by independent unions was a major factor in Senghor's thinking.

> [T]he intention (at least originally) was to provide for a moderate legal alternative party which might recruit among the government's own employees . . . [I]f the state's employees are in material terms still clearly a privileged elite, it remains equally clear that their strike action can immobilize the state apparatus . . . [I]f the trade union leadership could be divided and/or bought, the membership although quiescent since 1970 retains an acute enough sense of material grievance and political frustration. In these circumstances, it might not be altogether frivolous to suggest that the PDS opposition, with its widely-read newspapers, could be (presidentially) intended to provide at least a harmless distraction for restive state employees.[8]

Importantly, Senghor did not arrive at his decision to permit the reestablishment of political competition until after he had eliminated the oppositionist unions in 1973. In light of these points, it is entirely reasonable to advance that Senghor's re-democratization exercise was responsive to the problem of organized labor, particularly *fonctionnaires*, whom he recognized to be capable of forming unions in clandestinity as easily as in open view. To forestall a recurrence of this threat, he decided to create the less dangerous diversion of a loyally oppositionist political party. He stated his intentions quite clearly "in favor of a limited party pluralism, not a union pluralism."[9] The last thing that Senghor expected to see occur was a renaissance of independent unionism; he apparently believed that a legal political party would be perceived by restive workers as a viable alternative to some union. Ironically enough, union formation was the first thing that happened as a result of his democratization.

By 1975 Abdoulaye Wade had linked up with Mamadou "Puritain" Fall—an old warhorse of oppositionist unionism—to pursue the goal of launching a PDS-allied union alternative to the CNTS. They quickly formed the *Union des travailleurs libres du Sénégal* (UTLS), which in 1976 claimed a membership of ten thousand workers (probably an exaggeration), despite the government's refusal to grant it legal recognition.

The appearance of the UTLS outraged Senghor, who had clearly not anticipated that Wade would hold any appeal for workers. The UTLS was eventually accorded legal recognition in 1977, in part, no doubt, because Senghor realized that more dangerous alternatives existed to a PDS-sponsored unionism in the form of an increasingly cohesive underground coalition of radical politicians and disaffected unionists. The UTLS began to siphon large numbers of workers away from the largely inactive and corrupt CNTS. By 1980, however, UTLS pulled apart at the seams under the pressure of political disputes between cofounders Wade and Fall, coupled with increasingly serious attempts by radical underground parties to seize control of the union apparatus. Nonetheless, the minor victories of UTLS in the late 1970s amounted to a major delegitimation of the CNTS and embarrassment for a political regime bent on assuring social stability and fending off challenges from the opposition.

The true importance of the UTLS was that it served as an opening wedge against the regime's reluctance to admit independent unionism. Through that opening strode a renascent set of radical political parties that would begin to use unions in an increasingly well-organized assault on the primacy of the ruling party (which became the *Parti socialiste*, or PS, in 1976). Since the time of Senghor's effective banishing of multiparty competition (1966 to 1974), the old PAI had broken into two contending factions, the *Ligue démocratique/Mouvement pour le parti du travail* (LD/MPT) and the PAI-Sénégal (later renamed the *Parti de l'indépendance et du travail*, or PIT). They were divided by ideological and personal rivalries while simultaneously competing for the title of Senegal's "true" Leninist party. During the late 1960s a group of Senegalese students who had adopted Maoism while they were students in France formed *And-jëf/Mouvement révolutionnaire pour la démocratie nouvelle* (AJ/MRDN). Finally, Senghor's old *intellectual* rival Cheikh Anta Diop formed the *Rassemblement nationale démocratique* (RND), whose doctrine resembled a Bandung-style nationalism. While space does not permit a recounting of the disagreements and doctrinal battles that divided these clandestine parties, nor of the smaller political groupings that also began forming at the time, it remains important to note two major points: first, their membership was largely limited to the workforce of educated *fonctionnaires*, especially teachers; and second, they shared one overriding strategic goal, namely, to assail the edifice of power surrounding Senghor and his regime by winning control over labor unions.

Given the personal and doctrinal antipathies between these illegal parties—which were to become manifest once the parties were legalized and exposed to the light of day in the 1980s—it was amazing that during the late 1970s they collaborated in an effective oppositionist bloc. Two factors brought this about: (1) Senghor's continuing refusal to grant recognition to parties other than those he sanctioned, and (2) the legal possibility of forming an independent union. When it became clear during the electoral campaigning of 1977 and 1978 that Senghor would refuse to allow the free formation of political parties, they came together to pursue the only logical strategy open to them: a collaborative launching of a new union for teachers, the *Syndicat unique et démocratique des enseignants sénégalais*, or SUDES (see Table 2.1).

Teachers, when comprehensively organized, form the most politically important single workforce in Senegal (and this is probably true of most French-speaking African countries). They are simultaneously the largest group of wage earners—Senegal's primary school teachers alone grew in number from 5,813 in 1971 to 9,482 in 1981)—and the most prone to organize within strongly constituted unions. Earlier, the teachers' union the *Syndicat des enseignants sénégalais* (SES) had been the driving force behind the radicalized UNTS, and it was the chief target of Senghor's union repression of the early 1970s. Teachers were by far the most likely of occupational groups to belong to one or another of the underground political parties; indeed, many of the leaders of these parties were drawn from among teachers.

The approach adopted by the politicized union leadership of the late 1970s was to rattle the state into surrender by engendering a strong union challenge to its authority on the basis of purely occupational issues. The pull of SUDES's call for reform and better working conditions in the schools was so powerful it even drew in large numbers of PS members whose radical union leaders were bent on their party's destruction. From an early membership of around two thousand, probably representing the total number of clandestine party members among teachers at the time, SUDES's membership ballooned to six to seven thousand by 1981 and could count on the support of most of the remaining teachers.

The underground political leaders behind SUDES had also come to appreciate the strategic value of public support. Its theme of "the schools crisis" found considerable sympathy with a public that still harbored sentiments that the Senghor regime had done little to improve the lot of the common people. In addition, by the late 1970s Senegal was to enter perhaps the most severe economic crisis of its existence, provoked by the oil crisis of 1979.

Conflict between SUDES and the state began in earnest over the union's call for an "Estates-General for Education," which Senghor resolutely refused to consider. Even the normally pro-regime Mouride and Tijanya Islamic brotherhoods sided with the teachers' movement as it swelled and won public support. In short, through its leadership's adroit handling of internal organizing and public sentiment, SUDES quickly made itself into the spearhead of the most significant challenge to the Senghor regime's authority since the near disaster of 1968.

Beginning in 1979, under the capable generalship of Mamadou Ndoye, a school inspector who was also a leading member of the underground *Ligue démocratique*, the union carried out an intensive public information campaign, culminating in a "national day of action" on December second. When it held a twenty-four-hour warning strike on May 13, 1980, the government blundered into an overreaction, mobilizing the police and paramilitary forces to occupy schools and suspending the union's leaders from this job. In response, the union ordered its members to refuse to grade exams—a gesture which, in a system wherein students' futures were determined by school-administered tests, was bound to cause public outrage. Interestingly, public anger was directed not at teachers but at the Senghor government. To Senghor's increasingly peevish outbursts indicting the protests as politically motivated (which they were), Ndoye responded with calm dignity that SUDES's grievances only addressed years of the government's corrupt and inept management of the schools. The union was clearly winning the battle for public approval.

Matters were deteriorating rapidly for Senghor and his government. Although strikes—frequently led by the UTLS or by local CNTS delegates who had broken with a thoroughly corrupt national leadership—were becoming commonplace in the industrial sector, they did not constitute a threat on the order of magnitude of the SUDES challenge. At the same time, the economy was falling apart, partly the result of adverse terms of trade shifts, but largely the consequence of disastrous ineptitude in the management of the parastatal-dominated industrial sector. Confrontations with SUDES were growing increasingly violent. By October 1980 the schools were in an uproar, with thousands of students roaming the streets and engaged in sporadic acts of violence and vandalism.

The potential existed for a widespread social rebellion organized and led by the unions, which would have forced Senghor to declare marshal law and therewith nullify the liberal secular polity he believed he had built. The alternative, of course, would have been to recognize the demands of his political opponents, using the unions so effectively against him; but this he no doubt found equally repulsive. On the horns of this dilemma, he abruptly announced his resignation (in a *Le Monde* interview of October 21). It is likely that a number of causes lay behind his decision to leave office (he himself cited his advanced age—he was seventy-four in 1980—and his long-held intention to turn power over to a younger generation). But there can be little room for doubt that his own policies of political repression, coupled with a failed economic statism, had engendered a union-led social upsurge of discontent that threatened to cripple his regime. He had little option but to leave office with dignity while he still could.

The 1980s: Democratic Pluralism and the Unions

Abdou Diouf took office as president of Senegal on January 1, 1981, and found himself confronted with a sea of troubles. First, the coffers were dry: Senegal's economic debacle had forced it into the first of a series of stabilization agreements and adjustment loans with the World Bank and the International Monetary Fund in 1979. And their conditions for bailing out the bankrupt Senegalese state amounted to the end of rule by patronage (which continued, of course, but in a more subdued form than previously). Second, Diouf lacked any broad-based national constituency as a fall-back for political support; he owed his rise through the government hierarchy to the position of prime minister in the 1970s entirely to Léopold Senghor. Third, he inherited the seething social discontent being led by the unions, which threatened any chance he had of legitimating his rule in the near term.

Diouf solved his problems and consolidated his rule through a series of master-strokes aimed at the unions. He also took steps—which cannot be covered adequately here—to gain control of a ruling party apparatus that was firmly in the control of well-entrenched Senghorian "barons." On his second day in office he declared that the teachers could have their long-demanded Estates-General for Education. The event, which took place at the end of that month (January 1981), was carefully managed by the government to make it appear as if it had been its idea all along; and it resulted in nothing more costly than a promise to launch a set of commissions to study specific problems in the schools. Yet by making this concession, Diouf afforded SUDES enough of a sense of self-satisfaction that it abandoned militancy and gave the president the breathing space he needed.

Next, on May 6, 1981, the National Assembly passed a law at Diouf's request permitting unfettered rights of political party formation. The clandestine formations immediately filed for recognition, and by the end of 1981 there would be eleven parties in legal existence.

Up to this point in time the covert parties could collaborate in relative harmony, setting aside their rival claims to doctrinal turf and members so long as they had state oppression in common. SUDES had been launched and had risen to a position of considerable union power largely as a consequence of this cooperation (and this was true to a somewhat lesser extent of the UTLS). Under conditions of illegality despite Senghor's claims to political liberality, these parties had viewed their joint promotion and direction of unions as the most effective means to bludgeon their way into a degree of national power.

This collaboration had always been fragile at best. Now Diouf removed the reason for opposition party alliance by permitting parties to emerge into the open. There, as Diouf had almost certainly anticipated, they quickly fell to bickering over doctrine and primacy within the Left. As a result, their ability to contribute to union solidification was greatly diminished.[10] In fact, their disputes took on a particularly virulent form over rival claims to being the party of workers. The first—and most disastrous—manifestation of their discord occurred when Mamadou Ndoye and his *Ligue démocratique* faction were maneuvered out of the leadership of SUDES by a coalition of the other parties engineered by the PIT (which the PAI-Sénégal became upon legalization). This resulted in permanently splitting SUDES, for Ndoye created a faction that refused to recognize official union leadership and eventually (in 1987) departed to form a separate teachers' union, the *Union démocratique des enseignants sénégalais* (UDEN). With SUDES thus weakened, and the UTLS permanently splintered (various factions continued to exist as of 1990–91, but with very few worker memberships), the Diouf regime had, by instituting a major change in political structure, achieved its certain goal of gutting the force of labor's growing power.

The third step taken by the Diouf regime was to reform the moribund CNTS. In February 1981 there appeared on the streets of Dakar a *Manifeste du renouveau syndical* (Manifest for Union Renewal) signed by the leaders of twenty-five CNTS affiliate unions demanding the end of corrupt and inept leadership of the government-affiliated central. The name at the top of the list was Madia Diop, a veteran of militant unionism in the 1960s, who had brought his Union of Food-Processing Industries into the CNTS at its inception and gone on to become by far the most active and well-regarded of its leaders by the workers. (Senghor, who considered him an opportunist, had repeatedly barred his way to the top of the central organization.) Following a year of heated, and sometimes violent, jockeying for power, a CNTS convention in April 1982 elected Madia (I follow the popular convention in Senegal of referring to him by his first name), with the likely support of the Diouf regime. Madia immediately set about routing the well-fed rats from the attic of the union central, and he instituted measures that he claimed would make the CNTS a much more accountable and capable organization in the representation of workers' interests.

In the end, he did not: the CNTS of the late 1980s and early 1990s would remain as corrupt and internally divided as ever before. And with the arrival on the scene in full force of structural adjustment—which stipulated cutbacks in public sector spending, the privatization of parastatal companies, and a reduction in legal protections for job security—the union found itself relegated to fighting a series of defensive holding actions rather than winning major concessions for the working classes. Nonetheless, the presence of a CNTS that had promoted its most energetic, militant, and (to all appearances) honest leader to the position of secretary-general drew many members away from the autonomous unions (particularly within the UTLS) that had appeared in the late 1970s. For example, one of Madia's first acts as secretary-general was to win approval (through manipulating his ties to the government in this honeymoon period) of a sorely needed Interprofessional Collective Bargaining Agreement, replacing the scattered industrial agreements that had been in place in many cases since the colonial era.

Space does not permit of a full accounting of the evolution of the CNTS through the 1980s and into the 1990s. What is important to note is that the CNTS continued to dominate union membership in the industrial sector despite a singular lack of effectiveness in pursuing the collective interests of workers. For example, the Interprofessional Collective Bargaining Agreement had left open for negotiation specific provisions for worker rights and benefits at the level of different industrial sectors; these negotiations never took place, in most cases. It is equally important to note that Madia would increase his power within the union to the point of being inextricable: he remained until 2001, when his old enemy Abdoulaye Wade succeeded in having him ousted. He did so through weaving an intricate web of support both inside and outside the union, providing him with multiple bases of power that gave him a real measure of autonomy from the government and the ruling party. He gradually maneuvered his political opponents out of positions of union power by funneling patronage to their rivals within the union. (This would culminate in a violent confrontation with his internal enemies at the old *Bourse du travail* in 1984, with

Madia's forces winning the day at the cost of the death of one of their numbers.) Madia also formed external alliances with opposition political forces, and even their union allies. In doing this, he managed to blackmail the government into allowing him to remain at the top. The further point is that the nominal renovation of the CNTS, coupled with the splintering of the opposition parties occasioned by Diouf's democratization, had for the time being eviscerated the force of autonomous unionism.

The Late 1980s: The Autonomous Union Comeback

Following Diouf's masterful weakening of the several coalitions of radical parties and autonomous unions at the beginning of his presidency, opposition parties and their union allies alike spent a few years wandering aimlessly in the political wilderness. Diouf trounced the divided opposition in the 1983 elections, throwing them into a period of reflection and restructuring. While opposition parties may have truly believed that they could gain legislative seats following their legalization—and perhaps even a government ministry via the electoral process—the 1983 elections wiped away their illusions. By 1985 the opposition parties had reequipped themselves with strategies designed once more to ride to power on the union omnibus. Some of the parties (notably *And-jëf* and the *Ligue démocratique*) removed militant leaders and factions, reflecting a decision to do business in the open political arena in a more measured and publicly acceptable manner.[11] The most important outcome of this new pragmatism (duly justified with references to the works of Lenin) was the willingness of a critical node of radical opposition parties to hold truck with Abdoulaye Wade—a self-avowed economic liberal.

Senegal's politically savvy urbanites were to be repeatedly astonished in the late 1980s by a series of political alliances between Wade and his PDS and the *Ligue démocratique*, *And-jëf*, and several smaller parties. These coalitions of some mighty odd bedfellows make sense only if their real objective was to gain influence over unions. For, while working at odds with one another, few of the opposition parties could muster a majority of workers within any potential union; working together, they certainly could—and did.

Helping their attempts to gain influence within unions was a further factor: the arrival in full force of structural adjustment and wide resentment within the workforce against a seemingly acquiescent government. (The general public appears to have shared that resentment.) For the second structural adjustment program, which went into effect in 1986, explicitly sought privatization of the public and para-public organizations in which many potential members of autonomous unions were located, such as the Office of Posts and Telecommunications and the Dakar region transport society (SOTRAC). These employees were thus faced with loss of their semi-*fonctionnaire* status, with its prized employment security. The civil service was targeted for major staff reductions; teachers and health workers were being pressured into efficiency-producing measures, implying more work for stagnant pay. Once more, the combination of continued political intolerance and economic insecurity were to pave the way for reinvigorated opposition party–union coalitions and a new wave of labor militancy.

The holdout to these coalitions was the party claiming the true mantle of Leninism (which was indeed legitimated by its receipt of Soviet funding), the *Parti de l'indépendance et du travail*. The PIT, which retained its ability to proclaim itself unpolluted by alliance with an unabashed pro-Western liberal like Wade, was to spend much of the late 1980s consolidating its own autonomous union connections and pursuing a perhaps even less holy alliance than that of its Marxist competitors. This was the PIT's on-again, off-again coalition with Madia Diop, that shrewdest of union survivors who at the head of the CNTS was able to parley rumors of his alliances with the PIT into a palpable threat that forestalled the government's imposition of revisions to the Labor Code. These revisions, another element of the second (and then the third) structural adjustment plan, would have destroyed remaining job security provisions and (since he was, after all, a vice president of the National Assembly that would have to sanction the changes) completely undermined Madia's legitimacy within the industrial unions. These rumors took on real substance when, in the annual May Day parade in Dakar in 1990, Madia marched at the head of the worker delegations hand-in-hand with Amath Dansokho, the PIT's general secretary. Such brinksmanship on Madia's part underpinned his authority over the largely ineffective CNTS union apparatus; it confirmed the enmity of the old conservative core within the ruling party and kept Abdou Diouf forever guessing about Madia's loyalties. But his dalliance with the PIT made it too dangerous for the ruling party to attack.

The harbinger of renewed labor militancy under opposition party guidance came with the strike of government health service workers in the autonomous union SUT-SAS, whose secretary-general, Bakhao Seck, happened to be a ranking member of the *Ligue démocratique*. In July 1984, SUTSAS had heralded its presence with a two-day work stoppage, which won considerable public sympathy because (while working conditions and job security were the real issues) the union publicized grievances such as lack of medical supplies. The May 1985 strikes, from the sixth to the eighth and again from the thirteenth to the nineteenth, caused a public uproar—the result of the several deaths due to patient neglect that the strikes occasioned—whose target was more the government than the union. This evidently provoked a near panic within the regime; it constituted the return of a bogeyman that Diouf had thought dead and buried: a cohesive and aggressive public sector union. The danger lay in such a union's potential to rally further defections from the relatively passive CNTS, and in the capacity for this sort of event to serve as a touchstone to massive civil unrest. While the government acted quickly, through both threats and concessions to end the strike, it appears in retrospect as a point of departure. Soon the phosphate workers at Taiba engaged in a work stoppage. In May and June, bank and postal workers engaged in go-slows.

In July 1985 the *Alliance démocratique sénégalaise* (ADS) was formed by five opposition parties, including Wade's PDS, with its large electoral numbers, and *And-jëf* and the *Ligue démocratique*, with their union connections. Soon afterward, autonomous union formations either took form or took on new life. Facilitated by this new political alliance on the center-left that excluded the PIT, Mamadou Ndoye led a large group of teachers out of SUDES (which the PIT dominated) to form the *Union démocratique des enseignants nationale* (UDEN). At the university a group of professors (led by members of *And-jëf* and the *Ligue démocratique*) formed the *Syndicat autonome des enseignants du supérieur* (SAES). They would be joined in loose alliance by the workers of the national electric utility, whose union SUTELEC had a long tradition of militancy, and of the postal and telecommunications service whose union SNTPT had previously been a rare radical faction within the CNTS.

What remains of greatest interest about these autonomous unions is that despite the highly public political affiliations of their leaders, they adhered to a very real standard of autonomy. They had no choice, if they were to recruit successfully within their professional groupings. Past experience, particularly that of SUDES and the UTLS, showed that unions quickly fell apart when parties too overtly sought control. A large number of union members were, in fact, apolitical. As many of them averred in interviews, and as subsequent events would demonstrate, any sense within the rank and file that they were being asked to take risks in undertaking protests on behalf of party interests would lead them to defect from union action. It is important to note that the leaders of these unions were democratically elected on their merits as organizers and motivators. In fact, with the exception of one or two autonomous unions whose membership consisted mainly of adherents to a single party or coalition, the majority of members in these unions did not belong to the party of their union leaders. Nor, in this country where party loyalty is all but worn on one's sleeve, were union members misled or deluded about the affiliations of the leaders they elected. The point is that for any leader to win the union elections (which were regularly held in accordance with Senegal's labor laws), they had to demonstrate their capabilities as fighters on behalf of worker interests, rather than those of their parties; and so they did.

More importantly, perhaps, the logic of union recruitment had shifted with changing political and economic circumstances. Under conditions of overall state control of political and economic life—as existed in Senegal in the 1960s and 1970s—unions organized on a basis designed to affect state policy; that is, on as broad a front as possible. Therefore, comprehensive recruitment within any particular enterprise or government service mattered less than overall numbers of militants from as broad an array of workplaces as could be mobilized. The more democratic and less state-centric economic conditions prevailing in the late 1980s dictated a different logic of recruitment. With the withdrawal of the state from economic management, it became more logical to focus protest and bargaining efforts at the level of the firm or service; workers did not want their particular economic demands to be intermixed with and diluted by those of other kinds of workers. In addition, under conditions of democratic pluralism, rank-and-file members no longer saw the need to employ unions as outlets for political demands; most of them had long since made up their minds about their political convictions and considered them to exist in a different sphere from their life at the workplace.

As such, unions had become a powerful, but very blunt-edged, weapon for the opposition parties. Leaders like Bakhao Seck, Mamadou Ndoye, and others would have to base their recruiting efforts on achieving improved workplace conditions, not on political ideology, though this would always remain a factor among a core of party members surrounding the leaders in most of the autonomous unions. Under these circumstances these leaders, some of whom had received training in union organization either in Eastern Europe or elsewhere, emerged first and fore-most as superb strategists of labor activism.

The government, predictably, reacted with alarm. When the ADS coalition blun-dered into support for the simmering rebellion in Senegal's Casamance region, the government took it as an excuse to ban the coalition's activities. The government then attempted to drive the unions farther apart along preexisting fault lines, partic-ularly where the teachers were concerned. For example, things "happened" which made it easier for the UDEN splinter group to exist apart from SUDES—such as a research job at the Education Ministry that materialized for UDEN-leader Ndoye. UDEN tried to get doctors to form a separate union apart from lesser categories of health workers in order to break the inter-occupational power base of SUTSAS. In the postal service and the electric utility, the regime sought to wean workers away from autonomous unions through mounting well-funded "enterprise committees" (a form of quasi-union) to seduce members with promises of job preferences and other rewards.

Between these efforts and the feuds that still divided the opposition parties, autonomous labor organizations were kept in check—for a time. Major strikes were pretty well avoided in 1986 and 1987, despite a mounting tide of troubles among students at the university, a major strike of police (who were not unionized), and increasing insurgency in the Casamance.[12] The elections of February 1988, which once again were monopolized by the ruling PS, were the turning point.

Once more, troubles began with SUTSAS, which launched a forty-eight-hour strike in public hospitals across the country on August seventeenth. Although its leaders' political goals were transparent, the strike was predicated on the govern-ment's failure to honor promises it had made to the health workers to end the strike staged in 1985. When the government made a ham-fisted attempt to end the 1988 strike by withholding pay and seeking to negotiate a settlement—not with SUTSAS, but with the minuscule CNTS affiliate representing health workers—the strike went into a "rolling" phase in which health workers refused to come to work two days of every week. The advantage was that patients continued to receive care, thereby keep-ing public opinion in support of the union. The government ultimately had no choice but to bypass the CNTS and negotiate a generous agreement with SUTSAS. Stung by this official circumvention of the government's own union, Madia Diop soon thereafter unleashed the CNTS-affiliated bank workers union (SYTBEFS) in a twenty-four-hour strike on December 23.[13]

By early 1989 the real threat—as it had been so often in the past—was a revived alliance between the various organizations of teachers. In November 1988 the three autonomous teachers' unions—SUDES, SAES, and UDEN—announced plans for a strike in the new year. On December sixth they issued a common platform of teacher grievances centering upon the overall deterioration of quality in education, stagnant salaries, poor teaching conditions, and inadequate provision for housing. Following strained negotiations with the government, the unions struck on February 10, 1989. For political reasons of its own, SUDES pulled out at the last minute (the PIT, which now overtly controlled the union, was once more seeking a reconciliation with the government), meaning that an effective strike in the primary and secondary schools was impossible. But SAES, to which most professors belonged, was able to close down the university for seventy days, nearly causing the government to declare a complete closure (*année blanche*), as it had done the previous year in response to student demonstrations. Now SUDES, which was eager to prove its power in the schools without the breakaway teachers' unions, launched two forty-eight-hour strikes of its own, on March 17–18 and 24–25, closing schools throughout the country. It then gave warning of further strikes in April but promised a truce if the government would agree to parley. The government virtually scrambled to the bargaining table, inviting the participation of all national teachers' unions. There they received at least minimal satisfaction on all points of a sixteen-item checklist, which included creation of a unit within the Ministry of Education whose sole task was to monitor the government's progress in implementing agreements and an increase in teachers' housing subsidies.

This success brought preparations for strikes in other sectors that were, however, nipped in the bud when in late April 1989 a border war broke out between Senegal and its northern neighbor Mauritania. This caused a national mood that would not have sanctioned worker protest. Nonetheless, a critical goal had been achieved for at least one of the opposition parties. The PIT leadership, strengthened by its ability to claim credit for the success of the teachers' strike through SUDES's action, approached the government with an offer of "dialogue," whose goal was apparently some government post for the party in a national unity government.[14] While these talks led nowhere, they did portend things to come.

Events began to heat up again in early 1990. The major opposition parties other than the PIT once more condensed into a unified front around Abdoulaye Wade. On February 24, eight opposition parties, including Wade's PDS, *And-jëf*, and the *Ligue démocratique*, signed a declaration of unity. At a massive rally in Dakar on March tenth, the leaders of the alliance, known as CONACPO, called for "general mobilization," and Wade himself called for a general strike. The postal workers of the SNTPT embarked on a seventy-two-hour strike beginning March 21, and the teachers once more began to prepare for action.

By mid-1990, the unions associated with the CONACPO alliance had formed themselves into a *Union des syndicats autonomes du Sénégal* (UNSAS), while the PIT-affiliated autonomous unions constituted a *Coordination des syndicats autonomes* (CSA).

In the fall of 1990, a coincidence of economic and political events moved Senegal toward a major explosion of social anger, in which the UNSAS unions saw themselves as prepared to play a leading role. In the previous year, the government had passed changes to the investment code—with the acquiescence of Madia Diop and the CNTS—that made it possible for new investors to bypass the national Labor Code. In January 1990, the government implemented a new tax system, which was widely perceived (though somewhat inaccurately) to erode worker incomes. At the end of September 1990, a serious shortfall in government revenues forced President Diouf to decree a 5 percent surtax on all salaries. The incident coincided with the approach of nationwide elections for rural and municipal government offices.

The government, foreseeing disaster, reacted with an attempt to suppress the CONACPO-UNSAS alliance. In September Diouf personally approved the firing of fifty health workers for being absent from their posts during one of his inspection tours (a message to SUTSAS). In mid-November, the police broke up a CONACPO rally in downtown Dakar with considerable force. In early November UNSAS formally declared its intention to go on strike in early December. Anticipating the UNSAS move, and not to be outdone, SUDES—the most substantial of the CSA unions—had declared its own intention to strike two weeks earlier. The CNTS, which was under attack for its usual passivity, also made vaguely worded threats suggesting its readiness to strike.

Under these pressures, Diouf rescinded the income surtax on the eve of the November twenty-fifth elections. This prevented neither a massive abstention from voting nor the coming strikes. These began with a fairly effective strike by SUDES in the schools on December 3 and 4 (the issue being the government's failure to respect the 1989 accords with the teachers' unions).

The UNSAS strikes, which occurred on December 15–16 and again on December 18–22, were only partially successful by comparison. Still, UNSAS was able to all but shut down Dakar's large public hospital, *l'hôpital Dantec*, the university, and the *lycées*, while postal and electric utility workers engaged in a go-slow action. The strike, in the end, was badly coordinated, each union following a somewhat different strategy, and most appearing to exercise far from universal control over its rank and file. No popular upsurge of support, as called for by Abdoulaye Wade, attended the strikes; Dakar was generally calm on those days.

Yet, for all the weaknesses of the action, the strikes of December hit their mark: the government set in motion the process that would lead, the following March, to a declaration of a National Unity Government containing key members of the opposition. For, with all its failures, the UNSAS strike presented the Senegalese ruling elite with its traditional worst nightmare: a coordinated multi-sectoral strike in support of opposition party demands. Either during or immediately after the UNSAS strike, Diouf began negotiations with Wade toward his inclusion in a government coalition. In his traditional New Year's address to the nation, Diouf extended his hand to the opposition more generally, calling for a process of national reconciliation. In April 1991 Wade accepted Diouf's offer to become minister of state; the PIT's leader Amath Dansokho also received a government ministry.

Senegal's opposition parties, for the first time since the 1960s, had played the union card so successfully as to force open the door to power.

Unions and Politics in the 1990s and Beyond*

By sharing a degree of power with political formations influential in the most militant unions, Diouf bought himself nearly a decade of relative peace with labor organizations. Abdoulaye Wade continued in government, with a hiatus when he was arrested in 1994, followed by his acceptance in March 1995 of the post of minister of state, which he would occupy up until just prior to the legislative elections of May

---

*Note: This section covers events beyond the period covered in my dissertation; therefore, it is based on knowledge acquired, at a distance, from journalistic sources, notably *Le Soleil* and the *Economist Intelligencer Unit*, and from conversations with Senegalese contacts.

1998. He was joined in Diouf's cabinet by ministers from the *Ligue démocratique* and the PIT, although the latter would be ejected from the government in 1995. The notable holdouts from co-optation were Landing Savané and *And-jëf,* whose electoral popularity was to grow in these years due to its public image of refusal to give in to the patronage positions it was no doubt offered. Given the importance of unity among opposition forces in promoting collective worker action across a broad front in Senegal, Diouf's grudging acceptance of a unity government was to ensure the ruling PS roughly another ten years during which it continued to dominate national politics without any insurmountable challenges from labor. Significantly, it gave Diouf and his ministers the political space they required to enact and implement structural economic reforms that would probably have been impossible in the 1980s.

The 1990s were not to bring total quiescence on the part of labor, however; in fact, if anything, that decade brought with it more causes for labor action than any other decade since independence. The successive rallying points for labor in the '90s were, initially, the budgetary crisis brought about in the early years of the decade by a vastly overvalued CFA franc (which brought about a cut in civil service salaries) and, later, the wave of privatizations coupled with stagnation in wages and other benefits at a time of revived economic growth. Under these conditions, labor took to the streets repeatedly; however, with the exceptions of brief and largely ineffective general strikes in 1993 and again in 1999, the strikes of this decade took the form of one or another industrial union taking action, with little or no support from other unions or their political allies.

By 1995–96 the CFA devaluation of 1994 had led to the revival of exports, which were for the most part agricultural and mineral—thus having little impact on urban worker incomes—and had undermined the purchasing power of the largely urban-based unionized workforce. Urban unemployment in 1996 stood at 30 percent of the economically active population, and with wages largely frozen throughout most of the 1990s, even those with jobs were losing economic ground.

On top of this, the government from the mid-1990s onward launched a set of privatizations that targeted the major utilities, where militant unions with opposition party affiliations had long entrenched themselves. In 1997 it was announced that the parastatal telecommunications operation, SONATEL, would be sold to an international consortium (the deal would later fall through and the losing bidder, France Telecom, would eventually win ownership), and the workers struck, unsuccessfully, for higher wages. Later that year, the electric power utility, SENELEC, was put on the block, and the leader of its most militant union, SUTELEC (there were multiple unions at SENELEC), Mademba Sock, threatened to cause a seventy-two-hour blackout. In fact, the threat was later carried out. By this time, however, the government clearly felt it was in a position of power sufficient to carry out the transaction. Sock would be arrested and serve six months in prison along with a fellow labor activist; meanwhile, it was announced that SENELEC was being sold to a Canadian-led consortium (the deal later fell through, however). When the urban transit company SOTRAC was put on the selling block, and workers took action, the government simply liquidated the company.

Unions of civil servants fared little better in the 1990s. From January through May 1997 autonomous teachers' unions representing primary and secondary teachers joined forces in coordinated walkouts with SAES, which represented university professors demanding better housing allowances, an end to the hiring of "volunteer teachers," an extension of the retirement age from fifty-five to sixty, and the suspension of a 3 percent pension deduction pending an audit of the retirement fund's accounts. They were forced to accept an unsatisfactory settlement (with no concessions on the housing allowance or pension deductions and a mere modification of the volunteer teacher program) by the minister of education. This was none other than Mamadou Ndoye, erstwhile leader of the highly effective teacher strikes that united the opposition parties and public sentiment in the late 1970s, and now by virtue of his leading position in the *Ligue démocratique*, a member of Diouf's cabinet.

Gone, apparently, were the days when labor unions and their political allies could overcome their differences to launch effective collective action across a broad front, leading to major concessions and causing major change in political institutions. Nonetheless, a glimmer of the days of union glory emerged in the closing days of the decade when the PS, feeling its forty-year domination of government institutions slipping away, revealed its true colors by manipulating political institutions to ensure its continued hegemony. The PS was suffering from defections, mainly to its archrival, Wade's PDS, and mainly in the urban zones whose populations were slow to feel the benefits of the economic growth that followed the 1994 CFA devaluation. In 1996 it pushed through the National Assembly (where it continued to enjoy a majority) a decentralization law that, among other measures, brought about the division of Dakar and other urban areas into dozens of wards, divided in ways that would allow the PS to wield its power of patronage to carry elections; and the PS made strong gains in local elections in 1996.

However, after a weak showing in the legislative elections of May 1998, the PS returned to a one-party state mode of governance with a cabinet containing only one non-PS minister. In the lead-up to the presidential elections of 2000, the PS was to continue to maneuver by any means possible to retain its hold on power, including amending the constitution to wipe away the two-term limit on presidential tenure.

By February 1999 opposition parties overcame their divisions to unite behind Wade as the candidate with the best chances of overthrowing Diouf. The corollary of this renascent party cooperation was a degree of labor unity. Helping the effort, the privatization program had proceeded apace, and in a single three-day period in 1999, three thousand workers lost their jobs. In such circumstances, opposition party leaders called for collective union action, invoking even the long-dormant CNTS to action. Madia Diop, whose successful efforts to keep opposition parties—especially Wade's PDS—from winning control of CNTS-affiliated unions, had won him a sinecure within the PS (he was a member of its political bureau and a vice president of the National Assembly), apparently realized he would have to make a gesture of defiance to retain credibility. And he began to publicly denounce the privatization program. On June 28, 1999, the CNTS was in the vanguard of a general strike involving virtually all union formations in both private and public sectors—including the UNSAS and CSA autonomous union federations—demanding wage increases of 30–40 percent. Repeating past practices, Madia defected after the first day of the strike, and on behalf of the CNTS, he accepted the offer of both the government and the employers' associations for wage increases tied to GDP growth of 5–6 percent. Revealing labor's vastly diminished power, not to mention Madia's true loyalties, the failed general strike of June 1999 nonetheless heralded the unity of opposition to the PS.

Labor was not to play a pivotal role in the sea change of the political landscape betokened by Wade's victory in the 2000 presidential elections: the defections of PS barons Djibo Kâ and Moustapha Niasse, with their substantial voter followings, were to seal Diouf's fate. Nevertheless, the unions continued, albeit with diminished efficacy, to represent the discontent of the urban populations that were the losers in the political battles of the 1990s. Ironically, perhaps, the arrangement of political institutions that so undermined the ability of labor organizations to act collectively—characterized by PS power sharing with its former political enemies—had been brought about by the union victories of past decades.

Nor did labor power or militancy die with the 1990s. Wade's inclusion in his cabinet of virtually the entire array of opposition parties with union influence might initially be taken to suggest a defusing of labor militancy. And indeed, the government maintained largely cordial relations with trade unions throughout at least the first couple of years of Wade's presidency. Still, Wade lost an important battle when, in November 2001, his favored candidate to replace the retiring Madia Diop as secretary-general, Cheikh Diop, was defeated in CNTS leadership elections by Mody Guiro, a union leader with a reputation for combativeness and hostility toward the PDS. The CNTS since this time has been more distant from the government and remains close to a now-oppositionist PS. By late 2001–02, as political opposition to the PDS government began to coalesce, so too did union militancy, as strikes over continued loss of job security and purchasing power broke out in numerous sectors. In the first half of 2002 health workers, university professions, and teachers held strikes. Laid-off bus company (SOTRAC) workers took hostage the director general of the new company. In March postal workers brought the postal system to a complete standstill for a week in protest over salaries and poor management. Facing a rising tide of labor militancy, in May 2002 Wade's government agreed with united union federations (except for the CSA, still dominated by the PIT, which had departed Wade's government in its early days in 2000) on the creation of a new health insurance fund, improved retirement benefits for civil servants, an increase in workplace accident benefits, and other concessions. Despite this, and the signing in November 2002 of a social compact between the government and the main union federations that provided for regular consultation, strikes continued to plague Wade and his government. Those strikes intensified when, in March 2005, Wade dismissed the two *Ligue démocratique* ministers from his cabinet. With the *Ligue* and the *PIT* both in opposition, a loss of government control of the CNTS, and labor militancy on the rise, the question of labor's future cohesion and influence remains open and of critical importance to the future.

Conclusion

Several concluding points can be drawn from this account of union politics in Senegal.

First, in Senegal there is no such entity as "labor." Sociological divisions between industrial workers and *fonctionnaires* amounted to different preferences in union organization, which the government successfully played upon to keep workers from forming together as a united "class" in opposition. Even the *fonctionnaires* were kept from unity by ideological divisions reflected in their party preferences. This sociological condition was not lost on Senegal's power brokers, who from the 1960s onward played on these divisions to their advantage, and above all to avoid unified labor action.

Second, unions do not constitute an inherently powerful force. There is no union "calling" to militancy within Senegal that is perpetually present. What has brought workers into both an activist state of mind and a willingness to organize across social and ideological divisions is the conjunction of political intolerance (forcing ideologically opposed parties, with their influence over unions, together) and economic insecurity (providing union leaders with a cause). The connection with political parties has also proved critical to union power. Parties provided the trained leaders and organizational experience as well as a core of devoted cadres to help recruit and mobilize workers. Interestingly, however, it often appeared to be the union tail that wagged the party dog. With unions so central to their own power strategies, and with the majority of union members disinterested in the more radical aspects of their ideology, even the more avowedly radical parties subdued the more outrageous and violent aspects of their public statements in the 1980s. Public opinion is also a critical factor in the equation of union power. As the autonomous unions grew into greater sophistication over the years, they increasingly recognized that a key object of their battles with the government was to be sure the public was with them and against the state. Teachers and health workers, in particular, have been successful in their actions when they have formulated their claims in the language of public discontent with conditions in schools and health services.

Third, the importance of union control both to the state and to political parties has repeatedly and indelibly affected the form and content of political institutions. As this account has sought to show, the several iterations of progress toward a more liberal political regime have in fact been in direct response to the government's sense of threat from a unified union opposition. What is more, opposition party politics are thoroughly imbued with their desire to gain influence, if not control, within unions. This includes their political doctrines, which have in fact been tempered by the need to attract apolitical recruits to unions; it also involved their choice of coalition partners—extending to the repeated combinations of radical parties with centrist and economic liberal Abdoulaye Wade.

The final point is that behind the repeated upsurges of labor militancy in Senegal up until the election of Wade in 2000 was the ruling party's unwillingness to take the step that would amount to a transition to full democracy—sharing power (beyond largely token gestures), or even accepting the principal of, *alternance*, a change in the party in power. Above all, it was the desire to retain a monopoly of power on the part of the ruling party that promoted the union-party coalitions to form. The repeated concessions to demands for greater political liberalism—without ever taking the final step—bought time and political space for the regime; but in effect, they have created an institutional nexus of intolerance within which opposition parties and unions ultimately build solidarity and launch the next wave of assaults on power. And in this iterated process of union-led attacks on power, followed by institutional change, lies much of the story of political evolution in Senegal.

Notes

1. République du Sénégal, Situation Economique, 1988
2. Geoffrey Bergen, "Unions in Senegal: A Perspective on National Development in Africa" (PhD diss., Department of Political Science, University of California, Los Angeles, 1994), Annex 4. My estimates differ considerably from the unions' own claims, which tend to exaggerate membership (the CNTS has claimed from seventy thousand to one hundred thousand members), and are derived from internal union documents, interviews, and government figures reporting checkoff dues.
3. For theoretical and empirical underpinnings of this statement, see Seymour Martin Lipset, Martin A. Trow, and James S. Coleman, *Union Democracy: The Internal Politics of the International Typographical Union* (Glencoe, IL: Free Press, 1977); and Gary Marks, *Unions in Politics: Britain, Germany and the United States in the 19th and Early 20th Centuries* (Princeton, NJ: Princeton University Press, 1989).
4. Quoted in Dakar-Matin, June 16, 1969.
5. This speech is reprinted as "Le plan du décollage économique ou la participation responsable comme moteur du développement," in Léopold Sédar Senghor, *Liberté IV: Socialisme et Planification* (Paris: Editions du Seuil, 1983), 397–524.
6. As Jonathan Barker has shown for Senegal's rural areas, the factional leader is an intermediary between other factions lower and higher on the pyramid of clan groupings that exist between the individual and the state, whose personal status depends on the ability to provide flows of material resources. This authority, however, is highly precarious, since "factional leaders at lower levels can transform their loyalties from one higher-level faction to another with relative impunity." Barker, "Political Factionalism in Senegal," *Canadian Journal of African Studies* 7, no. 2 (1973): 292.
7. Loi no. 71–54 July 28, 1971, Journal Officiel du Sénégal, October 2, 1971, 945–46; and Loi no. 71–31 March 12, 1971, Journal Officiel du Sénégal, March 22, 1971, 302–6. These made mandatory arbitration procedures so time consuming as to make it virtually impossible to conduct a planned strike legally.
8. Donal Cruise O'Brien, "Senegal," in John Dunn, ed., *West African States: Failure and Promise* (Cambridge: Cambridge University Press, 1978), 179–80.
9. Senghor at Tunis in 1975, quoted by Christine Desouches, *Le Parti démocratique sénégalaise: une opposition légale en Afrique* (Paris: Berger-Levrault, 1983), 28.
10. For a highly cogent account of the splintering of the underground opposition following democratization, see Momar Coumba Diop, and Mamadou Diouf, *Le Sénégal sous Abdou Diouf* (Paris: Editions Karthala, 1990), 214–15.
11. "Changement à la tête de la LD-MPT," *Le Soleil*, April 10, 1984; Les dix-sidents d'And Jef, "Nos divergences avec la direction du mouvement maoiste et les véritables raisons de notre exclusion" (pamphlet, Dakar, September 1984).
12. As the elections of February 1988 neared, a new political alliance of the left, the SOPI alliance, was formed, this time including the PIT. However, discord between its leaders was

reflected when a planned schools strike that would have involved all the autonomous teachers' unions—including SUDES—fell apart when the latter refrained from striking on the agreed day.

13. By late 1988, Senegal's state banking system was on the verge of collapse due to years of mismanagement and appropriation of funds for political uses, and it was about to enter reforms that would inevitably lead to the loss of numerous jobs.

14. Parti de l'Indépendance et du Travail du Sénégal, Comité Central, "Déclaration de la XIe session plenière du comité central," Dakar, May 4, 1989.

CHAPTER 3

Labor Unions and "Democratic Forces" in Niger

Robert Charlick

The solution to the economic crisis can only be found in the political system. . . .
We must democratize our society as well as our strategies and policies for
development.

Laouali Moutari
General Secretary of the *Union des syndicats des travailleurs du Niger*
1990

It is widely accepted that labor unions and student unions played critical roles in
Niger's transition to multiparty democracy in the late 1980s and early 1990s.
Both Western and Nigerien social scientists saw them as a key element in the
"democratic forces"[1] that contributed to the reversal of authoritarian military and
plebiscitary regimes and that eventually, after several reversals, led to Niger's current
fragile democracy (Niandou Souley 1996; Wiseman 1996). With the hindsight of
more than fifteen years of "democratization" in Africa, a more sober conclusion must
be drawn: not only have the role of civil society and labor unions in particular
declined in shaping Africa's newly electoral democracies, there is good reason to conclude that in a country like Niger they never possessed the characteristics or resources
to sustain such a critical and leading role in political reform. Given the obvious
weakness of these groups and of "civil society" in general in Africa, when compared
to contemporary Asian and Latin American societies (van de Walle 2001; White
1995), this retrenchment is hardly surprising. What may be surprising is that this
temporary coalition ever had the success it did to begin with.

This chapter explores several aspects of the role of civil society in democratization,
with specific reference to organized labor. It does so using empirical evidence drawn
from a single case: Niger from 1960 to the present, a period that has witnessed the
creation of five republics, three military regimes, and a "transitional" government. It

makes three basic points about the role that labor unions have played, and are likely to continue to play, in Niger's democratization process.

1. With two brief exceptional periods (1952–59 and 1989–96), unions in Niger did not, in fact, lead the way toward democratic political reform;
2. Niger's labor unions have lacked the autonomy to be effective civil society actors, having always been politicized and partisan, whether in power or in opposition; and
3. While unions historically have been one of the only organized interest groups in Niger, they constitute a weak basis upon which to build a democratic civil society.

Theoretical Perspective on These Transitions

One of the most commonly employed perspectives in Western political science has been the "state-society" balance model. A variety of versions of this have been offered to explain the possibilities for pluralism and liberal political regimes, or for effective authoritarian rule, ranging from the state-centric analyses of Fatton (1992) and the notion of "strong societies and weak states" (Migdal 1988) to the concept of a "precarious balance" in which both state and society are in dynamic change with new "balances" being constantly established and compromised (Rothchild 1988). All along the way this "balance" analysis has had an air of unreality to it in the African context, where states were defined almost entirely as centralized governmental institutions, and societies were most frequently seen as localized forms of social organization and power. These perspectives had little real meaning to most African people. If, instead, we accept the definition of "governance" as the allocation of values and benefits and the making of rules to manage this allocation process at the national level and in the formal sector, then state-society balance takes on an entirely different perspective. The question becomes one of assessing the evolution of power in national institutions and in formal associational life operating at the national level and attempting to influence national policy. This is surely a much more restricted and largely elite game (Burton 1992).

In an earlier work, I have argued that at this level the true balance for a number of African societies, including notably Niger, is between a weak state and a weak society with all that that implies for consolidating "national power," for limiting the penetration of "foreign" influence, and for generating the capacity to achieve the broader goals of social peace and economic development (Charlick 1991). When both the state and the society are weak, small changes in the capacity of either can dramatically, and sometimes catastrophically, alter outcomes. These small changes, however, can logically also be reversed by subsequent small changes. A term that fits such a situation much better than the notion of "consolidation" is "institutional instability," in which it cannot be anticipated that either structures or existing outcomes will persist. This, I argue, is the situation of many African countries today, and I use the case of Niger to illustrate this unstable process. This notion of "precariousness" to indicate a highly "tip-able" balance among elite players is far superior in understanding the roles that specific actors—including labor, students, and the military—play in a series of changes that are all characterized by institutional instability than the notion of "balance."

The modern political history of the Republic of Niger has reflected this pattern well. For almost all of the period since formal independence in 1960, civil society in Niger has been so weak that it could easily be mastered even by a weak state, albeit one propped up by external actors. The period of exceptionality, in which labor emerged as a significant political actor, can be understood as having been associated with two phenomena: the weakening of the repressive capacity of the state, due to budget austerity and the change in leadership style from President Seyni Kountche to President Ali Saïbou and the growth of the anti-structural adjustment and pro-democracy coalition also supported in part by external actors led by elements of organized labor and students.[2] The balance was "tipped" again through a series of political maneuvers, including the weakening of unions through a combination of partisan politics and ethnic appeals that led to the return to authoritarian bureau-cratic-military national government in 1996. The cycle of institutional instability and labor's place in this process, however, is far from complete. As of late 2005, Niger's labor movement was fragmented and incapable of exercising any meaningful decision making, or even handling a watchdog function on the quasi-democratic regime that has persisted without *alternance*, or a change in the party in power, since 1999.

The Historic Development of Organized Labor in Niger during the Colonial Period

It is one of the ironies of history that colonial France, a regime with heavy partici-pation by the socialist Left, banned labor unions in its African colonies until 1947 (Bakary 1992). As soon as they were legalized, unions became partisan. Throughout Francophone Africa the unions that formed were supported by and closely associated with one or another French political party and tendency, principally through the *Confédération générale du travail* (CGT), a French labor federation associated with the French Communist Party. The first and subsequently largest labor federation in Francophone Africa during the 1940s and early 1950s, the CGT was led by the Nigerien Djibo Bakary. In Niger by 1954 the CGT quite naturally aligned with Bakary's political party, the *Union démocratique nigérien* (UDN) a splinter off the nationalist coalition party, the *Parti progressiste nigérien-Rassemblement démocratique nigérien* (PPN–RDA) (Niandou Souley 2000). In portraying the evolution of organ-ized labor in Niger, Boureima Maïnassara called the UDN a "workers' party, despite the fact that to win it clearly had to reach out far beyond Niger's tiny working class, making explicit alliances with traditional leaders and in places appealing to ethnic solidarity and fears" (Charlick 1991; Maïnassara 1989).

In 1956 Bakary made an effort to unify all of Niger's unions under a single fed-eration—the *Union nationale des travailleurs du Niger* (UNTN). (See Table 3.1, "Unions in Niger's Changing Political Landscape.") This effort failed when the PPN, after 1953 a party much more closely aligned with the gradualist strategy and the French colonial administration, countered with its own union organization. In 1957 many African unions affiliated with the new federation, the *Union générale*

Table 3.1 Unions in Niger's Changing Political Landscape

Period	Union federations	Independent unions	Government	Major political parties
Independent Niger- 1960–91	Union nationale des travailleurs du Niger (UNTN)	Syndicat national des enseignants du Niger (SNEN) Syndicat national des enseignants et chercheurs du supérieur (SNECS)	Single-party government of Hamani Diori Military government- Conseil Militaire Supreme, under General Seyni Kountche (4/1974) Second Republic under General Ali Saibou	Parti progressiste nigérien-Rassemblement démocratique africaine (PPN-RDA) Union démocratique Nigérienne–Sawaba outlawed Mouvement national pour la société de développement (MNSD-NASSARA)
First Democratic Period- 1993–96	Union des syndicats des travailleurs du Niger (USTN)	SNEN, SNECS	Third Republic- Alliance des Forces du Change- 9 party coalition government under president Ousman Mahamane	PPN-RDA Convention démocratique et sociale (CDS) Parti nigérien pour la démocratie et le socialisme (PNDS) Alliance nigérienne pour la démocratie et le progrès (ANDP-ZAMAN LAHIYA) MNSD
Military Regime- 1996–99	USTN		Military government under General Ibrahim Nassara Baré	Union nationale des independants pour la renoveau démocratique (party of General Baré) CDS, PNDS, ANDP, MNSD

Table 3.1 (continued)

Period	Union federations	Independent unions	Government	Major political parties
Second Democratic Period- 1999–present	*Confédération nigérienne des travailleurs* (CNT) *Alliance crédible aux exigences des travailleurs* (ACET) *Union des syndicats des travailleurs du Niger* (USTN) *Confédération démocratique des travailleurs du Niger* (CDTN) *Union général des travailleurs du Niger* (UGTN)		Fifth Republic–Elected Government of President Tandja and Prime Minister Amadou	MNSD CDS PNDS *Rassemblement pour la démocratie et le progrès* (RDP-JAMA'A)

des travailleurs d'Afrique noire (UGTAN). Headed by Guinea's Sekou Tourè, this group consistently led the anticolonial struggle in Francophone Africa, confirming the leftist orientation and rhetoric of African unions for decades to come. The PPN countered with its own federation, UGTAN *Autonome*, led by Hamani Diori, a leading PPN–RDA political figure and head of the postal workers union who would later become Niger's first president. The few "independent," or nonaffiliated, unions that emerged in this period, notably the teachers' union (*Syndicat national des enseignants du Niger*, or SNEN) was soon taken over by the PPN and led by one of the PPN's leading figures, Noma Kaka. From the very outset, then, Niger's labor unions lacked autonomy from the principal political parties, both in France and in Niger itself.

Post-Colonial Niger

The history of Niger's nationalist and anti-imperialist movements and its eventual formal independence have been discussed elsewhere (Charlick 1991). Independence and the events that precipitated it intensified the struggle throughout Francophone Africa for control of the organized labor movement. In 1960 the West African federation UGTAN split, marking the division between the "radical" states (Ghana, Guinea, and Mali) and the *Entente* states (Côte d'Ivoire, Dahomey, Niger, Senegal, and Upper Volta), with the *Entente* states heavily supported by Gaullist France. In Niger, where the PPN came to power with considerable French support, this immediately resulted in the creation of the new UNTN as the sole legal union federation. This labor federation was led by PPN militant Rene Delanne. Under the PPN regime, the UNTN was reduced to being an instrument of the one-party state, with virtually no autonomy or the ability to represent workers in the private or public sectors. It was during this period that the policies of internal democracy of Niger's labor movement were transformed into purely top-down decisions; member unions were not consulted. In recounting the history of this period, former UNTN Executive Secretary Maïnassara reported that union leaders who did not toe the party/state line were threatened and jailed, and the UNTN leadership learned of major economic decisions, such as changes in the minimum wage and in prices, on the radio (1999).

By 1969, when the drought had produced a nationwide economic crisis, UNTN leadership attempted to promote a series of policies that would have better reflected worker interests, such as the raising of the minimum wage, the nationalization of some French-controlled enterprises, and the reduction of French military and civilian personnel. The PPN crushed this effort, dismissing Delanne and replacing him with Siddo Hassane Hassane. Siddo, however reluctant he may have been, supported the repression of teachers and students, who were calling for a reduction of French presence and control (Maïnassara 1999).

Niger under the Military "Regime d'Exception" of General Kountche

When the army intervened and took power in April 1974, unionists at first hoped for better relations with the government. In 1975, at its 1st Extraordinary Congress, the UNTN adopted a more autonomous position from the regime, and its newly elected general secretary, Ahmed Mouddour, supported a strike of the uranium workers. Shortly thereafter, Mouddour was implicated in the March 15, 1976, "coup" attempt and, along with several other union leaders, was executed. This event produced a deep chill in the labor movement, with many union leaders fearing for their lives and an intensified split within the UNTN as to how to deal with the military regime. At UNTN's 9th National Congress in 1976, one faction insisted that it persist in its effort to assert its autonomy from the regime. It was at this meeting that the name of the federation was changed to the *Union des syndicats des travailleurs du Niger* (USTN), although this change appears to have had more to do with the personal power struggle within the federation than with policy differences (Maïnassara 1999). The military regime responded with rage, employing threats and bribes to bring union leaders back under control.

At its next Union Congress in 1978, USTN leadership capitulated totally, adopting a policy of "participation responsible," committing the unions to work much more closely with the military regime.[3] Under this policy, union leaders were invited to participate in some government meetings, but they were excluded from those most important to it (on housing and social security, for example). Some Nigerien analysts contend that this represented a democratically expressed view of unionists (Niandou Souley 2000), and USTN leaders even adopted a resolution asserting that "responsible participation" had in fact strengthened the hand of the unions. Others suggest that it was imposed without even the consultation of member unions and that it was part of a broader pattern of crushing union autonomy (Adji 1993, 2000). There is considerable evidence for this second position. The USTN was not even given a place in the National Council of the military regime's corporatist Development Society. Under the military regime, the USTN had four general secretaries (Ahmed Garba, Ahmed Mouddour, Boureima Maïnassara, and Mohamed Abdoulaye) within a ten-year period; the regime significantly interfered in the selection process each time. In addition, it pursued policies to end the "check-off system" for union dues, imposed a 3 percent "voluntary" wage giveback in 1985, banned strikes, arrested and imprisoned union leaders, and dissolved certain unions, notably the unions representing the police (Adji 2000). During this period Kountche also used organized labor as an instrument for supporting his foreign policy initiatives, such as the anti-Libyan demonstrations in 1981.

By the mid-1980s, however, the total dominance of unions by the military regime began to decline as the power of the Nigerien state succumbed to economic crises and internal political challenges. The rise of labor militancy, then, can be attributed largely to two things: the weakening of the state, and changes in the Nigerien workforce associated with the narrowly based uranium mining sector. By 1981 growth had slowed, and the grandiose plans to continue the expansion of the uranium and coal mining sectors—and consequently of the state—were in ruins. As Niger's debt and budgetary crisis unfolded, compounded by the tragedy of another disastrous drought in 1983–84, government spending fell and public employment began to contract. The regime began its negotiations with the International Monetary Fund (IMF) and bilateral donors to institute a deflationary "structural adjustment program," which it signed in October 1983. Much as it wished to protect relatively highly paid civil servants, however, the overall effect of these IMF policies involved deflation, the drying up of foreign investment, and a sharp decline in overall formal-sector employment (Gervais 1992). This weakened the state's capacity for providing patronage and buying loyalty. In addition, the structure of the Nigerien economy had changed significantly in the 1970s. From 1970 to 1991 the percentage of the population in urban areas tripled, paralleling the growth in the percentage of the workforce in industry. Until the 1980s, the mining city of Arlit, for example, bloomed in the desert, with a culture and life of its own unlike any other in Niger. The impact of Niger's northern mining towns would even affect very traditional urban areas like Agadez. Although the percentage of the GDP devoted to government spending had not increased significantly during this period, government employment, particularly in parastatal or mixed enterprises, grew during the "boom" years of the 1970s, producing a new class of managers and an expanded corps of teachers and health workers. These demographic and labor force changes provoked the beginning of new political movements whose leadership ostensibly sought to liberalize and rationalize the highly personal and authoritarian system and to gain some voice in public policy making.

Organized Labor under Ali Saïbou—
Organized Labor as a Force for Democracy

Immediately upon the death of President Kountche in 1987, the army named General Ali Saïbou, the close Kountche associate and chief of staff of the army, to the presidency. Saïbou had neither Kountche's stature nor his personal austerity, and the power of the state had been declining sharply during the 1980s as indicated above. In this context policies toward labor moderated. The USTN was able to distance itself from the newly created single legal party, the MNSD, and to adopt a posture of greater independence. Many union leaders and mid-level civil servants began to openly advocate reform beyond the initial state-controlled attempt, the National Charter, that fell far short of legitimatizing political competition. Some union leaders joined clandestine parties to promote reform. At the same time, conditions for labor continued to deteriorate as more than five thousand civil service jobs, nearly 15 percent of the public labor force, were lost from 1988 to 1992 due to weak revenues and tight budgets mandated by structural adjustment policies (Adji 2000). In 1989 some USTN affiliates emerged for the first time in decades as a voice for democratization when, at its congress in Maradi, key unions such as those representing customs (SNAD) and tax collection (SNAI) called for a return to multipartyism and adopted positions sharply critical of the government's structural adjustment policies. At USTN's next congress, in 1990, Laouali Moutari replaced Maïnassara as general secretary; the former was thought to be more independent and supportive of democratization.

During the 1980s, educated Nigeriens were increasingly radicalized by their perception of the causes and consequences of sharp economic recession. At the heart of the analysis were young technocrats in the previously growth-oriented sectors (uranium and coal mining). As their opportunities declined, they became increasingly nationalistic (Beckman 1992), attributing most of the blame to persistent foreign control of the Nigerien economy by the World Bank and the IMF, supported by other bilateral aid donors like the U.S. Agency for International Development, and to the incumbent regime that went along with these policies. One response was the formation of clandestine political movements that began to organize in secret to challenge the incumbents and perhaps the entire political economic orientation of the central state.

The history of these movements has yet to be written and can be discerned only through an oral tradition. Therefore, merely the broad outlines are known. Interviews with participants suggest two parallel and not unrelated analyses.[4] The first type was represented by the formation of the clandestine age groups, or "Gs," largely among young technically trained Nigerien "cadres," but also among teachers. These groups, characterized by their organization in small, secret cells of friends and schoolmates, initially were inspired by a neo-Marxist, anti-imperialist analysis of their position in the world system and by a long tradition of decentralized clandestine organization made famous by the National Liberation Front in Algeria. The second type followed a more traditional line, which emphasized the uneven pattern of investments and economic development and, hence, of positions of power along ethnic and regional lines. It particularly stressed the neglect and economic underdevelopment of northern Niger and of the Hausa people in southern Niger. Organizationally, these associations were ostensibly structured as ethnic and cultural associations, but they still needed to be clandestine because "ethnic associations" were formally banned. Although there were others, the two most important examples prior to 1991 were AMACA in Zinder and MADALLA in Maradi, both asserting Hausa ethnicity and dissatisfaction with a perceived Zarma domination of the national government. Although these differences in motivation and analysis appear to be major, in reality they were not nearly so separate. Even though this point is denied by some of the major players, the more radical "G" groups had elements of regional and ethnic appeal, as well as being highly personalistic organizations.

A second response was the linkage of these clandestine movements to labor unions and later, when it was politically feasible, to emerging political parties. The union most closely associated was predictably the teachers' union, SNEN, which had been hard-hit by reductions in national budgets for education. By 1990 the time was ripe for the formation of political parties that would reflect and attempt to capture these interests. The *Parti nigérien pour la démocratie et le socialisme* (PNDS–Tarraya), for example, attempted to build its core support around the clandestine groups and SNEN; it was led by Mahamadou Issoufou, the director of operations for the uranium mining company SOMAIR in Arlit.[5] Teachers and students, however, were never unified in a single political movement. A second, more radical party was the *Organisation pour la révolution démocratique nationale* (ORDN). Led by Maman Sani Adamou, a labor leader in the USTN, ORDN attracted a number of intellectuals as well as workers, but it never became an electoral force.

Throughout 1989 and 1990 the pace of demands for change accelerated. USTN called a series of strikes for better labor conditions, particularly in the mining sector. In February 1990 university and secondary school students demonstrated principally against the acceptance by the recently reorganized Ali Saïbou government of the World Bank's Third Education Project for Niger, with its reduction of spending and student benefits. The demonstration featured such slogans as "Down with the PAS" (Structural Adjustment Program) and "Down with the World Bank" (Adji 1996).

The Saïbou government responded with violence, shooting students as they crossed the John F. Kennedy Bridge from the university campus to downtown Niamey and killing at least three. The government's use of naked violence served as a catalyst to radicalize not only student associations but also a number of labor leaders, including the leadership of the labor confederation, USTN. It focused attention on student and labor's common analysis linking their condition to the "structural adjustment" and to the government's collaboration with it.[6] In response, the *Comité de coordination des luttes démocratiques* (CCLD) was formed, grouping USN, USTN, and several of the autonomous unions, in particular SNEN. Under the direction of USTN General Secretary Laouali Moutari, the CCLD committed labor openly to democratization of the regime. Laouali is quoted as stating that the unions had no choice but to enter the political fray because "the solution to the economic crisis can only be found in the political system. . . . We must democratize our society as well as our strategies and policies for development."[7] Despite continued cleavages among the USTN'S affiliated unions over the degree of militancy, Laouali promised strike action and even the use of force, if necessary, to secure the change in the Nigerien government. When the exiled former labor leader and head of the banned UDN (Sawaba) party, Djibo Bakary, was permitted to speak in Niger, addressing more than eighty thousand demonstrators, he evoked the legitimacy of a militant, independent, class-based struggle against the state (Adji 1993). The general strike that ensued, from November fifth to ninth, paralyzed the formal sector and the Nigerien government.

These actions were key steps in forcing the Saïbou government to accept the principal of multipartyism in November 1990, setting the stage for the USTN to break its official relations with the *Mouvement national pour la société de développement* (MNSD), the former single party of the military regime. It quickly led to the complete delegitimation of the MNSD government, and to calls for a Sovereign National Conference (SNC) that would essentially establish a parallel regime. During the period of preparation for the SNC in the spring of 1991, elite perceptions reflected the view that labor unions and student organizations held the most powerful positions in the transition. The head of the SNEN, Rabiou Daouda, chaired the commission preparing the conference, and threats of labor unrest, which the unions continued to make, no doubt played a crucial role in forcing the MNSD and the government of Niger to continue to allow the transition to unfold (Adji 1993). When in April the MNSD government proposed to give labor and student groups nine of the forty-eight seats on the preparatory commission, while reserving at least fourteen seats for the army and other government organs, the unions quickly scuttled this plan. So dominant was labor and its political allies in the eventual Preparatory Commission that labor unions and the USN, the student union, were accorded nearly 25 percent of the 883 voting delegates. During the conference itself, this numerical preponderance was reduced by the adoption of a unit voting rule under which each "sector" had one vote no matter how many delegates represented it. Nonetheless, USTN dominance was perceived to be so significant even with this rule that there was talk of a union dictatorship or at least of union rigidity in the proceedings of the SNC. USTN leader Ibrahim Mayaki fueled this perception when he openly acknowledged that the union would exercise a veto power over decisions it perceived to be contrary to democratic openness at the conference.[8]

Democracy and the Decline of Labor Power

Evidence of the limits of labor's power on the transition emerged immediately following the conference when, to the surprise of many, USTN President Mayaki was not elected to the transitional council (the *Haut conseil de la république*) and when the conference named Amadou Cheifou as prime minister of the transitional government.[9] He was an international technocrat thought to have the strong support of and connections to the international community. Clearly the message SNC delegates wished to present was not one of radical change in domestic or international economic policy. In fact, the transitional government was totally bankrupt and saw one of its principal tasks as imposing austerity measures, including delaying the payment of salaries of public sector employees and the armed forces. This, in turn, very quickly established a pattern of contestation and confrontation between the government and what had been leading interest groups in the transition. In February 1993 the government of the Alliance of Forces of Change (AFC) took power, naming Mahamadou Issoufou of the PNDS as prime minister and Mamane Ousmane of the *Convention démocratique et sociale* (CDS) as president. Not only did Issoufou have strong ties to SNEN and to the uranium workers' union but he and the PNDS had also campaigned as Social Democrats, appealing to unionized civil servants and promising better treatment for labor.[10] In his first major public speech, however, Prime Minister Issoufou threw down the gauntlet to labor by emphasizing the need to do something about the extreme inequity in the allocation of most public expenditures to a tiny segment of the population, namely, students and government workers. Although he promised to improve their lot by paying them regularly, he put them on clear notice that their dominance in policy terms was at an end (Charlick, Fox et al. 1994). This was followed immediately by the repeat of the pattern of delays in paying the salaries of government workers and in the imposition of a new labor agreement in October 1993. This obliged labor to accept a "temporary" salary reduction of 10 to 20 percent, an agreement that quickly came to be known in labor circles as *"L'Accord de la honte"* (the shameful pact). Some union leaders continued to defend Issoufou, however, arguing that as a minority partner within the AFC coalition, his party could have little real influence on policy.

The decision of the Ousmane government in early 1994 to accept the devaluation of the CFA franc, which created a 30 percent inflation in consumer prices, brought conflict between organized labor and the government to a head. Angered that after they agreed to the salary giveback they were not even consulted and their demands for salary adjustments and price controls were ignored, the unions began to call a series of strike actions. The Issoufou government responded by passing a new ordinance that significantly curtailed the power of government employees to strike, providing for governmental authority to requisition strikers and dismiss them if they failed to report for work (Charlick et al. 1994). Union leadership was so bitter about this and other "union-busting" tactics that in June 1994 the USTN effectively declared war on the government, announcing an "unlimited general strike" for all public sector employees until their issues were addressed. The result was disastrous for labor. In the three years since the National Conference had taken place, Nigerien labor unions had fragmented; multiple unions had formed in each sector of public service, including the police. The formation of these new unions appears to have been based on political party preference and, to some degree, on ethnic identity. And tensions over policy and ethnic coloration of leadership had surfaced at all levels: between local unions and branches, on the one hand, and the USTN central union, on the other. By the time the general strike was called, USTN no longer controlled a number of its nominal member unions, and it had still less impact on some branches in particular parts of the country, notably in Zinder and Tillaberry. As a result, the strike call was not uniformly respected, not even among members of some of the most powerful unions, that is, the teachers' union and the custom agents' union. By late July the USTN was forced to call off the strike indefinitely on the pretext that there would be a cooling down period and that negotiations would be reopened in the fall. Those renegotiations never took place.

Meanwhile, the strikes and heavy-handed government responses offered a golden opportunity to the MNSD. Beginning in the spring of 1994, it began to openly support the unions against AFC policies, while simultaneously courting rank-and-file PNDS members. Compounding the difficulties were personal conflicts between President Ousmane and Prime Minister Issoufou over a number of issues, including the terms of the World Bank adjustment loan being negotiated during the period of the general strike. When the World Bank's chief negotiator appeared on Nigerien television denouncing the strike and calling for labor discipline, Prime Minister Issoufou in effect found himself in an impossible situation.[11] It seemed that the Social Democratic and pro-labor party leader was taking orders from the World Bank regarding labor relations, which caused strains within the party that Issoufou himself could no longer tolerate. To further aggravate the situation, the opposition tabled a resolution of censure and no-confidence in the parliament in part over these policies. And while it was defeated on a straight party vote, backbenchers both in the CDS and in PNDS used it to attack Prime Minister Issoufou. On October third he resigned as prime minister and the PNDS pulled out of the AFC coalition, quickly realigning with the MNSD. New legislative elections were called for January 1995 and were won by the now reconfigured MNSD–PNDS alliance, an alliance of the old party of the military regime with the supposedly Social Democratic party. A new MNSD prime minister, Hama Amadou, was installed in a "co-habitation" regime in which Amadou and President Ousmane were at loggerheads on just about every issue. This situation led to constitutional crises and stalemates.

In the course of 1995 labor's conditions did not improve. There were a series of short strikes in different sectors to protest the declining standard of living. Confronted with deadlock and chronic budgetary crisis, the government found itself increasingly in arrears on salary payments to government employees. By the end of the year uranium workers were owed an average of three months' back pay, teachers five months', and support for scholarship students at the University of Niamey had been totally cut off. Although the PNDS was a leading element in the new government, labor had had little success working out its issues with the new parliamentary majority. A number of serious issues separated labor from the government. Under the AFC government a new flat wage tax, the *Impôt général cedulaire sur les traitements et salaries* (IGC) had been instituted. Amadou proposed a presumably fairer and more progressive tax, the *Impôt unique sur les traitements et salaires* (IUTS). This tax reform, which had been promoted by the World Bank, was closely tied to the negotiation of a new structural adjustment package. Organized labor contested both taxes. It opposed the IGC on the grounds that it had increased the tax burden without any consultation with labor. It reserved its most serious criticism, though, for the World Bank–proposed IUTS, which it claimed discriminated against labor because it placed the greatest burden for new revenue collection on public employees while leaving business virtually untouched.[12] In January 1996 organized labor was still trying to negotiate with the Financial Committee of the National Assembly on a plan to put an end to worker salary arrears and on the implementation of new taxes. At this very moment the National Assembly was debating a new law that would have further restricted the right to strike.[13]

On January 11 and 12, 1996, the USTN called for a strike specifically to protest the application of the IUTS. Discontent was so deep that many people began to talk of the possibility of civil war. On January 27, 1996, a military coup d'état overthrew the elected government and brought to power a military group headed by General Ibrahim Maïnassara Baré. By the time the coup took place the legitimacy and credibility of the democratic process and of its principal players was so thoroughly undermined that it was greeted in many circles, at least initially, with relief. The response to the coup on the part of labor and students was indicative of the weakness of these associations and their alienation from the elected regime. Even among these associations that had played so key a role in ending the previous military regime, there were no calls for mass demonstrations. USTN leaders, on the other hand, resisted efforts by the military to impose a new compulsory salary giveback. A few unions, notably the miners' union, called two-day strikes to oppose the decision on the part of the new government to implement the IUTS. Opposition by USTN central leadership was very temperate, however, as USTN leader Mayaki supported the notion of voluntary salary reductions. Clearly, top USTN leadership hoped that, given how poorly they had faired under the previous regime, relations with the military government would prove to be better. Both the USTN and the USN (student union) quickly announced their positions; they sought an early return to civilian constitutional government, but in both Niger and in France factions of both student and union organizations supported rallies welcoming the coup.

Initially, the USTN leaders tried to accommodate themselves to the junta by calling off the proposed strike, by supporting the putschists' position that elected leaders of the former regime should not be restored, and by agreeing to participate in the Coordinating Committee and later the National Forum organized by the military regime. By February and March 1996, however, the honeymoon was over. Newly named Prime Minister Boukari Adji met with union leaders to discuss salary arrears and made no promises, given the regime's dire financial straits. Instead, he proposed a voluntary contribution program whereby civil society would help provide funds to deal with the budgetary crisis. At the same time, he promised to make up one month of back pay for November 1995, offering some gesture of good will.[14] By February uranium miners at the two principal mines (SOMAIR and COMINAK) went on strike over nonpayment of wages. A temporary end to these strikes was brokered by mid-April, but relations between labor and the junta had deteriorated sharply. At the end of February the USTN went on record at its General Assembly as rejecting the government's plan for workers to lend it funds, or to pay monthly salaries now every forty-two days, thereby constituting a de facto 30 percent cut in public sector wages. USTN General Secretary Mayaki complained that labor was now worse off than before the coup, subject to both the IUTS tax and the wage cuts.[15] When in mid-June the USTN called a forty-eight-hour strike to protest that the government was not respecting the March agreement to pay wages even at this diminished level, the strike was largely unsuccessful. This demonstrated again the union's inability to effectively resist the implementation of these antilabor measures.[16]

Still more serious were the efforts on the part of the Baré government to "destabilize" the USTN by siding with dissidents within the union federation and supporting the creation of an alternative federation, the *Confédération nigérienne du travail* (CNT). This new grouping openly sided with Baré's personal political ambitions as he began to put together a campaign to win election to the presidency. The USTN naturally found itself once again in the opposition.

In the presidential election of July 1996, Baré suspended the vote counting in midstream, replaced the electoral commission, and then declared he had won a majority. Thereafter, relations with labor deteriorated still further. This time labor's response was quick and unequivocal. The USTN called an emergency meeting of all trade unions and denounced the election. It called for a general strike to stop all economic activity and produce *villes mortes* (dead cities) throughout the country until the electoral results were voided and opposition political leaders were released from jail. The government countered with its usual carrot and stick. It offered to pay all public sector workers one month's back pay effective immediately, and it arrested some top union leaders, including USTN head Ibrahim Mayaki. He was also sacked from his key position as head of the Social Security Trust Fund. The government formally acknowledged the right of unions to take "industrial actions," but it cautioned them against engaging in political strikes, warning that those who disobeyed would be subject to sanctions and would not get the promised make-up pay.[17] According to one story that circulated on various news services, Baré is reported to have stated on national radio, "Recess is over, and those who hide behind the unions to try to create trouble must be denounced."

The strike that followed was the most ineffective to date. Apart from the teachers union (SNEN), which closed down most of the schools in Niamey, few public sector, and almost no private sector, employees heeded the strike call. The USTN executive board was forced to reconsider its strike call, acknowledging its weakness in the face of the government's promises and threats. By 1998 the Baré government had introduced a series of new laws designed to weaken the civil service unions, including a 30 percent across-the-board wage cut and a rule for the mandatory retirement of public sector workers at the age of 50 (Adji 2000). These laws were hotly disputed throughout 1998 and failed to be implemented only because of the disruption caused by Baré's assassination. Sporadic strikes continued in various sectors, notably in the uranium and electricity production sectors and in truck transportation. The government's response was to arrest dozens of labor leaders and charge them with economic sabotage. Most of these were eventually acquitted in legal proceedings, some were quickly released, and others remained in jail long after their acquittal. The combined effect of these actions further weakened the unions.

Labor under the Post-Baré "Democratic Regimes"

In March 1999 General Baré was assassinated by forces led by his own army chief of staff, General Dauda Mallam Wanke. A brief transitional military government ensued, leading to an open competitive election in the fall that returned to power an MNSD president (Mamadou Tandja) and prime minister (Hama Amadou). Although the brutal repression of labor ceased under this new regime, the overall position of labor as an actor in civil society and as a force to defend the interests of Nigerien workers hardly improved. The period since 2000 has been characterized by the imposition of antilabor policies originated during the Baré regime, largely in response to conditionalities imposed by the World Bank and the IMF for the resumption of structural adjustment loans. These include the implementation of the Civil Service Reform Act with its provisions to cut civil service salaries by 30 percent and to mandate retirement at the age of 55.

It has also been characterized by the increasing politicization and fragmentation of union federations and by a deepening crisis in union internal organization and finances. Despite promises to the contrary, most Nigerien public sector workers experienced salary arrears of between five and eleven months since the new-elected government has come to power. In 2005, at the height of the ongoing food crisis in Niger, unions were unable to resist the imposition of a new 19 percent value added tax, making basic foodstuffs much more expensive for urban workers.

Nor did unions gain much in the way of bargaining power to meaningfully participate with the leadership of the regime elected in 1999 and again in late 2005. The style of interaction did change, however, as government seemed more open to consultation with the unions. In 2004, for example, in the midst of a continuing crisis in education, the government invited some of the unions to become partners (*la gestion parternariale*) in working out the issues that had kept the schools closed. This form of collaboration resembled the "responsible participation" policy of the Kountche regime more than a meaningful breakthrough in negotiating with the SNEN over the material condition of schools and teachers. In fact, the government did not even agree to respond to SNEN's concerns until after the fall 2005 elections.

Nothing illustrates the incapacity of unions to defend the interests of their members better than the course of the negotiations that the Tandja-Amadou government entered into with unions in July 2005. This was a critical period in a campaign for reelection, and the government agreed to meet with the four principal union groupings to discuss their demands. The unions were demanding a restoration of the 30 percent wage cuts, payment of back salaries, and the raising of the minimum wage, said to be the lowest in the world. They were also lobbying for a change in the mandatory age of retirement for public service employees from 55 to 60 and for an end to the practice of docking pay for employees unable to work due to strike actions that they themselves had not initiated. In September the government, through its interministerial committee, signed an agreement covering most of these demands. By November, however, Prime Minister Amadou made it clear that the government would live up to none of these accords. He offered instead only a 10 percent salary increase, a $4 (1,000 CFA) per month increase in family allocations, and a vague promise that if financial conditions permitted, they would revisit the retirement policy in 2008. The union federations discussed the possibility of striking over these issues but concluded that they were currently in no position to successfully do so. Thus, even in an election year, the force of the entire Nigerien union movement combined failed to be able to extract any real concessions from the government.

The period since the return to power of elected governments in 1999 has also been characterized by ongoing crisis in the country's largest union federation, the USTN, and by fragmentation and multiplication of the national union associations. USTN's Extraordinary Congress in 2000 was widely reported to be a disaster. Affiliated unions complained bitterly about the absence of internal democracy in USTN.[18] According to one Nigerien scholar, the union federations consulted very little with their affiliates and were not respecting their own bylaws for the periodic election of leaders (Adji 2000). These phenomena contributed to the USTN crisis in 2000 and to the ongoing defection of affiliates and efforts to form more effective union associations.

By 2000 the USTN had already been split, with the creation of the CNT during the Baré years. Now, as a result of this dissatisfaction with the UTSTN's 2000 congress, a second new union federation was formed: the *Alliance credible aux exigences des travailleurs* (ACET), which grouped together SNEN (teachers), SUSAS (health workers), SYNAJECS (youth and sport workers), SNAD (customs workers), SNAF (Finance Ministry workers), SNAT (Treasury Ministry workers), and SNAI (tax collection workers). Initially, the Amadou government banned this federation because of illegal strikes. There had, in fact, been a rash of strikes in the education sector, causing schools not to open for the 2004/05 school year until January, and in the health sector. Subsequently, the government recognized ACET and even included it in the negotiations discussed above.

Shortly thereafter, in 2001, a third new union association was formed—the *Confédération démocratique de travailleurs du Niger* (CDTN). This grouping represented still another split off the USTN. The rationale for this split was mainly the discontent over the USTN's inability to contest and mobilize opposition to government policies. A fourth union central has formed in recent years, namely, the *Union générale des travailleurs du Niger* (UGTN), representing still another fission among USTN affiliates. In addition to the fragmentation of national union associations, smaller groups of unions are coalescing, such as the *Federation inter-syndicales des douanes et de impôts* (FISDI), grouping workers from customs (SNAD), tax collection (SNAI), and customs warehouses (SNYTRAMAD). In addition, union bargaining is being weakened by the disaffiliation of many unions, which now have become "non-affiliated." This has been particularly true of white-collar worker unions that are abandoning all the federations. In 2001 there were at least twenty-one such unions.

Taken together, the fragmentation has both good and bad implications. It is surely evidence of a political climate in which state-dominated corporatist associations no longer have a monopoly on workers. On the other hand, it almost certainly represents a weakening of labor's already limited power. Analyzing the overall situation in Niger, a Nigerien sociologist at the University of Niamey wrote: "With the current deepening economic crisis, and the growing number of unemployed people and part-time workers . . . the break-up of the union movement is probably irreversible. Its fragmentation is made more likely by the failure of many union leaders to project a positive image of militant unionism to workers and the general public" (Adji 2000).

The Weakness of Organized Labor as an Actor in Civil Society

Elsewhere I have argued that unions and student associations constituted the best-organized and potentially most powerful actors in Nigerien civil society (Charlick 1991, 1996). It is indisputable that both played key roles in bringing down the military regime in the early 1990s and in supporting the transition to a more democratic political system. Why, then, have unions proven to be such a weak force both in consolidating democracy in Niger and in representing their own constituents and civil society more broadly, even during periods of democratic rule? Our analysis of the historical evolution of labor in Niger points to three factors that derive both from the internal characteristics of labor and from the international context in which it and the regime operate.

First, the organized workforce of Niger is extraordinarily small in comparison to the broader labor force and to the labor forces of more economically developed countries. As one of the world's least industrialized and developed economies, Niger has one of the smallest formal labor forces per capita of any country in the world. No more than 50,000 workers are formal sector employees, out of a total population of approximately 11 million and a labor force of about 7 million.[19] Of this number about 44,000 are government employees. One source reports that in 1995 about 12,000 workers were employed in industry (private and parastatal)[20] This number seems very unlikely at present given that, apart from the uranium and coal mining sectors that have about 2,500 employees, industrial employment is almost nonexistent. In 2003 one source estimated that fewer than 300 workers were employed in private sector manufacturing plants.[21] No doubt wage and salaried employment have declined since the 1980s with the contraction of both government service-oriented and industrial employment in response to declining uranium prices and production and to budgetary austerity under structural adjustment programs. In addition to being tiny, the salaried labor force is also highly dependent on the national government policies of taxation and budgetary expenditure. Even after a decade of "structural adjustment," at least 80 percent of formal sector labor in Niger still works for government or for parastatal enterprises. In this context class formation and class interests must be assumed to be weak and the position of organized labor in political life marginal. The majority of organized workers are always in a conflict between their own interests and those of the regime.

The tradition of an independent and nonpolitical bureaucracy is very weak in Niger. In 2004, for example, a number of unions, including customs workers, protested without effect against the use of their members by the dominant MNSD party in the electoral campaign and against the assignment and forced retirement of members based on political considerations. Our brief historical review demonstrates that labor leaders have clearly attempted to improve their relations with every new incoming regime, yet they have often wound up "in opposition," often identified with the coalition or parties out of power, as was the case during most of the Baré regime. This position has hardly benefited labor, but neither has the position of becoming too closely identified with the regime as a "responsible partner."

During the 2005 campaign, some union leaders joined elements in civil society and the media in protesting against corruption and purportedly illegal government procedure practices that they asserted were draining away public resources. Yet the USTN declared it would remain apolitical during the electoral campaign, taking no public position on the reelection of the Tandja-Amadou regime.

In any case, democratization has hurt the power of unions in several ways. As a tiny group, unions never could deliver large numbers of votes, and electoral politics in Niger has had remarkably little to do with class interests. Even a cursory analysis of election data reveals the persistence not of issues and economic interests but of ethnic and regional politics, with major parties still drawing most of their support from particular parts of the country and cultural-linguistic groups. In fact, ethnic appeals have been used to attempt to discredit unions by arguing that a single ethnic group—namely, the Hausa—have excessively dominated both the unions and the student associations.[22]

The second weakness of unions has been their own internal characteristics. Three stand out as limiting unions as effective civil society actors. First, most of the unions as well as their national associations have suffered from a lack of internal democracy and accountability. The origin of this pattern of maintaining tight control of information and decision making derives in all likelihood from the character of nearly all civil society actors as clandestine organizations during both the colonial era and much of the period of independence.[23] Unions adopted the practice and culture of the pattern of governance of Marxist cells, imposing "democratic centralism" on members as a way to limit the opportunities for external influence and to maintain "solidarity."[24] Relations between union centrals, like the USTN, and member unions became more and more strained as union leaders found themselves under increasing pressure by the sitting governments. Eventually, with democratization in the early 1990s, many unions, including the most sensitive security and police unions, split into separate ethnically based branches, defecting from USTN because of political loyalties and opportunities and because the internal processes of the centrals were considered so closed.[25] Thus, as Adji reports, many union leaders stayed on long after their elected terms had expired, resisting holding elections that could force them from office.

In addition, the organizational capacity of unions has been weak and deteriorating because they lack even the most basic infrastructure. During the period of single-party rule, corporatist unions benefited from a variety of subsidies that kept them going, including positions in the bureaucracy for their top leaders. With greater democracy, unions had to compete for resources. The subsequent dictatorship under General Baré found it fairly easy and inexpensive to buy union quiescence. Baré, for example, is reported to have offered the USTN one four-wheel drive vehicle and about $10,000 to accept the policy of "responsible participation" (Adji 2000). At the same time, Baré so drastically undermined the USTN's membership activities that by 2000 it had lost 87 percent of its revenue from the sale of membership cards, and only 10 percent of its affiliates were said to be current with their subscriptions (Adji 2000). In fact, by 2000 the USTN did not even have sufficient resources to pay its subscriptions to international unions, to hold its regular congresses, or even to pay for a telephone and fax machine (Adji 2000). With such minimal resources it could hardly be expected that unions could be effective associations lobbying for the interests of their members.

Finally, unions as well as other actors in Niger have had to deal with a very fundamental reality—the extreme dependency of the regime on international actors and their policy prescriptions. By the time the democratization movement began to accelerate in Niger, the state was utterly bankrupt. The elected AFC government and its new prime minister, Issoufou, saw no alternative to putting Niger back on a track where it could get World Bank and IMF loans and could increase the scope of bilateral assistance linked to its conformity with structural adjustment policies. So, no matter how pro-labor Issoufou may have been, his first task was to attempt to reduce expenditures and increase tax revenues. Given the structure of Niger's formal sector, there could be little alternative to compressing civil service salaries and benefits and to opposing all of labor's efforts to protect its members from the consequences of devaluation and deflation. Several recent studies demonstrate that in most African countries, and even in Niger, the impact of these policies on expenditures and on employment has been exaggerated (Gervais 1992; van de Walle 2001). Nonetheless, it does appear to have been significant, with major delays in payment of salaries, in government salary givebacks, and in the loss of a significant number of public sector jobs. In this climate, it is hardly surprising that labor's demands have been more and more modest and its ability to achieve even the most modest improvements in conditions of its members extremely limited.

Notes

1. The terms "forces democratiques" (Niger: Souley Niandou 1996), "forces vives" (Madagascar: Fox 1994), or "rainbow coalition" (Frederick Chiluba, Zambia: White 1995) describe a loose coalition of antiregime actors including labor unions, students, opposition politicians, intellectuals, some businessmen, commercial farmers, and in some cases, religious leaders.
2. For the most complete account of the transition from 1990 to late 1994, see Charlick 1994. See Bjorn Beckman (1992, 324) for the argument that, contrary to the expectations of governance experts at the World Bank, the greatest pressure for regime reform, for liberalization, and eventually for democratization came from mass-based interest groups, notably organized labor and students, that were opposed to structural adjustment. For the case of Niger, a similar argument has been made by Niandou Souley (1992) and by Souley Adji (1996).
3. Niandou Souley (2000) suggests that this policy shift was democratically decided upon by union leaders, but Maïnassara (1999) stresses the heavy pressure and threats that union leaders confronted.
4. For reasons of preserving the personal security of those interviewed, most of the oral sources will not be specified here. One key player who was interviewed in January 1993

and again in July 1994 was Mohamed Bazoum, a high-ranking official in the PNDS who was second vice president in the first elected parliament and then became minister of foreign affairs after January 1995.

5. See the interview with Issoufou in the weekly newspaper *Haske*, 51, January 7, 1993.
6. It was not until its thirteenth congress in 1992, however, that the USTN officially rejected the Structural Adjustment Program.
7. See *Haske*, 4, August 15, 1990.
8. *Haske*, 19, September 9–16, 1991.
9. In fact, as a former regional director of the International Civil Aviation Organization, Amadou Cheifou was not the best connected Nigerien to play this role.
10. Based on interviews conducted in Niamey in June 1996 with Ali Moussa (deputy director of USTN), Habou Souley (leader of SNEN), and Abdou Maigandu (national secretary for worker education of the USTN).
11. I personally observed this television broadcast.
12. Maarouf Elhadj Sani, "Si Sacrifice on doit consenter, cela doit concerner tous les citoyens," interview with the General Secretary of USTN in *Le Democrate*, February 26, 1996.
13. *Le Sahel*, January 19, 1995; and personal interviews with USTN leaders in June 1996.
14. *Le Sahel*, 5119, February 14, 1996.
15. Interview with USTN General Secretary Ibrahim Mayaki, in *Le Democrate*, February 26, 1996.
16. *Agence France-Presse*, June 14, 1996.
17. Idi Mama Kotoudi, "Niger Unions Call Strike Over Muddled Polls," *PanAfrican News Agency*, July 10, 1996.
18. Adji 2000. I also observed this process firsthand when I conducted research in Niamey in May and June 2000.
19. Labor statistics for Niger are notoriously unreliable and vary significantly according to the source. The ICFTU reports that there are forty-four thousand government workers and a total of seventy thousand formal-sector workers in all. (International Confederation of Free Trade Unions, online, July 3, 1997.) This seems very unlikely given the tiny size of the private sector.
20. United Nations Development Program, *Human Development Report, 1995* (New York: Oxford University Press, 1995), Table 11, 176–77.
21. Hayden Wetzel, "Country Commercial Guide—Niger" (Ottowa: Industry Canada, October 2003). Also available at http://www.strategis.gc.ca.
22. Bachir Attouman, "Reflexions sur le regionalisme et le tribalisme," *Haske*, 13, April 15–30, 1991.
23. See Bakary 1992 and Mainassara 1989.
24. Based on interviews with union and student leaders in Niamey, June 2000.
25. Based on interviews conducted in July–August 1994, including with the previously highest ranking woman in the Nigerian national policy, Mme Barry Bibata.

References

Adji, Souley. 1993. Les successions politiques: L'exemple du Niger. Unpublished paper.
———. 1996. Démocratisation, PAS et Production de la violence populaire au Niger. Unpublished paper presented at the colloquium Transitions in Africa, Violence and the Politics of Participation, Niamey, Niger, June.

————. 2000. Globalization and union strategies in Niger. In *Organized labor in the 21st Century*, ed. A. V. Jose. Geneva: International Institute for Labour Studies.

Bakary, Djibo. 1992. *Silence: On décolonise—itinèraire politique et syndical d'un militant africain*. Paris: L'Harmattan.

Beckman, B. 1992. Empowerment or repression? The World Bank and the politics of African adjustment. In *Authoritarianism, democracy and adjustment*, ed. P. Gibbon, Y. Bangura, and A. Ofstad, 83–105. Uppsala, Sweden: Scandinavian Institute of African Studies.

Burton, Michael, Richard Gunther, and John Higley. 1992. Introduction: Elite transformations and democratic regimes. In *Elites and democratic consolidation in Latin America and Southern Europe*, ed. John Higley and Richard Gunther. New York, Cambridge University Press.

Charlick, Robert. 1991. *Niger: Personal rule and survival in the Sahel*. Boulder, CO: Westview Press.

————. 1996. "Democratic forces" in African civil society: The role of labor and student organizations in Niger's recent political transitions. Unpublished paper, November.

Charlick, Robert, Sheldon Gellar, Tina West, Leslie Fox, and Pearl Robinson. 1994. *Improving democratic governance for sustainable development: An assessment of change and continuity in Niger*. Washington DC: Associates in Rural Development.

Charlick, Robert, Leslie Fox, Maureen Covell, Jean Rakotorisoa, and Charles Rabenrivo. 1994. *An Assessment of Politics and Governance in Madagascar*. Washington DC: Associates in Rural Development.

Fatton, Robert. 1992. *Predatory rule: State and civil society in Africa*. Boulder, CO: Lynne Rienner.

Gazibo, Mamoudou. 1997. Gloire et misères du movement syndical nigérien. *Politique africaine* 69 (1997): 126–34.

Gervais, M. 1992. Les enjeux politiques de ajustements structurels au Niger, 1983–1990. *Canadian Journal of African Studies* 26 (2): 226–49.

Maïnassara, Boureïima. 1989. *Pratiques syndicales et conscience de classes au Niger*. Niamey: Imprimerie Nationale du Niger.

————. 1999. *L'evolution du mouvement syndical au Niger—De la periode coloniale à nos jours*. Niamey: Presses de la Nouvelle Imprimerie du Niger.

Migdal, J. S. 1988. *Strong societies and weak state: State society relations and state capabilities in the third world*. Princeton, NJ: Princeton University Press.

Miles, W. F. S. 1994. *Hausaland divided: Colonialism and independence in Nigeria and Niger*. Ithaca, NY: Cornell University Press.

Niandou, Souley A. 1992. Economic crisis and democratisation in Africa. Symposium of Ibadan, Nigeria, June 15–19.

————. 1996. De l'Instabilité du modele compétitif à la conquete violente du pouvoir: Le case du Niger. Unpublished paper presented at the colloquium Transitions in Africa, Violence and the Politics of Participation, Niamey, Niger, June.

————. 2000. Syndicalisme et démocratie au Niger: Suivi longitudinal. Unpublished paper.

Rothchild, Donald, and Naomi Chazan. 1988. *The precarious balance: State and society in Africa*. Boulder, CO: Westview.

Schmitter, P. C. 1992. The consolidation of democracy and representation of social groups. *American Behavioral Scientist* 35 (4/5): 422–49.

White, G. 1995. Civil society, democratisation and development (II): Case studies. *Democratisation* 2 (Summer): 56–84.

Thomson, Alex. 2004. *An introduction to African politics.* 2nd ed. London: Routledge.

Van de Walle, Nicolas. 2001. *African economics and the politics of permanent crisis, 1977–1999.* New York: Cambridge University Press.

Wiseman, John A. 1996. *The new struggle for democracy in Africa.* Avebury, UK: Aldershot.

CHAPTER 4

Trade Unions, Democratization, and Economic Crises in Ghana

Jon Kraus

We cannot be concerned about strengthening democracy inside our union without being concerned about democracy. . . . The people of Ghana . . . reserve the historical right to determine how their affairs are run and who governs them. . . . We must exercise our democratic right to choose our rulers.

L. G. K. Ocloo
General Secretary of the Industrial and Commercial Workers Union
1987

What role have trade unions and workers played in Ghana's move toward political liberalization and democratization, in the past and in the recent1990–93 democratic transition? Have unions been important, either through their beliefs and protest behavior or as a consequence of their structural position in civil society? Were economic conditions key factors in the unions' behavior? Since Ghana's return to democracy, have the unions become more active on behalf of their interests in civil society and in the political system than under authoritarian rule? Have they helped to consolidate democratic processes?

I argue that the trade union movement in Ghana made a major contribution to political liberalization and democratization between 1983 and 1992. It did not do so through an outburst of strikes and demonstrations, as occurred in some other countries, though protests and resistance were important. The union movement did so by struggling to retain its institutional autonomy and power, by protesting continuously against violations of union rights and the economic policies of the Provisional National Defense Council (PNDC) government, and by demanding to be consulted on economic policies affecting workers. The Trade Union Congress (TUC) and its national unions persisted in these struggles against a highly repressive, antiunion regime, which had quashed all public opposition and the ability of other societal groups to articulate their interests or mobilize members. The TUC's persistent struggles had several impacts. They enlarged the public political space where societal groups could demand a voice and accountability from the government. They demonstrated visibly—through meetings, consultation, and election of leaders—an alternative democratic ethos to the PNDC's authoritarianism. In their acts of opposing PNDC policies and mobilizing members, unions demanded the restoration of democratic assemblies and constitutional government. Unions were moved by the desperate economic conditions of workers and their rights to speak for workers, which the state denied. And unions were the only substantial group in the mid-1980s onward to demand full democratic and constitutional rule. Union movement resistance widened the public arena and by doing so allowed other organizations to become more publicly active and opposition groups to reemerge in 1990–91 without suffering deadly repression. The union movement was weakened by PNDC coercion, but it was the one large, democratic group to remain independent and capable of demanding its rights. It drew other associations (of teachers, nurses, civil servants) into public forums with itself to broaden its base, giving these groups the courage to articulate their interests. It compelled the PNDC to deal with its capacity to mobilize protests when the PNDC had imposed a "culture of silence" in Ghana and other protest was moribund.

Since the return of constitutional rule in 1993, the unions have become even more involved in demanding their rights to represent worker and public interests and in mobilizing workers behind their policy stands. Unions have threatened general strikes and wide-ranging opposition on many occasions. Unions have sought to use the new democratic institutions (parliament), civil rights (press freedoms, protest rights), and legal rights and institutions to advance their policy interests and institutional autonomy, thus strengthening democratic institutions in Ghana.

Trade unions in Ghana have not always been highly supportive of democratic political systems. Indeed, in the early 1970s they were very unhappy with the civilian democratic government and extended them low levels of support. They were joyous in 1972 to see the overthrow of a hostile, ineffective democratic regime. The Progress Party government tried to weaken and destroy the union movement in 1971. It made the unions deeply suspicious of this party and unwilling to support it when its leaders campaigned in 1977–78 to remove the military government, which had given the unions exceptional benefits. Union leaders supported the democratic renewal in 1979–81, but its economic policies alienated workers.

In this study, I first examine existing theory that discusses the role of trade unions in political liberalization and democratic transitions. Second, armed with some analytical approaches, I briefly survey the experience of trade unions with the different regimes in Ghana since independence in 1957. This historical experience has shaped the attitudes of unions to democracy and union rights and power. I assess trade union–state relations in terms of the growth of union strength and rights, achievement of union autonomy and interests, operative union political norms, and union responses to regime labor control strategies. In this context I look at the relationship of the trade unions to class forces, state power, and transnational power.

Third, and most importantly, I assess the impact of trade unions in restoring political liberties and democratic life under the authoritarian ruler Flight Lieutenant Jerry Rawlings and his PNDC government from 1982 through 1992. It tried to destroy the union movement. Last, I examine trade union behavior in Ghana since democratic rule in January 1993 to discern (1) whether the unions have supported democratic political processes and institutions, and (2) whether or not the experiences of the TUC and its member unions with democratic rule have been advantageous, and how this has affected union and worker support for the democratic regime.

Theory and Analytical Perspectives on Trade Unions in Africa's Democratization

The sources of political liberalization in authoritarian regimes and democratic transitions have been examined with diverse theories and analyses. Recent theorizing, however, has been unable to attribute the wave of democratic transitions to any single economic or political factor (Diamond, Linz, and Lipset 1988; Huntington 1991, 34–106; Shin 1994). Some analyses suggest that political liberalization began with elite concessions in Latin America but mass political protests in Africa (Bratton and van de Walle 1997; O'Donnell and Schmitter 1986). Controversies in interpretations occur because of different analytical approaches and a focus on different actors or periods of political transitions, for example, the weight given to mass protests vs. elite transactions (see introduction).

I am primarily interested in the behavior and conflicts of the major social/political actors or social classes as a means of explaining immediate outcomes. One also has to look to the major economic and political factors that animate the behavior of these actors. Although Bratton and van de Walle (1997) do not find economic factors systematically related to the mass protests that led to democratization in Africa, many analysts of democratization movements in Africa and Latin America locate the source of political protests that unseat old regimes in harsh or deteriorating economic conditions (Bermeo [1997] and Haggard and Kaufman [1995] on Latin America; Bratton [1994], Chikhi [1991], and Heilbron [1993] on Africa). I agree and have written so in the introduction to this volume.

In Africa, it was evident that the most important source of political liberalization was mass protests against the old regimes, which was closely associated with the numbers of trade unions, protests, and strikes (Bratton and van de Walle 1997, 148–50, 185; Kraus 1995). Despite this, and that unions are the single largest associational group, little attention has been paid to the impact of trade unions or their protests on the processes of political liberalization or democratic transition in civil society literature (Harbeson, Rothchild, and Chazan 1994), including in Ghana. In part this may be because trade unions were often not directly involved in the political process after their initial protests had unhinged the old regime and forced the restoration of political liberties (Barchiesi 1996). Also, the explosion of protests was relatively brief in many cases. Nonetheless, some scholars have emphasized the significant role of trade unions in some stages of democratization in Africa, Latin America, and southern Europe (Adler and Webster 1995; Bermeo 1997; Collier and Mahoney 1997; Valenzuela 1989). I argue that trade unions played the most important role of any political actors in restoring political liberties in Ghana by 1990–91, although the unions did not engage in massive protests and force immediate changes.

Rueschemeyer, Stephens, and Stephens are the foremost analysts who have argued that the organized working class (not the middle class) has been the key class actor in the development of full democracy almost everywhere, though it could not bring democracy into being by itself. Rueschemeyer et.al. develop extensive historical studies and focus analytically upon the interactions of three clusters of power—class, state, and transnational structures—to explain how and under what circumstances democratic forms emerge from capitalist development (1992, 1–27, 40–75). They regard social class interactions as crucial for explaining patterns of democratization. Capitalist development, which creates a bourgeoisie, a middle class, and a working class, "is related to democracy through changes in the balance of class power." The relatively low crystallization of class formation and class power in most African states suggests that it might be difficult for African trade unions to play a central role in the generation and consolidation of democracy. However, despite the crucial role of ethnicity in African political conflicts, many African struggles do involve relations of class, state, and transnational structures of power, such as markets and multinationals (Sandbrook 1981; Sklar 1979; Waterman 1983). We use these structures of power to discuss trade union–state relations in Ghana.

Some studies that argue that trade union protests have been central to the wave of democratization in southern Europe and Latin America in the late 1970s and 1980s often do not discuss at length *why* they have played such an important role (Bermeo 1997; Collier and Mahoney 1997). They regard *collective or mass actors* as crucial. The forceful protests and strikes give trade unions and other mass actors their preeminent roles. Collier and Mahoney specifically argue that trade unions play a central role only in the initial stage of democratization, when protest forces authoritarian regimes to concede civil and political liberties. They see the process of democratic transition itself "necessarily dominated by elites establishing rules for the actual transfer of power and designing the institutions of new democracies" (287), which is often so. But it seems unlikely that a full transition would occur without the continuing presence of pro-democratic mass actors, which push regularly and impatiently for fulfillment of their demands (Bermeo 1997).

It is not only the mass protests of unions that generate political liberalization and democratization. *Trade unions struggle to come into existence and to organize mass support and hence often arouse continuing, fierce antagonism to their organized power from the state and private sectors. They struggle to acquire and maintain institutional autonomy, legal rights, bargaining capabilities, and representation of worker interests. When trade unions do these things in authoritarian societies, and succeed, they broaden the boundaries of legal and civil rights.* They raise the costs of repression to state and society because of their size and resistance. Moreover, unions understand that they need political liberties to protect their rights of association and protest, representation, and bargaining. Other organized groups in society then perceive that unions are being successful and renew attempts to have their interests represented. It is precisely in these respects, I will argue, that the labor movement provided a major impetus to the renewal of political liberties and democratic demands in Ghana.

Clearly, the significance of trade unions in political life increases in proportion to their relative strength. Some of the key **measures of trade union strength** I discuss include the following:

(a) total size of the union movement, or size in specific industries;
(b) strategic salience and location of union members, for example, in a key export industry or city;
(c) a union movement's collective capabilities, such as centralization vs. fragmentation of trade unions, ideological/ political division vs. unity, bargaining and legal rights won, and financial strength;
(d) unions' collective capacity to mobilize support, as indicated by strikes or protest activity, indicating leverage, and historical memory of union struggles;
(e) autonomy of trade union organization from the state, and persistence of this;
(f) democratic or authoritarian norms and practices in the union movement, which influence rank-and-file responsiveness; and
(g) linkages to other collective actors and political parties.

Alternative labor control strategies are used quite self-consciously by the state to control labor and to prevent it from developing independent power or from allying itself with a political opposition (Crisp 1984, 3–7; Valenzuela 1989). The **corporatist strategy** involves state creation or support of trade unions, which it then controls by means of restrictive legislation, state-sanctioned finances and required membership, political alliances, cooptation or selection of leadership, and state monitoring and repression of dissident labor behavior. A **market strategy** is most frequently an exclusionist one; labor is outside the coalition of support and "free" markets are emphasized. It seeks to weaken trade unions as representative organs and as bargaining agents. It involves restrictive legislation that narrows the scope of legal union prerogatives (e.g., strike and bargaining rights), decentralizes bargaining, foments union splits to solicit allies, restricts political activism, and represses unions or leaders it considers hostile.

Trade unions are often posed between a strategy of resistance and accommodation and have some choices. Union leaders in Ghana and other countries frequently confront coercive choices and have not been co-opted when, on some issues, they choose accommodation. Beckman (1995) explains why the Nigerian trade unions at first launched a fierce *resistance* of strikes and protests to structural adjustment policies (SAPs) in 1988–89 and then seemed to end this resistance and accept an *accommodation* with the Babangida government, based on minor concessions and promises of a new minimum wage. The *context* was one in which the unions had accepted a legal structure; the military government had power and *could—and later did—*simply abolish the labor federation and put in caretaker leaders. The decision whether to resist in militant protest and put the labor movement and bargaining rights at risk or to accommodate itself to less than what is sought is *a contingent decision based on a calculation of risks and gains.*

The literature on trade unions in Ghana has not dealt with the question of the impact on democratization (Gyimah-Boadi and Johnson 1993). Haynes offers an extended examination of the efforts of the Railway Workers Union (RWU) to reverse the assaults of the PNDC and Workers Defense Committees (WDCs) upon the roles of trade unions and why the RWU remained nonmilitant and bargained with the

PNDC (1991). Herbst attempts to explain why the union movement in Ghana was acquiescent—but it was not—in the face of structural adjustment policies. He explains the acquiescence in terms of the PNDC's assault upon the union movement, repression, and "chance" (1993, 58–75). A number of studies discuss the origins of the conflict of unions with the PNDC and WDCs (Adu-Amankwah 1990; Graham 1989; Yeebo 1991). Akwetey argues that the trade unions contributed to democratization by their protests and by calling for constitutional rule, but that its resistance declined by 1987–88 once the PNDC conceded to consulting it on key policies (1994). All these works help observers understand Ghanaian unions. But many greatly underestimate trade union resistance to the PNDC government, and none link this resistance and demands for autonomy and representation to democratization in Ghana.

It is often argued that rank-and-file workers, not allegedly unresponsive national union leaders, initiate strikes in Africa. But in authoritarian regimes, national and some local union leaders are under coercive pressures to avoid strikes. National leaders often countenance and support strikes, but not openly. And it is the existence of union organization that creates the feasibility for this collective class activity, regardless of leader and rank-and-file frictions.

Trade Union–State Relations, Union Autonomy, and Democracy, 1957 to 1981

In this section I briefly examine (1) some major characteristics of the trade union movement in Ghana, and (2) the experiences of trade union relationships with the class, state, and transnational power structures (e.g., markets, financial institutions, the International Labor Organization [ILO]) under democratic and authoritarian regimes from 1957 to 1981. I discuss such issues as:

- Has the union movement become stronger under democratic or authoritarian regimes, and with what impact on union thinking?
- Have democratic norms been important, historically, to Ghanaian unions?
- Has the union movement expressed a preference for political democracy and, if not, why not? How have unions aligned themselves in past democratic struggles in Ghana, and why?

Ghana's wage/salary sector was estimated at 20 percent of the total labor force in 1960, one of the largest in Africa. Most of its members belonged to Ghana's working class, some of which was rural (on cocoa farms). The largest employers were the mines, government, and commerce. There were 41,447 mineworkers in 1941, and 34,100 in 1954. Formal sector recorded employment (firms with ten or more employees) was 343,752 in 1960, which drastically underestimates the wage sector, since there were already about 320,000 paid-up union members in 1961, as noted in Table 4.1 (Kraus 1979b, 119). Ghanaian artisans and lower civil servants were forming trade unions before World War I, but organizing efforts were largely suppressed until after World War II. Ghanaian workers have a fairly rich labor history of union organizing, long "recognition" strikes in mines opposed by the Chamber of Mines, and Railway Workers Union (RWU)–led general strikes in 1950 and 1961 (Crisp 1984, 35–120; Jeffries 1978; Kraus 1979b, 109–16). By the mid-to-late 1950s the previously migrant labor force was largely a permanent one. Most workers, blue and white collar, occupied the lower rungs of the wage pyramid. Workers and union membership were concentrated in the coastal cities of Sekondi-Takoradi, Accra, the capital, and the nearby new port and industrial center, Tema. The percent of *formal sector* wage workers, private and government, actually declined from the mid-1960s to 2000 because of economic failures in the 1964–83 period and IMF-enforced shrinkage of parastatal and government employment during 1984–2005. A large labor force of self-employed artisans and petty-commodity producers in towns and cities provide goods and services. They employ wage workers and many apprentices. Hawkers, the unemployed, drivers and mates, and hundreds of thousands of market women swell the urban labor force. This sector is clearly distinct from the Ghanaian working class but is linked to it socially, spatially, and economically. The number of itinerant urban hawkers increased massively as formal sector wage opportunities shrank.

Trade unions have a long history in Ghana, having developed prior to and independent of the nationalist movement. In the British colonial tradition, unions were essentially decentralized house unions, with the exception of the RWU, starting in the late 1930s, and the Mineworkers Union (MWU), in 1945. Unions and membership grew rapidly in the postwar period, along with the economy, going from fourteen unions with a mere 6,030 paid-up members in 1946 (far more were unpaid members) to forty-one unions with 38,135 paid-up members in 1949. Many dismissals and repression of unions followed the January 1950 general strike. Unions, nurtured by the nationalist era, increased to ninety-one with 67,473 paid-up members by 1955–56. However, the union movement was still relatively weak, despite the ability of key unions to strike for employer recognition and higher wages. The colonial regime followed a liberal market labor control strategy. It encouraged unions, but in an environment that kept the TUC weak and unions small and poor. Political linkages were strongly discouraged. In 1956, fifty of eighty-one active unions had under 250 members; seven had 1,000–5,000 members, and only one (the MWU) had more than10,000. Few employers were willing to engage in collective bargaining; unions had few funds or paid staffs. The TUC was decentralized, with little power (Kraus 1979b, 124–25). Leadership was elective at branch and national levels. The idea of democratic representation became a union norm in this era.

Unions and the Convention People's Party Government, 1957–66. The early nationalist movement, the Convention People's Party (CPP), was the vehicle of Ghana's actual and aspiring petty-bourgeoisie. Its leaders were teachers, traders, pharmacists, and middle school dropouts, with no property outside of state power. The CPP embodied a multi-class, populist expression of Ghanaian nationalism. Its leaders became split between those who saw CPP nationalism and government as the instruments to fulfill petty bourgeois ambitions (e.g., in business) and those who saw them as a mechanism for transforming Ghana's economy structurally and instituting egalitarian social change. Trade unionists were among the early supporters of the populist, militant CPP when it arose in 1949. Together they organized the "positive

Table 4.1 Estimated Trade Union Membership in Ghana, 1961–2004

National unions	1961	1967	1974	1977	1984	1987	1991	1995/96	2004
Industrial & Commercial	62000	85000	80000	115020	134405	130000	120502?	104521	58000
Local Government	32000	17799	28000	36000	41870	35000	35000?	26100	26100
Health Service Workers	14000	1718	7795	12000	28684	32000'	20141	28148	19600
Timber & Woodworkers	17000	13000	14000	20850	22232	20000	18120	24219	27052
Railway Enginemen	1000	800	816	701	898	898	892	850	300
General Transport, Petrol & Chemical Workers	10000	7405	4500	10000	28684	29185	29260	15219	5316
Teachers & Educ. Workers		13000	14000	34000	31822	40300	37000	31878	40000
National Union of Seamen		2000	7000	5716	5011	4999	1566	1871	2000?
Railway & Ports Workers*	11000	6218	10180	13587	8955	8955	5761	4495	2500
Private Road Transport	7000	5383	20000	21700	56138	93617	37400	12000	12000
Mineworkers	21000	23500	23074	21200	27003	22500	23051	17050	12715
Public Service Workers	16000	15000	15600	28000	62933	105574	136822	89064	19723
Public Utility Workers*	27000		12000	18000	25730	20000	10036	8468	8204
Construction & Building	56000	33566	40000	68820	52443	50437	34333	36046	Est 20000
General Agricultural Workers	38000	28760	42000	111184	123586	101212	101203	86602	15102
Maritime & Dockworkers	8000	12000	18600	22250	31085	31085	28000	28379	6250
Post & Telecommunication Workers		5000	7422	11200	11119	7056	6500	6026	5769
Textile, Garment, & Leather Workers*							ca. 10000	ca. 7500	2000
Union of Industrial, Commercial & Financial Workers									7000
Total	320,248+	270,149	345,047	550,260	698,491	732,818	655,472	520,936	Est 283,131

Sources: Ghana, Labor Department 1960–61, 93; TUC, Exec. Board 1968, 5; TUC, Exec. Board 1978, 28; TUC, Exec. Board 1988, 19; TUC, Exec. Board 1992, 3; TUC, Exec. Board 1996, 54; TUC, Exec. Board 2004, table. Some data in 1990–2004 adjusted in interviews; all data on TGLWU obtained in interviews, 1994–2004. Total in 1961 includes membership for the unions whose individual data is not given, since they were parts of other unions then. Data for 1991, 1996, and after is probably exaggerated for several unions that have lost members through layoffs. This is noted by a ? after the figures. At least four unions in addition to the two with question marks may have much lower membership; the 1996 total could easily be 50,000 fewer members. Est.=estimate.

*The Public Utility Workers Union (PUWU) split from the Public Service Workers Union (PSWU) in 1968; the Ports section of the Railway and Ports Workers Union split and joined the Maritime and Dockworkers Union in 1982–83; the Textile, Garment, and Leather Workers Union (TEGLU) split from the ICU in 1991. And the Union of Industrial, Commercial, & Finance Workers split from ICU in 2004. TEGLU is not a member of the TUC, UNICOF is. Their members are included in 2004 totals only.

action" 1950 general strike, which was animated by union and nationalist grievances. In the 1950s pro-CPP unionists allied themselves with the CPP, in part in order to create a more powerful union movement, with fewer, larger, more powerful unions. There was substantial class empathy between the unions and the populist CPP leadership but also substantial union opposition to a union-CPP alliance. John Tettegah's election in 1955 as TUC secretary-general was organized by the CPP. Tettegah used his alliance with Kwame Nkrumah and the CPP to overcome some union resistance and get the government to push through an Industrial Relations Act (IRA) in late 1958, though many CPP leaders feared it gave the TUC too much power. This drastically changed the structure of unions and collective bargaining in Ghana and involved, with the CPP-TUC alliance, a corporatist labor control project. During 1958–61 the unions became a core CPP political constituency and base for Nkrumah's socialist project. Tettegah aggressively sought to increase TUC leader influence within the CPP.

The IRA gave major advantages to the unions. It reduced the number of small unions from eighty-five to twenty-four (and later to sixteen) industrial unions. It established a contracting-out dues check-off system and, in 1960, a union shop, thus giving the unions and TUC for the first time a regular financial base for organizing, which was pursued. The act required employers to bargain with unions, which received bargaining certificates from the minister of labor, who could extend to other employers accords reached in that sector. And the act established a disputes mechanism that included resort to compulsory arbitration, which union leaders wanted and from which they benefited. Thus, the act empowered trade unions with enormous new powers, at least temporarily. Union membership jumped from 67,473 in 1956 to 320,248 in 1961 (see Table 4.1).

The IRA and the bargain also cost the unions dearly. Legal strikes were difficult, if not impossible, but in reality unions have rarely been punished for strikes. Some authority was vested in the TUC over the member unions, and Tettegah's implicit bargain with Nkrumah was that the unions would be faithful CPP allies or subject to political control. But labor protests could threaten the government, as evidenced by the large Accra protest in June 1960 and the 1961 general strike based at Sekondi-Takoradi. The latter led to a harsh crackdown on strikes (Drake and Lacy 1966). The government had prerogatives regarding bargaining certificates, audits, and freezing accounts that could be used punitively. A 1959 amendment required all unions to merge with the TUC (several had resisted). The IRA's real costs cannot be disentangled from the CPP government's authoritarianism during 1960–66. This, plus the CPP influence among union leaders, curtailed sharply the unions' ability to assert their independent interests after 1961. Although most unions continued to elect their own leaders, four union leaders were removed politically in 1964. The government imposed leadership at the TUC level (ousting Tettegah for Magnus George in 1962, then Kwaw Ampah in 1964) It spied on internal union activities, including TUC Executive Board meetings. Leadership abuses went unchecked (Crisp 1984; Ghana 1969a). Union subordination to party and state was stressed. Demoralization was high (interview, Kumadey 1973; TUC, Bentum 1966). Union resources rose, but from 1962 onward, union capacities to act fell. State power was not entirely unfavorable to unions. Unions raised private sector wages by bargaining. The CPP development project added some key benefits, greatly increased employment, and created enormous public goods for workers (such as free primary education, health care).

Ghanaian union leaders after 1966 learned from this period that trade union independence and a democracy that permitted it were very important—though also not sufficient for fulfilling union goals. In periods of democratic rule (1951–57, 1957–60, 1969–71, 1979–81, 1993–present), trade unions were far freer to speak out forcefully and employ strikes as a bargaining weapon to improve their leverage vis-à-vis government and private employers (Table 4.2). The periods with the fewest average strikes and days lost are clearly in the Nkrumah dictatorship (1960–66) and three military regimes (1966–69, 1972–79, and 1982–92). But, union leaders embraced the IRA as invaluable: it helped to create large industry-wide unions, a strong TUC, and crucial collective bargaining rights.

Unions and the National Liberation Council Government, 1966–69. The military-police NLC overthrew the Nkrumah government in February 1966. It ruled largely with senior civil servants and recruited as its political advisers and allies the leaders of the ex-opposition, who represented Ghana's merchant-professional bourgeoisie. Neither the NLC military-police leadership nor their political allies, who came to lead the Progress Party (PP) government (1969–71), had any sympathy for the workers or unions. There was substantial social distance between NLC and PP leaders and the national trade union leaders, who at most had secondary educations.

The coup changed the union movement dramatically and permanently. Benjamin Bentum, a young, highly energetic, ex-general secretary of the General Agricultural Workers Union (GAWU), who had been ousted in 1965 by the old TUC leadership, was appointed as TUC secretary-general by the NLC. Bentum set out to re-create a democratic trade union movement. He insisted on new elections in all national unions, involving genuine competition. Bentum had the NLC arrest and briefly detain some dissident holdover leaders, so new leaders were elected in most of the then sixteen national unions (interviews 1972). A TUC Delegates Congress was held shortly thereafter in 1966, where Bentum was elected secretary-general in a competitive election and acquired more legitimacy. During 1966–72, the TUC and all national unions held biennial delegates' congresses to elect leaders; after that they were quadrennial. Bentum argued to union delegates in 1966 that a union must be responsive to "and draw its authority from the workers themselves." Unions must be self-reliant, keep out of party politics, freely determine their own policies, and take a stand on public issues important to labor. "Genuine trade unions can only thrive in a democratic environment" (TUC 1966, 56). Prior union leaders had placed the unions "in chains" (TUC, Bentum 1966). The TUC under Bentum became, by 1968–71, an aggressive, articulate voice for worker and working-class interests.

The NLC government laid off 60,000 government workers and decreed that civil servants need no longer belong to unions. Thus, union membership fell from perhaps 400,000 to a bit over 200,000 in 1966. New organizing brought membership back to 270,000 by the end of 1967 and 342,000 by 1970 (see Table 4.1). The seventeen national unions that emerged and have remained since then issued new membership cards and have run their own unions without TUC intervention since 1966–67. The TUC does not intrude in national union elections, or normally in

Table 4.2 Strikes, Strikers, and Days Lost in Ghana, 1945–2004

Years	Number of strikes	Number of strikers	Work days lost (in thousands)
1945/46–1950/51	av. 25	av. 23491	av. 348.8
1951/52–1956/57*	av. 48	a. 20302	av. 474.9
1957/58–1959/60	av. 50	av. 15606	av. 30.5
1960–65	av.12.5	av. 5562	av. 38.3
1966–69	av. 40.5	av. 25764	av. 86.8
1970–71*	av. 68.5	av. 34091	av. 140.1
1972–78	av. 42.0	av. 26080	av. 81.7
1979–81*	av. 63	av. 64985	av. 308.5
1982–91	av. 17	av. 8390	av. 16.2
1977	61	47304	205.2
1978	65	42913	196.2
1979	50	40606	170.6
1980	62	89989	260.0
1981	69	50736	292.7
1982***	10	4706	11.7
1983	16	19901	40.7
1984	9	10550	17.0
1985	13	2830	8.0
1986	19	8229	24.9
1987	26	11826	23.8
1988	11	1472	3.2
1989	20	9854	18.8
1990	24	8492	7.2
1991***	24	5557	9.7
1992	24	5531	42.1
1993–2004*	av. 33.6	av. 28370	av. 233.886 or 70.476 (excludes 1999)
1993	24	35125	n.d.
1994	27 (23)**	n.d.	n.d.
1995	27	10456	204.5
1996	40	14929	64.6
1997	35 (31)**	12428	32.8
1998	46	7821	56.4
1999	42	154167	1764.6
2000	29	16460	94.99
2001	25 (23)**	14756	47.8
2002	35	14213	37.99
2003	38 (30)**	20263	59.3
2004	38 (30)**	11455	35.97

Source: Kraus Data Set, from Ghana, Dept. of Labor, Strike record book. Av. = average for this group of years. The number of years in the averages are, respectively, 6, 6, 3.25, 5.5, 4, 2, 7, 3, 10, and 12 (for 1993–2004) varying for years for which data is available.

*Indicates regimes that have been democratic and includes the period of internal self-government, 1951–57.

**Strikes cited are total, those in parentheses are the ones for which the other data—strikers, days lost—are available.

***The number of strikes and lockouts, strikers involved, and days lost greatly exceeded these numbers. There was turmoil at many workplaces, with demonstrations against management. In 1991 there was a huge teachers strike, not recorded here.

internal affairs, except by invitation or in the case of intra-union conflicts or major strikes; any other interventions are strongly resented. Since 1966 the TUC secretary-general is elected by a delegates' conference but draws his continuing authority from the consent of national union leaders. This has sometimes produced cautious, consensual TUC leadership.

Although the NLC government restored some political and civil liberties, it was an authoritarian government. It demanded industrial peace. It believed that debt renegotiation and economic renewal required IMF stabilization loans and policy conditions, such as layoffs. General Emmanuel Kotoka insisted that strikes were illegal and must be controlled by union leaders. Bentum and national union leaders cooperated with the NLC initially, given the poor economy and the NLC's restoration of union rights, autonomy, and collective bargaining. But as the levels of NLC harshness to strikers increased (arrests, trials, fines, dismissals) and the NLC proved to be nonresponsive to claims to arrest the sharp fall in real wages, union-state conflicts accelerated. When 2,000 dockworkers were locked-out in 1968 and protesting mineworkers were shot at and killed by police at Prestea, Obuasi, and then Tarkwa gold mines in 1968–69, Bentum threatened a general strike if there were more shootings (Crisp 1984, 150–64; Ghana 1969b; Kraus 1979b, 141–42). State pressures upon TUC and union leaders to moderate worker demands and behavior became less important, as rank-and-file demands, wildcat militancy, and government ineffectiveness made TUC and national union leaders more responsive to local worker/union claims (Kraus 1979a; Jeffries 1978, 102–39). This made the unions more democratic, too. The TUC insisted on the rights of the minimum wage workers to higher wages and on the injustice of the widening wage gap. It spoke publicly and critically on social security funding, low cost housing, tax policies, and ministerial performance, arousing wide worker support (Kraus 1979a, 276).

Unions and the Progress Party Government, 1969–71. The democratic election of the PP government in 1969 averted a more intense union-state clash, as PP and union leaders acted initially in a conciliatory way. The unions had made an explicit decision to be nonpartisan in the election. But, the business-professional PP leadership manifested a profound disdain for union leaders on a class basis and pursued a growth strategy that favored domestic and foreign capital. The PP argued that urban workers were overpaid relative to the rural poor.

The key issues in the union-state conflict were the high level of strikes, TUC/union demands for wage increases to offset large real wage losses, and PP attempts to intervene in the unions. The PP pursued a liberal market control strategy and, as state power, was initially less labor-repressive than the NLC was. But the PP was utterly indifferent to dealing with labor claims against government departments and parastatals. Ministers blithely ignored them until the unions, six months later, issued strike ultimatums and proceeded to strike. In 1970–71 wage claims were a key issue in 60 percent of the strikes. By 1967 the real minimum wage had fallen to 69 percent of its 1963 level; by 1971 it fell to 56 percent (Kraus 1979a, 277). The average number of strikes in 1970–71 rose by 69 percent over the 1966–69 average, strikers by 32 percent, and day-lost by 61 percent (see Table 4.2). PP ministers were constantly trying to avert or end strikes. In 1971, 43 percent of strikes were against the central government, and another 31 percent were against parastatals. The PP was also powerfully opposed to increasing the minimum wage—which was the equivalent of only 3.5 percent of a member of parliament's pay. The PP intervened directly in union affairs, supporting two breakaway splinter unions, the attempt to create a new labor federation, and a rival candidate in the 1970 TUC election for secretary-general. In 1971 the government refused to raise the minimum wage and launched a new wage tax. The TUC mobilized workers around the country in protests, moving toward a general strike. The PP government response was to repeal suddenly the Industrial Relations Act, thereby abolishing the TUC; it froze all union and TUC bank accounts and required a new registration of unions, new elections, and a contracting-in form of check-off. A halfhearted general strike failed. The PP totally disrupted and sought to destroy the union movement (interviews: Ahinful-Quansah, Ashiley 1972). Trade union leaders have not trusted these leaders of Ghana's merchant-professional bourgeoisie ever since, despite their role in struggles for democratic rule.

Unions and the National Redemption Council Government, 1972–79. Facing an economic crisis, the PP government in 1971 had cut budgets and benefits, alienating many groups, including workers, civil servants, the military, businessmen, and students. An IMF-dictated devaluation in December 1971 cut living standards harshly. The NRC military coup quickly followed. Renamed the Supreme Military Council (SMC) in 1976, it was composed entirely of junior military officers, whose grievances were military interests and nationalist.

Colonel I. K. Acheampong and the NRC/SMC sought legitimacy through multi-class appeals and rewards to, and relationships with, diverse Ghanaian groups, including unions and workers, students, civil servants and the military (higher wages, perks, promotions), cocoa farmers (higher prices), and indigenous businessmen (decrees reserved some sectors for Ghanaians). The NRC won its widest support with major nationalist appeals against foreign dependence and the IMF: it repudiated certain foreign debts regarded as tainted by corruption, unilaterally rescheduled others to ease the debt crisis, and promoted food self-sufficiency. It nationalized some industries and promoted indigenous business and farming. The SMC improved the economy's performance for several years. But by 1975 to 1976, SMC rule displayed an erratic, personalist, and highly corrupt economic mismanagement. The hyperinflation of 53 percent in 1976, 116 percent in 1977, and an average 64 percent in 1978–79 impoverished all classes; it destroyed the economy.

Nevertheless, in 1972–74 the NRC/SMC cemented an important relationship with the trade unions. Although NRC/SMC imposed a corporatist style of labor control and intervened to quell strikes between 1972 and 1973, it restored the Industrial Relations Act and hence the TUC and the union structure. The unions were able to elect their own leaders and largely to maintain their institutional autonomy, but they lacked the freedom to act aggressively in industrial relations. As trade-offs the NRC wanted no strikes, higher productivity, and support for the NRC/SMC. In exchange, the NRC in 1972 quickly raised the minimum wage by 33 percent (and other wages as well), revalued the currency value (raising purchasing power), and imposed price controls on key consumer items, especially imported food, house rents, and public transportation. It raised wages again in 1974. It helped the TUC get scarce food and other commodities to distribute to members through co-operatives. Some government departments became state corporations, where unions organized. Jobs increased. Union membership soared by about 61 percent, from 342,800 in 1970 to 550,260 by 1977, adding to union resources and organizing (Table 4.1; TUC 1970, 6). The SMC publicly raised TUC status, gave it representation on public boards, and canceled major TUC debts, such as the one on the Trade Union Hall.

Given the TUC-SMC relationship, trade union leaders tended to believe initially that this authoritarian military regime served the interests of workers and unions better than the prior democratic regime. But, the NRC/SMC's economic mismanagement so wrecked the economy that it destroyed the incomes of workers. The real minimum wage plunged by two-thirds from its high of 75.2 in 1975 to 25.6 in 1978 (Kraus 1991, 123). Still, the unions under the consensual leadership of Issifu rebuilt union capabilities and created political space in civil society for union initiatives. When trade unionists began to strike at a higher level in 1974–76, strikes were not suppressed nor were workers jailed. Annual strikes averaged eleven in 1972–73, thirty-one in 1974–76, and fifty-nine in 1977–79, as the number of strikers and days lost soared (see Table 4.2).

As the economy collapsed in early 1977, the SMC was confronted with a rising level of protests, led by university students, the Ghana Bar Association (GBA), and the Association of Recognized Professional Bodies (ARPB). Economic demands quickly turned into political demands by the GBA and ARPB for the SMC to hand over power by the first of July to a transitional government, or face a major strike. It was launched, with the support of students. But on July 1 the SMC doubled the minimum wage from ₵2 (cedis) to ₵4, with other wages raised, too, a blatant and successful attempt to stop the unions from joining political protests. Given the SMC's pro-union policies, the TUC did not come out in support of demands for constitutional democratic rule, or the political movement organized to protest Unigov, the SMC's scheme for nonparty government. Opposition to Unigov was led by ex-PP politicians who, the unions knew, had sought to destroy them in 1971–72. In 1976 the TUC essentially accepted the Unigov idea but argued that it must involve a mass movement and socialism, not SMC ideas (TUC 1978, 61–62).

General Fred Akuffo ousted Acheampong in July 1978. Reluctantly, and under pressure of political protests and major strikes, he promised to restore constitutional rule. But the grievous economic conditions had created great discontent with the TUC and union leaders among rank-and-file and local leaders. They were angry at their horribly diminished wages and at union leaders, as well as the government, for their inability to prevent this. But most unions were cautious. Ghana's most militant union leader, Richard Baiden of the Maritime and Dockworkers Union (MDU), challenged Issifu for the post of TUC secretary-general at the 1978 TUC Delegates Congress. He challenged existing leadership as "too complacent, too ready to compromise on issues of principle, too weak to fight back, merely reacting to government proposals" (Arthiabah 1978; Baiden 1978, 2, 4). Almost all union leaders backed Issifu, but Baiden's critique resonated with some of the rank and file.

Unions, SMC II, and the Armed Forces Revolutionary Council, 1978–79.
The brief rule of the second Supreme Military Council (SMC II) government had little impact. Its technocrat and economist ministers faced massive budget deficits,

hyperinflation, and no foreign exchange. The IMF required a stabilization plan and a severe currency devaluation. This increased prices on all items and generated a new round of strikes, including one by civil servants in December 1978. The SMC II could not afford a tactical alliance with unions. The unions faced a weak state and hostile market and international forces (IMF). Leaders pushed catch-up wage demands much more aggressively. Faced with the prospect of a new democratic system, the TUC leadership decided to support none of the three major parties: two associated with the disliked PP and one with the old guard CPP, the People's National Party (PNP). At Issifu's initiative, the TUC seemed to give its support to a Social Democratic Front (SDF) party, which profoundly misread political realities. Union support for the SDF was nonexistent. It received almost no votes in the cities of southern Ghana and only a couple of ethnic-based National Assembly seats in northern Ghana. Some union leaders were openly pro-PNP.

Before elections, the Armed Forces Revolutionary Council (AFRC)—under a youthful Jerry Rawlings—seized power on June 4, 1979. It was a revolt of junior officers, NCOs, and other ranks against senior military leaders. AFRC represented the soldiers' fury at the corruption and misrule of senior officers, which sullied the military's reputation. Rawlings spoke with great moral passion against corruption and misrule and rallied the military against the senior officers and the people against its institutional rulers. Senior officers were quickly placed on "trial" before military tribunals and found guilty. Eight were swiftly executed, including three former military heads of state. As tax records were examined for corruption, fear spread among the merchant-professional bourgeoisie; few paid taxes. Many fled the country.

Rawlings's populist outrage against governmental incompetence and corruption targeted the soaring prices for food and basic goods—a legitimately pressing subject for many Ghanaians. Encouraged to hold their leaders responsible, workers were soon demanding that managers explain their actions, and the possible diversion of goods, and show their accounts. AFRC's anger embraced the common man's anger against all leaders, including union leaders. Rawlings was appalled at the disorder of strikes and constant wage demands. But he permitted the 1979 elections to take place, and the Third Republic was inaugurated in September 1979. But Rawlings left behind an expectation that justice must be served and rebellion was justified. AFRC left the state more enfeebled than it found it. Senior officials were afraid to act. AFRC soldiers had reimposed unenforceable price controls and beaten women in the markets. Goods fled the market.

Unions and the People's National Party Government, 1979–81. Ghana's third constitutional, democratic regime came to power in 1979 under the worst circumstances: a deeply depressed economy, huge budget deficits, no foreign exchange, large debt arrears, hyperinflation, and enfeebled state capacities. It faced multiple contradictory policy pressures from the consuming public, party leaders, the military, civil servants, the IMF, businessmen, and the trade unions. The PNP had a divided and often weak leadership, which made the economy even worse (Chazan 1988, 112–15; Kraus 1988b, 478–82). The PNP was the creation of the CPP old guard. Its leaders came from a new generation of a business-professional bourgeoisie, whom President Hilla Limann appointed to cabinet positions. But the ex-CPP leaders controlled the party. The government made major efforts to eliminate price controls and to establish policy changes to elicit IMF and Western aid. But the government was divided over reforms, and struggles for power led to policy vacillation and corruption. One opposition party promised its support to the PNP in order to provide stability for this new chance at democracy, which the union leaders also wanted.

Under democratic rule, unions were much more assertive. Workers agitated more freely for wage increases to offset the deeply depressed real wages (inflation was 54 percent in 1979, 50 percent in 1980). The average number of strikes in 1979–81 rose by 50 percent over the prior regime, strikers rose by 150 percent, and days-lost to strikes leaped by more than 300 percent (see Table 4.2). Strikes were no longer all wildcat, led from below; national union leaders felt free to threaten strikes.

The PNP government, unlike the PP, tried to work with the TUC and union leaders, meeting with them regularly to discuss union claims. The PNP strongly supported celebrating May first as Labor Day, agreed to distribute some scarce goods through cooperatives, forbade layoffs without permission from a TUC-government committee, and did not repress strikers. But some serious tensions arose from key PNP-TUC differences. The PNP was trying to liberalize the economy, but scarce essential goods had outrageous prices. Ultimately, in April 1981 the TUC threatened a general strike, demanding a more fair distribution of goods, quicker approval of collective agreements, and ending delays in paying the new minimum wage. The TUC cancelled the strike threat when the PNP promised to distribute fifteen essential goods at controlled prices through various worker/civil service offices. The TUC also wanted to avoid weakening the government (Labor Dept., Ghana, File KD-5). Union leaders demanded an increase in minimum wages to ₵12–₵15 but, in reality, were willing to accept ₵8–9. They knew that the government had no funds and that higher increases would stimulate inflation. The PNP government's resistance to higher wages was undermined when, in September 1980, the members of parliament (MPs) in the National Assembly gave themselves salaries of $18,000 per year, thirty-eight times the $1.50 per day minimum wage. The government conceded to labor's now insistent demand for ₵12. But high strike levels persisted because of government slowness in implementing the tripling of salaries. This barely sustained real wages but created inflation of 116 percent in 1981.

The newly aggressive leadership of union leaders was insufficient to assuage the deep discontent of rank-and-file workers with constant shortages of goods and government slowness in paying salary arrears and approving collective agreements. The AFRC period had encouraged workers to be more militant and critical of leadership, as did democracy. Thus, overt challenges to union leaders increased. When five thousand workers at GIHOC demonstrated in 1980 against wage arrears and escalating prices, they marched on Parliament House, entered, disrupted proceedings, and caused some minor mayhem. They then besieged TUC headquarters, trashing some offices and threatening to assault leaders of the Industrial and Commercial Workers Union (ICU). The PNP government quickly dismissed about a thousand of the demonstrating workers, led by Amartey Kwei. He later helped organize the Association of Local Unions (ALU), which challenged the TUC under the PNDC. ICU-TUC efforts to challenge the dismissals in court did not lessen worker anger. Members of the Public Utility Workers Union (PUWU) were so opposed to their general secretary that they physically removed him from the union office in 1981.

The Struggle between Unions and the PNDC Government

On December 31, 1991, Rawlings and a small group of ex-military overthrew the elected PNP government. Rawlings said that he had returned to make a revolution. Although the PNDC first articulated its mission in the language of radical populism and identified with workers' interests, it was highly hostile to unions and challenged their right to represent workers. With a few union dissidents it overthrew all existing union leaders, briefly crippled the unions and collective bargaining rights, and set up People's and Workers Defense Committees (PDCs and WDCs). The WDCs were PNDC allies to replace unions as worker representatives at work. Thus, there developed over the eleven years of PNDC dictatorship a ferocious struggle between the PNDC and the union movement, revolving around the unions' insistence upon their institutional independence, their representation of workers, and their right to be heard by the state on key matters of workers' welfare. The PNDC fought the union movement on all these, first with a corporatist labor control strategy, then a market one. The unions were the only significant group with the capacity to persistently insist on its rights, though the GBA, the National Union of Ghanaian Students (NUGS), and churches protested intermittently. A reluctant PNDC had to accept the existence and voice of the TUC, again and again, as representative of workers' interests. In the process, the trade union movement created a considerable "space" for resistance in civil society. Moreover, the TUC in 1985 and after widened this space by bringing into it other groups of working people: the large Ghana National Association of Teacher (GNAT), the Registered Nurses Association (GRNA), and civil servants union (CSA). The democratic norms of the trade unions and the TUC's demands for political democracy were a standing rebuke to the authoritarian PNDC.

Jerry Rawlings seized power with the help of a small part of the military and some radicals (Yeebo 1991, 47–56). Rawlings said he had returned to bring revolution and called upon people to form PDCs and WDCs in order to mobilize people for radical change. Ghana's economy was in a ravaged state, and it was further devastated by the worst drought in fifty years in 1982–83 (Kraus 1991; Nugent). The PNDC unleashed a quasi-revolutionary situation since it unmoored key institutions through its assaults on the military officer corps and on existing social hierarchies. Popular mobilization was organized by Ghanaian leftists in the PDCs, WDCs, the Interim National Coordinating Committee, and Public Tribunals to impose revolutionary justice. The PNDC launched populist economic policies to renew economic life. The PNDC itself was composed of seven very disparate individuals, reflecting the military, student, dissident union, and small leftist group bases. It had important cleavages: five of its seven members were gone—in exile, jail, or resignation—by December 1982, leaving Rawlings and his security chief.

The cabinet of government secretaries was only initially more broadly based. Harsh implementation of price controls led to soldiers, police, and PDC groups seizing goods from market women, beating them publicly for price violations, and forcing farmers in the rural areas to sell food at set prices. The small Left worked hard at organizing PDCs and WDCs, which challenged business and state managers and did indeed give some workers and others a sense of power and ability to demand accountability from managers (Graham 1985; Yeebo 1985, 64–76). But PDCs/ WDCs, which were highly disruptive and acted often without authorization, and soldiers' arbitrary violence soon lost the PNDC's public support. Before the end of the first year, populist economic policies had clearly failed; financial resources were unavailable. Reluctantly, Rawlings and his team of Left technocrats changed course and accepted IMF funding and a totally different economic strategy, which IMF conditionalities required (Kraus 1991; Martin 1991). It now focused on liberalizing all sectors of the weak economy, including foreign exchange and prices, restoring export growth by continuous large devaluations, restricting budget deficits and state economic roles, raising interest rates, and promoting domestic and foreign private capital investment. By 1983, these policies had alienated most workers and unions. This required the PNDC to seek new constituencies of support, among rural exporters, and local capital. *But the most important players in its political constituency of support became the IMF, the World Bank, and Western aid donors* who funded the regime and dictated its key economic policies.

An early PNDC ally was the small, dissident labor group ALU, headed by Amartey Kwei, the dismissed GIHOC union leader. Kwei rallied to the association some union locals who were angry at their national unions and some individuals (such as Korang Opare-Ababio) who had lost elections for union office. Few of the ALU leaders held union office, though some were branch leaders. ALU's key support was among the Accra branches of the PUWU and the refinery union. The leaders of the PUWU had physically and unconstitutionally ousted their leaders in 1980, then found themselves isolated within the TUC Executive Board, and were thus highly hostile to existing leaders. Led by Christian Agyei, they backed the ALU dissidents in the effort to oust existing union leaders. But these ALU leaders, few in number, were *trade unionists*. Fed by their new power via the PNDC and their own ambitions for office, they wanted all the general secretaries and the TUC head, I. M. Issifu, to be driven from office; new elections to be held; and the reorganized unions to become populist and militant. But Rawlings and the soldiers around him disliked unions from the beginning, especially union demands for higher wages and strikes. Hence, Rawlings's support for ALU forces and Kwei was temporary.

After the PNDC's seizure of power, it ordered as an economy move, without union consultations, the suspension of leave allowances over ₵250 and all collective bargaining. The unions protested and quickly rejected this idea. After the ouster of union leaders, Rawlings suggested that the secretary of labor simply *appoint* another TUC secretary-general, which indicates Rawlings's ignorance of the idea of democracy in unions (Yeebo 1991, 90–91). The soldiers in 1982 were very antiunion and assured unionists that the WDCs were there to replace the unions (interview, Abloso 1985).

Backed by the PNDC, ALU worked in early 1982 to overthrow the union leadership. ALU tried to cancel a TUC rally to support the PNDC; it then joined it to launch verbal and then physical attacks on the union leaders, forcing them to withdraw. In late January, Rawlings and Kwei had the union general secretaries and Issifu and Issifu report to Burma Camp Barracks in Accra where Kwei and other PNDC leaders hectored them as betrayers of the workers—except for Agyei of the PUWU and Baiden of the MDU. TUC head Issifu feared for his life and decided to resign, as did another union head. The other leaders promptly elected the most militant, Baiden, as acting TUC secretary-general, hoping thus to weaken ALU's attacks. Baiden was determined to maintain the TUC's independence. The Executive Board also announced new elections of all union leaders. There were many acts of intimidation against union leaders at all levels, including violent demonstrations and molestation. ALU published repeated "resolutions" demanding the removal of the present union leaders for betraying "the interests of the workers." On April 23 it "resolved" that all national union leaders were to be suspended from office, the TUC constitution was to be suspended, and all officers were barred from union headquarters. In response, leaders of all seventeen unions in Sekondi-Takoradi, the port and historic union center, met the next day and condemned the "so-called ALU" resolution, resolving that workers in the TUC were the only ones who should decide who should be their leaders, "not the PNDC" (Sekondi-Takoradi workers). Their protest delegation to Accra of seven workers from each union was stopped on the way out of Takoradi by the military and beaten. On April 28 hordes of ALU workers and armed soldiers, backed by armored carriers, descended upon the TUC hall, trashed it, and expelled union leaders, who avoided a confrontation because of PNDC weapons. The union general secretaries faced arrest; about half did not flee Ghana but surrendered to the police, confident that international union protests would lead to their release, which occurred (interview, Yankey 1985). The two unions whose headquarters were outside Accra, mineworkers (MWU) and railways (RWU), refused for months to abandon their offices, until their leaders were arrested (Haynes 1991, 141).

Union Resistance, 1982–83. Resistance to PNDC and ALU control persisted in 1982–83. Interim Management Committees (IMCs) were elected to run each of the seventeen unions and the TUC. Although many ALU leaders inserted themselves into their unions and the TUC's IMCs, union branches were asked to *elect* leaders to represent them on the IMCs. Thus, some of the new IMC leaders, such as the MDU's Seth Abloso, were opponents of the ALU takeover. Some IMC secretaries were allies of the ousted leaders, such as Amoah of the General Transport, Petroleum and Chemical Workers (GTPCWU). Although ALU leaders at first dominated the TUC-IMC and were important in some union IMCs, elected members of IMCs were representatives and hence responsive to major pressures from below. In contrast, Rawlings had supported the creation of WDCs, which radicals in major cities helped to organize. The now weakened local union leaderships were constantly faced by attacks by the pro-PNDC WDCs, which demanded unions turn over union resources and roles to them and supported all PNDC policies. The situation in Tema was different, with some WDCs more popular and representative (Graham 1985). To undermine the RWU, the railway WDC declared that union dues would be reduced to 40 pence from 1 percent of wages, union affairs would be probed, and the RWU-IMC would be dissolved (Labor Dept., RWU files). In July the railway WDC physically seized the offices.

Resistance to ALU and PNDC control of unions occurred among many ousted national union leaders and also in international union bodies. The ex-general secretaries sought support among their union networks. International union secretariats, the International Confederation of Free Trade Unions (ICFTU), the ILO, and the

Accra-based Organization of African Trade Union Unity (OATUU) made persistent inquiries regarding the violations of rights of Ghana's trade unions. By late June 1982 Amartey Kwei, who had led the ALU takeover, met with some ousted union general secretaries and insisted that efforts had to be made to hold new national union elections by October. Responding to ILO pressures, he said that the TUC constitution was fine and he deplored the current ALU management of TUC. He encouraged the former leaders to get in touch with their locals and prevent further problems within the TUC. In August Kwei drafted letters to respond to ILO, international union secretariats, and OATUU pressures and promised free elections for the unions, which anyone could contest. He noted that a reformed TUC-IMC was being set up, composed of seven of the former general secretaries and seven interim heads of unions to guide the TUC. Kwei and the Labor Department were under pressures from Ghana's Foreign Ministry with regard to timely responses to the ILO protests (Labor Dept., Ghana, File KD-5, vol. 15). In June the PNDC secretary for labor met in Kumasi with senior industrial relations officers for the unions, saying that the "ALU is claiming to be the mouthpiece of the Labor movement in Ghana." The real issue at stake, said Secretary Stephen Kwayie, was whether they had given the ALU a mandate to act on behalf of all the unions and how best to organize democratic elections. Union leaders responded: since ALU was formed without consultation on a national scale and its decisions were taken by only a few people in Accra, its activities amounted to a dictatorship (timber union); it was dictatorial for ALU to change the TUC constitution; ALU was not a union and could not engage in collective bargaining (ICU); all agreed ALU was unrepresentative (Labor Dept., Ghana, File KD-5, vol. 15). The Labor Department regarded the ousting of union leaders as illegitimate.

Despite populist rhetoric, many workers involved at the local and regional levels in union branches quickly reacted sharply against the PNDC. The PNDC violated democratic norms in using force and violence to overthrow elected leaders and seeking to replace local unions with WDCs. It attacked such union rights as strikes and collective bargaining. Resistance occurred very quickly in many unions, including the railways, railway enginemen, maritime and dockworkers, mineworkers, timber, general transport, public utilities, and sectors of the ICU. When ALU leaders showed up in Cape Coast in May 1982, they summoned all branch leaders and PDCs to meet with them. After less than three minutes of talking, a unionist interrupted an ALU leader to inquire by what authority he was there to address them and if it was democratic for a few workers to unseat elected union leaders. With these words, the union leaders rose and departed. When the ALU leaders tried to go to the TUC regional office, they were greeted with such contempt that they regarded themselves as in danger and left quickly (Labor Dept., Ghana, File KD-5, vol. 15).

Local unions sent representatives to regional consultative conferences held by each union to obtain support for the new IMC members and to select delegates for national conferences to elect new leaders. While many IMC leaders got consent for resolutions that they provided, assembled delegates frequently dissented. At the mineworkers' conference, more than 25 percent of delegates refused to support the new mineworkers' IMC. At the General Transport workers meeting in Ashanti, resolutions criticized strongly the soldiers who were attacking, cheating, and molesting defenseless people and demanded the return of all ₵ 50 notes that the PNDC had forced Ghanaians to surrender. The ICU Ashanti consultative meeting resolved to embed safeguard in future constitutions "to prevent the unconstitutional overthrow of the executive by a few individuals." When E. K. Aboagye met with PUWU delegates in Cape Coast, he was quickly challenged whether holding the chair of both the TUC-IMC and the PUWU-IMC "was not a monopoly of power." A delegate said he did not endorse Aboagye as PUWU chair because Aboagye was a trustee in the old PUWU's national executive (NEC), which he now denounced! Delegates rejected the person Aboagye tried to impose on them for the IMC and elected someone else. Aboagye later failed to win any office at the PUWU national delegates' conference. At a Construction Workers Union (CBWU) meeting, IMC member Foli Amekor made such statements as: "Members should not think that TUC is no more." "The present IMC members do not support the ALU's actions." "A coup has no procedure. It only has to be staged and support sought." CBWU resolutions were critical, demanding that all collective agreements in the pipeline be approved. The TUC should remain independent and democratic. And at the CBWU national congress, only Foli Amekor among the IMC members won office (Labor Dept., Ghana, files KD-13-TJ, KD-273-TJ, KD-246-TJ, KD-294-TJ, KD-238-TJ).

The March 1983 PNDC budget raised food prices, started to reduce price controls, accepted an IMF plan as condition for loans, and devalued the cedi against the dollar by 90 percent, driving up all local prices (Kraus 1991, 124–28). While some of these economic reforms were certainly necessary, they constituted a sharp reversal of the PNDC's prior policies and further reduced workers' living standards. Disputes over this prospective budget had alienated the radical Left groups, stimulating several coup attempts in late 1982. The budget outraged union leaders and workers, forcing the ALU leaders to support workers or lose their base entirely. The Accra PSWU branch demanded in late April a suspension of the budget and of the "unrealistic and unfair" minimum wage. If these demands were not met by May 5, "we shall advise ourselves accordingly," that is, a strike threat (Labor Dept., Ghana, File KD-294-TJ). Indeed, there were protests and strike threats from many segments of labor if the budget was not withdrawn. Acceptance of IMF conditions was central to the PNDC getting foreign aid, but it directly undermined its popular support. The GBA, the ARPB, NUGS, and the Christian Council saw the budget as the last straw. They demanded that power be handed over to a transitional government to arrange a return to democracy.

The PNDC government responded to these demands by violence and coercion against these groups, including the TUC. It harassed and jailed leading lawyers who headed the GBA and ARPB, causing others to flee from Ghana. On May 4 the PNDC sent some nine hundred mineworkers in trucks from Obuasi to Kumasi, a center of PNDC opposition. The miners attacked university students, who through NUGS had protested the PNDC budget. Days later University of Ghana students marched into Accra in large numbers to protest the PNDC and demand it hand over to the chief justice. Workers there and back at the university campus attacked the students and closed down the campus. Students were sent home, and NUGS leaders soon had to flee the country, breaking NUGS protests for some years (*West Africa*, June 6, 1983, pp. 1343–44; July 18, 1983, pp. 1654–55). On May 9 union leaders who had negotiated with the government on the budget were meeting when about a thousand workers and others, organized by the WDC/PNDC, entered the TUC with guns and cutlasses, attacked the leaders, and trashed offices. The WDC mob then headed the short distance to the Calvary Methodist Church, where a synod had convened; the mob attacked some assembled clergy, who had also called for the PNDC to resign. Letters protesting these events were read in churches throughout Ghana in the following weeks. Anti-PNDC sentiment rose. Although multiple incidents of violence in Kumasi occurred between the military and churches, the churches did not mobilize overt opposition. Nonetheless, the voices of Christians and Catholic archbishops councils' were heard once again in 1990.

This left the unions as the only large organized oppositional force in Ghana. Even the pro-ALU unionists and some WDCs were opposed to the violence and the budget. The TUC-IMC protested vehemently to the PNDC on "the unprovoked siege and attack" but portrayed itself as only opposing the budget peacefully (Labor Dept., Ghana, File KD-5, vol. 16). There was talk of a nationwide strike, which the TUC-IMC avoided. But the language of dissenting unions became harsher. On May 12, nine union leaders in Kumasi criticized Rawlings and "the deceptive slogans" of the PNDC "in working on the emotional sentiments of . . . ordinary people . . . against their fellow countrymen. . . . The PNDC continues to destroy . . . properly designed structures." They demanded the withdrawal of the budget and that the PNDC hand over power to a "National Government" ("Statement on the Present State of Affairs" 1983).

This wide level of resistance to ALU leadership and the attack upon the TUC was expressed sharply in the elections of leaders to the seventeen national unions that occurred during 1983. In seven of the seventeen unions, prior general secretaries or their deputies were elected as the new general secretaries. In several others, such as the RWU and the MDU, the new general secretaries were leaders in highly independent unions. The strongest pro-ALU leaders elected were Korang Opare-Ababio of PSWU, L. G. K. Ocloo of ICU (the largest union), and the chairman of the Private Road Transport Workers Union (PRTWU), a semi-union of owner-drivers allied with the PNDC because it provided import licenses for spare parts, which got their trucks back on the road. The second indication of union resistance came at the TUC Delegates Congress in December 1983. IMC chair E. K. Aboagye boasted that he would surely get elected, but, when opened, the nominations from the national unions overwhelmingly favored the old guard team of A. K. Yankey for TUC secretary-general and Frank Adjabeng for TUC chairman. A. K. Yankey handily beat his pro-ALU opponent, Korang Opare-Ababio, 163 to 45 votes; Adjabeng beat Aboagye of ALU—plus two other candidates—for Executive Board chairman, 144 to 25. The PNDC now faced a TUC leadership it could not manipulate.

The core of the TUC's struggle with the PNDC up to 1992 involved trying to regain its autonomy of action, to raise minimum wages to offset massive real wage losses over the past decade (Table 4.3), and to retain major benefits won in the past. The TUC also insisted that the government consult it on key economic policies that affected workers. This explicitly involved the assertion that the TUC, not the PNDC, represented the interests of Ghana's organized workers in national life. The constant common struggles on these issues brought a somewhat divided union leadership together. Raising the minimum wage led directly to increases in the wages of

Table 4.3   Ghana Minimum Wages, 1960–2004

Year	Nominal minimum wage (cedis) (% increases = increase from prior year)	Nominal consolidated minimum wage**	Inflation rate (%)	Real minimum wage index	Cedi-dollar exchange rate (cedis)
1960	0.65			120	
1963	0.65			100	
1966	0.65		13.5	58.3	
1967	0.70		−8.5	68.6	
1968	0.75		7.1	67.9	
1971	0.75		9.3	56.0	
1972	1.00		10.0	68.1	
1973	1.00		17.5	57.1	
1974	1.50*		18.4	73.2	
1975	2.00		29.7	75.2	
1976	2.00		53.0	48.1	
1977	3.00*		116.3	33.4	
1978	4.00		73.7	25.6	
1979	4.00		53.9	16.7	
1980	6.00*		50.1	16.6	
1981	12.00		116.5	15.4	
1982	12.00		22.3	12.6	2.75
1983	21.75*		122.8	9.9	30.0
1984	32*		39.6	11.5	50
1985	70		10.4	21.4	60
1986	90		24.6	22.0	90–128
1987	112.50		39.8	19.7	153–176
1988	146.25 +30.0%		31.3	20.5	
1989	170.00 +16.2%		25.2		280–375
1990	218.00 +28.2%		37.2		310–370
1991	292.55 +34.2%	460	18.1		
1992	292.55 0%	460			
1993	292.55 0%	460	27.4		
1994	502.27 +71.7%	790	24.9		
1995	763.2 +52.0%	1,200 Jan.***	59.6		
1996	1,081.2 +41.6%	1,700	32.7?		1,637
1997	1,271.6 +17.6%	2,000	20.8		2,050
1998	1,271.6 0%	2,000	15.7		2,315
1999	1,843.8 +45.0%	2,900	13.8		2,358
2000	2,670.3 +44.8%	4,200 Nov.***			3,970
2001	3,497.8 +31.0%	5,500			7,098
2002	4,769.8 +36.4%	7,500			7,869
2003	5,851.0 +22.7%	9,200	31.1		8,631
2004	7,123.0 +21.7%	11,200			8,900

Table 4.3 (continued)

Sources: Kraus 1991, various issues of TUC, *Report(s) to Quadrennial Delegates Congress* 1988, 1992, 1996, 2000, and 2004.

*Nominal minimum wages in these years are average of the minimum set at different times of the year. Raise in 1980 was to ₵12, in 1983 to ₵25, in 1984 to ₵40.

**In 1991 the PNDC negotiated a Consolidated Minimum Wage. It included rent, transport, and canteen allowances, at 20%, 16.5%, and 20.5%. So total allowances of an extra 57% were added to a revised minimum of ₵292.55. The basic minimum is about 63.57982% of the consolidated minimum.

***Month new minimum wages came into effect.

all workers. The consequent large increases in wage bills were also why the government resisted: it had to comply with budget deficit and inflation limits set by the IMF.

Union-PNDC Struggles, 1983–92. The PNDC government employed a coercive liberal market labor control strategy. First, the PNDC used police coercion to deter or break up any strikes or planned demonstrations. It commissioned extensive Labor Department and police surveillance of labor activities: for example, labor officers sat in on meetings of District Councils of Labor (DCLs). The PNDC had some allies in a few unions whose leaders sat on the TUC's Executive Board, composed of all union general secretaries and chairmen as well as the TUC SG and department heads. On some occasions, when major TUC protests were threatened, the PNDC backed down (e.g., on food prices in 1984). But at times it sent thugs into the TUC headquarters, surrounded the TUC headquarters with armed police and military personnel, and threatened to arrest the top leaders. Despite many union protests, *because of coercion there were fewer strikes and people on strike under PNDC rule than under any regime since 1945, except Nkrumah's in 1960–65* (see Table 4.2).

Second, once the PNDC takeover of the TUC had failed, it sought to undermine the TUC's legitimacy as the workers' representative voice, often by media attacks, other times by pitting the PDCs and WDCs against union power. The PNDC control of all media until 1991 made it difficult for the TUC to make its case to the public and its own members.

Third, it used the threat of disruption of the unions, as in the 1982 takeover, to induce union leaders to exercise caution and not challenge the PNDC's main policies with forceful protests.

Fourth, the PNDC used intimidation against various levels of leadership and workers to work its will: it demanded that leaders come to security headquarters, it threatened them with arrests or financial audits, and, ultimately, it arrested those whose political actions it feared.

Fifth, one means of refusing the TUC a policy role was endemic to the PNDC political style: it denied the public all information on public policy, then suddenly announced policies (budgets, minimum wage levels) over radio and TV. It often failed to reply to TUC letters or memoranda. The unions always had to react belatedly to measures that had been taken. A Tripartite Committee existed to discuss changes in minimum wages, but for many years Finance Minister Botchwey would simply arrive and announce the new minimum wage. This forced the TUC to begin private and then public protests in order to have a voice in this decision.

Sixth, the PNDC worked to oust union leaders whom it thought too forceful and to limit contestants for top TUC posts, though it was usually unsuccessful.

Seventh, the PNDC used divide-and-rule tactics to break up union solidarity, providing special rewards to deflect unions in the most strategic areas from going on strike—the railway, gold mine, electric and water works, and oil refinery workers. For some years, food supplies from foreign aid were funneled through their unions in order to deter demands for higher wages.

The PNDC also sought to weaken the unions by liberalizing the labor markets: it decentralized bargaining in certain sectors, especially commerce and mining; sought to impose the criteria of "ability to pay" to break up bargaining among state industries in the same sector; moved to freely permit layoffs, which led to a huge decline in formal sector employment during 1984–95; de-unionized parts of government services (e.g., customs); and periodically sought to cancel by fiat past gains won in collective agreements.

Despite this array of intimidations, the TUC started to challenge the PNDC soon after Yankey was elected. In December 1983, acting under IMF pressures, the PNDC government started to decontrol basic food prices by raising them dramatically, from 166 percent (maize/sugar) to 254 percent (rice) in the midst of the drought and semi-famine conditions in Ghana. Individual unions, DCLs, and the TUC protested loudly. Based on the new prices, the TUC estimated the minimum daily food costs for a family of four at ₡416 vs. the then ₡25 per day minimum wage. The TUC asked for an increase to ₡300, given the massive devaluation and food price shocks (TUC 1984a). The TUC suggested that a wide-scale strike might be launched if prices were not reduced, which they were on February 13. That night Rawlings took to the TV and airwaves and ridiculed the TUC for its demand for a ₡300 minimum wage. He said it was "rubbish" and the TUC leaders were misleading the workers and were "enemies of the people." The TUC criticized Rawlings for this unjustified attack, saying the minimum wage could not feed a family a single meal, not to mention rent and clothing (TUC 1984b, 1984c).

There was a dynamic to union-PNDC conflicts that were animated by union protests against low minimum wages, beatings and harassments by soldiers and WDCs, and rising costs because of the early structural adjustment (SAP) measures. PNDC responses included hostility (with coercive threats), occasional negotiations, or at times announcements of policy reversals in order to avert protests. The protests escalated during 1985–88 as new SAP measures focused on core labor concerns, such as huge retrenchments, arrests of union and political leaders, and government's efforts to eliminate key gains won by collective bargaining, such as end-of-service benefits (EOSBs). EOSBs involved two months of pay, at final year wages, for each year worked; hence, they could be huge, and they assumed gigantic proportions as inflation and increased nominal wages drove up their size in state-owned enterprises (SOEs), which were heavily subsidized by government. The PNDC was under huge IMF/World Bank pressures to privatize many state firms, which first required reducing employment levels. Some of the most adamant voices came from unions deeply affected by retrenchments, namely, the PSWU and ICU, headed by Korang Opare-Ababio and Ocloo, respectively. But these issues affected all the unions. The years between 1985 and 1988 saw protests from union leadership as well as from below, where DCLs brought together local unions and often initiated protests (TUC, DCL/Tema 1991).

After prolonged negotiations in the spring of 1984, the government agreed to a 60 percent minimum wage increase, to ₵40, equal to the erosion in wages since the 1983 budget. Then in a Tripartite Committee meeting the TUC found that the finance minister had revised it down by fiat to ₵35, arguing that the higher figure included allowances. This was a "rationalization" wage to low-income workers, with much smaller increases to higher-income workers. The consequence during 1983–86 was that wages in the private sector and government became incredibly compressed. Thus, the highest paid worker (excluding allowances) was often paid no more than two times the minimum wage. The TUC had also protested a newly created Prices and Incomes Board (PIB), whose job was to keep down wage increases in collective agreements.

On October 10, 1984, the TUC Executive Board distributed a resolution noting Ghana's grave economic conditions arising from "government's submission to the dictates" of the IMF and the World Bank. It noted the consequent "unbearable conditions of life" and their implications for "the sharpening of class conflicts." The government must "wrestle the economy from the grips of the IMF" and the World Bank (TUC 1984a). In October the TUC gave evidence of a 100 percent inflation increase over fifteen months. Offered a 30 percent minimum wage increase, the TUC asked for a 100 percent increase to ₵70 to reverse massive real wage losses. It won its request, one of the few times after 1982. Real wages rose from a pathetic 11.5 percent of the 1963 level in 1984 to 22 percent in 1985 (see Table 4.3).

By 1985 the PNDC government started massive retrenchments, using force and arrests to avert opposition demonstrations. In January eight union leaders of the Post and Telegraph Workers Union (PTWU) were arrested as they sought to avert the dismissal of more than three hundred workers. On February 18 the TUC distributed a "Position Paper on the National Situation," which sharply attacked PNDC policies of submission to the IMF (TUC 1985). We "cannot justify the present economic, social, and political situation . . . to our mass membership." The TUC criticized PNDC failure to implement its economic recovery plan, cuts in subsidies, mass retrenchments, escalating utility and commodity costs, absence of a union role in policy formation, and no palpable gains from "submitting" to IMF and World Bank dictates. Between 1983 and 1985 water costs rose by 150 percent, postage by 365 percent, and electricity by 1,000 percent (Ephson 1986a, 78). In July 1985 the military beat to death a Cocoa Board worker, arousing widespread anger in the ICU, TUC, and DCLs; many DCLs wished for a massive protest. PNDC leaders threatened union leaders with arrests and a direct conflict if a protest was mounted, insisting instead that the TUC protest a current case of CIA spying. The TUC accepted a closed government probe of the death without a demonstration, a decision that angered some union leaders.

In November 1985 news of the imminent layoff of nineteen thousand Cocoa Board workers led the ICU and TUC to consider major protests. The PNDC preemptively whisked off to the police some ICU and Cocoa Board leaders and threatened them against any protest. The government then announced the retrenchment on the radio. It surrounded the TUC hall and the Cocoa Board headquarters with military armored cars and police to avert protests. The PNDC's—and IMF's—only concern was to reduce the wage labor force. There was no further talk of "deployment" to other jobs. There was no employment policy of any kind.

The militant Tema DCL organized demonstrations in January 1986 of some twenty thousand workers in the industrial port city, thirty miles from Accra. The workers were protesting against the low increase in the minimum wage and new devaluations. This startled the government. To cut expenditures, it announced on Friday, April fourth, the cancellation of leave allowances in their entirety, about 15 percent of worker incomes. Protests started over the weekend. By Monday, the TUC directed that all workers put on red armbands and raise a red flag—indications of readiness to mount a protest or strike. The TUC called together the National Consultative Forum, which included leaders of GNAT (teachers), CSA (civil servants), and GRNA (nurses). It told government that cancellation of leave allowances must be abandoned, promising resistance. The Tema DCL promised to go on strike by Friday, and it was rumored that a strike would occur in Accra. At 6 o'clock on Friday morning, the government restored leave allowances (Correspondent 1986a; TUC 1988).

Believing that the TUC was being animated in its protests by the activities of small leftist groups, such as the New Democratic Movement (NDM), on April 16 the PNDC arrested Kwesi Pratt, secretary-general of the Kwame Nkrumah Revolutionary Guards (KNRG), Akoto Ampah (NDM), and two other activists. Rawlings said on radio: "This would have been a real nasty and shameful affair for all of us . . . that such a national strike should come about over leave allowances." He accused "individuals within the labor front and others with close links [of] plotting and planning . . . and manipulating the rest of the workers by preying on their ignorance" (Ephson 1986b, 920–21). The PNDC went public with an argument on the high cost of leave allowances. The TUC passed "Views on Economic, Social and Political Affairs" at its April Executive Board meeting, which included its first call for democratically constituted "peoples assemblies" at all levels. To avert a conflict, the PNDC initiated talks with the TUC. Two meetings held in June created a TUC-PNDC Standing Consultative Committee (TUC 1988a, 32). This was clearly to deflect the TUC into talking channels; few meetings were ever held.

PNDC charges that the planned strike had been politically motivated put the unions and GNAT on the defensive. In October, armed police invaded the precincts of the Asene Household Factory near Accra and arrested five trade union and CDR leaders who were leading a peaceful sit-down strike (Correspondent 1986b). Press attacks upon the TUC accused it of doing nothing for workers, making unrealistic demands, and protesting retrenchments of nonproductive jobs. Censorship denied the TUC a public response.

In late November 1986 the PNDC launched a new attack upon workers benefits, issuing a letter that instructed all employers to end the present method of calculating EOSBs. With TUC Executive Board support, acting secretary-general, L. G. K. Ocloo, sent a tough letter to the PNDC, demanding an immediate withdrawal of the letter or the "TUC would advise itself," that is, a strike threat. The PNDC temporarily withdrew this order, fearing a strike.

Many union leaders were not intimidated. Korang Opare-Ababio, PSWU general secretary, opened its delegates conference in January 1987 by denouncing the neoliberal policies as sharply lowering the workers' standard of living. The retrenchments and threats to suspend benefits were an effort "to undermine, weaken, and eventually destroy the trade union movement and its class representation" (*West Africa*, January 26, 1987, p. 152). The TUC leadership was fighting to prevent PNDC attempts to tax allowances and curtail severance payments. Forty-five thousand public workers were scheduled for retrenchment in 1987–89. In March 1987 ICU general secretary Ocloo blasted the PNDC government at length in opening the ICU Delegates Congress. "We cannot be concerned about strengthening democracy inside our union without being concerned about democracy for the popular masses. . . . The culture of fear is beginning to reassert itself . . . because [of] repression, harassment, and intimidation." Ocloo asserted the right of Ghanaians to choose their own leaders and to do so under conditions of free speech, assembly, and association. "Those who seek to destroy the trade union movement must take their cue from history, that the workers' movement can never be destroyed" (ICU 1987).

This clear demand for democracy echoed those of the TUC in April 1986, which were repeated in the December 1986 TUC paper "The Trade Unions and Democracy." Then, on May Day 1987, Yankey reiterated the call. The PNDC's call for district assemblies "must necessarily be linked to election of leaders at the national level and election of the government by the people as a whole." He repeated the proposals of April 1986 for a people's assembly to draft a constitution and "for constitutional rule" by December 31, 1988 (Correspondent 1987a, 1243–44). Trade unions leaders at most levels understood that their ability to represent the interests of workers without fear required democratic freedoms. The PNDC's response to this was to arrest on May 17 and 20 Kwesi Pratt (KNRG), Akoto-Ampah (NDM), and Kwasi Adu-Amankwah (NDM), head of the TUC's political department. This became a source of continuous union protests (Correspondent 1987a, 1243).

A new dispute arose over the government's attempt to tax travel, leave, transport, and canteen allowances, which Ocloo protested by sending letters to all firms organized by ICU, saying they should resist any illegal deductions. Then, on June 4, CDR elements organized by the PNDC and led by a police jeep invaded TUC headquarters again, attacked some people, and occupied it for twelve hours, without police intervention. Ocloo (Yankey was abroad) protested harshly against "this wanton display of anarchism by organizations with so close affinity to the government." He warned that if this "criminal act" against the TUC was not dealt with, the TUC might have to retaliate. He repeated the TUC demand for a return to "constitutional rule by December 1988" and called upon all unions to resist trade union violations (Correspondent 1987a, 1244). Again, the union militants wore red armbands and unfurled red flags. The police canceled a planned TUC rally on June 9, claiming the NDM was behind the rally. To break leftist support for the unions, on July 14–15 the police arrested several other leftist leaders. Tensions rose with threats from the army commander, who warned "elements in the student and worker fronts" against incitement and rumors of a strike set for July twenty-first, which Yankey denied (Correspondent 1987b, 1429).

The government was determined to contain TUC protests. By some accounts, the PNDC had a heavy influence at the 1988 TUC Delegates Congress in March 1988. Union delegates were pressured not to elect the more militant ICU head, Ocloo, over

A. K. Yankey, secretary-general, who the PNDC had previously opposed but was now thought less combative. PNDC security head Captain Kodwo Tsikata made threatening remarks in his speech to delegates. Yankey did handily win reelection as TUC secretary-general (interviews: Abidi, Akoto Ampah, Arthiabah 1991; *West Africa*, May 2, 1988, p. 775). However, TUC conferences tend to elect more conciliatory rather than militant leaders as secretary-general (e.g., in 1973, 1978, and 1992). And many union general secretaries, who influenced their unions' voting, respected Yankey's negotiations with the government and his conciliatory leadership within the TUC. The union delegates again condemned the PNDC's adherence to IMF/World Bank economic conditionalities and the massive retrenchments. It demanded a much higher minimum wage (₵370). It also reaffirmed its call for a constitutional convention, full civil liberties, free elections, and the return of democratic rule by the end of 1988—not the voice of a coerced labor movement (TUC 1988b).

The PNDC also sought to undermine individual union leaders. Exploiting differences within the MDU, it helped to manage Seth Abloso's loss as general secretary at the 1987 MDU conference. It especially targeted Ocloo of the ICU who helped animate strong TUC resistance. Ocloo changed dollar aid from a foreign union into Ghanaian cedis in Lome, Togo (for a higher rate than obtainable in Ghana), a common practice. The National Bureau of Investigation (police) made persistent inquiries about a dispute in ICU over what happened to this money. Ocloo was hounded and finally fled the country, creating a leadership vacuum in ICU. Powerful ICU locals protested the ICU National Executive's appointment of acting officers. The ICU then tried to organize an emergency delegates' conference to elect new leaders; the government said no, fearful that Ocloo would be reelected. The ICU was thus weakened (interview, Yankey 1991; Sackey 1989).

In 1990–91 there was a decline in overt resistance among TUC and union leaders to key structural adjustment policies and, critics charge, to pushing democratization (Akwetey). There was discontent among some top leaders that Secretary-General Yankey was being dictated to in his negotiations with the PNDC. The argument was that he no longer listened to the TUC Executive Bureau—which would be contrary to his leadership style—and no longer fought hard enough (interviews: Abidi, Korang Opare-Ababio 1991). But Yankey seemed to be an exceptionally able SG during the period between 1983 and 1992 and was not intimidated by the PNDC. He was a leader and a conciliator among the sometimes rancorous general secretaries who were divided by ambitions (e.g., to replace Yankey), ideology (pragmatists vs. anti-imperialists), and leadership styles (militancy vs. accommodation). He negotiated well with the government, some said. Critics were rightly angry that the Executive Board named Rawlings "Worker of the Year" at the 1990 May Day celebration, and that when union leaders met Rawlings, Yankey said on TV that the TUC "supports the [PNDC's] economic program" (Owusu 1990). His major ambition was to ensure the survival, independence, and unity of the labor movement. He was a quietly tough pragmatist.

The TUC's brief shift from militant resistance to temporary accommodation was mirrored, and perhaps prompted, by behavior in the Nigerian Labor Congress (NLC), which was familiar to Ghanaian unionists. The NLC fiercely resisted the military regime's increase in gasoline prices in 1987–88 and other SAP policies demanded by the IMF. It mobilized massive strikes and resistance to the oil price hikes, actions that were supported by university students and others. After first arresting union leaders, the government backed down. Then, in March 1988, taking advantage of a division in elections in the NLC, the government declared that the NLC leadership was illegal, suspended all national union heads, and appointed an administrator to manage the unions. It then raised the gas prices again and anticipated further hikes, leading to a renewal of major strikes from local and regional unions all over Nigeria. There were massive arrests of union leaders. Because of the economic disruptions, the government met with the dominant NLC unions and arranged a truce, but it did not withdraw the oil price hikes. And the NLC accepted a smaller minimum wage hike than it wanted. As Beckman notes, the unions saw that the state could inflict huge damage on their activities, that unions required state consent for industrial relations, and that tactical accommodation was called for (1995). This did not remove the NLC's or TUC's belief that SAP policies were ruinous or their opposition to military rule. Accommodation temporarily replaced militancy. And Ghanaian labor militance persisted in 1991–92 in strikes, demands from below by DCLs, and the challenge by militants in the hotly contested TUC leadership race in 1992 (Adu-Amankwah 1992).

Moreover, the TUC's political demands helped to push the PNDC into launching a limited political reform in 1990, which quickly came unraveled. The political space that the TUC fought hard to open up permitted old and new political groups to emerge and seize upon existing political traditions to jump-start democratization in 1990. The transition of Ghana's quasi-personalist authoritarian regime to democratic rule occurred through a pattern where *resistance* leads to *a regime controlled transition* (see conclusion). The transition did not take place as the PNDC had planned because of the sudden rise of pressures from below. The PNDC regime had engineered the relatively apolitical creation and partial election in 1988 of people to district assemblies. In July 1990, pushed by domestic demands for change and political riots in nearby Francophone states, the PNDC's tame National Committee on Democracy (NCD) suddenly began to hold public forums in regional capitals to elicit public views on what kind of government they would like. The PNDC's idea was to develop support for a no-party system and, in effect, an extension of PNDC rule. The PNDC had only announced the initial public forums a few days before they met and only invited regime supporters. The holding of the first two forums suddenly elicited a great burst of new political activity. The Catholic Bishops Conference in early July issued a call for a national debate on Ghana's future. The KNRG held a press conference within days, demanding an immediate lifting of the ban on political activities and denouncing the PNDC's forums as one sided. On August first, despite threats of arrest, a small band of politicos led by professor Adu Boahene and KNRG representatives, including Kwesi Pratt, announced the creation of the Movement for Freedom and Justice (MFJ). It demanded a return to democratic, constitutional rule and an immediate end to restrictions on civil liberties. On August 31 an emergency TUC Executive Board meeting reaffirmed its 1988 call for a "return to constitutional rule" in Ghana, with full civil liberties and competitive elections. On September 3 the NDM supported the MFJ's demands. On the next day NUGS reiterated its calls for democratization. On September 6 GNAT representatives called for restoration of democracy at the first NCD regional forum open to non-PNDC groups. The Tema DCL and others demanded that no PNDC or government members should attend these forums because their presence created a climate of fear. Clearly the formation of the MFJ and the refusal of Boahene, Pratt, and others to be intimidated by immediate arrest were crucial in the inauguration of a national debate. But the space had been created by the TUC's protest activities and demands for democracy.

All regional forums now heard dissident voices. The Christian Council in December urged that the PNDC take immediate steps to return constitutional rule to Ghana. Thousands of party leaders from earlier democratic regimes were ready to organize again in 1991. In response, on December 31, 1990, and January 1, 1991, Rawlings made two speeches in which he laid out a program for return to constitutional rule, after creation of a constitution, though a free press and parties were still illegal. Although Rawlings designed a consultative assembly that involved a built-in PNDC majority, the draft constitution it considered was crafted by a group of lawyers, under public pressure, along the lines of Ghana's past constitutions. The constitution provided a strong basis for democratic rule and Supreme Court oversight of civil liberties. Despite the PNDC ban on parties, in August 1991 a small private press started to publish again and the leaders of prior Nkrumahist and PP party traditions launched political "clubs" and started to openly hold organizational meetings, which the police did not disturb.

The unions provided consistent public support for the unfolding democratic process, reiterating fully its support for democratic institutions at DCL meetings, the Consultative Assembly, and its 1992 Delegates Congress (TUC 1992a, 25–29). It regularly argued for the removal of all PNDC barriers to speech, a free press, and political competition prior to the 1992 election. Ten union leaders were designated to serve in the Consultative Assembly and did so. At the 1992 Delegates Congress the TUC reiterated that it would not participate in partisan politics, which might divide union members; it insisted, however, that it would have a loud voice in public policy debates. Any union leader who wished to participate, or hold office, in party politics had to resign his or her position (TUC 1992b), but union activists did participate in election monitoring.

Trade Unions under Democratic Rule in the 4th Republic: NDC, NPP, and Unions, 1993–2006

The outcome of the 1992 presidential and parliamentary elections created a political environment that induced the TUC to develop an activist public posture on budgetary and other policy debates. Rawlings turned the PNDC apparatus of rule into a new party, the National Democratic Congress (NDC). As NDC presidential candidate, Rawlings beat Adu Boahene, the candidate for the renewed Busia political tradition, the New Patriotic Party (NPP), with 58 percent to 30 percent of the vote. The NPP deeply believed that it had been defrauded of the election (Jeffries 1993; Oquaye 1995; Ninsin 1993). Hence, the NPP refused to participate in the parliamentary elections. Thus, there was no opposition party in parliament.

(Rawlings won the presidency again in 1996 with 57 percent in an election deemed fair.) This and labor-state conflicts, said the TUC, "put further stress on the [TUC] . . . as the TUC had to take on additional advocacy roles on major national issues" (TUC 1996a, 1). The political environment improved after the 1996 election, when NPP opposition MPs took their seats. But the TUC thought in 2000 that "at the political level . . . democracy and constitutionalism continued to remain fragile" (TUC 2000a, 1).

The 1993–96 political environment had several key qualities. First, the NDC ruled in much the same way as it had when it was the PNDC, except that it accepted important constitutional constraints. Thus, for important public groups, government decision making remained non-transparent, and the government itself remained largely unaccountable and unresponsive to public pressures and questions from key constituencies (interviews: Agyei 1993; Brimpong 1993). Indeed, the structures and occupants of the executive branch remained remarkably the same. The NDC MPs were largely tame and did not hold ministers responsible in any sense. The NDC government frequently met requests for information with silence. Second, however, the 1992 constitution reestablished some basic constitutional civil liberties, such as free speech, press, and association, which have enormous support in the Ghanaian public. The TUC, Ghana Bar Association, and the NPP used these liberties to establish more firmly the reality of these freedoms. The private (non-state) newspapers were biweeklies, at best, and of poor quality, with a few exceptions. The real end to state control over information was the widening access of the public to Ghana radio and TV and the expansion in FM radio stations after 1995. These were listened to widely and featured critical political debates.

The TUC and others could now freely criticize the government, with their views given in the newspapers and on FM stations. The political environment improved in 2000 with the election of the opposition NPP, labor's well-remembered nemesis as the PP in 1969–71. Some union leaders believed that democracy was more secure, and speech and union activities were freer, once Rawlings and the NDC lost in 2000 (interview, Yinsob 2004). Despite the historical antagonism between unions and the NPP leadership, relations have not been bad. Union leaders know that they do not have the same interests. After the 2000 election a delegation of NPP leaders visited the union leaders and made clear their intentions to try to consult with the TUC and have decent relations (interview, Yinsob 2004). The NPP has not tried to intimidate the union movement.

With renewed freedom to act in 1993, the TUC and national unions acted vigorously in the public arena. In December 1993, the TUC initiated the first of many forums to assess the impact of SAP, attended by many, including the IMF and the World Bank but not NDC ministers. In the 1990s the TUC continued to organize anti-SAP conferences, critical of government policies, though it had accepted the state enterprise privatizations. In mid-1995 the TUC Executive Board requested the government to organize a nonpartisan forum to assess the economy. A three-day conference was belatedly organized a year later. The TUC continued to convene the Consultative Forum, bringing teachers, civil servant, and nurses' groups into discussions on wages and taking them into the Tripartite Committee meetings with the government. TUC interests were clearly broader than those of trade unions. It intervened in 1995 in a strike of hospital doctors with the government in order to ensure medical services. The TUC also intervened in the large gasoline price increases in 1993, which always generated large transport fare increases. The DCLs protested that they would resort "to all powers at their disposal to back their demands." The National Assembly responded, and the price increase was reduced (TUC 1996a, 56). But in this area success was infrequent: the IMF and the World Bank insisted on market prices for fuel and large taxes to build budget revenues.

The TUC was involved in mobilizing its national unions and rank and file on behalf of union and wider issues. For instance, soon after the 1992 TUC elections, the TUC mobilized workers around the country through rallies of DCLs and issues regarding the 1991 wage consolidation and to demand settlement of claims for the EOSBs for the many laid-off workers. These protests induced the PNDC government to concede to paying the EOSBs over three years. In early 1993 Rawlings used Ghana Radio and TV to blast the three largest entrepreneurs in Ghana and urge boycotts of their products on grounds that they helped to fund the opposition. The TUC protested Rawlings's attack and joined with the Association of Ghana Industries to mount a "Buy Ghana Goods in Order to Save Jobs" (TUC 1996a, 56). When, in 1993, the NDC government laid off 10,400 more workers from the Cocoa Board, it ignored the collective agreement and cut severance pay sharply. Cocoa Board workers went on strike. The TUC demanded compliance with legal labor agreements and organized the DCLs to mount nationwide demonstrations to support Cocoa Board workers. The government then agreed to eighteen months of severance pay (TUC 1996a, 58).

The NDC government also used some force to intimidate opposition. A coalition of elements from the opposition parties launched a *Kueme Preko* campaign ("Kill Us Now!") to protest the government's adoption of the IMF/World Bank–imposed value-added tax (VAT) of 15 percent, a campaign the TUC also supported. The NDC government used remaining thugs in the CDRs to interrupt the large protest in Accra; they shot and killed four protesters. This outraged the public. The TUC demanded from the minister of the interior a full explanation of the state violence, which he refused. So the TUC also pushed the new Commission on Human Rights and Administrative Justice to pose the same questions; it too sought to compel government accountability, ultimately through the courts. The introduction of VAT had to be postponed for several years because of the wide support for *Kueme Preko* demonstrations all over Ghana.

In each democratic period in Ghana, governing parties have tried to penetrate the labor movement, either to capture support or to dampen opposition. Since 1993, the union leadership has prevented this. The closely fought 1992 TUC elections created important strains among the leaders. But the "Alliance for Change" candidates have since been drawn into the top TUC leadership, and TUC elections have been less contested due to accords among the general secretaries of the national unions. Unions also avoided involvement in partisan politics. The NDC's efforts to liberalize the labor laws took place gradually, with consultation with the TUC, as in the long negotiations over a new labor act that legalized strikes. Two breakaway unions from the ICU were not politicized. The TUC has been able to cope with unions outside the TUC and the organization of a new, small Ghana Federation of Labor.

During 1993 to 2006 the TUC was a significant participant in democratic institutions in Ghana. It invigorated democratic practices by the breadth and level of its activities. The TUC has sought to increase its institutional capabilities by upgrading its research and by building the capacities of its top and secondary leadership through its union education and through labor programs with Cape Coast University. From the mid-1990s it has joined, and lent office space to, the Coalition against Water Privatization, an extremely important debate for all Ghanaians. The TUC has paid far more attention recently to developing clear, explicit guidelines regarding what it values as democratic practices and liberties in Ghana, including explicit democratic norms for unions. The democratic process has worked imperfectly in unions. Some union leaders manage to use their power to discourage challenges to their reelection. Secretary-General Adu-Amankwah recommended to the TUC in 2004 that the tenure of a secretary-general be limited to two four-year terms, which would open up the democratic process at the top. But the union heads disliked the idea, which could later be applied to their unions. It was defeated at the 2004 TUC conference.

The TUC has detailed, as part of its policies, conditions that facilitate and militate against democracy, and its need to "intervene consistently to safeguard and promote conditions that promote democracy in Ghana" (TUC 1996b, 51–65; TUC 2000b). The support for these ideas evidenced among the top and secondary trade union leadership militates against future support for coup leaders who promise economic salvation by overturning democracies, as occurred in 1972.

The TUC has been involved in voter education, especially within the unions, to deepen understanding of the issues. In 1996 and 2000 it joined with key civil society groups to organize election monitoring. In 2000 it invited the flag bearers of the political parties to the TUC Delegates Congress in Kumasi to address the delegates. TUC demonstrated its electoral importance and wanted presidential candidates to say what their parties could do for workers.

Since 1993 the TUC has had a staff member involved in tracking bills that come before the National Assembly. The TUC has made regular representations to the relevant committees on key items of legislation relevant to labor, such as the annual budget, taxes, VAT, public holidays, free trade zones, public utility, and national minimum wage bills. An NPP committee chair cited the TUC as the major interest group lobbying the assembly. It has met informally with a group of labor-friendly MPs, and it has organized retreats with government and business leaders to deal with the new labor code and minimum wage conflicts.

There has been a significant increase in strikes under democratic rule. Comparing the PNDC years with the 4th Republic (1993–2004), the number of strikes has doubled, the number of strikers more than tripled, and the number of days-lost more than quadrupled (see Table 4.3). However, the strike levels are much lower than in the last two periods of democratic rule, when frustration over desperate economic conditions boiled over. What is important—and bears on democratic rule—is that the TUC and individual unions have the capacity to threaten to hold strikes or demonstrations in order to get the government or SOEs to negotiate seriously and resolve problems. During 1993–2000 the TUC was regularly frustrated with NDC inaction in bargaining over minimum wage increases. But its capacity to signal its anger in protests and demonstrations has meant that real minimum wages did not fall. And under the NPP rule, it has been successful, again through pressures, to raise the real minimum wage (see Table 4.3).

Conclusion

The trade union movement in Ghana has fought for its independence and worker rights for well over forty years and has enjoyed the norm of internal democracy since its emergence after World War II. The 1958–65 TUC leadership sought to—and did, briefly—enhance union power by linking itself to a dominant party system, where ultimately it lost its autonomy. But since 1966 virtually all TUC and national union leaders have recognized that the independence of trade unions and their capacity to fight aggressively for workers and egalitarian policies is bound up with political democracy. Still, it was a democratic regime (PP, 1969–72) that sought to disband and enfeeble the union movement, a fate from which it was saved by an initially populist military coup (NRC/SMC). It learned over several periods of democratic and authoritarian rule that democracy is not a panacea for union success. And it has struggled since the return of democracy in Ghana in 1993 to rebuild the real wages of workers and stave off the decline of the organized labor force as government and private sector firms laid off workers. This sharply reduced the size of the union movement (see Table 4.1), which fell to about 285,000 members by 2004, despite efforts by unions to recruit atypical types of workers. Still the PNDC period seared into the minds of union leaders at most levels that authoritarian regimes, regardless of rhetoric, bode ill for the vitality and well-being of the union movement.

The long history of union autonomy in Ghana and general patterns of democratic leadership selection within unions gave the union movement the collective capability, norms, and values to withstand the attempt of the PNDC to first emasculate and then control it. The at least *intermittent periods of democratic rule* up to 1982 were also crucial in teaching unionists that democracy gave them a freedom to pursue their interests that dictatorship did not. *Union leadership* was also key: all the union leaders had long experience within a democratic union movement and rose up through its ranks; they were attached to their unions and their rights. In countries without these democratic experiences, the political environment is such that union leaders are more readily coerced, corrupted, or bought off by dictatorships. Other factors that contributed to the TUC's ability to defend its autonomy and then demand democracy was the *existence in laws and institutions of labor regulations that protected union rights* and, in 1982–83 especially, of *external union organizations interested in supporting trade union independence.*

The unions' relatively large size, experience of autonomy, and organization gave them the capability under several authoritarian regimes to withstand repression, assert the rights of non-state collective actors, and embody norms of democratic participation. They could and did *create political space* that ultimately enabled other, more political, actors to organize for democratic rights. The union movement in Ghana, unlike those in South Africa, Zambia, and Zimbabwe, has not sought to play a direct role in organizing political power since the disastrous experience in 1960–66 under the Nkrumah regime. However, the unions have asserted a loud and persistent voice in the political arena regarding a range of economic and social policies that structure the well-being of the lives of Ghanaian workers and other Ghanaians as well. Unions see themselves as the key representative of the interests of a substantial portion of the modern public in Ghana's democratic life. The unions' insistence upon this role has given vitality to Ghana's democracy.

References

Abidi, J. O. 1991. Interview.

Adu-Amankwah, Kwasi. 1995, 1996, 2004. Interview.

Adu-Amankwah, Kwasi. 1990. The state, trade unions, and democracy in Ghana, 1982–1990. Master's thesis. The Hague: Institute of Social Studies.

———. 1992. Report on the 4th Quadrennial Congress of the TUC. Unpublished manuscript.

Agyei, Christian, 1993. Interview.

Ahinful-Quansah, J. 1972. Interview

Akwetey, Emannuel O. 1994. Trade unions and democratization: Comparative study of Zambia and Ghana. PhD diss. Stockholm: University of Stockholm, Dept. of Political Science.

Arthiabah, Peter. 1974. The politics of the 2nd Quadrenniel Congress of the Ghana Trade Union Congress. *Legon Observer*.

Ashiley, E. T. 1972. Interview.

Baiden, Richard. 1978. The Ghana TUC—why leadership and structural changes are necessary and urgent. Mimeograph. Accra, Ghana: Maritime and Dockworkers Union, June 9.

Beckman, Bjorn. 1995. The politics of labor and adjustment: The experience of the Nigeria Labour Congress. In *Between liberalization and oppression*, ed. T. Mkandawire and A. Olukoshi, 281–323. Dakar, Senegal: Codesira.

Bergen, Geoffrey. 1994. Unions in Senegal. 2 Vols. PhD dissertation. Ann Arbor: UMI Dissertation Information Service.

Bratton, Michael. 1994. Micro democracy? The merger of the farmer unions in Zimbabwe. *African Studies Review* 37 (April): 9–37.

Bratton, Michael, and Nicholas van de Walle. 1997. *Democratic experiments in Africa*. New York: Cambridge University Press.

Brimpong, John. 1993. Interview.

Chazan, Naomi. 1988. Ghana: Problems of governance and the emergence of civil society. In *Africa*. Vol. 2 of *Democracy in developing countries*, ed. L. Diamond, J. Linz, and S. M. Lipset, 93–139. Boulder, CO: Lynne Rienner.

Collier, Ruth Berins, and James Mahoney. 1997. Adding collective actors to collective outcomes: Labor and recent democratization in South America and southern Europe. *Comparative Politics* 29 (April): 285–303.

Correspondent (A). 1986a. Resurrection after Easter. *West Africa*, April 21, pp. 812–13.

———. 1986b. Protect our rights. *West Africa*, October 27, p. 2254.

———. 1987a. Current concerns. *West Africa*, June 29, pp. 1243–44.

———. 1987b. In a fighting mood. *West Africa*, July 27, pp. 1429–30.

———. 1988. Worker-power ousted. *West Africa*, December 12, pp. 2326–27.

Crisp, Jeffrey. 1984. *The story of an African working class*. London: Zed.

Dagadu, E. 1989. Labor under fire. *West Africa*, June 5, pp. 918–19.

Diamond, Larry. 1988. Introduction: Roots of failure, seeds of hope. In *Africa*. Vol. 2 of *Democracy in developing countries*, ed. Larry Diamond, Juan Linz, and S. M. Lipset, 1–32. Boulder, CO: Lynne Rienner.

Drake, St. Clair, and Leslie A. Lacy. 1966. Government versus the unions: The Sekondi-Takoradi strike, 1961. In *Politics in Africa*, ed. Gwendolen Carter, 67–118. New York: Harcourt, Brace, and World.

Ephson, Ben. 1986a. Paying the price. *West Africa*, January 26, pp. 78–79.

———. 1986b. Margins for maneuver. *West Africa*, May 12, pp. 920–21.

———. 1986c. Give and take. *West Africa*, November 10, 1986, pp. 2347–48.

Eshun, Issac. 1987. Collision course. *West Africa*, July 13, pp. 1344–45.

Fashoyin, Tayo. 1990. Nigerian labor and the military: Towards exclusion? *Labour, Capital and Society* 23 (April): 12–37.

Ghana. 1969a. *Report of the Commission of Enquiry into the funds of the Trades Union Congress*. Accra, Ghana: Government Printer.

Ghana. 1969b. *Report of the Committe of Enquiry into the recent disturbances at Prestea*. Accra, Ghana: Government Printer.

Ghana. 1971. *Report of the Commission of Enquiry into the Obuasi disturbances*. Accra, Ghana: Government Printer.

Ghana. 1993. *Rural communities in Ghana* [Ghana Living Standards Survey, 1991/92]. Accra, Ghana: Ghana Statistical Service.

Ghana, Labor Department. Various files. Various dates.

Graham, Yao. 1985. The politics of crisis in Ghana: Class struggle and organization. *Review of African Political Economy* 34:54–68.

———. 1989. From GTP to Assene: Aspects of industrial working class struggle, 1982–86. In *The state, development and politics in Ghana*, ed. Emmanuel Hansen and Kwame Ninsin, 43–72. Dakar, Senegal: Codesria.

Gyimah-Boadi, E., and A. Essuman-Johnson. 1993. The PNDC and organised labor: The anatomy of political control. In *Ghana under PNDC rule*, ed. E. Gyimah-Boadi, 196–210. London: Codesria Books.

Haggard, Stephen, and Robert Kaufman. 1995. *The political economy of democratic transitions*. Princeton, NJ: Princeton University Press.

Harbeson, John, D. Rothchild, and N. Chazon, eds. 1994. *Civil society and the state in Africa*. Boulder, CO: Lynne Rienner.

Haynes, Jeffrey. 1991. Railway workers and the PNDC government in Ghana, 1982–1990. *Journal of Modern African Studies* 29 (1): 137–54.

Herbst, Jeffrey. 1991.Labor in Ghana under structural adjustment: The politics of acquiescence. In *Ghana: The political economy of reform*, ed. Donald Rothchild, 173–92. Boulder, CO: Lynne Rienner.

Higley, John, and Richard Gunther. 1992. *Elites and democratic consolidation in Latin America and southern Europe*. Cambridge: Cambridge University Press.

Huntington, Samuel. 1991. *The third wave: Democratization in the late twentieth century*. Norman: University of Oklahoma Press.

International Confederation of Free Trade Unions. 1994–2005. *Annual survey of violations of trade union rights*. Brussels: International Confederation of Free Trade Unions.

Industrial and Commercial Workers Union. 1987. Address by the general secretary, L. G. K. Ocloo, at the 4th Quadrennial Delegates Conference. Mimeograph. March 4.

Jeffries, Richard. 1978. *Class, power, and ideology in Ghana: The railwaymen of Sekondi*. Cambridge: Cambridge University Press.

Jeffries, Richard, and C. Thomas. 1993. The Ghanaian elections of 1992. *African Affairs* 92:331–66.

Kraus, Jon. 1979a. Strikes and labor power in Ghana. *Development and Change* 10 (April): 259–86.

———. 1979b The political economy of industrial relations in Ghana. In *Industrial relations in Africa*, ed. U. Dimachi, H. Dieter Seibel, and L. Trachtman, 106–68. London: Macmillan.

———. 1988a. The political economy of trade union-state relations in radical and populist regimes in Africa. In *Labour and trade unions in Asia and Africa*, ed. Roger Southall, 171–210. New York: St. Martin's Press.

———. 1988b. Political party failures and political responses in Ghana. In *When parties fail: Emerging alternative organizations*, ed. Kay Lawson and Peter Merkl, 464–99. Princeton, NJ: Princeton University Press.

———. 1991. The political economy of stabilization and structural adjustment in Ghana. In *Ghana: The political economy of reform*, ed. Donald Rothchild, 119–55. Boulder, CO: Lynne Rienner Publishers.

———. 1995. Trade unions and democratization in Africa. In *Africa contemporary record, 1989–90*, ed. Marion Doro and Colin Legum, A53–A72. New York: Africana.

Kumadey, Patrick. 1973. Interview.

Labor Department, Ghana. various years, 1939–1974. *Annual report*. Accra: Government Printer.

Labor Department, Ghana. Various files. Various years.

Martin, Matthew. 1991. Negotiating adjustment and external finance: Ghana and the international community, 1982–89. In *Ghana: The political economy of recovery*, ed. Donald Rothchild, 235–63. Boulder, CO: Lynne Rienner.

Ninsin, Kwame. 1993. Some problems in Ghana's transition to democratic governance. *Africa Development* 18 (2): 5–20.

Oquaye, Mike. 1995. The Ghanaian elections of 1992. *African Affairs* 94:259–75.

Owusu, K. 1990. Caring and sharing. *West Africa*, July 23, pp. 2151–53.

Public Agenda [Ghanaian weekly paper]. 1995–97.

Reuschmeyer, D. E., H. Stephens, and J. D. Stephens. 1992. *Capitalist development and democracy*. Chicago: University of Chicago Press.

Sackey, W. 1989. Trouble for the ICU. *West Africa*, March 13, pp. 389–90.

Sandbrook, Richard. 1981. Worker consciousness and populist protest in tropical Africa. In *Research in the sociology of work*, ed. Richard Simpson and I. H. Simpson, 1:1–36. Greenwich, CT: Jai Press.

Sekondi-Takoradi Workers. 1982. Statement. Mimeograph.

Shin, Doh Chull. 1994. On the third wave of democratization: A synthesis and evaluation of recent theory and research. *World Politics* 47 (October): 135–70.

Sklar, Richard. 1979. The nature of class domination in Africa. *Journal of Modern African Studies* 17 (4): 531–52.

Statement on the present state of affairs in the country issued in Kumasi on 12th May 1983 by workers of the undersigned establishments and unions in Kumasi. 1983. Mimeograph.

Trade Union Congress. 1966. *Extraordinary [delegates'] congress of the TUC (Ghana): Comprehensive report*. Accra, Ghana: Trade Union Congress, mimeograph.

———. 1970. *Report on the activities of the TUC to the 3rd Biennial Congress*. Winneba, August.

———. 1978. *Report on the activities of the TUC to the 2nd Quadrennial Congress*. September 1978, Parts 1–2.

———. 1984a. Resolution by the executive board on the appraisal of the economic situation, to chairman of PNDC. TUC/SG/41/27. Mimeograph.

————. 1984b. Economic and research dept. to secretary general. Memorandum. April 6.

————. 1984c. Press statement by the TUC (Ghana) on the recent price increases of some commodities. February 22. Mimeograph.

————. 1985. Position paper of executive board of TUC on national situation, to chairman of the PNDC. TUC/SG/A.41/31. Mimeograph.

————. 1988a. *Report on the activities of the TUC to the 3rd Quadrennial Congress of TUC, Cape Coast, 1988.* Accra, Ghana: Trade Union Congress.

————. 1988b. Resolutions adopted by the 3rd Quadrennial Delegates Congress. University of Cape Coast, March 16–18.

————. 1992a. *Report on the activities of the TUC to the 4th Quadriennial Congress of the TUC.* Cape Coast, August.

————. 1992b. *Record of the proceedings of the 4th Quadrennial Delegates Congress.* August 26–28.

————. 1996a. *Report of the executive board of TUC to the 5th Quarrennial Delegates Congress.* Cape Coast, August 18–22.

————. 1996b. *Policies of the Trade Union Congress adopted at the 5th Quadrennial Congress of TUC.* Mimeograph.

————. 2000a. *Report to the 6th Quadrennial Congress of TUC.* September 12–16.

————. 2000b. *Policies of the Trade Union Congress (Ghana) adopted at the 6th Quadrennial Delegates Congress.* September 12–16.

Trade Union Congress, and Benjamin Bentum. 1966. *Trade unions in chains.* Mimeograph. Accra, Ghana: Trade Union Congress.

Trade Union Congress, and DCL/Tema. 1991. Report of the activities of the Tema District Council of Labor for the period August 1985–October 1991. Mimeograph.

Valenzuela, J. Samuel. 1989. Labor movements in transitions to democracy. *Comparative Politics* 21 (July): 445–71.

Vormawor, Dennis. 1996. Interview. Deputy secretary general, TUC, July, December.

Waterman, Peter. 1983. *Aristocrats and plebians in African trade unions: Lagos port and dock worker organisation and struggle.* The Hague: Peter Waterman.

West Africa. Weekly (London). Various issues.

Yankey, A. K. 1985, 1991. Interviews. TUC secretary general.

Yeebo, Zayo. 1985. Ghana: Defense committees and the class struggle. *Review of African Political Economy* 32:64–72.

Yeebo, Zayo. 1991. *Ghana: The struggle for popular power.* London: New Beacon.

Yinsob, Benjamin. 2004. Interview. Assistant to TUC secretary general.

CHAPTER 5

Trade Unions, Development, and Democratization in Zambia: The Continuing Struggle

Emmanuel Akwetey and Jon Kraus

Apart from being a labor movement, ZCTU is also a political institution because it deals more with political issues. Let those saying [for ZCTU to leave out politics] know that even the Church supports a political party and that poorly paid workers cannot give good tithe in Church. The way we are governed has a bearing on the livelihood of people in the country and those calling on the labor movement not to support a political party of their choice should revisit their history. Our concern has been that our party [MMD] has failed to deliver and that is why we want to support a party that is labor-friendly. We used our resources to obtain independence and to change the government in 1991 and I see no reason why people should get worried when we say will support a single political party this time.

Sylvester Tembo
Secretary-General, Zambia Congress of Trade Unions
2004

Introduction: Beyond Mobilization Roles?

The years between 1989 and 1991 may be regarded as the period during which the Zambia Congress of Trade Unions (ZCTU) reached the height of its perceived influence in Zambian politics. The organization's public campaign for the democratization of Zambian politics, initiated in December 1989, culminated in the electoral defeat of the United National Independence Party (UNIP) at the multiparty polls of October 1991. Prior to that election, UNIP's control over the governing institutions of parliament and the executive organ had been so effectively unchallenged that the ruling party equated itself with the state as well as with Zambian civil society. But all this changed when active trade union support for the

Movement for Multiparty Democracy (MMD), the political opposition which Frederick Chiluba led to electoral victory in October 1991, decisively brought to an end the authoritarian party-state regime.

Although this mobilization role was linked to the movement for democratic political reforms in Zambia, it is less clear whether the specific issues that led the ZCTU to play such a role formed part of a purposeful agenda to jointly promote democracy and development. The mobilization of unionized workers and the public at large ensued from years of trade union opposition to government policies, especially the adoption of structural adjustment programs (SAPs) (Akwetey 1994). But there was little indication that alternatives to UNIP's policies were at the center of any future political pact between the ZCTU and the MMD. It was not clear how specific aspirations of the labor organization and its members were going to be fulfilled within the liberal democratic framework of Zambia's Third Republic, with the MMD, not UNIP, in government. In the five years after the formal transition to multiparty democracy, the record of relations between the ZCTU and the democratically elected MMD government showed that neither the political aspirations nor the desired public policies of the ZCTU had been fulfilled. In the next decade, the ZCTU again moved into an oppositional posture to the MMD government that it helped into power in order to forcefully pressure the government to alter its policies.

This chapter explores two major questions and their minor corollaries. First, what role did the ZCTU play in the overthrow of the old regime in Zambia and the renewal of democratic politics? What was the relationship between the prior authoritarian, single-party UNIP regime and the trade union movement that enabled the ZCTU to play this dynamic role? And how important were economic conditions in Zambia to the ZCTU's mobilization of labor forces against UNIP rule? Second, given that the relationship between the union movement and the MMD government in democratic Zambia after 1991 was clearly unsatisfactory for the unions, will trade unions continue to mobilize support for democratization and economic reforms when their aspirations appear unfulfilled by these processes? How is their role in the transition to democracy affected when economic reforms appear to undermine living standards of unionized workers?

Trade union roles and attitudes are normally a fluid mixture of support for or opposition to government as determined by the trade unions' independent, rational assessment of the structural and dynamic conditions that affect their ability to fulfill their interests and aspirations. We examine the Zambian union experience during 1992–2006 and how the ZCTU and the union movement adjusted their political attitudes and relationship to the MMD government and democratic life as economic "reforms" were implemented that severely damaged the interests of unions and workers.

Background to Democratization in Zambia

We examine the background to Zambia's transition to a multiparty democracy in October 1991 by assessing union-state relationships during the period before the creation of the party-state and during the tenure of the party-state.

Prior to the Party-State Regime (1964–73)

The emergence of wage earners as a social group in Zambian society developed with the large-scale exploitation of copper that began in the 1930s and in the policy of the colonial government to control the unionization of workers. But the expansion of unionized labor in Zambia was the direct result of the labor and development policies of the UNIP regime that ruled Zambia from 1964 to 1991. The policies of the UNIP and the colonial governments contrasted sharply in one major area, UNIP's promotion of "developmental trade unionism."

The colonial state did not articulate a direct relationship between trade unionism and the development of the colony over which it ruled. Indeed, it was not until the late 1940s and early 1950s that it departed from its largely "night watchman" function as the enforcer of law and order. It began to sponsor a limited development of socioeconomic infrastructure in the country (Liatto 1989; Sklar 1975). Generally, colonial government's public expenditures on such social projects as schools, hospitals and clinics, housing, transportation, communication, and manufacturing remained minimal (Crawford 1988). After forty years of direct colonial rule (1924–64), the colonized society that became independent Zambia in October 1964 had little to show in terms of socioeconomic and political-institutional development.

The scale of neglect and the scope of widespread poverty support the argument that the Colonial Office's policy to promote supervised unionization of indigenous workers was intended to prevent the possibility of militant resistance to the autocratic labor regimes of the mines from linking up with the anticolonial movement (Burawoy 1985; Davies 1966; Jeffries 1978). Colonial labor policy forcefully insisted upon nonpolitical unionism. It facilitated administrative regulation and control over workers' activities by decentralizing unionization and encouraging intra-sectoral rivalry and divisions. These undermined efforts to build a strong and coherent labor organization. After independence, the UNIP government implemented its national development agenda through a series of development plans. The Transitional Development Plan of 1965–66 and the First National Development Plan (FNDP) of 1966–70 made the modernization of Zambia a primary objective through socioeconomic infrastructure development, industrialization, and the creation of jobs. Together, they facilitated the creation of thousands of new jobs and the growth of an educated workforce.

By 1970 many more Zambians were educated, better paid, and enjoying a vast range of social welfare services than had ever been the case under colonial rule (Bates 1971; Molteno 1974, 31; Pettman 1974, 133; Sklar 1975). The government also implemented an affirmative policy of Africanization. The government was thus able to tackle the problem of underrepresentation of Zambians in the middle- and top-management levels of industry. It systematically increased the number of Zambians in such positions. Later, the government drew on the support of the unions to reform the despotic and autocratic management regime that had been used to humiliate and exploit indigenous Zambian workers. By the end of the 1960s, a policy of affirmative action had been so effectively implemented that the government shifted greater attention to its economic development programs. It was in pursuit of this objective of building a modern economy, state, and nation—as well as consolidating UNIP power—that UNIP government's relations with the ZCTU and unionized workers were profoundly affected.

In 1964, the UNIP government had responded to union demands for reform of labor legislation in order to enhance the unionization of workers and the building of a strong labor center, which could direct workers to support national development programs (Meebelo 1986). The Trades Unions and Trades Disputes Act (1964) was passed to amend colonial labor legislation to achieve that purpose. The new act formulated a new organizing principle of unionization. This "one industry, one union" idea moved the union movement from a decentralized structure to a more centralized one. This was evident in the reestablishment of the Zambia Congress of Trade Unions (ZCTU) as the sole trade union center, funded regularly through compulsory dues check-off. A new labor law also tried to control industrial disputes by attempting to control their outbreak and their resolution. As in other African states, the government offered the central trade union benefits in exchange for political cooperation with the party and government.

Partly as a result of the new labor law and the implementation of the government's development plans, unionization and union membership grew, enabling the ZCTU to increase its affiliated membership to 184,000 workers by the end of the 1960s. With the number of national unions reduced to eighteen, the ZCTU—designated the sole representative of workers—appeared to be in a powerful position to represent workers to the government (Gupta 1974, 297–98; Meebelo 1986). The positive impact of its labor and development policies on the growth of unions led the government to believe that it had created the basis for a long-term development partnership. UNIP needed workers' support for its objective to develop a national state and modern economy. Union-government ties were strengthened by the fact that some unions supported the struggle for independence and the UNIP as a party and were reinforced by the increased pay and promotions after independence. Hence, the government assumed that workers would also support its implementation of development programs.

The UNIP government was determined to ensure industrial peace and was greatly concerned with the high level of strikes that occurred after independence. Strikes numbered in excess of two hundred per year in the mid-1960s. The government insisted on labor peace in the copper mines, the bedrock of government revenue and thus of hopes for economic development. Hence, it continuously intervened in strikes, using party, government, and, sometimes, union officials to force strikers back to work. Despite the close ZCTU-government ties, union leaders were often unhappy with government and party interventions.

Trade unions were expected and urged by the UNIP government to move away from consumer orientations to more production orientations and to promote industrial peace (Bates 1971; Sklar 1975). The ZCTU was also to ensure that workers gave practical support to government development policies by educating workers to understand the goals of such policies. Restraints on wage demands were thus as important as refraining from wildcat strikes or planned industrial actions. However, strikes continued throughout the second half of the 1960s, and wildcat strikes, in particular, threatened to spread from the mining to the public utility sectors. In the post-independence flush of high worker expectations, the strikes persisted, and the

ZCTU appeared unable either to control or to deter their spread. Thus, the government responded with a series of measures ranging from the arrest and detention of mineworkers to statutory banning of strikes and lockouts in essential industries such as electricity, health, water, food, fuel supplies, mining, construction, and transportation. Despite such interventions, the government continued to support the ZCTU and its existing pro-UNIP leadership as the powerful center of trade union control in the country.

In 1971 the government enacted a new Industrial Relations Act (IRA) that amended the elements of voluntarism in unionization, as defined in the 1964 act, by making them more mandatory and sanctionable when violations occurred. As a result, membership in trade unions became mandatory and affiliation with the ZCTU obligatory. This yielded a labor regime of growing political intervention and the potential centralization of control over the national unions by the ZCTU. This trend toward increased state control was also manifest in political institutions. By 1970 a systematic movement toward a new regime of "developmental dictatorship" was gaining momentum. A concentration of powers in the executive arm of government was paralleled by unbridled repression of formal political opposition. In the early 1970s, multiparty politics was proscribed, together with the freedoms of expression, association, and assembly (Sklar 1986).

In 1973 Zambia was formally declared a one-party state under a new constitution that both legitimated the concentration of powers in the party and government and abrogated representative parliamentary democracy and a wide range of civil and political rights (Tordoff 1974). All these had major implications for unions and their roles in Zambia.

During the Party-State Regime (1973–90)

It was believed that centralizing power in the party-state would enhance the capacity of government to secure law and order while accelerating economic and social modernization. By design or accident, some positive changes in organizational growth and development were recorded. There was rapid expansion of the public sector economy, as several parastatal enterprises were established. These, together with the reform of local government structures, boosted employment.

In response, membership of the trade unions grew by almost 80 percent as mandatory unionization of workers on the basis of "one industry, one union" increased total membership from 184,000 in 1969 to 352,900 in 1989. The expansion in membership accelerated in the 1970s but slowed down somewhat in the 1980s in the face of economic crisis, stabilization plans, and public sector downsizing. The largest unions in 1989 were the National Union of Public Service Workers (NUPSW), with 65,610 members; the Mineworkers Union of Zambia (MUZ), with 58,808 members; the Zambian National Union of Teachers (ZNUT), with 36,230; the Civil Servants Union (CSUZ) and the National Union of Commercial and Industrial Workers (NUCIW), each with 27,000; the National Union of Building, Engineering and General Workers (NUBEGW), with 25,000; and the Zambia United Local Authorities Workers Union (ZULAWU), with 25,000 (Akwetey 1994, 52). Four of the seven largest unions were composed entirely of public sector workers.

A qualitative growth of the ZCTU organization also occurred during the mid-1970s to the late 1980s. A skillful, more professional leadership emerged to lead skilled white-collar workers and semi- and unskilled blue-collar workers. The new leaders perceived the ZCTU's roles and obligations differently from both their predecessors and those prescribed by the government. Some of their predecessors had campaigned together with UNIP for independence and were committed to UNIP's political and development agenda. The new generation of leaders emphasized professionalism, union interests, and union autonomy. The changes associated with the party-state dictatorship and the 1971 IRA law inadvertently produced conditions that shaped trade unionism in a way that was different from what the UNIP government had intended.

Despite the UNIP domination of a one-party state, the long pre-independence tradition of trade union autonomy and democratic elections persisted, a tradition particularly strong in MUZ. In 1974–75 the ZCTU and some national unions elected new, younger leaders who were critical of the excessively close relationship between the ZCTU and the UNIP and articulated a more vigorous assertion of union interests. In 1974 Newstead Zimba, then-president of ZNUT, was elected as ZCTU secretary-general. In 1975 Frederick Chiluba, then head of the building workers union (NUBEGW), was elected ZCTU chairman-general. Though still pro-UNIP, Zimba and Chiluba provided strong leadership insistent on worker-union interests until 1991, when they led the MMD in elections to oust the UNIP government. Zimba was critical of past ZCTU leaders and thought they had demonstrated insufficient commitment to workers' interests. In particular, the ZCTU had failed to support the teachers/ZNUT strike in 1970 until after teachers' union leaders were arrested. He regarded the prior ZCTU leadership as too deferential to UNIP, with many interested in obtaining UNIP political appointments (Akwetey 1994, 50). The new ZCTU leadership had the effect of greatly strengthening ZCTU autonomy from the ruling party by strongly asserting workers' interests when they came into conflict with UNIP government policies in 1975–90. This would reoccur as new ZCTU and other union leaders elected in the late 1990s, and afterward, threw off MMD influence, reasserted union autonomy, and acted militantly in behalf of workers' concerns.

Trained leaders, an educated and numerically strong workforce, regular funding from dues-paying members, and a legally imposed decision-making framework further enhanced the ZCTU's capabilities. All these qualities together engendered a feeling of organizational autonomy and a belief in the capability of the ZCTU to defend distinct workers' interests from those of the party-state.

The situation steadily generated opposition, confrontation, and repression in UNIP-ZCTU relations, as the national economy receded into a crisis that grew worse from the mid-1970s onward. In the period between 1974 and 1989, copper export revenue fell sharply. It accounted for 90 to 95 percent of the foreign exchange earnings of Zambia's parastatal dominated economy. The "total real earnings from copper declined by some 73 percent" between 1973 and 1984 (Loxley 1994, 137). The economy steadily declined. The shortfall in government export revenue accelerated in the face of mounting import bills for manufactured goods, fuels, food items, and fertilizers. Import shortages developed. Serious distortions were thus produced in both the industrial and the agricultural sectors, leaving the government unable to implement its 1972–75 development plan.

In response to the escalating crisis, the government approached the International Monetary Fund (IMF) and agreed to enforce austerity measures in the economy as one of the conditions of the IMF's sponsored "stand-by arrangement." Between 1973 and 1988 the government agreed to a total of six such IMF "stand-by arrangements" and one "extended fund facility." Each was aimed at facilitating access to IMF loans and future donor aid, which could offset the balance of payments deficits. Each successive agreement incorporated more and more conditionalities, covering devaluation, wage freezes, slashes in government spending and borrowing, liberalization of import-export trade, decontrolling domestic prices, and cutting subsidies on consumable goods. Because of the adverse social impact of these measures, especially on vulnerable middle- and lower-income groups, mass mobilization of opposition seemed likely. The government, for its part, felt vulnerable to disturbances that could potentially undermine political stability and its authority. This put organized workers' support for UNIP's austerity measures on the spot. Support could enhance the political legitimacy of government austerity measures; opposition could create a legitimization crisis.

The government took the ZCTU's preparedness to support its measures for granted. Thus, it expected trade union leaders to either directly influence their members' support for the policies or at least to acquiesce in their implementation. Within the party-state regime, UNIP considered itself to be the superior social and political organization. Thus, UNIP regarded all other organizations as subordinate to the party; they should obey directives to support party and government policies. Instead, the ZCTU publicly voiced opposition to the economic austerity measures. This clearly responded to rank-and-file sentiments and interests. ZCTU leaders argued that stabilization measures like the reduction of subsidies on imported maize, the liberalization of prices, and the wage freeze would not affect all Zambians equally. Unionized workers would be the losers since the government's development policies had thus far increased income inequality and widened the gap between the low-income workers and the politicians, businessmen, and bureaucrats. ZCTU leaders believed that the IMF austerity measures would only promote "a capitalist way of life," not humanism and equality, values that Zambia's president, Kenneth Kaunda, had articulated.

Zambia's many accords with the IMF for stabilization plans or SAPs led to increased levels of national union and ZCTU resistance to government policies and the launching of protests and strikes. The ZCTU understood that the interests of workers were distinct from those of the UNIP government. Table 5.1 on strikes in Zambia indicates that the number of strikes—127 to 159 per year—was quite high during 1969–71, though the number of strikers and days lost to strikes were not so high. The 1971 Industrial Relations Act, as noted above, greatly increased government powers to intervene in strikes and to prohibit them altogether in "essential services." It also increased the powers of the ZCTU over its member unions; the government hoped that the ZCTU would help to control strike activity at the rank-and-file level. The crackdown had some initial impact, as there was a large decline in the number of strikes and strikers in 1972–74. However, the adoption of a new stabilization accord

130 • Emmanuel Akwetey and Jon Kraus

with the IMF in 1978 reduced subsidies and increased costs substantially on key consumer goods. It led to union demands for wage increases and a huge increase in the number of workers on strike (up to 42,067) and days lost (see Table 5.1). The UNIP government's expectation of acquiescence from the ZCTU was misplaced.

ZCTU resistance also led in late 1977 to a renewal of UNIP demands that the ZCTU support the government's austerity package since it was subordinate to UNIP—an idea ZCTU leaders resisted then and each time it was raised. Zambia's 1986 SAP involved subsidy reductions, in particular on the food staple, maize meal, budget cutbacks, layoffs, and real wage erosion. The removal of subsidies on maize meal led in November 1986 to widespread demonstrations and then riots in major

Table 5.1 Strikes in Zambia, 1969–97

Years	Number of strikes	Number of strikers	Total work days lost
1969	159	16,944	20,773
1970	128	17,040	122,951
1971	127	14,964	18,894
1972	74	10,453	20,874
1973	68	9,892	6,453
1974	60	7,725	38,334
1975	78	17,121	51,003
1976	59	5,619	6,527
1977	51	9,166	15,990
1978	50	42,067	297,331
1979	44	10,846	42,916
1980	121	28,434	79,896
1981	156	76,776	556,408
1982	39	4,056	7,702
1983	54	9,217	8,170
1984	507	27,750	31,382
1985	50	23,749	66,176
1986	35	5,344	8,932
1987	70	19,437	154,325
1988	39	9,794	51,009
1989	69	19,963	32,173
1990	103	51,606	219,375
1991	102	31,788	258,061
1992	91	25,658	110,713
1993	31	9,581	23,568
1994	35	13,165	37,266
1995	24	8,228	24,226
1996	36	10,606	37,148
1997	60	20,513	81,707

Source: ILO Labor Statistics, online, http://laborsta.ilo.org/cgi-bin/brokerv8.exe.

cities and on the copper belt, where workers joined in. The UNIP government retracted the withdrawal of the subsidy. Others aspects of the SAP led to an explosion of strikes in 1987, with huge increase in strikers and days lost (see Table 5.1).

In 1980–81 the UNIP government had attempted a local government reform, which in the copper-belt townships merged the social facilities (health, education) offered by the mines with those of the local governments. The unions involved—MUZ and ZULAWU—strongly resisted this merger because they believed that it would reduce the significant social services provided by the mines. When the government went ahead anyway against ZCTU opposition, the ZCTU ordered that its local union leaders not participate in the elections, which only UNIP members could contest. The ZCTU suspended these union officials who went ahead and contested the elections. UNIP's Central Committee harshly attacked ZCTU leaders. It dismissed the union leaders from the party, saying that they had also lost their union positions, since only UNIP members could hold such posts. It then arrested ZCTU President Chiluba and Secretary-General Zimba as well as MUZ leaders. Mineworkers on the copper belt broke out in a spontaneous strike and local government, postal, and bank workers joined them. It almost became a general strike (Akwetey 1994, 58). This was the largest outbreak of strikes and strikers since independence (see Table 5.1). The government had to release the union leaders from jail and to drop the merger of the social services of the mines and townships.

These protests and strikes encouraged the ZCTU and its unions to perceive their interests as distinct and to resist the government by the sheer size of the strikes and their economic significance. The state's inability to quell these protests and rank-and-file support for the unions and their leadership enabled the ZCTU to act autonomously and to resist government policies. The unions were the only effective opposition in a one-party state.

Job losses through redundancies linked to the austerity measures appeared to support the ZCTU's arguments. According to Loxley, between 1975 and 1990 there was a 4 percent drop in employment that translated into a 10 percent decline in the membership of the unions (1994, 137). Growing threats to workers' pay and job security, as well as losses in the union revenue derived from the dues paid to the ZCTU, only intensified the ZCTU's critical voice and opposition to the stand-by agreements. The ZCTU also attributed its refusal to acquiesce to the austerity program to the exclusion of ZCTU leaders from the stabilization policy-making process. Economic stabilization decision making involved only IMF experts and a "cross-section of senior civil servants and national politicians" (Callaghy 1989; Gerzel, 1984). UNIP did not accept the trade unions' claim to separate representation in the policy-making process since, it believed, it represented all Zambians.

Consequently, the government ignored ZCTU protests against exclusion and proceeded to implement the stand-by agreements of 1973, 1976–77, and 1978–80 in defiance of trade union protests. In response to persistent ZCTU opposition and strikes such as those in 1987–88 (see Table 5.1), the government proposed a number of measures aimed at controlling the ZCTU. An attempt was made to formally integrate the ZCTU with the party through an amendment of the UNIP constitution. The proposal aimed to facilitate direct political and administrative control over the trade union leaders. It would enable the party to appoint such leaders and hold them accountable to UNIP leaders rather than the unionized workers. The ZCTU opposed the proposal and argued that it was a voluntary "trades" association that was completely independent of the party in terms of its "restricted membership" functions. It effectively resisted all attempts to "dilute" the professional character of trade unions by transforming them into a mass organization subordinate to the party. The proposal was shelved in 1978 but revived in the late 1980s.

In the meantime, trade union opposition to government economic policies persisted and even extended to other sectors, such as the local government reforms of 1980 (Akwetey 1994; Liatto 1989). Clearly, as opposition to economic policies and local government persisted, UNIP and the government no longer perceived the trade unions in terms of "support or acquiescence" to government development programs. Rather, the ZCTU was increasingly seen as the illegal "opposition" in the party-state that must be either controlled or crushed. In the period between 1982 and 1989, repressive measures were carried out to tackle the "political threat" posed by opposition trade unionists, ranging from intimidation in public and routine arrests and detentions to the political co-optation of outspoken trade unionists. Invariably, these administrative measures proved ineffective because ZCTU officials devised a variety of strategies of evasion, and they successfully mobilized sympathetic international support for their side. However, matters came to a head in the late 1980s when the UNIP government decided to enhance its measures of control by threatening to unilaterally amend the 1971 Industrial Relations Act or, failing that, to abolish the ZCTU (Akwetey 1994).

In 1988 the government decided to amend the act by submitting proposals that aimed to break up the ZCTU by amending the mandatory rules of affiliation that had required unions to belong to the ZCTU. Since it failed to win the support of both the ZCTU and the Zambian Federation of Employers (ZFE), the proposal was shelved for two years. In early 1990, however, the government revived the issue of amending the 1971 Industrial Relations Act. This time the government decided to circumvent joint ZCTU and ZFE opposition by using the UNIP-controlled parliament to enact the amendment bill into law. Trade union leaders then concluded that the new legislation was designed to destroy the organizational cohesion of the unionized workers. Consequently, the ZCTU moved to open advocacy and agitation for democratic political change.

Transition to Formal Political Democracy (1990–91)

On New Year's eve 1990, the ZCTU issued a statement calling for the restoration of multiparty politics in Zambia and declaring its intention to campaign in support of such a reform. That declaration initiated the democratization process that quickly progressed from the phase of political liberalization to the inauguration of a new liberal democratic constitution in November 1991. By openly undertaking to lead a campaign for political liberalization, the ZCTU ruptured its relations with UNIP. ZCTU officials openly contested not only the legitimacy of the party-state but also the basis of the labor organization's relations with UNIP. ZCTU leaders argued in 1990 that the subsequent evolution of the relationship from its early anticolonial links with UNIP had been shaped much more by the "progressive" impact of public policies on workers than by any formal obligations. Once the trade unions felt that the policies of the government were not progressive enough and did not enhance material benefits for the workers, unions were free to end the alliance.

The ZCTU also maintained that cooperation in the era of the nationalist campaign was shaped by a common interest in terminating colonial rule and securing independence. There had been no formal agreement on the specific development objectives. In the absence of a formal contract of relations, they did not feel obliged to associate with UNIP when the party no longer served workers' interests. The future roles of the labor organization could no longer be determined merely on the basis of historical relations with a ruling party.

Civil Society Coalition for Political Liberalization

By mid-1990, the initiative taken by the ZCTU to campaign for the restoration of multiparty politics in Zambia had expanded into a mass movement that attracted businessmen and women, disaffected UNIP members, university lecturers, clergymen, traditional rulers, and leaders from an array of occupational- and community-based associations. Widespread support of the campaign facilitated the emergence of a coalition for democratic political change that called itself the Movement for Multiparty Democracy (MMD). It was constituted in July 1990 by business leaders, church leaders, intellectuals, ex-ministers, and disaffected UNIP members, together with the leaders of the ZCTU (Mbikusita-Lewanika et al. 1990). The shared objective of this group was for a peaceful political change. But beyond that, each of them had specific interests whose practical realization required organizational capabilities that none of the actors alone could adequately provide.

The Zambian business community, the "unofficial bourgeoisie," had earlier felt the pinch of the donor suspension of funds in 1987–89. But they stood to benefit from the market-oriented reforms of the 1989 stabilization program, which gave greater scope to private capital and enterprise. It provided no assurance in the long-term, however, that external funding would be forthcoming if the one-party state regime remained in office.

Kaunda's abrogation of the 1989 IMF accord, under pressure, led bilateral donors and the IMF to begin to perceive the government as weak, lacking in the political resolve to implement stabilization measures. Their loss of confidence in the ability of the government to deliver on its international economic obligations further aggravated the Kaunda regime's image within the domestic business community. Donors hardened their attitude toward the government on the issue of its debt service obligations. Zambia's financial situation seemed hopeless, intensifying pressures for change.

With its total debt in 1991 approximating US $8 billion, and the debt service ratio (debt service/exports) recorded at 105 percent, there developed a widespread belief that a political change of government was necessary to obtain external credits and donor grants (Mwanakatwe 1994, 30). The political mood in civil society suggests that anything short of changing both the government and the party-state regime would be highly unacceptable. Peaceful change depended not only on the government's recognition of formal political opposition and attendant civil and political liberties but also on the value the opposition attached to peaceful campaigning and electoral contests. The role of church leaders was at this specific conjuncture highly critical. They intervened in conflicts over general election dates and recommendations of the Mvunga Constitutional Commission, and they facilitated the resolution of issues. But it was the ZCTU that brought its huge organizational capabilities to bear decisively on the mobilization of electoral support for the MMD.

Leading the MMD

The ZCTU commanded the organized support of more than three hundred thousand unionized workers based in the urban townships. That number could decisively translate into a block vote that could win elections. In addition to the membership capability, ZCTU leader Chiluba was widely known and generally regarded among Zambian politicians as the uncorrupted "Mr. Clean." That made him a leader acceptable to a wider constituency of Zambians. Trade union leaders enjoyed the support and protective advocacy of international labor organizations like the International Labor Organization ILO and the International Confederation of Free Trade Unions (ICFTU). Finally, the long resistance to UNIP political control had taught ZCTU unions useful lessons in public campaigning. Compared to the other members of the coalition, the organizational capabilities of the ZCTU were immense and could be mobilized quickly. What the other actors lacked in organizational and popular support, the ZCTU could provide. But compared to the financial clout of UNIP, the financial resources of the ZCTU were minimal. Finance was the greatest asset used by Zambian business interests to complement the ZCTU's limited funding of the MMD's campaigns.

Defectors from UNIP, some of whom were previous cabinet ministers, also contributed the knowledge required to anticipate and influence decisions within UNIP's leadership at a time when the party was declining. Together with the intellectual input made by university lecturers, the experienced politicians who defected from UNIP provided the cutting-edge strategies adopted by the MMD to control the trajectory of the transition to formal political democracy. It was the complex interplay of these collective efforts that contributed to the victory of the MMD over UNIP in the October 1991 elections. Thus, it would be inaccurate to claim that the ZCTU played the sole or indispensable role in bringing about political liberalization and the inauguration of the new democratic regime in Zambia. Nonetheless, the mobilization presence of the ZCTU within the pro-democracy movement was tremendous. The ZCTU joined the alliance as the most coherently organized and unified political force backing Chiluba's candidature for the MMD presidency and the presidency of Zambia. A charismatic alternative to Kaunda, Chiluba was the leader who pulled "over 100,000 people" to mass rallies for multipartyism (Bratton and van de Walle 1992, 429). Union grievances with the government and employers were also expressed in an explosion of strikes, which increased by 49 percent between 1989 and 1990. The number of people who went on strike rose by 153 percent, and the days lost to strikes increased by 581 percent (see Table 5.1). Strikes and days lost remained at the 1990 levels in 1991, the only time in the last twenty-five years that days lost to strikes exceeded two hundred thousand two years in a row. Kaunda's flagging government could not stop the surge of strikes and protests. The intensity of the MMD campaigns and divisions within UNIP weakened the government's ability to mobilize comparable political support against the movement for democratic change. But at each stage, Kaunda's UNIP government was reluctant to give up the prerogatives of one-party rule. UNIP introduced a variety of delaying tactics to stave off the momentum for democratic institutions. In mid-1991, the government gave up on the idea of submitting the question of restoring multiparty politics in Zambia to a national referendum. It later reached agreement with the MMD over the electoral register and the date for the general election. This enabled Zambia's first multiparty general elections since 1969 to be held on October 31, 1991. The MMD won by a landslide, and Chiluba was elected president. He took over the presidency from Kaunda immediately.

After the Transition and toward Union Renewal (1991–Present)

In the five years after the formal transition to democracy, the ZCTU shifted from the mobilization role it had played in support of the MMD. By 1995–96, the labor organization not only stood apart from the MMD but also was actually opposed to the economic reform programs of that government. Looking divided and effectively weakened, the ZCTU no longer appeared to constitute the political force that initiated and led the pro-democracy movement. It had failed to attain the major organizational and political goals that had earlier informed and shaped its opposition campaign against the UNIP regime. How and why did the ZCTU and the organized labor movement become the loser in Zambia's post-transition democratization and economic reform processes?

By the period between the late 1990s and 2006, however, the ZCTU and many of its national unions had elected new leaders who were not nearly as cooperative with, or intimidated by, the MMD government of President Frederick Chiluba or his successor in 2000, Levy Mwanawasa, as were the union leaders during 1991–97. As in the 1974–75 period, the democratic elections of new leaders expressed the will of union leaders and rank and file to assert the autonomy of union interests more forcefully. Indeed, the split of major unions from the ZCTU in 1994 constituted a decisive vote of no confidence in the ZCTU's continued support for the MMD government, under whom unions had suffered dearly. The union movement was now more divided than in the period between 1985 and 1990 and had lost many members through extensive layoffs. It had also lost the leadership of a key union, the MUZ, which was hit most severely by the dismissals. The 1994 split in the union movement, which also led to the splintering of many unions, was only partly healed after 1995–96. But three of the four major unions that had left ZCTU rejoined it in 1999. And the ZCTU, along with the other union federation, the Federation of Free Trade Unions of Zambia (FFTUZ), recovered much of the ZCTU's former independence and militance, challenging repeatedly the MMD government on SAPs, nonaccountability, neglected wage claims, and violations of labor agreements. What factors explain this renewal of union strength and strikes, and has that renewal contributed to democracy in Zambia?

The ZCTU and Market Economic Reforms

First, what factors explain the relative decline of ZCTU and its influence under the MMD government in 1991–96 and after? Prior to the elections, Chiluba and his ZCTU colleagues argued that adding value to workers' real incomes, ensuring job security, and creating more jobs required policies that attracted foreign private investment. The hard choice, Chiluba argued, had to be made between economic recovery and continued economic decline. In his view, "economic restoration is restoration of our salaries and wages" (Chanda 1993, 24–27). As president and leader of the MMD government, Chiluba implored ZCTU's leaders to seek to represent the "true interests of workers" within the broader national interest (Chanda 1993, 26). He argued that workers, "like everybody else," have to take their share of the collective sacrifice to promote Zambia's economic recovery through growth, management efficiency, and development. Thus, he expected the ZCTU and unionized workers to support the MMD and the implementation of its economic reform program.

The labor movement sympathized with the difficulties Chiluba faced in his task to "revive the economy" after years of mismanagement (Alexander 1993, 13). He had to fulfill the conditionalities of the IMF and the World Bank loans while simultaneously managing domestic economic and social pressures. That sympathy posed "an acute strategic dilemma" to the post-election ZCTU leaders (Alexander 1993). They had to decide on how long organized labor should support the MMD's economic recovery program and how unfavorable aspects of the program could be criticized in public. Early criticism, in Alexander's opinion, could be viewed as undermining the MMD government, while speaking out later could similarly weaken rank-and-file confidence in union leadership. The challenge was how to sustain support for the government through constructive criticism without undermining government trust and workers' confidence in the ZCTU leadership.

Meeting the challenge, in practice, initially required the ZCTU to reverse itself to support the broad array of market-oriented policies that the union movement had consistently opposed since 1975. Even if supporting government policies was the logical choice for the ZCTU as part of the MMD, and whose immediate past leader was now Zambia's president, such a decision had practical consequences. Would support for government economic policies affect the organizational autonomy of the ZCTU from the ruling party in which ex-ZCTU leaders held high offices? And how would opposition affect access to key decision-making processes and influence over decisions?

Initially, the new union leadership decided to support the government's economic programs by practically refraining from public criticism. In December 1991, the MMD government began to implement the stabilization package of its SAP with great speed and enthusiasm. There is no evidence of ZCTU engagement in the funding negotiations with the World Bank and IMF. In its determination to reduce inflation from its peak level of 191 percent in 1991, the MMD government announced in early 1992 the removal of food subsidies, liberalization of export and import trade, restrictions of public sector wage increases, abolition of all tax-free allowances, and curtailment in public expenditures. In response, the ZCTU attempted to control unionized workers' opposition to the measures. It did so by cautioning "union members to avoid going on strike as management may either send them on early retirement or dismiss them" (Simutanyi 1995). Then, when the government authorized the retrenchment of workers, the ZCTU issued guidelines to the affiliate unions on how to conduct negotiations on labor redundancies and secure fair redundancy packages (ZCTU 1993). Still, there were many strikes and days lost in 1992 in response to these measures. The government's pressures led to a sharp fall in strikes, strikers, and days lost in 1993 to 1996.

Although systematic stabilization measures had a negative impact on workers' job security and living conditions, it was the impact of the retrenchment policy and privatization that decisively awoke the ZCTU to the dangers inherent in its silent support of the government's economic policies. During May 1990 to May 1994, drastic retrenchment of workers in so-called distressed public sectors such as construction, transport, mining, and finance caused internal rifts within the ZCTU. Members of the affected sector unions became restive and voiced criticisms. But the ZCTU leadership's silence discouraged them from public action. More than thirty-eight thousand workers, or 10 percent of the ZCTU's membership in 1992, lost their jobs between 1992 and 1995 in the toughly implemented retrenchments.

As thousands of workers were laid off, trade union membership also declined, as did the revenues accruing to the ZCTU from the dues paid by its affiliated unions. Such effects raised questions over why the ZCTU supported the MMD's economic programs when its immediate constituency of unionized workers had only suffered losses rather than benefits in employment, wages, and welfare services. The inability of ZCTU to deliver goods valued by union members undermined its authority and its mobilization capabilities. In an attempt to reclaim its lost authority and trust with its members, the ZCTU leadership took a more critical stance against the policies of the MMD government. In October 1992, the ZCTU shifted from its policy of tacit support for the government's economic policies to a critical, nonpartisan relationship with the MMD. It had decided, it said, to engage constructively but critically in the democratic and development processes because of the lack of democratic consultation and deliberation in the making of orthodox "SAP policies." These were affecting "workers and other vulnerable groups," with "no apparent regard to issues of employment and labor incomes" except "over-concentration on the profit motive" (ZCTU QC/D No. 1, October 26–29, 1994, 5). The ZCTU later intensified its criticism of economic policies when the government launched its privatization programs. The ZCTU observed critically that privatization "may not be a panacea to the poor performance of the parastatal sector." And government seemed to be in a hurry to privatize state-owned enterprises even where firms were not ready for privatization.

ZCTU said that unrestrained privatization had "brought a lot of anxiety to enterprises and greatly affected operations since both managers and workers feel uncertain about their future" (ZCTU QC/D No. 1, October 26–29, 1994, 6). ZCTU questions suggested that the cost of privatization was too high. But the ZCTU was even more concerned that care had not been taken to secure the success of privatized enterprises after they had been massively undervalued and sold (ZCTU File, January 18, 1996). Still, the ZCTU did not reject the MMD's privatization program. Rather, it argued that practical solutions to the problems should be found through open consultation among the social partners (ZCTU File, January 18, 1996).

The MMD government and President Chiluba did not take kindly to the ZCTU's growing critical stance toward their economic policies. Hence, they reacted by freezing direct contact between the organization and the presidency. Throughout 1993, Chiluba avoided all contact with the most outspoken leader of the ZCTU, Chairman-General Fackson Shamenda. So, like the predecessor UNIP government, the MMD government found it more convenient and punitive to isolate and insulate spheres of policy making from the critical ZCTU leadership.

The MMD government's isolation of the ZCTU leadership coincided with negotiations on amendments to the Industrial and Labor Relations (ILR) Act that UNIP had legislated in 1990. When the negotiations ended, the MMD government, the Zambian Federation of Employers (ZFE), and the ZCTU had agreed on changes that had unequal effects on the three parties. In the new ILR Act enacted in 1993, both mandatory unionization of workers and compulsory dues check-off were abolished. Conflict-resolution procedures, including compulsory arbitration, were likewise adopted. Collective bargaining was institutionalized, and a new tripartite body, the Tripartite Consultative Labor Council (TCLC), was set up. The greatest prize that the government and business extracted from labor was the agreement to restrict the workers' right to strike and to ban inter-sector solidarity strikes. Like the economic recovery measures, the ZCTU's negotiated concessions in the ILR Act have had an adverse long-term effect on the ZCTU. The introduction of voluntary unionization and dues subscription enabled individual workers to leave the unions and for sector unions to disaffiliate with the ZCTU. Hence, when workers felt disappointed with the ZCTU's support for the economic stabilization measures of 1991–93, they quietly made their exit, thereby causing further decline in membership and revenue to the ZCTU.

Dissent, Division, and Decline

By 1994 the disappointment of sections of Zambian trade unions was gradually translating itself into open rebellion or rifts within the ZCTU. The disappointed unionists questioned the wisdom in the ZCTU's political support for the MMD's economic reforms. They also doubted the intentions underlying some of the concessions given to government and business in the renegotiation of the ILR Act. Internal disputes over the concessions made in the new act (1993) eventually split the ZCTU in November 1994. Financial sector workers were the first to experience the folly of the ZCTU leadership's compromise of the right of workers to organize inter-sector solidarity strikes. In late 1993, five hundred bank workers went on strike in an attempt to resolve an impasse of wage increases and conditions of service. The government swiftly dismissed all the workers, arguing that they had not complied with the dispute resolution procedures of the 1993 ILR act. When the government tried to rescind its decisions, the Zambian Union of Financial Institutions and Allied Workers (ZUFIAW), with 11,700 members (1989), called for solidarity strikes to compel a more favorable response from the government.

The ZCTU leadership's support, however, was critical if solidarity strikes were to take effect. But declaring such a strike would have been illegal under Section 78 of the 1993 ILR Act, which stipulated that workers could not go on a solidarity strike "unless the union agrees with the employer." So instead of leading a solidarity strike, the ZCTU opted for a judicial resolution of the dispute. It offered to engage lawyers to defend workers who petitioned against their dismissal in the courts. As this approach turned out to be drawn out and ineffectual, ZUFIAW raised its voice against the ZCTU leadership. It accused ZCTU leaders of "remaining silent over the matter [dismissals] instead of coordinating with other unions to save the sacked workers through solidarity action" (ZCTU File, January 18, 1996, 8). Unionized workers called for Section 78 to be scrapped. Lack of progress on this issue intensified the feeling that the ZCTU had failed to provide the leadership for dealing effectively with the MMD government. For national unions that had been severely affected by the government's economic and labor policies, the ZCTU's preferred approach to relations with the MMD government had clearly failed and backfired. Rather than participating in government policy making, the ZCTU looked more marginalized than it had ever been.

The obvious failure was compelling enough to motivate other national unions to make claims to the powerful positions within the ZCTU, that is, the posts of chairman-general and secretary-general. In 1994 four sector unions that together accounted for 46.8 percent of the total membership of unionized workers decided to challenge the incumbent holders of the two key positions. These unions were MUZ (mineworkers, historically the most powerful union), ZNUT (teachers), NUCIW (commercial and industrial workers), and ZUFIAW (banks). Despite their numerical strength, the four unions failed to get their preferred candidates elected at the 9th Quadrennial Congress of the ZCTU, held in late October 1994. After losing the elections, they declared their joint disaffiliation with the ZCTU. Some suggested that the organizations involved were merely "bad losers" of the democratic elections.

However, it is important not to lose sight of the linkage between the disaffiliation and the crisis of leadership that unfolded within the ZCTU after Chiluba and other union leaders joined the MMD government. Chiluba, Zimba, and Sampa led the ZCTU for nearly two decades, holding the positions of chairman-general, secretary-general, and deputy secretary-general (Finance), respectively. Indeed, so entrenched were they in these positions that their departure enabled all eight of the positions on the ZCTU Executive Board to be contested—for the first time since 1974—at the 1994 Quadrennial Congress. Chiluba and Zimba had symbolized both the organizational coherence of the ZCTU and the effectiveness of confrontational strategy in its relations with the UNIP government. Their leadership style had been specifically personal, yet relevant to the circumstances of the party-state regime under which they operated. Thus, their departure created a leadership vacuum. The legacy of precedents and experience they bequeathed increasingly appeared to be inadequate for making an effective response to the challenges of the post-UNIP era.

The limitations of the leadership culture of the party-state era showed clearly also in the nature of the MMD government's own response to the critical position taken by the ZCTU leaders. As the ZCTU claimed the right "to question and contest certain government decisions that affected the life of workers and the vulnerable in society," Chiluba and the MMD government decided to isolate the ZCTU leaders from their rank-and-file members (ZCTU Files, October 1992 and January 1996). However, acts of direct political intervention remained discreet until the elections of the Quadrennial Conference in 1994.

Officials of two of the "dissenting" national unions, MUZ and NUCIW, alleged that MMD Minister for Labor and Social Security Zimba and his deputy, Golden Mandandi, openly campaigned for the reelection of the incumbent ZUTC office-holders, Chairman-General Shamenda and Secretary-General Chirwa. However, followers of Shamenda and Chirwa also claimed that President Chiluba and Minister of Interior Sampa actively encouraged Kunda of MUZ and Alikipo of ZUFIAW to challenge Shamenda and Chirwa for their respective positions. The officials involved have rejected the specific allegations against them. But it could be inferred from both the allegations and the apparent confusion over which side was actually supported by the MMD government that there may have been no coherent strategy. Still, since the factious unions announced their disaffiliation from the ZTCU, the government initially withheld formal recognition of the breakaway unions. Their attempt to register a rival trade union center, called the "Confederation of Free Trade Unions [of Zambia]" in early 1995 failed because the 1993 ILR Act provided only for the ZCTU and did not recognize or approve of the existence of a rival center (*Times of Zambia*, August 9, 1995).

The government initially resisted calls for the act to be amended to enable another trade union center to be registered, though this occurred eventually. The MMD government was determined not to make life easy for unions that broke away from the ZCTU on the grounds of excessive MMD government influence over the unions and intervention in the ZCTU elections. Frustrated but determined to succeed, the fractious unions registered a Federation of Free Trade Unions (FFTUZ) under the Societies Act (Chapter 105) in January 1996. But the FFTUZ could not initially function as a trade union unless its registration was recognized under the ILR Act of 1993. From 1994 to 1999, the ZCTU was clearly divided and both financially and organizationally weakened by the split. Having lost membership and influence over the unionized workers of Zambia, it risked a further loss in influence as a formidable source of opposition to government policies.

The MMD government's successful initial implementation of the economic recovery program strengthened donor and IMF/World Bank support for these programs. Growing external funding, and deepening dependence of the MMD government on that facility, constituted a great constraint on the ability of the ZCTU or rival trade unions to influence government economic decisions. Growth in the external funding accessible to the government usually enhances the relative autonomy of the state and insulates economic decision makers and policy processes from domestic political pressures (Herbst 1993).

The Renewal of Trade Union Opposition and Protests

The MMD government was highly successful in developing a series of lending programs with the aid of the IMF and the World Bank, including Extended Structural

Adjustment Facilities (ESAF) loans and Poverty Reduction and Growth Facility (PRGF) loans. In exchange for carrying out the extensive tariff, foreign currency, and labor market liberalization measures and privatization of the state sector, these loans were supposed to help finance economic renewal in Zambia. Despite the inflow of a certain amount of foreign aid from the IMF, the World Bank, and foreign governments, the economic reform program has been a massive failure in Zambia, judged by the economic performance during 1990 to 2002, or thereabouts. The growing immisseration of blue- and white-collar workers, the rising unemployment, the falling real wages and living standards, and the nonresponsiveness of successive MMD governments have fueled the mounting opposition of the major Zambian unions and the union federations, ZCTU and FFTUZ. For some years the national union and ZCTU leaders listened to the pleas of Chiluba's government to give it a chance, to make sacrifices for future economic progress. But the future never came. As ZCTU's president in 2002, Leonard Hikaumba, observed: "They wanted people to sacrifice, and we agreed, all of us. That sacrifice . . . to give [a] chance to the Government was . . . perceived as a weakness, because even on things that we could have fought against in the previous administration, we allowed them to go" (Larmer 2005, 38).

It was not only the cumulative evidence of economic distress and failure that led over the years to the development of persistent ZCTU and FFTUZ opposition to government measures. It was also the rising evidence of government corruption and the breaking of faith with the unions in the matter of mines privatization, which led to collapse of rather than growth in parts of the copper sector. Ultimately, it was the renewal of union leadership in the ZCTU and some national unions—as occurred in 1974 and 1975—which revived a consistent critical stance toward the MMD government and a willingness to support opposition political parties in their quests to oust the MMD government in elections in 2000 and after.

The evidence of economic failure of the MMD government and of IMF/World Bank/Western reform programs has been overwhelming. Despite the implementation of massive "reforms" at the behest of the IMF and the World Bank, real gross domestic product (GDP) per capita fell by 20.3 percent between 1990 and 1995 and by 12.6 percent between 1990 and 2000. Real domestic income fell by 31.9 percent between 1990 and 2000. Government share of real domestic income fell from 41.8 percent in 1990 to 10.2 percent in 2000 (Situmbeko and Zulu 2004, 36). This reflected a collapse in government capacity to provide public services. The whole economy continued to shrink for some years. One of the earliest measures, the removal of subsidies on maize, led to higher prices and an erosion of living standards. This, plus the removal of subsidies on fertilizer, did not lead to any significant increases in agricultural production, however. A 2000 World Bank study accepted that the removal of subsidies on maize and fertilizer under the IMF/World Bank program led to "stagnation and regression instead of helping Zambia's agricultural sector" (cited in Situmbeko and Zulu 2004, 34). As a result, wage employment in agriculture fell from eighty thousand in 1990 to a mere fifty thousand in 2000. The devaluation of the Zambian currency to reflect market rates should, presumably, have expanded exports, but exports as a percent of GDP fell from 36 percent in 1990 to 27 percent in 2000. This is explained partly by the low world price of copper and partly by the incompetent and probably corrupt ways in which part of the state copper company was privatized (Larmer 2005, 32–37). The privatization of the Zambia Consolidated Cooper Mines (ZCCM) between 1997 and 2000 severely delegitimated the privatization process in the eyes of Zambians and the trade unions. They had gone along with it in the hopes of reinvestment and renewal. The Luanshya mine complex was sold not to a major copper company but to a London firm in commodities trading. It breached its agreement with the state and unions, closed down social service facilities, laid off workers, and refused to pay "terminal benefits." When MUZ raised the issue in 1998 with the management of RAMCoZ (the new firm), management sacked the MUZ branch chairman, which led to a major eight-day strike by six thousand workers. That strike was violently put down by the security forces. The stink of betrayal and corruption, with reputed regular RAMCoZ payoffs to the MMD, undermined the MMD government and created MUZ member discontent with its leadership (Larmer 2005, 35–36).

The various liberalizations of foreign currency, trade, and labor markets did not generate the entry of new productive forces. Despite the privatization of 257 state firms between 1994 and 2001, most do not seem to have been turned into effective private enterprises. This did not reduce, however, IMF/World Bank/Western country zealous insistence, on pain of withdrawal of aid, for even further privatizations in 2002 to 2005. Direct foreign investment inflows *fell* from the pre-reform 1990 level of $203 million to $97 million in 1995 and to $122 million in 2000. And some of that, as in the case of RAMCoZ "investment" in the Luanshya mine complex, led to asset stripping, unpaid debt to state electricity and other utilities, and bankruptcy. The extraordinary IMF/World Bank–imposed reduction and "rationalization" of tariffs has led directly to undermining Zambia's remaining industry, as would be utterly predictable when existing industry was operating at low levels of capacity utilization. Formal sector manufacturing employment fell from 75,400 in 1991 to 43,320 in 2001, while paid employment in mining and manufacturing together tumbled by 41.5 percent, from 140,000 in 1991 to 83,000 in 2000 (Situmbeko and Zulu 2004, 33). All of this lost formal sector employment had a huge effective drag on economic demand and growth, while reducing drastically the number of trade unionists. Even the Human Development Index (HDI) declined in Zambia: slightly, between 1980 and 1990, and then sharply, between 1990 and 2001, from .461 to .386. Zambia's position in the HDI ranking of countries fell from 130th of 170 in 1990 to 163rd of 175, while life expectancy plummeted from 54.4 years to 33.4 (partly because of AIDS).

The only thing that is absolutely certain is that no democratic government, which has to be responsive to its citizens, could possibly have conceived and carried out an economic program of such destructiveness. As Finance Minister N'gandu Magande explained, "We are running the country but the budget is controlled by the donors" (Larmer 2005 42). It was not just the budget, however, but also the shape and extent of major macroeconomic and sector programs that were extensively determined by the donors. It was not so much the democratically elected government as the IMF and the World Bank policy makers who designed and imposed these policies, even if the MMD government enacted them. Over time, the MMD governments have been more reluctant to carry out "reforms" as protests, strikes, and confrontations with unionists, civic groups, and other protesters have occurred.

The sources of the renewal of trade union strikes and confrontations with the MMD government also originated in the souring of the democratic promise renewed with such enthusiasm and expectations in 1990–91. By 2001, after ten years of Zambia's new democracy, the government had had two sets of declarations of states of emergency (targeting the political opposition); two deeply flawed and controversial national elections that reduced competition (1996 and 2001); violence against political opposition members; manipulation of promises of constitutional reform; attempts to change the constitution so that President Chiluba could extend his presidency to a third, constitutionally forbidden term; and many efforts to circumscribe the opposition (Simon 2005, 201–5). There has also been some harassment of the media. The weakness and failure of opposition parties to cooperate has reduced challenges to the MMD leaders. Chiluba's attempts to run for a third term involved months of political and party turmoil and, finally, the threat by a third of the members of parliament to impeach him. Yet the opposition could not coalesce behind any candidate. So Mwanawasa, the MMD candidate, won the presidency in 2001 with 29.2 percent of the vote, with the second-place candidate receiving 27 percent, and three dissident MMD candidates receiving, collectively, 21.5 percent (Simon 2005, 206). Moreover, the executive largely dominates all policy making, and this does not include the authoritarian intervention in the democratic elections of ZCTU national leaders in the 1994 and 1998 quadrennial conferences. The government did this in order to keep in power ZCTU leaders relatively friendly to Chiluba and MMD rule.

Still, the democratic changes in the constitution and public life made in 1991 have meant that regular elections do occur, opposition parties are quite active, a private press persists, the Supreme Court is not supine, and important civil society groups are active in political life. These include the bar association, student groups, the churches, the unions, and coalitions of civic groups. These are the mobilizers of active dissent to executive power.

Toward Union Autonomy and Rising Union Militance

How was the union movement—including the ZCTU and FFTUZ—able to increase its relative autonomy to act more forcefully in behalf of its interests than it did in 1991–96? First, it is important to observe that the ZCTU was never under the control of the MMD government, even though three major leaders of the ZCTU went into the MMD government in leading positions, as noted above. Initially, Chiluba, Zimba, and Sampa retained strong relationships with their union successors and played upon the loyalty of union leaders to their ex-leaders. Despite the growing dismay with the impact of economic reforms upon workers, some ZCTU and union leaders continued to give residual support to Chiluba and the MMD. At the same time, the new MMD government demonstrated clearly that it could—and did—reward friends and punish enemies, inside and outside of labor.

Second, pressures from the rank and file at the declining economic conditions and the major retrenchments in the public and private sectors led to reassertions of union autonomy. As noted, in 1994 four major unions seceded from the ZCTU and created a decidedly more oppositionist FFTUZ. This led for some years to schisms within unions—often because of worker discontent with the performance of their leaders in dealing with harsh economic conditions—and the new unions joined FFTUZ. This initially weakened the ZCTU and increased the animosity between the two federations. But it also compelled union leaders, over time, to recognize that if they did not act more militantly in behalf of worker and union interests, they would lose the support of their rank and file to other unions in another federation.

Third, the attempts of the MMD to intervene in ZCTU elections gradually alienated some union members and leaders, led existing leaders to turn back to the union base for support, and ultimately brought new leaders into power, in both the ZCTU and FFTUZ. They were a new generation, not bound to Chiluba loyalists. The interventions in the 1994 elections have been noted. In 1998 some union leaders wanted to contest Facksom Shamenda for president and Sylvester Tembo for secretary-general; both were perceived to be MMD or Chiluba loyalists, despite their criticisms of government policies. Austin Liato, who was ZCTU vice president in 1998, did contest Shamenda for the presidency, as others contested Tembo. The MMD again appears to have used its influence within the ZCTU to ensure the victory of Shamenda and Tembo. The MMD government then punished the challenger, Liato, who was president of the Zambia Electrical and Allied Workers Union (ZEAWU): he was dismissed from his job with the Zambia Electrical Company; the government de-registered ZEAWU; and Liato was also dismissed as minister for the copper belt province (*The Post*, December 9, 2005). While Chiluba supporters remained in power, within the next several years union discontent from below forced the ZCTU union leaders to strike a more independent position. In 1999 this was helped by the return to the ZCTU of three of the four large trade unions that had seceded in 1994: ZNUT (teachers), MUZ (mineworkers), and NUCIW (commercial/industrial workers).

Ultimately, this discontent led to the election of a new and much more militant leadership in the ZCTU and FFTUZ. At the 2002 ZCTU quadrennial conference, Leonard Hikaumba was elected president on a specifically militant platform of trying to prevent the MMD government from engaging in further privatizations. At thirty-eight years old, Hikaumba was a break with the older generation of ZCTU leaders. He had been a student leader at the University of Zambia in the mid-1980s, from which he was expelled for leading protests. He later became president of the large Civil Servants Union of Zambia (CSUZ). Under his leadership CSUZ had a series of strikes: a two-month strike in 2001 led to an 80 percent pay increase (Larmer 2005, 39). Sylvester Tembo was reelected as secretary-general but became markedly more militant in the company of the younger ZCTU leadership. Joyce Nonde was elected secretary-general of the Zambia Union of Financial Institutions and Allied Workers (ZUFIAW) in 1997, a full-time position, and was later elected president of the FFTUZ. Nonde soon emerged as one of Zambia's most outspoken and combative trade union leaders in conflicts with the MMD government and the IMF. She helped to launch the protests against the nationalization of the Zambian National Commercial Bank (ZNCB) and two other state-owned corporations in December 2003, a landmark in forcing the government to reverse, at least temporarily, its compliance with IMF dictates. Nonde complained pointedly about the outrageous salaries of some forty ministers and huge retirement gratuities paid to MPs after a mere three years of work, while the government refused to pay contractual wage increases to civil servants (Pan African News Agency, February 18, 2004). And in mid-2004 she argued that some Zambian leaders who were supposed to advise the government on national programs were, in effect, marketing officers for the IMF and the World Bank (*The Post*, August 10, 2004). In 2005 the MMD government, led by the labor commissioner, launched attacks upon Nonde, as the MMD did in 1998 on Liato, to try to have her removed from her position as secretary-general of ZUFIAW and, barring that, at least to stop her from running for reelection in 2006. The government indicated that it had assembled a team to stop her and her FFTUZ vice president, Teza Nchinga, from contesting any executive office in FFTUZ elections in October 2006. The MMD government clearly wanted Nonde out of office before the MMD itself faced elections for the presidency and National Assembly in 2006 (*The Post*, December 9, 2005).

Past MMD interventions, new union leadership, a protesting rank and file, and debilitating MMD economic policies made the task of reasserting union autonomy much easier.

How can one explain the progressive distancing of the union movement from the MMD as a party and a government and toward a more militant approach to the government? One of the most important factors, as noted, was the growing anger and despair among the rank and file of national unions about the declining standard of living and threats of continuing layoffs. The total formal sector wage labor force had shrunk dramatically, by 13 percent, during the decade of the 1990s; in mining and manufacturing the percentage decline was 41.5.

Second, the MMD government support for intra-union schisms within national unions that led splinter unions to join FFTUZ increased distrust for the MMD and forced national unions and the ZCTU to act more militantly in behalf of union interests. Union militance was necessary in order to retain the loyalty of the rank and file. Part of the escalation in strike threats, strikes, and protests during 2000–2005 was probably due to the need of union leaders to act more militantly. In the period between 2001 and 2005, splinter unions from ZCTU affiliates in the education, mining, broadcasting, and energy sector joined FFTUZ. When the state-owned Zesco thought it found corruption in the ZCTU-affiliated union, Zesco withdrew its recognition from the ZCTU affiliate and recognized a new FFTUZ affiliate. ZCTU President Hikaumba regretted that FFTUZ seemed to be thriving on splits among the ZCTU affiliates.

Third, opposition among civil society groups to the corruption and antidemocratic trends in the MMD government grew in the late 1990s and after, which undoubtedly encouraged the ZCTU unions. The Oasis Forum, which had the support of churches, the bar association, student groups, and trade unions, initiated some protests. On other occasions the ZCTU or FFTUZ initiated protests that were joined by other civil society groups. In 2001 civil society groups and unions had been successful in opposing Chiluba's bid for a third term in office. They later mounted major protests before parliament, demanding that it lift Chiluba's immunity from prosecution to permit investigations of corruption. Parliament and the government conceded to popular pressures and voted to lift his immunity. (Chiluba was convicted by a British court of embezzling $46 million while serving as president of Zambia during 1991–2002. Zambia was still trying to put him on trial in mid-2007). ZUFIAW (financial workers) in FFTUZ and ZCT organized the protests against the privatization of the ZNCB and two other state companies in December 2002; they were joined by opposition parties and civil society groups. When parliament voted against the privatization and the MMD government's policy, the demonstration became a victory celebration. The success of this protest was taken as rewarding militant behavior against government's submission to IMF policies, even if months later the government reversed itself (Larmer 2005, 29). The unions were a major contributor to, and a beneficiary of, the rise in militant protest behavior.

A fourth and major source of rising militant union opposition to the MMD government involved the MMD's continuing acceptance and implementation of economic policies dictated by the IMF, the World Bank, and foreign donors. Only forceful opposition had any impact in interrupting the MMD government's endless implementation of these policies. The gathering strength of pervasive anti–IMF/World Bank sentiment among the attentive public and even MMD members compelled Levy Mwanawasa, elected president in 2001, to begin to speak out in nationalist terms against the IMF and the World Bank. He has talked of the need for Zambians to make their own decisions and has started to rely upon nationalist and moral exhortations to Zambians. In 2003 he said that "[The IMF's privatization program] has been of no significant benefit to the country . . . privatization of crucial state industries has led to poverty, asset stripping, and job losses" (quoted in Situmbeko and Zulu 2004, 25). Still, the MMD government continued to submit to IMF and World Bank ultimatums on major privatizations and on keeping budget deficits to strict limits or else face cut-offs in IMF and World Bank loans. Mwanawasa has pursued this path even though doing so has meant that the state breaks its own collective agreements with unions and fails to pay contractual benefits. This has brought the government into direct and continuous confrontation with the unions during 2002–2006.

The ZCTU and FFTUZ realize that the source of some of their key problems has been IMF/World Bank–dictated government policies. This was clear in the privatizations that led to huge numbers of worker layoffs and in the decisions in 2003 where a direct IMF threat forced the government to go ahead with the partial sale of the state commercial bank that it had just canceled. It was also an explicit IMF ultimatum to the Zambian government that made it renege on a decision in mid-2003 to raise civil servant wages and housing allowances. This in turn led to several years of strike threats, strikes, and demonstrations by civil servants and local government workers. The IMF resident representative bluntly noted publicly in December 2002, "If they don't sell [ZNCB], they will not get the money" (Situmbeko and Zulu 2004, 42). FFTUZ President Nonde correctly argued that the IMF and the World Bank both influence officials at all levels of government with direct payments of salaries, ministerial expenses, and trips and perks. "No domestic constituency can compete with this organized, insider voice lobbying, which has the constant power to cut off loans and loan disbursements and now debt cancellation. . . . There is no sovereignty at all" (*The Post*, August 10, 2004). FFTUZ Vice President Nchinga voiced union distrust when, in 2005, he said that Zambia did not have its own economy; others were running it (*The Post*, January 24, 2005).

The outstanding issues that led to the high levels of protests, strikes, and confrontations with the MMD government between 1999 and 2004 actually involved two sets of issues. One directly involved labor interests and grievances, the second a broader set of concerns animated by Zambia's depressed economy and government behavior. Clearly, the trade unions and their rank and file were most directly aroused by grievances that directly affected their declining standard of living and union rights. These included issues of wages and benefits, privatization and job losses, violations of collective bargaining agreements, IMF and World Bank restrictions, the right to strike and protest, and threats to or actual de-registration of unions. The other set of issues regularly intersected these and engaged the unions because they helped to ensure their rights to exist, to remain autonomous, and to protest and strike. This set of issues included the degree of democracy in Zambia, the capacities of opposition political parties, union rights to support political parties, the freedom of the press, and the problem of government responsiveness on key policy decisions. We primarily discuss the role of the first set of issues in the renewed militancy of Zambian unions from 1999 to 2006. We discuss the other set of issues more briefly. Nevertheless, union participation in both sets of issues constituted a significant contribution to Zambia's democratic life.

With respect to wage and job issues, the two-month strike by CSUZ under Hikaumba's new leadership led to a victory in June 2001, with an 80 percent pay increase largely to overcome past inflation. The strike heralded a new militancy by civil servant unions. The financial workers union in FFTUZ helped spark the struggle against privatization of the Zambia Commercial Bank in December 2002. It was strongly supported by ZCTU and the political opposition. This also suggested that a protest strategy was critical. The right to protest this privatization was at first contested by the police and only granted when the ZUFIAW threatened a strike by financial workers—suggesting workers had to be combative in order to exercise their rights. In 2003 the civil servant union came into a major conflict with the MMD government when it reneged on a collective agreement signed in 2002 that provided for increased wages and housing allowances. The IMF had informed the government that paying these increases would lead to a budget overrun of $125 million, which violated the guidelines of the IMF's PRGF loan. The IMF insisted that loan dispersals would then be halted; this would also damage the government's attempt to fulfill conditions for debt cancellation under the Highly Indebted Poor Country (HIPC) program.

ZCTU's Hikaumba warned that "we are ready to make the government grind to a halt if they dare touch what has been agreed upon" (Pan African News Agency, July 2, 2003). Still, the government—as usual—submitted to the IMF and the World Bank. This prompted the finance minister's utterance, quoted earlier, that "We are running the country but the budget is controlled by the donors." The civil servants did, in fact, go on a nationwide strike during August–September 2003, which the government promptly declared to be illegal. Union leaders were harassed, and the ZCTU called it off in mid-September in order to launch legal challenges to the government's contractual failures. Still, the political cost to the MMD government was heavy. Feeling that the government was generally acting in bad faith, the ZCTU threatened to pull out of its participation in the Constitutional Review Commission. Its composition—largely appointed by the government—was already heavily under attack by the opposition political parties for being stacked in favor of the MMD. In the midst of the civil servants strike, ZCTU Secretary-General Tembo warned that there were strong signs that the president "will again hijack this constitutional review process" (*The Post*, August 6, 2003). By November the labor minister warned that unions that engage in politics risk being de-registered; he then registered three new unions that had split from ZCTU affiliates. He warned that the president "is not amused with labor leaders pursuing illicit ambitions" and "Do not mix trade unionism and politics because your members need bread and butter and not politics." The new unions had apparently been organized by MMD leaders who argued that "The time of paralyzing government to demand better services is gone" and "Trade unionism [is] not about confrontation but harmony" (*Times of Zambia*, November 3, 2003).

In December 2003 Hikaumba promised the government an even worse time in 2004 than in 2003 because the unions would not again accept a wage freeze and tax increases (*The Post*, December 27, 2003). A week after promising that there would be no new taxes in the 2004 budget, the finance minister introduced new taxes on all workers and maintained the wage and housing allowance freeze. He argued that the government had no option in order to get back on track with the World Bank's Poverty Reduction Growth Facility. At this time the government was paying large allowances and housing costs for forty-eight ministers and deputies. Anticipating the taxes, the ZCTU met with its union affiliates. With FFTUZ support, the ZCTU called for a one-day national strike by all public service workers, preceded by demonstrations outside parliament, in order to lobby the MPs to vote against the budget. Members of the opposition parties and some MMD leaders said they would join the protests (*Times of Zambia*, February 11, 2004). The government threatened to dismiss any workers who joined an "illegal strike." But the government bowed to the pressures of civil society groups and the unions who had vowed defiance of the threat. The ZCTU grandly overestimated that half a million workers would go on a nationwide strike beginning February nineteenth. (The last general strike had been in 1988, against Kaunda's government.) The major demonstration before parliament took place, and a nationwide strike briefly closed government offices, local government, commercial banks, and state corporations.

This confrontation led to an escalation of MMD denunciations that the unions and the ZCTU were acting politically and in their leaders' personal interests. The ZCTU and FFTUZ submitted a joint memorandum on financial alternatives for reducing government bills so wage increases could be paid; it was ignored. The union leaders accepted that the country faced extremely hard choices, that it was important to fulfill the HIPC program conditions so that $3.8 billion in debt would be eliminated—which did occur in 2006 (*Times of Zambia*, April 4, 2004). The ZCTU and FFTUZ responded tartly to government denunciations of the movement's desire to support a political alternative to the MMD. The ZCTU's Tembo freely acknowledged that "The ZCTU is a political institution, since it deals with political issues" "Our concern has been that our party [MMD] has failed to deliver and that is why we want to support a party that is labor-friendly. We used our resources to obtain independence and to change the government in 1991 and I see no reason why people should get worried when we say we will support a single political party this time" (*Times of Zambia*, April 12, 2004). FFTUZ's Nonde observed: "In 2006 the labor movement is at absolute liberty to abandon the MMD for any other progressive opposition political party which has a program to save workers from extinction. . . . In any event, the MMD government should resign now because it has abdicated its mandate to govern the country to the [World Bank] and IMF" (*Times of Zambia*, March 16, 2004).

These were powerful warnings to a president who won power in 2001 with 29 percent of the popular vote. President Mwanawasa was clearly outraged, saying that the "unions could go to hell with their support." There followed a confrontation between ZCTU leader Hikaumba and Mwanawasa at the ZCTU's May Day celebration, which the president attended. Hikaumba told the poorly attended May Day rally that the president owed unions an apology for saying publicly that the "unions could go to hell." Mwanawasa responded that unions should be the first to apologize, accusing the ZCTU of denying that it was "politically inclined." The ZCTU said it was embarrassed at the president's behavior (*Times of Zambia*, May 3, 2004). These disputes persisted, with Hikaumba saying that he would support strikes or any actions by civil servants to win their wage increase and housing allowance. ZNUT (teachers), now headed by ZCTU Secretary-General Tembo, threatened to go on nationwide strike if the housing allowances were not paid by the end of August. The government pretended it had no money (*The Post*, July 19, 2004). When a conciliator could not settle the differences between CSUZ and the government on wages and housing allowances, Hikaumba requested, as the law provides, that the Labor Department issue a strike ballot; it simply refused.

The outstanding issues between the MMD government and both the CSUZ and the ZCTU continued throughout 2004 to 2006 and in some ways became more rancorous. Hikaumba blasted the government for its failure to prepare labor laws for amendment, to remit funds to the Public Services Pension Fund, and for the labor minister's ludicrous promise to create 1 million jobs. The government was serious, the minister said, "except for the fact that it lacked the resources to implement many promises" (*Times of Zambia*, August 19, 2004). Hikaumba also attacked the president for his complaints about "numerous wildcat strikes and work stoppages," laying the blame on government behavior (*The Post*, January 19, 2005). FFTUZ's Vice President Nchinga, warned that if there was not a pro-worker budget in 2005: "There will be rolling strikes; it is going to be rough for the government this year if workers' lives are not improved" and lamented that "Last year we were humiliated left, right, and center, and disadvantaged by the wage freeze" (*The Post*, January 24, 2005). And in February there was a nationwide strike by local council workers because poor government funding meant workers could not be paid. And the MMD government decided that the president and secretary-general of FFTUZ were so antagonistic that it launched a major (unsuccessful) campaign to remove Nonde and Nchinga from their offices in FFTUZ and their own unions.

Despite ZCTU criticisms, Hikaumba was concerned not to appear too political and to subject the ZCTU to severe government sanctions. He also criticized the disarray of opposition parties. The ZCTU was not opposed to talking to the government about constitutional reforms, but it threatened to encourage nationwide civil servant demonstrations if the government obstructed constitutional reform. Hikaumba warned the government against threatening civil servants about exercising their right to hold demonstrations (*The Post*, December 20, 2004).

Despite the angry impasse over wages and housing allowances, Hikaumba and ZCTU leaders did meet with President Mwanawasa in June 2004 to discuss the Constitution Reform Commission and labor matters. Nonde furiously attacked the ZCTU for this kneeling before the government and making a U-turn in their common strategy without informing FFTUZ. She said that FFTUZ was not bound by "ZCTU's blackmail reconciliation with the government." Such discussions were inconsistent since the MMD government had imposed wage and housing-allowance freezes. Furthermore, Nonde said FFTUZ had supported ZCTU protests against government policies. A conflict erupted between the ZCTU and FFTUZ, which had been cooperating closely with each other for several years. ZCTU's Tembo said that the ZCTU met with the president "to find out from him insinuations that the government wanted to de-register the ZCTU and its affiliate unions." This had been occurring among affiliates; a new splinter from the miners' union had just been registered, which is what Nonde meant by "blackmail." ZCTU and FFTUZ leaders met and reconciled, however, arranging a joint full executive meeting to mend relations (*The Post*, June 28 and July 12, 2004).

In December 2005 the ZCTU joined the major protests of civil society groups and all opposition parties in Zambia's capital to demand a constituent assembly to approve a new constitution. The Constitutional Review Commission, created after strong public pressures in 2003, came up with recommendations that the MMD government rejected in November. The MMD disliked the dilution of presidential powers and scrapping of the first-past-the-post electoral system, which the opposition supported. The opposition wanted constitutional changes in place before the October 2006 election. ZCTU president Hikaumba denounced "the protracted debate" and called on the government to enact a new constitution through a constituent assembly (*Africa News*, December 12, 2005). The government's appointment of a team of government members to study the adoption process was far short of the ZCTU's demands. Nevertheless, the ZCTU said this was a good start. The Oasis Forum and other opposition parties, on the other hand, criticized government domination of the Constitutional Review Commission (*Times of Zambia*, February 17, 2006).

While the unions have recovered their capacity for autonomous action and militant opposition to government policies, there was no real sign that the ZCTU and FFTUZ were willing to join in, or lead, the opposition in systematic confrontation with the government, as had occurred in 1990 and 1991. There was some caution in Hikaumba's behavior toward the government, and for good reason. The liberalization of labor relations has led, with some government prompting and use of its legal powers, to fissures in the labor movement and significant fragmentation of labor strength and capacity to mobilize workers. There has been a deep splintering and weakening of the labor movement, despite the fact that the ZCTU remains the preeminent federation. There are now five different unions in the teachers sector; previously there was one. MUZ is relatively weak and miners are divided among unions; they are no longer the huge threat they were when copper was economic king.

ZCTU and FFTUZ leaders had threatened to support opposition parties in the presidential and National Assembly elections in 2006. While the ZCTU refused to support the MMD in both the 1996 and the 2001 elections, it adopted a nonpartisan stance and did not support any party. Several opposition parties merged in 2005 and 2006, making them a slightly more coherent electoral threat than before. Indeed, after the sudden death of its leader in 2006, the party that became the United Democratic Alliance asked Hikaumba if he wanted to be among their presidential choices. He waited three weeks before declining. The offer suggests the oppositions' view regarding labor's electoral potential. In mid-2006 ZCTU and FFTUZ leaders still criticized opposition parties for their divisions and infighting.

Clearly, there were profound divisions within the two labor federations regarding what party, if any, to favor or whether they should remain nonpartisan. In late July, Hikaumba said that the ZCTU had resolved to back a political party in the presidential and National Assembly elections. Shortly after, Hikaumba said the ZCTU would back a presidential candidate but let workers decide on their party choice—an attempt to compromise an internal conflict. A week later Hikaumba and the ZCTU backed away from even this political engagement. Rather, he said, the ZCTU would be nonpartisan in the election. FFTUZ and its member unions were similarly divided. The FFTUZ Executive Board and its unions met in early August and voted their party preferences: there were seven votes for the Popular Front and its populist candidate, Michael Sata; four for the MMD; and three for the United Democratic Alliance. FFTUZ concluded that three parties were very important to FFTUZ members, who should support one of these (Xinhua News Agency, August 13, 2006). The Secondary Teachers Union (SESTUZ) in FFTUZ dissociated itself quickly from even this stance, saying that it was nonpartisan by policy. "Whoever wins will be responsible for paying salaries of our members." SESTUZ then thanked the MMD government for releasing long-time arrears on housing allowances and salaries to teachers—a month before election day (*The Post*, August 21, 2006). Both the FFTUZ and the ZCTU still tried to force the parties to be responsive to workers' interests. Attempts to mobilize labor's rank behind one party and candidate would have deeply divided the unions. FFTUZ leadership sent long questionnaires to the three parties, asking that they state their positions on key labor concerns. The ZCTU made its final decision regarding its nonpartisan approach on August 30, less than a month before the election. It later published a manifesto of labor's goals and a list of MPs from the past assembly to vote for because of their past support for labor. Still, it became clear that many union activists and leaders—especially within FFTUZ— did support the Popular Front and Sata for president. Sato won a large majority of the votes in Lusaka, the capital, and in townships along the copper belt.

The MMD won the election, with about 43 percent of the presidential vote for Mwanawasa and 40 percent of parliamentary seats. The Popular Front, with its populist presidential candidate and the largest FFTUZ Executive Board support, came in second, with 30 percent of the presidential votes and 32 percent of MP seats. The United Democratic Alliance trailed with 25 percent and 14.6 percent, respectively.

The failure of the opposition to unite and an economic upswing in 2005 and 2006 helped to re-elect a government very unpopular with the unions.

Conclusion: Trade Unions, Democratization, and Economic Reforms

The Zambian trade union movement was unique in Africa: it created and led a political party that forced the renewal of democratic liberties and elections and came to power, led by the ex-union leaders. Although UNIP made major efforts to embrace the union movement within the party-state, key factors ultimately enabled the unions to resist:

- the relatively large size of the union movement;
- a strategic sector, copper, where strikes could arrest the whole economy;
- the pre-independence tradition of democratic union life, where rank and file had the will and capacity to pressure leaders who might be tempted by party affiliations and power; and
- the union movement's ability to generate new leadership, which insisted upon worker/union interests with protests.

This established significant space for unions to exercise their autonomy of party/state pressures. As UNIP supporters, unions were awarded some major advantages that gave them check-off, larger membership, and resources.

There are some patterns in Zambian union history. The movement of unions to fight energetically for union autonomy and workers' interests occurred in the period of the independence struggle, the struggle against UNIP domination in the 1980s, and since the mid 1990s there were renewed efforts to reestablish autonomy. The latter two periods were ones of increasing economic crisis. The two eras when the unions had reduced autonomy and were less militant were when they aligned themselves with a political party—the authoritarian UNIP party-state, and the MMD government after 1991. Union leaders initially believed that alignment with a party would increase union resources, organization, and power. It did initially, in the 1960s and 1970s, but the party insisted upon the priority of its interests and upon union subordination to these. In the 1960s and 1970s, Zambia still had resources; copper prices were high; and the government could reward union alignment with laws, resources, and political status. But in the 1990s, burdened by low copper prices and exports, no growth, and huge budget deficits, the new democratic government could offer unions and workers little for their support.

Thus, in this latest democratic era, the union movement and workers do not appear to have benefited from democratic life or the economy. The depressed real wages, massive layoffs, increased joblessness, and decline in living standards testify that unions and workers did not gain. This was less a reflection of democracy than of the depressed economy and the state's adoption of a liberal market labor control policy. Still, given the overextended Zambian state, profound erosion in copper exports, and reduced government revenues, there was bound to be economic contraction unless foreign private investment magically transformed things. The laissez-faire public policy, privatization experience, and low capital inflows have failed to generate alternative sectors of employment. In addition, political pressures from the MMD government and residual union loyalty to ex-leaders now in top government offices induced lower levels of protest than would have otherwise occurred.

However, profound political discontent among the rank and file, dissident break-away unions, and newly elected leaders in national unions and in the ZCTU and FFTUZ have reanimated the union movement and made it an important part of the democratic public. But, even a democratic environment offers no guarantee that the unions would have unfettered freedom to mobilize their resources to pursue the interests of unions and workers.

The government has been able to use legal change to reduce the resources and cohesion of the movement. It has used the legal power of de-registration to eliminate local unions and leaders it disliked; it has even targeted national union and ZCTU and FFTUZ leaders whom it found dangerous (e.g., Liato in 1998 and Nonde in 2005). It has also withstood public pressures on policies, despite the growing weak-ness of MMD in presidential and parliamentary elections. The IMF, the World Bank, and the Western country aid donors are more powerful coalitional partners than any combination of domestic groups—except at election time. Their financial resources have made the MMD governments less politically accountable.

On major issues of interest, the union movement has not been very effective, or only marginally so. Thus, *has democratic politics failed as far as trade unions and workers are concerned? In turn, have trade unions failed to support democratic institutions and norms?*

First, whatever the erosion in jobs and living standards in Zambia since 1991, this is only one test regarding the possible benefits of democratic life for the union move-ment. It was inevitable that the economic "reforms" envisaged by the IMF, the World Bank, and Western donors would lead to an erosion in wages and benefits and a loss in state and private sector jobs. But the absence of growth during 1991–2000 con-stituted a massive failure. Second, the democratic environment has made it possible for trade unions to deepen their own democratic institutions and norms and to greatly increase the organizational autonomy of the unions. Despite the capacity of the ZCTU to resist intermittently the UNIP government's policies, its autonomy was limited until it went into full-scale opposition. The autonomy of the two labor federations, ZCTU and FFTUZ, is undoubtedly greater than it was in the 1980s, even if they seem to have been less effective in blocking some government policies. *All governments* try to withstand the powers of significant groups in civic society, espe-cially if the costs (e.g., increased budgetary expenditures) are heavy. The authoritar-ian UNIP government did so by trying to capture and control the ZCTU and the unions to create policy autonomy for itself. The MMD government has used a dif-ferent strategy, a liberal market labor control regime, which includes "liberalization" of labor law and engaging in divide-and-conquer policies. This has helped to weaken the ZCTU and fragment the union movement. But the ZCTU could not have main-tained the level of mobilization of opposition that it offered in 1990–91 and imposed its policy preferences when the state was largely broke.

Still, the lack of success of union leadership in fulfilling their demands has induced union members to blame their union leaders more than the government. Rank-and-file frustration has led to dissent, division, and schisms within organized labor. While the breakaway unions have weakened some national unions, they should also have increased leadership accountability to rank-and-file pressures. It is clear that the top ZCTU leaders held office too long (1974–75 to 1991 and 1991 to 2002). Still, the union movement has managed repeatedly to inflict heavy political costs upon the government for pursuing policies that violated their interests. The unions reversed their early accommodation with the MMD government and, since the late 1990s, have mobilized major protests and strikes in behalf of their goals. The unions have clearly relearned the dangers of close alignment with any party.

If the economic life under democracy has not been favorable for workers and unions, the union movement has been highly beneficial for Zambia's democratic life. The major activities of the unions have contributed to the vitality of Zambia's civil society and democratic life in myriad ways. The union movement has nurtured democratic leadership and norms through union institutions and supported democratic structures and rules. It has insisted on autonomy from state power and worked, through its own efforts and its cooperation with other groups, to hold governments accountable for their public policies and behavior. It has also supported the idea of opposition political parties, a free press, and active civic participation while it has scrutinized government policies and disseminated information to its members. The union movement has insisted upon seeking redress of grievances.

Ultimately, the unions have continued to embrace democratic political norms and institutions even when these have not appeared to reward workers and unions.

References

Akwetey, Emmanuel O. 1995. Democratization and labor regime reform in post-transition Africa. Paper for the Joint Workshop on Labor Regimes and Liberalization: Restructuring State-Society Relations in Africa. Harare, Zimbabwe: Institute of Development Studies, University of Zimbabwe.

Akwetey, Emmanuel O. 1994. Trade unions and democratization: A comparative study of Zambia and Ghana. PhD diss., Political Science Dept., Stockholm University (bound).

Alexander, David. 1993. Workers' education and political change. Occasional paper no. 42, Center of African Studies.

Bangura, Yusuf. 1992. Authoritarian rule and democracy in Africa: A theoretical discourse. In *Authoritarianism, democracy and adjustment: The politics of economic reforms in Africa*, ed. Peter Gibbon, Yusuf Bangura, and A. Ofstad Uppsala, Sweden: Nordiska Afrikainstitutet.

Bangura, Yusuf, and Bjorn Beckman. 1991. African workers and structural adjustment with a Nigerian case study. In *The IMF and the south: Social impact of crisis and adjustment*, ed. D. Ghai et al. London: Zed.

Bates, R. H. 1971. *Unions, parties, and political development: A study of mineworkers in Zambia*. New Haven, CT, Yale University Press.

Bratton, M. 1994. Economic crisis and political realignment in Zambia. In *Economic change and political liberalization in sub-Saharan Africa*, ed. Jennifer A. Widner. London: Johns Hopkins University Press.

Bratton, Michael, and N. Van de Walle. 1992. Popular protest and reform in Africa. *Comparative Politics* 24 (July):19–42.

Burawoy, M. 1985. *The politics of production: Factory regimes under capitalism and socialism*. London: Verso.

Callaghy, T. M. 1989. Lost between state and market—the politics of economic adjustment in Ghana, Zambia and Nigeria. In *Economic crisis and policy choice: The politics of structural adjustment in the third world*, ed. Joan M. Nelson. Princeton, NJ: Princeton University Press.

Dansereau, Suzanne. 1995. Unions in southern Africa: Structural adjustment and reorganization. *South African Labor Bulletin* 19 (September).

Davies, I. 1966. *African trade unions*. Harmondsworth, UK: Penguin.

Gertzel, C. 1984. Dissent and authority in the Zambian one-party state. In *The dynamics of the one- party state in Zambia*, ed. C. Gertzel, C. Baylies, and M. Szeftel. Manchester: Manchester University Press.

Gupta, A. 1974. Trade unionism and politics in the copperbelt. In *Politics in Zambia*, ed. W. Tordoff. Manchester: Manchester University Press.

Huntington, S. P. 1991. *The third wave: Democratization in late twentieth century*. Norman: University of Oklahoma Press.

Liatto, B. 1989. Organized labor and the state. PhD diss., Department of Politics, University of Leeds.

Jeffries, Richard. 1978. *Class, power, and ideology in Ghana*. New York: Cambridge University Press.

Larmer, Miles. 2005. Reaction and resistance to neo-liberalism in Zamiba. *Review of African Political Economy*, 32 (March): 29–45.

Loxley, John. 1994. Rural labor markets in a mineral economy. In *Structural adjustment and rural labor markets in Africa*, ed. V. Jamal. New York: St. Martin's Press.

Maree, Johann. 1982. Democracy and oligarchy in trade unions: The independent trade unions in the Transvaal and the Western Province General Workers' Union in the 1970s. *Social Dynamics* 8 (June): 41–52.

Mbikusita-Lewanika, Akashambatwa, and Derrick Chitala, eds. 1990. The hour has come: Proceedings of the national conference on multi-party option. Lusaka, Zambia: Zambia Research Foundation.

Meebelo, H. S. 1986. *African proletarians and colonial capitalism*. Lusaka, Zambia: Kenneth Kaunda Foundation.

Molteno, R. 1974. Cleavage and conflict in Zambian politics: A study in sectionalism. In *Politics in Zambia*, ed. W. Tordoff. Manchester: Manchester University Press.

Mwanakatwe, John M. 1994. *End of Kaunda era*. Lusaka, Zambia: Multimedia Zambia.

Pettman, J. 1974. *Zambia: Security and conflict*. Sussex: Julian Friedmann.

Przeworski, A. 1992. *Democracy and the market: Political and economic reforms in eastern Europe and Latin America*. Cambridge: Cambridge University Press.

Rasmussen, T. 1974. The popular basis of anti-colonial protests. In *Politics in Zambia*, ed. W. Tordoff. Manchester: Manchester University Press.

Rothchild, D., and R. Curry. 1978. *Scarcity, choice, and public policy in Middle Africa*. Berkeley: University of California Press.

Sklar, R. L. 1975. *Corporate power in an African state: The political impact of multinational mining companies in Zambia*. Berkeley: University of California Press.

Simon, David. 2005. Democracy unrealized: Zambia's third republic under Frederick Chiluba. In *The fate of Africa's democratic experiments*, ed. L. A. Villalon and P. VonDoepp. Bloomington: Indiana University Press.

Simutanyi, N. 1985. *The politics of structural adjustment in Zambia*. Paper presented to the workshop Governance and Economic Policy Making, ECPR Joint Sessions of Workshops, Bordeaux, France, April 27–May 2, 1985.

———. 1995. Political opposition and democracy in Zambia: Problems and prospects. 8th CODESRIA General Assembly on Crisis, Conflicts and Transformation Responses and Perspectives, Dakar, June 26–July 2.

Situmbeko, L., and J. J. Zulu. 2004. *Zambia: Condemned to debt*. London: World Development Movement, April.

Sørensen, G. 1993. *Democracy and democratization*. Boulder, CO: Westview.

Tordoff, W., ed. 1974. *Politics in Zambia*. Manchester: Manchester University Press.

Tordoff, W., and R. Molteno. 1974. Cleavage and conflict in Zambian politics: A study in sectionalism. In *Politics in Zambia*, ed. W. Tordoff. Manchester: Manchester University Press.

Valenzuela, J. S. 1989. Labor movements in transitions to democracy. *Comparative Politics* (July 1989): 445–71.

Zambia Congress of Trade Union Files

1992. Minutes of the General Council meeting, Katilungu House. Kitwe, Zambia, October 18.

1994. Submission of the ZCTU to the Zambia Constitutional Review Commission. September 29.

1994. Report of the Secretary General, 9th Quadrennial Congress. QC/D no. 1–3. Livingstone, Zambia, October 26–29.

1996. Zambia Congress of Trade Union chairman general's introductory remarks. Tripartite Consultative Labor Council meeting. Lusaka, Zambia, January 18.

1996. Minister of labor and social security's speech. Tripartite Consultative Labor Council Meeting. Lusaka, Zambia, January 18.

1996. Zambia Federation of Employer representative's speech. Tripartite Consultative Labor Council Meeting. Lusaka, Zambia, January 18.

1996. Split within the ZCTU: An account of the events as they happened before, during and after the Ninth Quadrennial Congress in 1994. Kitwe, Zambia: Zambia Congress of Trade Unions.

Other Publications

Zambia. 1993. *Labor and industrial relations act*. Lusaka: Government Printer.

Zambia. 1993. *Implementation of economic recovery program—efforts and policies*. Report Zambia: Presented to the Consultative Group for Zambia, April 6–7. Government of Zambia.

Zambian Newspapers

Times of Zambia. Various dates.
The Post. Various dates.

CHAPTER 6

Trade Union Struggles for Autonomy and Democracy in Zimbabwe

Richard Saunders

It is not possible to reform the economy without political reform. The demand for participation and consultation, for accountability and openness in government and for open debate on national issues is one that can only be realized by ourselves making this happen . . . Workers are demanding effective and democratic organizations, whether in government or in the unions. . . . People are actively discussing political, economic, and social issues. The sleeping giant is beginning to wake up in Zimbabwe.

Gibson Sibanda
President, Zimbabwe Congress of Trade Unions
May Day, 1991

Introduction

The labor movement in Zimbabwe has maintained a precarious existence for several decades. The target of succeeding governments, political factions, employers, and economic policies, trade unions have faced these challenges armed with weak organizational structures and often a lack of unity. Before independence in 1980 this was especially the case. After 1980, new obstacles were put in the way of the labor movement by the post-colonial state. In independent Zimbabwe's second decade, neoliberal policies provided a range of new challenges for labor organizations and their allies in civil society. Recently, the emergence of populist authoritarian government in the midst of political-economic crisis and creeping globalization has erected new obstacles for the labor movement and redistributive politics.

In some respects, post-independence trade union struggles for autonomy and democracy mark a return to the past. They elicit familiar questions regarding the relationship of organized labor to the nationalist movement, other social forces, and the state. Early analyses of state-labor relations in the 1980s highlighted the corporatist, paternalist, or authoritarian aspects of the Zimbabwe African National Union-Patriotic Front (ZANU-PF) government's engagement with the labor movement. They stressed the weak union structures inherited from the pre-independence period and identified the new government's commanding presence in labor structures in the early 1980s. But recently it has been important to give equal consideration to the movement's resilience, autonomy, and contributions to democratic struggles, such as its contribution to the creation in 1999 of the Movement for Democratic Change (MDC), Zimbabwe's main opposition political party.

The labor movement's revival began in the late 1980s when Zimbabwe's trade unions stepped up their struggle for survival and independence in the face of economic and political reforms. Government's neoliberal policies imposed new constraints on workers and ordinary Zimbabweans, but they also created space and provided new grievances for mobilization. The second decade of independence was marked by episodic bouts of illegal strikes, slowdowns, lockouts, demonstrations, and other labor actions—and by repression, retrenchments, and pressures from the state and employers. Regular resort by workers to protest and labor action slowly chipped away at the state's powers and the ruling party's authority. It helped sections of the union movement build a degree of autonomy in the workplace and strengthened the national labor center. This autonomy and purpose erupted more fully in the late 1990s, as social unionism redefined the labor movement.

This discussion considers the historical and political terrain on which labor's struggles for autonomy and democratization have occurred. It focuses on the shifting relations between the union movement and the state in its different phases—colonial, nationalist, neoliberal, and populist-authoritarian. It traces the vulnerabilities and strengths of the labor movement as it has engaged with the state and social partners and developed capacities to pursue agendas and to lead broad social forces in challenging the state. The discussion explores how the labor movement thrived in a hostile environment and attempted to reshape it into a more democratic space.

A Problematic Inheritance

Several decades of industrial development and labor activism under colonialism bequeathed a weak, divided, and politically marginalized union movement to Zimbabwe in 1980 (Brand 1976; Shadur 1994). This weakness was the result of several factors. Long-standing state control and repression were the most important. Thus, black workers were prevented from organizing trade unions and bargaining collectively with employers for much of the colonial period. African labor unions were also undermined by persistent internal fragmentation against the backdrop of regional, sectoral, and political differences. The state and foreign organizations played an aggravating role. Hence, workers' capacity to contest the state and employers was weakened.

From the time of their first emergence in the 1920s and '30s, African workers' organizations were severely constrained by concerted repression on the part of the colonial state and employers. This process began with the introduction of the first labor regulations soon after colonization in the 1890s. The *Masters and Servants Act* of 1901 mandated that African labor could not be unionized. It specified that workers could enter into individual contracts with employers only "voluntarily," in which the rights of workers were severely curtailed. The *Industrial Conciliation Act* of 1934 (ICA) granted only white workers the right to form free trade unions, excluding blacks from the category of "employee." Associated measures, including the banning, arrest, and detention of labor leaders, and the disruption of organizing activities, buttressed these legislated controls.

This did not prevent sporadic collective action, day-to-day challenges to the harshly oppressive labor process, or the development of labor consciousness among workers (van Onselen 1974). An initial attempt at forming a trade union–like organization in the 1920s and early 1930s, the Industrial and Commercial Workers Union (ICU), foundered due to leadership divisions, poor organizational capacity, and severe state repression (Ranger 1970).

The 1940s saw renewed labor militancy as African workers and the wider black urban community mobilized in response to growing socioeconomic crises. A 1945 strike by railway workers under the leadership of the Rhodesia Railways African Employees Association was followed by a widespread general strike in 1948, which seized upon plummeting living standards. A government commission of inquiry documented the hardships of African workers and recommended broad improvements in labor conditions but not recognition of African trade unions.

It was only in 1959 that the ICA was revised to allow limited recognition of black unions. This came after a decade of increasing labor activism, including formation in 1954 of a national African center, the Southern Rhodesia Trade Union Congress (SRTUC). The modified ICA of 1959 reflected an emerging state strategy that mixed repression with co-option; it would remain in place until 1980. Under the remodeled ICA, white unionists were given controlling power within officially "multi-racial" unions. The state was given extensive supervisory powers over the internal and external links of unions, and strike action was effectively preempted as illegal. Crucially, African unions were barred from engaging in political activities— and risked deregistration if they did. The resurgent nationalist movement was then challenging the colonial state.

Despite legal restrictions, black labor organizations developed close links with the nationalist movement at leadership and lower levels.[1] However, questions of nationalist political affiliation and union autonomy soon emerged and led to intense internal friction within worker organizations. Union leaders like the SRTUC's president, Reuben Jamela, attempted to avoid the submersion of workers' issues and structures within the broader alliance of social forces represented by the nationalist movement; they were increasingly marginalized as a result. The limited workplace rights conceded to African trade unions by the state was a contributing factor, opening divisions within the movement over the issue of alignment with the nationalists. By the early 1960s, a labor-nationalist alliance option was pursued by the dominant section of the labor movement but was attacked by nationalist leaders. They rejected the principle of union autonomy and mobilized to discredit "workerist" union leaders.

Such interventions helped provoke a series of splits within the already fragile labor movement. The first of these occurred over the degree of affiliation to the broader nationalist movement and saw the defeat of the autonomy-minded leadership. This splintering was soon followed by others, as the political wing of the nationalist movement split into ZANU and Zimbabwe African People's Organization (ZAPU)—prompting parallel splits within the nationalist-aligned trade union movement. The 1962 split of the SRTUC saw the formation of the African Trade Union Congress (ATUC). The two bodies merged the next year, under the ATUC label, following the settling of SRTUC leadership disputes. When a 1963 split in the nationalist movement yielded Joshua Nkomo's ZAPU and Ndabaningi Sithole's (later Robert Mugabe's) ZANU, a parallel split within the labor movement created the ZAPU-aligned Zimbabwe African Congress of Unions (ZACU). All this rendered the new fledgling labor centers highly susceptible to the Cold War maneuvering of international labor institutions like the International Confederation of Free Trade Unions (ICFTU). This led to further factionalism and fragmentation within black worker organizations (Raftopoulos 1996).

The African labor movement was also increasingly marginalized by the directions of the nationalist struggle. The military aspect of the liberation struggle assumed greater importance in the late 1960s and 1970s. The nationalist leadership moved closer to the rural peasantry that formed the bedrock of the military campaign and would constitute the heart of the ZANU's constituency once the war was won. Thus, the political vitality of the divided urban labor movement fell.

In labor relations the creeping political frailty of African unions compounded other deeply structured problems. In the first case, chronic macroeconomic weaknesses in the national economy saw the entrenchment of substantial structured unemployment, particularly after World War II. Moreover, the colonial labor market was characterized by a preponderance of low-skilled labor, dominated by large numbers of unskilled (and difficult-to-organize) workers in the commercial agricultural sector. Until the 1950s, the bulk of the urban industrial workforce were migrant workers from neighboring colonies.

African unions also experienced considerable organizational difficulties in penetrating the labor market, quite aside from the heavy restrictions imposed by the state. Poorly skilled officials occupying thinly financed structures meant union management capacity was generally low. This limited the unions' ability to expand and mobilize their membership (Shadur 1994, 62).

While the number of registered black unions increased rapidly in the early 1960s from six to twenty-six, union membership and density remained chronically low until 1980. One observer calculated that only 6 percent of the total formal sector labor force of 900,000 in 1975 (or 54,000) could be classified as paid-up union members. Overall membership had grown only marginally since the early 1960s (Davies 1975). An interpretation of 1979 data showed a total of 88,000 unionized industrial workers in fifty-seven unions—twenty-three of them white-dominated—yielding a union density of 11 percent (Wood 1987, 1988). The Riddell Commission in 1980 found forty registered unions with 79,000 members, and seventy-one unregistered unions, membership unknown (Riddell 1981, 243, 256). At that point the highest union density was in the mining and urban industrial and commercial sectors. Even then, it was no higher than 29 percent. Moreover, union membership in these sectors was spread across at least six different "federations," which were little more than branches or fragments of unions held together by small leaderships (Riddell 1981, 256; Shadur 1994, 68–69).

It was in this context—and that of a sharp intensification of repression under the minority white Rhodesian state, with union activists detained and banned—that African unions failed to establish a strong national presence in the labor market and black politics prior to 1980. One of the enduring consequences—and emblems—of this failure was the inability of African unions to arrest the decline in workers' living standards in the 1970s.[2] Independence therefore brought with it heightened needs and expectations on the part of black workers, who looked impatiently to the new government to deliver that which their own unions had not.

New Order?

The crisis situation that confronted the ZANU-PF government even before it took power in April 1980 accentuated the defining characteristics of the colonial inheritance and set the tone of labor relations during the following several years. Less than two weeks after the independence elections of March brought ZANU-PF to power, the first in a series of strikes took place. The strike quickly spread throughout the country, enveloping several sectors. Over the next eighteen months, thousands of workers in the public and private sectors engaged in succeeding waves of strikes, demonstrations, and protests in the face of the state's hostile rhetoric and occasional brutality.

Initially the new ruling party had no coherent policy on how to manage the situation. Its emerging strategy of containment and control included attacks on both workers and the existing federations and the unilateral creation of a single new national labor center closely linked to ZANU-PF. These measures signaled the party's widening "ownership" of labor movement politics and policies in the early 1980s. While the ruling party and state could initially impose "solutions" on workers, these created tensions and the basis for the reemergence of autonomous unions later.

ZANU-PF's first experience of labor relations took place under conditions of pressure and urgency. The wildcat strikes of early 1980, the largest and most sustained since the general strike of 1948, threatened the fragile stability of the productive sector. They also posed a direct challenge to the untested governing abilities of the nationalist movement in an environment of political uncertainty. Early accounts estimated there were as many as 171 strikes over a two-year period, and possibly many more. Most took place independently—and beyond the control—of existing union structures (Raftopoulos 1994; Sachikonye 1986; Wood 1988; all have higher estimations based on regional reports). The walkouts of 1980–81 underscored the pent-up frustrations and high expectations of a large section of formal sector workers, born of poor pay and working conditions, abusive management, and continuing decline in living standards.

ZANU-PF's promises of a new mass-oriented agenda aimed at redressing peasant and worker interests were an additional factor. In the 1980 election campaign ZANU-PF's broadly socialist politics were mixed with more specific concrete promises, including the long-denied right to strike. Prime Minister-elect Mugabe told the nation in 1980: "We are socialist . . . basic wages and working conditions of black and white must be based on an equal footing" (Wood 1988, 288–89). The new government also promised in a series of policy documents that the private sector would be preserved and respected as the engine of economic growth (Zimbabwe 1981, 1982). Mugabe argued that "whilst the main thrust of the National Development Plan is socialist . . . ample room has been reserved for performance by private enterprise" (Zimbabwe 1982, i).

If the socialist pronouncements by ZANU-PF created political space for workers' organizations, it was less clear that the latter would be able to seize the opportunity by mobilizing their membership and weak structures to deal effectively with management and government. Indeed much of the open terrain in labor relations was quickly occupied by the state, employers, and white-dominated trade unions, which quickly called for rebuilding workers' organizations. The state's aim, however, was clearly to establish organized control over labor relations.

Sachikonye (1986) and Wood (1988) note that the widespread labor unrest of 1980–81 provided ZANU-PF with an opportunity to launch concerted efforts to harness the post-independence trade union movement. The state's repressive response involved threats and the use of the police and military to break up strikes and demonstrations (Astrow 1983; Mitchell 1987; Shadur 1994; Wood 1987). In May 1980 Labor Minister Kumbirai Kangai warned a thousand striking transport workers, "I will crack my whip if they do not go back to work." In the longer term, the government turned to policy initiatives to placate, suppress, and marginalize workers' demands.

In May, in the midst of a wave of labor unrest, government announced a National Minimum Wage Bill and new minimum wage levels to take effect July 1, 1980. This started an annual exercise in wage setting, undertaken unilaterally by the state, which still failed to address workers' demands. As a result, real wages did rise rapidly for a brief time in some sectors, like mining and agriculture, because of the prior subsistence levels common in those sectors. But workers in most areas of industry were soon adversely affected. After initial average increases, by 1986 most workers' real wages were in decline, following a wage freeze, reduced subsidies on essential commodities, and rising levels of annual inflation. By 1989 average real wages had dropped 13 percent from 1980 levels, due to accumulated inflation of more than 330 percent (Tsvangirai 1990b). Manufacturing workers were especially hard-hit (Herbst 1990, 203–5; Wood 1988, 293).

Other early interventions by the state met with mixed success. Rules restricting retrenchment did protect workers but did not help speed up employment growth. It stagnated after the initial post-independence mini-boom. "Liaison Committees" (later workers committees) were encouraged by the ministry in 1980 to improve communications between workers and management and to thwart the continuation of wildcat strike action. Unfortunately, however, employers, the state, and more militant workers alike often circumvented those committees. The state also faced management problems that stemmed from the low skills capacities of its own inadequately trained, relatively inexperienced officials (Raftopoulos 1994). This left considerable space for interventions in day-to-day labor relations by party officials and others, who had no legal role in the labor dispute process.

ZCTU Established

But the most important intervention by the state would be its formation of a unified national labor center, the Zimbabwe Congress of Trade Unions (ZCTU), in 1981. The prolonged labor unrest of 1980, the weakness of existing union structures, and the popular authority enjoyed by ZANU-PF as a result of "independence euphoria" together underlay the ruling party's moves to establish a unified center under its partisan tutelage. By mid-1980 the Ministry of Labor was developing plans for the creation of a new trade union body, but not without criticism and opposition from key veteran leaders in the existing union federations.

In the ministry-driven process leading up to the inaugural ZCTU congress in February 1981, much of the labor movement old guard was marginalized. At the same time, government recognized—and therefore empowered—a number ZANU-PF–aligned unions, activists, and repackaged opportunists, many of them with questionable status within labor circles. By these means ZANU-PF asserted its early control over the emerging national labor structure and extinguished a furtive attempt by a group of more independent-minded union officials to establish a nonaligned body, the United Trade Unions of Zimbabwe. The ruling party leaders handpicked the new ZCTU's interim organizing committee, and it became increasingly dominated by ZANU-PF members. This and clear evidence of irregularities in the accreditation of unions for the body's first congress meant that the launch of the new ZCTU represented more the influence of ZANU-PF than that of the workers.[3]

With ZCTU's political capture by ZANU-PF, the Ministry of Labor played a direct role in manipulating factional disputes within the body (Shadur 1994, 104–5). Weak administrative structures, elitist tendencies among the executive, and intense factionalism nurtured in part by several splinter unions sympathetic to ZANU-PF rendered the organization exceedingly vulnerable to the state and ruling party. There was a series of leadership squabbles and changes and a pervasive environment of mismanagement. A 1984 Ministry of Labor report (Zimbabwe 1984) described a chaotic situation in which twenty-one trade unions were without adequate records of membership. Many unions had no financial accounts. Only about one-quarter of the fifty organizations surveyed held regular branch meetings. Union penetration of workers' committees stood at equally low levels. Thus, the ZCTU, most affiliates, and their branches proved ineffective in mobilizing most shop floor workers and combating the power of employers (Cheater 1988).

Consequently, the labor movement failed to meet the challenge of responding to the state's new labor code, the *Labor Relations Act* (LRA), introduced in 1985. The LRA stood as the defining industrial relations legislation of the 1980s and '90s, broadening the scope of labor relations management. There was little evidence of the labor movement's participation in its design. The LRA included notable advances for workers, including the right to join trade unions and workers' committees, freedom of association, and protection from victimization. But it also undermined these by enshrining wide-ranging powers in the Labor Ministry. The code gave government the authority to set maximum wages; to cancel collective bargaining agreements; to investigate, certify, decertify, and administer trade unions; and to rule proposed industrial actions illegal (Sachikonye 1986, 261–63). And the LRA severely undercut labor rights by banning strikes in "essential services," which government defined so broadly that the vast majority of workers were included.

As one senior unionist put it, the labor movement's "role as mediator for the workers [had] been hijacked by government" (*Moto* #47). Later, government's assumption of broad powers over labor relations through the LRA would form a key target of attack for union activists struggling for greater ZCTU autonomy. Yet when the LRA was drafted, the ZCTU had not been in a position to mobilize its constituency for a campaign around the code. Banners at the ZCTU's 1985 May Day rally gave telling testimony of those times: "Workers and Employers are one!" some read.

ZANU-PF's strategy of penetrating, encircling, and undermining the ZCTU's senior ranks led directly to growing tensions and mismanagement within the organization. Mounting allegations of corruption, nepotism, and theft, combined with a new minister of labor in 1984, ushered in a wave of criticism from government and its semiofficial media. They also prompted growing cooperation between government and factions within the ZCTU that wanted to see the organization attain a degree of coherence and perform as an autonomous, representative institution accountable to its labor constituency. In late 1984 the ministry, actively supported by many of the better-organized union affiliates, led a process in which the ZCTU's leadership was supplanted by a ministry-appointed administrator working with a select group of senior unionists. In March 1985 the ministry put a new interim executive in place. At a second national congress in July, a new ZCTU leadership was elected, one dominated by officials from some of the better-organized unions favoring greater accountability within the ZCTU (Sachikonye 1986, 265).

Despite government's possession of decisive power in defining the limits of trade union action, the ouster of a leadership, which unquestionably owed its position to ZANU-PF patronage, marked the beginning of new phase at the ZCTU. From 1985 onward, the organization would seek to put increasing distance between itself and the state and ruling party. This pursuit of autonomy initially took the form of efforts by the ZCTU to improve administration and to build membership. But it would expand rapidly in the late 1980s to include a critique of government's labor relations policies and the state's emerging neoliberal economic program. Both aspects of this attack seized upon the redistributive policies enunciated by ZANU-PF at the outset of independence, using these to attack the performance of ZANU-PF in government. ZANU-PF's early promises therefore created space for a new labor-led activism.

Rebuilding and Resurgence after 1985

The ZCTU's emerging role as an important pole of social critique and democratic activism in the late 1980s stemmed from organizational developments within the ZCTU, changes on the national political and economic terrain, and shifts in regional and international politics. The labor center began to develop as one of very few viable national "civic" organizations,[4] aiming to represent not only its own constituents' interests but also the concerns and needs found in the mass constituencies of black civil society (Saunders 1995; Saunders et al. 1995). For the ZCTU this exercise in building mutual support provided new means of bringing pressure to bear on the state, thus forcing concessions on questions of participation and accountability. A key need was to develop effective social coalitions to advance the ZCTU's position and defend it against counterattacks.

The initial revival of the labor movement's national political presence was based on the ZCTU's improved internal management and ZANU-PF's relaxation of control over political debate. Management improved slowly after 1985, but it accelerated after a July 1988 biennial congress at which a restructuring program was approved. This created a full-time secretary-general and staff and proper accounting and administrative procedures. Improvements were immediate.

Improved management generated a growing presence of union affiliates. Though union membership remained static at about 163,000 workers in the mid-1980s, the number of registered unions increased by eleven between 1984 and 1987 (Shadur 1994, 113). Between 1988 and 1992, official union membership rose by approximately 25 percent, to more than 200,000 (see Tables 6.1, 6.2, and 6.3). This increase occurred with the rising urban industrial content of unionized employment and despite overall stagnant growth in formal sector employment in the 1980s.

But it was only with the merger of ZANU-PF and ZAPU at the end of 1987, and the ensuing period of relative *glasnost* or political openness, that room was created for freer debate and activism. For the ZCTU, this freedom initially involved increased action on the imperiled state of free collective bargaining under existing labor laws and ZANU-PF's foot-dragging over its redistributive development program. In the first case the ZCTU called for widening tripartite consultations on the LRA and the distancing of the ministry from wage setting and collective bargaining. In the second, union officials demanded explanations from ZANU-PF in an attempt to extract continued—if only rhetorical—commitment to a socialist program (*Financial Gazette* September 30, 1988; *Ziana* August 15, 1988). There was concern at the detention and deportation of twelve expatriate Trotskyites accused of inciting militant socialist positions within a ZCTU union. Consultations with government and employers through tripartite structures improved but led to few substantial advances for workers. Demands for participation in government's social and macroeconomic policy making met with hostility.

Clearly, there were limits to how much pressure the labor movement could apply on its own, even in the context of political openness. Constitutional changes in 1987 permitted the president to appoint 20 MPs to the 150-member parliament. In light of "socialist" ZANU-PF's failure to represent workers' interests, the ZCTU argued, workers should have their own specially appointed delegates to the National Assembly. ZCTU leaders noted that government had already appointed some MPs to represent "minority interests," notably whites. Therefore, they called for a limited number of MPs to be appointed on the ZCTU's recommendation to represent the large constituency of workers. ZANU-PF's response was emphatic and negative: the ruling party alone would decide on special interest representation, and ZCTU-designated MPs would sit in the assembly only by defeating ZANU-PF candidates in the course of elections. When ZANU-PF finally anointed

Table 6.1 Membership of ZCTU Affiliated Unions: 1998, 1992, 1988

	1998	1992	1988
1. Associated Mineworkers Union of Zimbabwe	32,000	26,000 (35,000)	26,000
2. Zimbabwe Construction and Allied Workers Union	n.d.	25,000	15,000
3. Federation of Municipal Workers [Zimbabwe Urban Councils Workers Union]	15,000	15,355	9,282
4. General Agricultural and Plantation Workers Union	80,000	15,000	10,000
5. National Engineering Workers Union	22,000	15,000	8,500
6. Zimbabwe Amalgamated Railwaymen Union	n.d.	12,000	12,000
7. Commercial Workers Union of Zimbabwe	22,000	10,000 (21,000)	7,000
8. Zimbabwe Textile Workers Union	6,000	10,000 (12,000)	6,345
9. Zimbabwe Catering & Hotel Workers Union	15,000	9,500 (12,000)	9,500
10. National Union of the Clothing Industry	5,000	7,000 (10,000)	6,245
11. Zimbabwe Motor Industries Workers Union		6,410 (10,000)	6,410
12. Zimbabwe Post and Telecommunications Workers Union	6,500	5,775	5,628
13. Zimbabwe Tobacco Industrial Workers Union	n.d.	3,800	2,658
14. Zimbabwe Leather, Shoe and Allied Workers Unions	6,500	3,725 (5,000)	2,556
15. Zimbabwe Chemicals, Plastics, and Allied Workers Union	3,000	3,723 (5,000)	1,588
16. United Food and Allied Workers Union	6,000 (12,000)	6,000	n.d.
17. Zimbabwe Graphical Workers Union	3,812	3,602	n.d.
18. Iron and Steel Workers Union of Zimbabwe [Ziscosteel Workers Union]	3,300	2,080	n.d.
19. Transport and General Workers' Union	3,000 (7,000)	3,000	n.d.
20. Zim Education, Scientific, Social, & Culture Workers Union	2,800	4,001	n.d.
21. Zimbabwe Furniture and Allied Workers Union [Zimbabwe Furniture & Cabinet Workers Union	11,000	2,500	2,300
22. Zimbabwe Electricity and Energy Workers Union [National Union of ZESA Workers]	3,000	2,000	2000
23. Zimbabwe Banking and Allied Workers Union [Zimbabwe Society of Bank Officials]	4,500	1,390	1,169
24. Air Transport Workers' Association	747	650	n.d.
25. Zimbabwe Radio & Television Electronics Manufacturing Workers Union	560	560	n.d.
26. Zimbabwe Pulp & Paper Workers Union	543	n.d.	n.d.
27. Cement and Lime Workers Union of Zimbabwe	500	n.d.	n.d.
28. Zimbabwe Union of Musicians	400	400	n.d.
29. Air Transport Workers Union	350	356	n.d.
30. Zimbabwe Union of Journalists	200	200	n.d.

Table 6.1 (continued)

	1998	1992	1988
31. National Local Authorities and District Development Fund Workers Union	200	n.d.	n.d.
32. Domestic and Allied Workers Union	3,000	9,000	n.d.
Total	200,590 (243,232)	162,835	n.d.

Sources: Makanya, Ngirandi, and Schiphorst (1993) and ZCTU (1998).
Compiled from union affiliation returns recorded by the ZCTU Accounts Department in 1992 and 1988; the 1998 figures, which are incomplete, were compiled from affiliate interviews. In [brackets], the name under which a trade union was previously known is given; figures in (parentheses) are *actual* estimates of Union Affiliate membership from Makanya, Ngirandi, and Schiphorst (1993). n.d. means there is no data available for this time period.

Table 6.2 Membership of Public Service Unions

	1998	1992	1985
1. Zimbabwe Teachers Association	54,000	42,800	30,000
2. Zimbabwe Nurses Association	n.d.	14,000	5,000
3. Government Workers Association	n.d.	n.d.	8,500
4. Public Services Association	45,000	35,000	n.d.
Total	n.d.	91,800	43,500

Sources: for 1985: (Wood 1988, 296); for 1992: Makanya, Ngirandi and Schiphorst (1993); for 1998: ZCTU (1998)

Table 6.3 Trade Union Membership (ZCTU Affiliates) Trends: 1990–2001

Year	Membership (× 1000)	Employment (× 1000)	Unionization rate (%)
1990	200.1	1,192.1	16.8
1991	191.4	1,244.0	15.4
1992	200.6	1,236.2	16.2
1993	200.8	1,240.3	16.2
1994	192.1	1,263.3	15.2
1995	197.8	1,239.6	16.0
1996	152.5	1,273.8	12.0
1997	184.3	1,323.3	13.9
1998	193.3	1,348.5	14.3
1999	197.9	1,314.4	15.1
2000	165.0	1,290.0	12.8
2001	180.0	1,185.3	15.2

Source: LEDRIZ, databank (Harare 2004)

a "trade union MP," it chose a pro–ZANU-PF ex-ZCTU official who later became labor minister.

Both the government's domination of labor relations and the "united" ZANU-PF's unassailable presence in state politics helped push the ZCTU toward seeking allies and space for mobilization in civil society. In the late 1980s more autonomous civic organizations reemerged, concerned with issues of democratization and government accountability. They grew and proliferated rapidly in the early 1990s. This development was fueled by public revelations of high-level state corruption and mismanagement, the opening of political space as a result of the changing domestic and international political environment, and declining social and economic conditions in the 1990s. Initially, it was also provoked by the limitations on political freedoms still in place after the ZANU-PF/ZAPU merger.

The civic resurgence in Zimbabwe was carried forward by focal themes, debates, and agencies that shifted in their prominence as the social and economic crisis deepened during the 1990s. First, the locus of civic activism was centered on government corruption, unaccountability, and ZANU-PF's ideological drifting from its redistributive program. That focus was fueled by increasing evidence of high-level public corruption, as seen, for example, in the "Willowgate" scandal of 1989, which led to the resignation of five government leaders and demonstrated the vulnerability of ZANU-PF to public criticism and challenge.[5] Civic campaigns then moved to encompass rights-based campaigns against proposals for a legislated one-party state and the continuation of emergency powers. ZANU-PF's formal conversion to neoliberalism in 1990–91 marked a new phase of critique and organizing around issues of the social economy. This gradually challenged the government in ways that helped provoke a general crisis of governance and legitimacy. By the end of the 1990s, a broad civic coalition with interorganizational networks emerged to directly confront the crisis situation posed by an increasingly remote, violent, and elite-driven state.

Civic campaigning quickly became an accepted and growing feature of national social life in the early 1990s. The coming of majority rule in South Africa, the collapse of allies in Eastern Europe, and the ruling party's assumption that no substantial political project could challenge it for control of the state coaxed ZANU-PF in the direction of controlled liberalization of a political space.[6] Emerging from the weighty influence of interests aligned to the ruling party, the civil society organizational terrain involved a limited but growing array of social groups and institutions, including university students, churches, women's groups, human rights activists, and professional and consumer groups. The ZCTU was positioned at the leading edge of this informal civic "movement."

A key factor in the ZCTU's leading civic role was its established organizational strength. In 1990, the labor movement was one of the few nationally organized institutions with an identifiable, relatively coherent membership and a capacity to mobilize it around policy issues (Sachikonye 1995a; Saunders et al. 1995). In addition, several ZCTU leaders recognized the strategic importance of developing links with other civil society interests in order to press for the consolidation of (and later, a return to) redistributive, pro-worker social and economic policies. To do this, the

ZCTU needed to connect the core issues of its labor agenda with the concerns of the emerging civic movement.

> The workers should not advocate the principle of "workerism" at all, because eighty percent of our population are peasants. What they should do is try to link up workers and peasants into strong structures to advance their interests. . . . The role of such a group would be that of the leading force in society, through the arm of popular organizations. . . . Other mass organizations—co-operatives, peasants, students—must organize as well, though generally these groups are not as conscientized, organized and self-directed as the ZCTU. This is why the ZCTU would like to step in and help others mobilize . . . (Tsvangirai 1990a).

Already in 1988, some in the ZCTU had seen the value of using the movement's organizational base to force broad concessions from government on political issues of interest to workers. ZCTU leaders threatened action, for example, against mismanagement in several urban councils. "We will ensure that the working class control the councils," said ZCTU's secretary-general, Morgan Tsvangirai. "Councilors must start jumping around" (*Herald* December 22, 1988).

The clear risks in this strategy increased sharply along with the rising voice of public criticism against ZANU-PF. In late 1989 Tsvangirai was jailed for six weeks for subversive intent under emergency powers regulations. He had expressed support for University of Zimbabwe students who had demonstrated against government corruption and cutbacks, leading to their arrest and closure of the university. "My own detention was part of the targeting of the labor movement. . . . the most potent force of dissent," noted Tsvangirai (1990a).

This hostility was an obstacle for the ZCTU, which was keen to keep channels of communication and negotiation with government open as a means of influencing government policy, especially on market liberalization policies. And the labor movement's changing relationship with government was a cause for polarization within the ZCTU, as some affiliates and leaders who favored close links with ZANU-PF challenged the emerging, more autonomy-minded ZCTU leadership. At the 1990 ZCTU Congress the split opened more widely, likely leveraged by political interventions by the ruling party. One result was the fueling of a bitter internal campaign by a dissident faction sympathetic to the ruling party against the leaders reconfirmed at the congress. Another was the important victory won by the latter in moving the ZCTU explicitly toward a position of political nonalignment and support for the practice of multiparty democracy.

At the same time, the labor movement pursued a parallel path of political engagement with its emerging civic allies, seeking democratic reforms at the level of state politics and basic human rights. One instance involved a campaign against the retention of emergency powers; a second, efforts to dissuade ZANU-PF from imposing a legislated one-party state (Mandaza and Sachikonye 1991; Raftopoulos 1992). Both came after the 1990 elections, which ZANU-PF won handily and hoped to use as a springboard for the rapid enactment of a one-party state. Through public seminars, an aggressive media advertising campaign, and direct education of civic membership, the loose civic coalition succeeded in winning on both issues. In July 1990 the state of emergency was finally permitted to lapse by government after twenty-six years of continuous enforcement. And in September ZANU-PF abandoned plans to legislate a one-party state. Concurrent political changes in apartheid South Africa and the former Eastern Bloc helped facilitate this political liberalization.

These civic successes enhanced civil society's emerging presence and greater leverage in national political debates while temporarily diminishing the state's legal powers of censure. They also placed the ZCTU and civic critics at the center of attacks by the ruling party on its opponents.

The New Era of "Reform"

ZANU-PF signaled its decisive abandonment of a mass-oriented redistributive development program in 1989 with the introduction of trade liberalization measures aimed at loosening market controls, hopefully to facilitate employment growth (Zimbabwe 1991a). In 1991 a full package of neoliberal reforms, the Economic Structural Adjustment Program (ESAP), was announced. ESAP was launched with strong backing from the private sector and its representative institutions—and considerable financial and political support from the World Bank, the IMF and Western donor countries.

ESAP scrapped ZANU-PF's broad development program that in the 1980s had included high spending on social services and equity programs, the protection of employment, and close regulation of capital flows, trade, and investment (Stoneman 1988). Despite claims by government that the new program was homegrown, most of ESAP's key macroeconomic components were standard boilerplate. They included removal of consumer subsidies, lifting of price controls, devaluation of the Zimbabwe dollar, trade and currency deregulation, and promotion of export production. Standard, too, were the World Bank's and the IMF's recommendations for fiscal and public sector reform, including slashing the deficit in half, to 5 percent of GDP, primarily by the retrenchment of more than 20,000 of the state's 190,000 workers; the commercialization and privatization of public enterprises; and the reduction of social spending. Finally, there was the string of large loans and credit facilities from the World Bank, the IMF, and international donors, aimed at supporting the country's short-term balance of payments and new domestic investment. These basic prescriptions were not fundamentally altered by later policy initiatives that succeeded ESAP after it officially expired in 1995: the Zimbabwe Program for Economic and Social Transformation (ZIMPREST) in 1998, and the Millennium Economic Recovery Program (MERP) in 2000.

In exchange for ESAP austerity, Zimbabweans were promised sustained economic growth and employment creation. Zimbabwe would be "Africa's first Newly Industrialized Country," said Finance Minister Bernard Chidzero. An optimistic target of 5 percent annual growth in GDP was set, with 30 percent new growth coming from manufacturing. It was argued that a modernized industrial sector would attract foreign investment, employ more highly skilled workers, and enable the country to compete in foreign markets. To cushion the expected shocks to consumer markets and employment, a special ESAP "safety net" program was enacted at the insistence of donors (Zimbabwe 1991b). In late 1991, schemes were announced for the retraining of retrenched civil service employees and the provision of consumer food subsidies for the poorest urban families and educational and health fee exemptions for poorer households. Most of these programs were not fully implemented or funded.

In reality, ESAP failed to foster growth, and the short-term shocks turned quickly into a chronic and worsening social crisis. Growth reached 5 percent in only one of the five years of the program (1994) and averaged only 0.9 percent in 1991–95. Heavy government borrowing, high interest rates, and devaluation led to a swelling state debt (from 45 percent of GDP in 1989 to more than 100 percent in 1995). High repayments contributed to budget deficits of around 10 percent—double the 5 percent projected. Inflation shot to previously unseen levels. During the 1992 drought it surpassed 40 percent, and it averaged nearly 30 percent over 1991–94. In 1991–92, food prices for lower income households rose more than 50 percent, while typical wage increases averaged only 10 percent.

State spending cutbacks were up to 40 percent in real terms. Demand for services rose due to increasing impoverishment, declining real incomes, and the growing AIDS pandemic. Nongovernmental organizations (NGOs) and other observers agreed that health and education services were crumbling and that social indicators were in chronic decline (Berridge 1993; Chisvo and Munro 1994; Lennock 1994). In 1980 government spent $11.80 per person annually on health, in 1990 $11.45, in 1992 (in constant 1980 dollars) $9.66, and in 1995 only $9.14—far below the internationally recommended level of $13. Education per capita real spending also stagnated or fell back. Meanwhile, government's introduction of various "user fees" for health care and education also barred access to needed services to increasing numbers of people.

As Zimbabweans paid higher taxes, rates, and fees for diminishing access to poor services, the impact on the majority quickly became clear. In the 1990s, life expectancy fell on average by twenty years. The rate of maternal deaths due to pregnancy and childbirth rose by a factor of five, and infants were 33 percent more likely to die than at the start of ESAP. In Harare, a startling 22 percent of deaths in 1999 in children one to four years of age were from malnutrition (Saunders 2000, 64). HIV/AIDS was partly to blame for these rising mortality figures, but a large part is explained by reduced spending on rural clinics and prevention strategies.

Another key outcome of the growing crisis was a sharp decline in average real wages, which fell from Z$8,600 (Zimbabwean $) in 1990, to Z$6,700 in 1992, and by nearly 25 percent by 1995. In October 1992, the minimum wage of domestic workers was less than 50 percent of a basic food basket for a family of four (Kanji and Jazdowska 1993). By the mid-1990s, average real earnings, which contracted nearly 10 percent per year between 1991 and 1994, would fall to the lowest levels since the early 1970s (ZCTU 1995a). ESAP, one study argued, was dragging ordinary Zimbabwean workers to the brink of widespread destitution (Gibbon 1995, 30). Worse off were retrenched workers, some of whom lost their jobs because of business failure and public service cutbacks. Thousands of others were squeezed out in the course of rationalization programs. The Ministry of Labor estimated that thirty-two thousand formal sector workers were retrenched during 1991–96 (Zimbabwe 1996). But ZCTU officials claimed the real figure was probably twice that number (interviews, ZCTU Economics Dept. staff 1995–96).[7] All employment sectors bore the brunt of ESAP austerity.

Popular Response and State Containment

An important and direct result of the ESAP-inspired economic and social crisis was an extended period of popular activism against the program—and a significant decline in ZANU-PF's political credibility. Indeed, such was the unpopularity of the neoliberal reforms that public condemnation of them even came from within the ranks of the ZANU-PF senior leadership. The main locus of complaint and mobilization, though, was civil society. It entailed the rapid development of community-based organizations, spontaneous street protests, widespread critiques of the state's pared-back social programs, and unprecedented outbreaks of labor action.

The political schism with the ruling party's established allies in the labor movement, radical intellectual circles, and other popular institutions was apparent with the first moves toward trade liberalization in the late 1980s. It quickly resulted in demonstrations and criticism from university students, intellectuals, and labor leaders. The gap was substantially widened by government's anxious, heavy-handed response in the short term—and was stretched to the breaking point by the state's institutionalization of constraints on its critics. For example, the government in 1991 redrafted the University of Zimbabwe's legislated constitution to give it enhanced and unmatched power to oversee the broad policy and narrow disciplinary procedures of the university.

At the ZCTU, the first economic reforms of 1989 were met by stridently nationalist and radical policy critiques. The ZCTU "alternative" mixed calls for greater state-led nationalization, expropriation, and indigenization of leading productive sector and financial institutions, with demands for ideological, administrative, and fiscal vigilance in government (ZCTU 1989). Government's introduction of ESAP in 1991 presented intense challenges to the labor movement, since organized labor and the old industrial relations regime stood clearly in the way of neoliberal reforms, which included the "freeing" of labor rights in industrial relations.

The state's strategy involved a direct assault on the organizing capacity and shop floor rights of unions and workers by means of new industrial relations interventions that sought to cut off the national labor center and affiliates from the rank and file in the workplace. It augmented the power of employers in workplace labor relations. The state also exacerbated existing divisions within the ZCTU and its affiliates, further diminishing the political profile of the labor center. This attack demanded a flexible approach by labor to retain its autonomy and effective power.

The ZCTU's initial responses to the neoliberal challenge focused on rolling back the pace and scope of reforms through demands for consultative discussions. When this approach failed, and government first formalized its comprehensive reform program, the labor movement emphasis shifted increasingly to defending unions and workers' rights while building new structures for mobilization within and outside the labor movement.

Even before ESAP-related retrenchments and financial pressures threatened the capacities of the national labor center and many of its affiliates, there was evidence in the early 1990s that structural weaknesses and divisions within the ZCTU undermined unity and efficiency. Slow progress had been made in facilitating low-level participation in union organizing and skills training, particularly at the level of workers' committees. Effective communication links among national, union, and worker committee structures were often poorly developed (Makanya, Ngirandi and Schiphorst 1993). Much of this was also the direct outcome of growing union and shop floor autonomy, bolstered by waves of successful local labor actions in which the national labor center did not play a decisive role. When workers did mobilize, they were most effective when organizing through their branches and union affiliates; when they did not, they often fell victim to employers' strategies of co-option and marginalization. Without solving these problems, ZCTU would not be in a position to organize and sustain a campaign against neoliberal incursions into workers' rights.

Against this backdrop the ZCTU's combative October 1990 Congress resolved to place new emphasis on the consolidation of union structures at the national and affiliate levels (ZCTU, 1990). New departmental and regional structures were announced, including a health and safety department and, later, organizing and information units. There were calls for the negotiated merger of the public sector and industrial workforces under one labor law and one united national union center. The building of alliances with civil society groupings and local communities was recognized as a critical strategic goal: through such linkages the institutional weaknesses of the ZCTU could be more quickly and comprehensively addressed. As the secretary-general observed in 1990:

> When issues like corruption and price increases come up, the ZCTU does not have the national organizational ability to mobilize people fully around that, to reach all progressive groups on such issues. The most we can usually do to reach out across the country is release a position statement—but without supporting grassroots structures, it just becomes a statement of a position. . . . What is needed is to organize first, and then, back up your public position with action. That sort of approach is much more effective. . . . We want to see grassroots groups and workers organized more closely, side by side, in the regions, and also district committees (Tsvangirai 1990).

These path-breaking initiatives, which helped redefine the institutional shape and politics of ZCTU in the 1990s, were confirmed in the midst of a simmering struggle involving the ZCTU and some of its stronger affiliates closely associated with the agenda of the ruling party. This struggle emerged precisely because of imbalances between the national and affiliate structures of the organization. At the 1990 Congress conflict had erupted in the form of a challenge by a minority faction led by ZCTU's former president, Jeffrey Mutandare, under the auspices of a dispute over affiliate dues and labor center financing. This unsuccessful dissident attack on the national executive strongly suggested that the organizational challenges confronting the ZCTU went beyond the issue of strengthening union capacities.[8] Meanwhile, financial troubles precipitated by the ZCTU "dissidents" through their withholding of union dues—troubles that were resolved only at the 1995 Congress—exacerbated divisions within affiliates at a time when they were under increasing attack from the state. They hampered the ZCTU's rebuilding program.

For its part, government moved to utilize a range of instruments, including legislation and harassment, to corrode the labor movement's potential capacity to challenge ESAP. Initially this involved an increased tempo in ZANU-PF's political attacks on the ZCTU's legitimacy. In April 1991, Labor Minister John Nkomo announced without warning that the government would de-register the ZCTU and demand changes to its constitution before considering renewed recognition (*Sunday Mail* April 28, 1991). The ZCTU was forced to seek a temporary interdict in the high court to prevent the minister from making further allegations and de-registering the body.

The union leadership took the occasion to sound its own warning. "We want to avoid the politics of frustration, strike action, demonstrations and spontaneous street politics that occurs when democracy breaks down and people are no longer listened to," cautioned ZCTU's president, Gibson Sibanda, on May Day in 1991, in what turned out to be a prophetic speech.

> Workers are demanding effective and democratic organizations, whether in government or in the unions. People are actively discussing political, economic and social issues. The sleeping giant is beginning to wake up in Zimbabwe. . . . We have given too much power to the state and now we are watching helplessly while it runs out of control with our jobs and our lives. In 1980 we gave the state power to redistribute the wealth in Zimbabwe, but some misused that power to distribute jobs and opportunities to their own friends and family, and built up areas of political patronage. . . . We need independent watchdogs and checks on central state power. One of those watchdogs is the trade union movement.

Sibanda then identified the locus of the current democratic struggle and ZCTU's role in it.

> It is not possible to reform the economy without political reform. The demand for participation and consultation, for accountability and openness in government and for open debate on national issues is one that can only be realized by ourselves making this happen. . . . We call for an economic convention for all national patriotic organizations and all economic interest groups in Zimbabwe to come together to identify and find solutions to our current crisis (Sibanda 1991).

ZANU-PF rejected this idea and chose instead to use its own arsenal of state power and political suasion to subdue the "waking giant." Here, its interventions on the terrain of industrial relations under the auspices of structural adjustment reforms led to critical, wide-ranging consequences.

Neoliberalization of Labor Relations

Under the cover of structural adjustment, the state made substantial changes to the labor code and related regulatory instruments in an attempt to undermine organized labor politically and practically. In the early 1990s, government announced its gradual withdrawal from the collective bargaining process as part of the liberalization of the labor market. In reality the state's diminished role would be less striking than claimed. Most "liberalization" reforms had the tendency of increasing the balance of power on the side of employers and the state, and against workers.

New statutory instruments (379 and 404) in 1991 gave shop floor workers' councils the right to negotiate codes of conduct and retrenchment regulations at the shop floor and industrial council levels without the approval of the Ministry of Labor, ZCTU, or national employers' organizations. Such measures lessened the likelihood of industry-wide standards of employment being maintained and invited the fragmentation of collective worker action within and across industries. The attack was intensified when government unilaterally amended the LRA in 1992, after dropping most of the draft amendments agreed upon in tripartite meetings in 1987 and 1990.

The new amendments removed the ZCTU from the collective bargaining process, cutting it off from the grassroots membership. The regulations placed additional constraints on union power at the shop floor level and favored management and Ministry of Labor officials. On the other hand, the shop floor workers' committees mandated to lead collective bargaining lost many of their most qualified workers, now designated as "managerial employees." The amendments also asserted the primacy of agreements on retrenchments and codes of conduct made by management-worker committees ("works councils") over those reached by sector-wide bodies comprised of union and employer representatives ("employment councils"). This created such chaos that by 1993 sector-wide minimum standards were effectively put in place with government's consent. Finally, the amendments made collective job action almost impossible, by giving the state the right to issue blocking "show cause" orders and retaining wide definitions of "essential services."

These attacks on the labor movement, and ESAP's negative impact on workers' living standards, led to a period of escalating government-ZCTU conflict. The labor movement's strategy in support of demands for greater democratization was increasingly combative and involved demonstrations, information campaigns, lobbying initiatives targeting backbench MPs, and threats of wider "mass-action" (Tsvangirai 1991). The state's response was the application of greater pressure and force in a seemingly deliberate effort by government to provoke new conflicts.

A benchmark in this process came in June 1992, when police broke up a ZCTU anti-ESAP demonstration in Harare that had been banned. It led to a successful constitutional court challenge by the ZCTU against laws used by the police to suppress freedom of speech and association.[9] Relations with the state worsened when two hundred unionists walked out of a meeting with the minister and deputy minister of labor after it became clear that ESAP policies were not negotiable. Minister Nkomo responded that the ZCTU represented probably "less than ten percent of the workforce," and he warned that "from now on government will have to amend Bills without consultation because we are dealing with people who might be illiterate" (*Sunday Mail* June 21, 1992). The government then curtailed constructive communications with the ZCTU for the next three years, pushing the LRA amendments through parliament against the combined voices of workers and employers. It used state-dominated media and other outlets to allege the ZCTU's "political ambitions" (*The Worker* June 29, 1992).

The ensuing period of cold war between the state and the labor movement was characterized by sharp public exchanges and successive waves of strikes in the public and private sectors. Many came in response to ESAP-related workplace pressure from employers. One survey of publicly reported industrial actions in the 1990s reported a marked rise in the quantity and duration of actions as well as the number of workers participating (Table 6.4).

New features of industrial action were emerging that pointed to the entrenchment of labor militancy due to the harsh economic environment: more national or cross-regional actions took place, across a greater variety of sectors. Strikes were increasingly illegal or wildcat in nature and were used with regularity as part of the collective bargaining process.[10] Well-organized affiliates were under increasing pressure to agitate; less well-organized sectors saw waves of grassroots militancy that were relatively successful.

The spiraling cycles of strikes into the mid-1990s—now including public sector actions—rendered the terrain of labor relations increasingly volatile. ZCTU warnings

Table 6.4 Labor Actions in the 1980s–90s

Year	Number of labor actions	Number of workers participating
1988	10	3,600+
1989	5	800+
1990	15	10,000+
1991	9	10,000+
1992	10	12,000+
1993	19	18,500+
1994	17	13,000+
1995	25	20,000+
1996	28	235,000+
1997	55	1,073,000+

Source: Survey of national newspaper reports of strikes, demos, go slows, and so on. ZCTU mimeograph (1998) and Saunders (2001).

Note: + symbol after these figures indicate that they are an underestimation of labor actions due to under-reporting arising from the limited geographical scope and coverage of only larger actions.

"Success" of Industrial Actions, 1993–97

Year	Number of actions	Success	Failure	Discussion or unclear	Unreported
1993	19	7	3	5	4
1994	17	8	1	4	4
1995	25	16	1	6	2
1996	28	13	2	11	2
1997	55	34	6	7	8

at the time of the LRA amendments about the destabilization of industrial relations and the resurgence of shop floor militancy appeared to be borne out. The 1992 reforms and ESAP's dismal performance paradoxically strengthened a bargaining position for labor: as militancy expanded and the economic crisis deepened, some in government came once again to see the ZCTU as a potentially valuable social partner. On one hand, the state presumed, the ZCTU could help mediate and stabilize growing conflict within labor relations; on the other, it showed interest in helping reshape ESAP into a more effective, labor-friendly program that a collection of constituencies could be rallied to support. Co-option engineered in this manner held the additional advantage of preempting closer links between the ZCTU and key ZANU-PF constituencies, which ESAP's dislocations threatened to cultivate, for example, pro–ZANU-PF black capitalists. By late 1994, the first moves toward state-union reconciliation were under way. At the ZCTU's 1995 Congress both government and the labor center acknowledged the benefits of tripartite cooperation and pledged closer working linkages. The ZCTU moved toward a dual-pronged approach to relations with the state. It recognized that key tripartite initiatives—such as the National Social Security Authority and its plans—depended on renewed, closer working contact with the state. But the ZCTU continued to pursue alliances with a range of civil society groups in opposition to state unilateralism (ZCTU 1995a).

The hallmark of the first prong of this new approach was "Beyond ESAP," a ZCTU research program developed to provide alternatives to the ESAP *status quo* (ZCTU 1995b). It was premised on greater influence in policy-making circles, a dubious possibility. But it was also meant to serve as the ZCTU's efforts to educate and mobilize labor's other civic partners in order to demand greater political and economic concessions from the state. For the ZCTU the price of regaining access to government was its tacit commitment to carry its membership into the process of cooperation, foreswearing the more combative tactics of the early 1990s. But there were doubts about the ability of the ZCTU to carry its constituency with it. The links reaching from the shop floor through union affiliates to the national labor center remained uneven and sometimes weak. More importantly, the intensification of economic hardship, anger at ESAP, and heightened antagonisms between management and workers made effective interventions by outside labor representatives a waning prospect.

The second prong of the ZCTU leadership's emerging strategy involved nurturing the existing and burgeoning links with popular civil society to engage in the deepening of democracy through wider civic and "stakeholder" participation in policy making. The ZCTU's secretary-general argued that a key factor in ESAP's crisis was the state's failure to include an array of social forces in shaping and overseeing the implementation of its policies. "There is a need for the role of the state to be properly defined. The state has a role to play in the economy—we in the ZCTU don't believe in the complete withdrawal of the state from the marketplace and society. But we think the state needs to intervene to empower, not to control; to redress imbalances, and do so under a consensual process" (Tsvangirai 1995).

But it was unclear how to reconcile the demands of the market with the interests of social fractions adversely affected by ESAP reforms. There was growing interest within the ZCTU for the establishment of a national tripartite authority, modeled roughly on South Africa's. Exploratory proposals for such an institution in 1996 were rejected by government, however, which resisted external constraints on its power by civil society and even disgruntled elements within ZANU-PF. Government's preferred solution to this political dilemma came with the 1997 establishment of the National Economic Consultative Forum (NECF), a pseudo-tripartite structure that had no legal and little political-moral authority. Crucially, government stipulated that the NECF's membership would be held on an individual rather than representative or institutional basis. NECF's deliberations would be nonbinding and nonofficial. Thus, the ZCTU refused to join the NECF, deriding it as a diversionary, government-friendly "talk shop." Government refused to participate in meaningful tripartite negotiations until cycles of labor militancy by ZCTU national structures forced it to accept the establishment—if not the spirit—of the Tripartite Negotiating Forum (TNF) in late 1998, but government did not abandon the NECF.

Government's prevarication about, and opportunistic resort to, tripartism reflected the more profound dilemma both it and the labor movement faced as the social, economic, and—by 1997—*political* crises of the 1990s ensued. These crises undermined the institutional and political authority of government and energized social forces opposed to market-oriented policies.

For the labor movement, a parallel set of tensions emerged: militant workers and civil society allies demanded not just productive consensus with government but also greater direct challenges to business and the state, to attack its corruption,[11] and to roll back measures that were behind growing inequality. The explosion of wildcat industrial actions and civic protest in the mid-1990s showed, above all, that workers' grievances and anger needed to be addressed if the support of grassroots constituencies was to be maintained. Increasingly this calculus influenced the ZCTU's strategic engagement with the state. By 1998 a broad-based informal alliance of civil society groups emerged under ZCTU leadership, which demanded greater accountability of the state. This alliance catalyzed into a formal political movement that challenged ZANU-PF power in the 2000 elections.

Social Unionism and Civic Alliances

The ZCTU's growing commitment to social unionism and political restructuring in the late 1990s was driven by the convergence of several factors: the rapid deterioration of economic and social conditions; a series of disastrous politically motivated state expenditures in 1997–98; and government's break with its former international financial partners. The ZANU-PF leadership also consolidated a new strategic alliance with powerful security interests and effectively abandoned dialogue with perceived antagonistic civil society groups. In turn, the labor movement was increasingly driven by grassroots demands to play a lead role in mounting mass actions to achieve political objectives.[12] By the late 1990s the national political role of the ZCTU leadership was increasingly inextricable from its industrial relations one.

In the early 1990s ESAP provided the initial, yet ambiguous, basis for the emergence of the civic movements. The ESAP-inspired austerity helped to create a large "natural" constituency of disaffected people. It also impoverished already weakened civic institutions representing popular interests. Funding of local organizations was imperiled by high inflation. It opened stark differences of capacity between the few civics with internal or foreign resource bases and the large majority of local organizations that typically had only volunteers and limited organizational reach. The labor movement, in contrast, had a voluntary mass membership to run union activities, professional capacities to organize, affiliate contributions, and regional and international aid.

The leading role of the ZCTU as a *civil society organization* (not simply a labor-oriented one) evolved quickly, as the labor center focused on issues of social participation and state accountability. The ZCTU moved to consolidate and strengthen its regional and national structures. In the first half of the 1990s, Zimbabwe witnessed an explosion in the number, variety, and geographical spread of civic groups, including many focused on local government accountability, food security, and health alliances (Saunders 2000, 49–84). ZCTU structures and members regularly provided critical political, logistical, and technical inputs that helped incubate and sustain other new initiatives. In this formative period of cooperation, the unparalleled capacity and grassroots presence of the ZCTU and its members helped imbricate the movement's agenda and its personnel into the heart of the emerging loosely formed civic "movement." Few national civics were established in this period that did *not* include the ZCTU or its activists as key members.[13]

While civil society organizations' capacity and popular legitimacy generally strengthened in the 1990s, ZANU-PF's reliance on and use of increasingly coercive state power expanded dramatically. It focused its attack on leading edge civics. The failure of formal political opposition to hold the ZANU-PF government to account also meant the ruling party could employ the state unilaterally against the civic opposition. Concerned at the growing level of civic protest,[14] in 1995 government amended the *Rhodesian Welfare Organizations Act*, renaming it the *Private Voluntary Organizations Act 1995*, or *PVO Act*. It attempted to narrow the room within civil society organizations for critiques of government and autonomous engagement with communities and donors.[15] Among other provisions, the PVO Act gave the minister near arbitrary powers to decertify, change the executive, or otherwise circumscribe the activities of any nongovernmental organization registered as a "welfare organization"—which included most civics and "service organizations."[16]

The PVO Act marked a new phase in government's strategy to control the space of civil society and national political debate. The act enabled an immediate attack on a well-established, nonpartisan civic organization, the Association of Women's Clubs (AWC), and the raiding of its assets by ZANU-PF's own Women's League.[17] The attack was highly symbolic: if a comparatively nonpolitical organization like the AWC was vulnerable to state intervention, all civic groups were. However, the act's unintended consequences were more profound: in 1996 the AWC challenged the constitutionality of the act, eventually winning a Supreme Court decision in 1997 that struck down the law on the basis of its infringement of rights to association and communication. The victory over government marked not just a victory for the AWC but also a new turning point for civil society-state relations: for many leading civics, government's blatant transgression of constitutional rights with the PVO Act suggested government itself would have to be confronted more directly. More effective constraints on the state's capacity to undermine constitutional rights were needed. This realization was the basis for the emergence of a powerful civic constitutional movement, with the leading participation of the ZCTU, concretized in the formation of the National Constitutional Assembly (NCA) in 1998. At the same time, civil society was increasingly polarized between organizations more willing to appease government (for example, the National Association of NGOs) and those like the NCA, which sought to challenge it.

Mass Action Politics

Civic and labor mobilization for expanded rights, government accountability, and higher living standards erupted in the form of unprecedented national mass actions in 1997–98. These followed new waves of large-scale, high-profile industrial actions in the public and private sectors in 1996 and 1997. This period witnessed the largest national strikes since 1948, involving more than 1 million workers and hundreds of thousands of others.

In August and September 1996 Zimbabwe saw its biggest strike since independence, when more than seventy thousand public sector workers walked out for more than two weeks in the latest in a series of "illegal" industrial actions. The dispute centered on the state's nonpayment of promised wage increases and its failure to make headway in harmonizing public and private sector labor laws by creating negotiating structures for public servants. Unions won significant gains in most cases, with salary increases and new negotiating structures with public service associations. While some portrayed the strike as a spontaneous display of anger, in reality it followed an extended period of intense organizing and mobilization within the workers' organizations, notably the Public Services Association and the Zimbabwe Teachers Association. In the year leading up to the 1996 strike, the associations had negotiated with government, linking regularly with their membership around their collective demands and the frustrations of the negotiation's progress. The strike, therefore, reflected the improved organizational strength of most public sector workers' associations and their renewed determination to normalize industrial relations in that sector.

Critically, the public sector strikes also reflected both an important political break with the ruling party and the growing organizational links between public and private sector workers. Public service workers, once the bedrock of ZANU-PF support following the post-1980s' de-racialization state-sector expansion (Raftopoulos and Phimister 2004, 358), now largely defied the party. At the same time, there was closer coordination between them and the ZCTU and private sector unions. At the outset of the new relationship, in late 1996 the ZCTU publicly aligned itself with public sector workers by calling for a two-day general strike in support of striking health workers. Although this wider action fizzled in disarray due to organizational confusion and differences, it both cemented public-private sector labor cooperation and provided important lessons around the need to create a consensus and strong internal channels of communication between levels of the labor movement (ZCTU 1996).

In 1997 a broad and rising wave of private sector strikes in response to deteriorating real wages notched up pressure on government to redress the economic crisis.

However, an emerging political crisis soon overtook industrial militancy as the key concern of government, business, civil society, and the labor movement. Explosive revelations of a scam became public in which senior ruling party and government officials quietly looted millions of dollars from a war veterans compensation fund. The ZANU-PF leadership came under enormous pressure from former liberation fighters within its ranks to make amends by channeling new resources to their ranks. Under threat of internal party rebellion, the leadership secretly negotiated a package of unbudgeted gratuities and pensions for up to fifty thousand ex-combatants, amounting to more than Z$4 billion in new government spending. Given existing state budget constraints, the payouts necessitated the emergency collection of new taxes and levies, including a 5 percent war veterans levy and higher petrol taxes.

There was an immediate public outcry over the punitive nature of the taxes for working and poor people, especially given the corrupt ruling party leadership. The situation worsened in November when government, seeking to rebuild its populist credibility, announced it would compulsorily acquire and resettle at least fifteen hundred commercial farms. In response, financial markets dumped the Zimbabwe dollar, which in one day—dubbed "black Friday"—fell 75 percent against international currencies. The beginning of a long period of sharpening economic instability began. It was exacerbated in 1998 by Zimbabwe's large-scale and costly military involvement in the Congo conflict and by the subsequent cutting off of most aid from foreign agencies and donors.

On December 9, 1997, a ZCTU-organized national mass action against the new taxes and levies constituted the first cross-sector national strike since 1948, and it involved more than a million formal sector workers. The strike shut down all significant commercial and industrial activity in the country. It included well-attended street demonstrations supported by a wide range of civil society groups, including business.[18] Despite intense government harassment, threats, and misinformation designed to derail the ZCTU and its allies, follow-on "stay-aways"[19] (workers who strike but stay home, foregoing public demonstrations) in March and November 1998 were nearly equally successful in attracting broad observance. In the March and November actions, nearly 80 percent of unionized workers went out for three days, affecting 90 percent of business (ZCTU 1998a; see Table 6.5).

Trade union affiliates and ZCTU regional and national structures reported in this period a rising tide of interest in the labor movement by formal and informal sector workers, civic activists, and community organizations. The strengthening and flexing of labor's muscle around political mass actions also helped to build the national profile of the workers' agenda, and there was sharp growth in dues-paying membership and increased rates of workplace unionization from 1997 to 2000 (see Table 6.3). One ZCTU study of grassroots labor views after the March 1998 actions found that political mobilization and mass action were also raising levels of expectation and commitment among workers, with a broad range of the membership expressing support for moves toward more explicit political confrontation with the state and ruling party (ZCTU 1998a).

Within the national labor center leadership there was renewed interest in pursuing a dual path of tripartite consultation *and* sharpened public critique of government around corruption, human rights, and poor governance. The ZCTU would

Table 6.5 Worker Participation in the March 3–4 Stay-away: Selected Estimates

	Total number in sector	Number union members	% sector on Strike[a]	Number of workers unions on strike
General Agricultural and Workers Union of Zimbabwe	300,000	80,000	7	20,000
Associated Mine Workers Union of Zimbabwe[b]	65,000	32,000	—	—
Commercial Workers Union of Zimbabwe	150,000	22,000	60	90,000
Furniture, Timber, and Allied Trades Union	20,000	11,000	75	15,000
Medical, Professional, and Allied Workers Union	15,000	1,200	60	9,000
National Engineering Workers Union	34,000	22,000	98	33,000
National Union of the Clothing Industry	22,000	5,000	100	22,000
Public Services Association (Adex, CSEA, GWA, Protech)[c]	80,000	45,000	80	65,000
Railway Association of Enginemen	750	750	100	750
Zimbabwe Amalgamated Railwaymen's Union	10,000	8,700	100	10,000
Zimbabwe Bankers and Allied Workers Union	8,000	4,500	70	5,600
Zimbabwe Catering and Hotel Workers Union	19,500	15,000	85	16,500
Zimbabwe Chemical and Plastics Workers Union[d]	80,000	13,000	100	80,000
Zimbabwe Electricity and Energy Workers Union	8,000	3,000	75	6,000
Zimbabwe Leather, Shoe, and Allied Workers Union	9,000	6,500	99	9,000
Zimbabwe Posts and Telecommunications Workers	10,000	6,500	100	10,000
Zimbabwe Railway Artisans Workers Union	1,200	1,200	100	1,200
Zimbabwe Teachers' Association[e]	96,000	54,000	70	67,000
Zimbabwe Textile Workers Union	12,000	6,000	95	11,400
Zimbabwe Urban Council Workers Union	21,000	15,000	75	15,000
Total of Unions Surveyed	961,450,	352,350	51%	486,450
Total of Unions Joining March Stay-Away	896,450	320,350	54%	486,450
Total Industrial (non-rural) Unions	596,450	240,350	78%	466,450

Source: ZCTU, Staying Away to Move Forward (1998)

[a] In cases of different rates of participation on the two days, this figure represents the average rate of participation.

Table 6.5 (continued)

---

[b] The AMUZ did not participate in the March stay-away.

[c] PSA figures are rough estimates only, based on compilation of regional and national estimates.

[d] Estimates of the number of workers varies between 55–80,000, depending on whether small companies are counted.

[e] ZIMTA estimates are rough estimates only.

negotiate but also retain the threat of mass action as a bargaining tool and not rule out the possibility of heightened political challenges to ZANU-PF. By the end of 1998 this strategy resulted in government's acceptance of the TNF and the opening of negotiations with unions to set minimum wages and establish consensus on the poverty datum line. Simultaneously, the ZCTU played a lead role in the newly formed NCA and helped prepare the ground for a February 1999 national convention of popular groups and civic organizations, focused on developing a *Working People's Agenda for Change.* This confirmed the ZCTU's return to a pro–poor redistributive development agenda.[20] Within six months a new political entity, the Movement for Democratic Change (MDC), was formed on the basis of this agenda. Leading up to this, the ZCTU had convened an extraordinary national congress at which it unanimously resolved to support the formation of the new political party. The MDC was publicly launched on September 11, 1999, in Harare. Of the MDC's interim executive, approximately half came from the national labor movement, including ZCTU President Sibanda and Secretary-General Tsvangirai. They became MDC vice president and president, respectively.

The ZANU-PF government responded to this growing challenge with coercion and conciliation. In December 1997, after the first mass action, ZCTU Secretary-General Tsvangirai was severely assaulted in his office by suspected ZANU-PF militants. In March 1998 the ZCTU's Bulawayo offices were firebombed. In coming years, as the MDC rose to challenge ZANU-PF, the level of physical violence and intimidation unleashed openly by state security officials, party activists, and their paramilitary allies rose dramatically. The targets included not only MDC leadership and activists but also trade unionists and civic organizers. The intensity and scope of violence rose in 2000, when a constitutional referendum in support of government was defeated. ZANU-PF was then challenged in parliamentary elections by the MDC—the ruling party's first authentically national, competitive opponent since independence. In 2000–02 alone, more than 150 opposition activists and suspected MDC supporters died at the hands of ZANU-PF-allied agents; thousands more were victims of extreme political violence.[21]

Conciliation was a complementary and sometimes disarming component of ZANU-PF's strategy for containing the labor movement and civics. With the TNF, for example, some progress was made for a brief period in gaining state cooperation in agreeing to minimum wage scales, establishing tripartite structures, and engaging in discussions for the development of a "social contract" (Kanyenze 2004). But state cooperation was always tentative, and in practice ZANU-PF tended to engage with an increasingly narrow range of civil society interests and organizations. Some of these it created as protégé, compromised, pseudo-civics under the heavy hand of a state that intended to displace institutions and initiatives established outside of state structures. But even limited forms of cooperation with critical civil society halted abruptly by February 2000, with government's constitutional referendum defeat at the hands of a civic alliance led by the NCA and backed by the MDC and ZCTU.

Militarized Politics and the Labor Movement

ZANU-PF's defeat in the February 2000 referendum—its first defeat in a national vote—sent shock waves through the political leadership and provoked a series of state-led actions aimed at bolstering ZANU-PF's advantage before parliamentary elections in June 2000. Foremost among ZANU-PF's moves was the violent invasion of commercial farms—and later mines and other productive enterprises—by self-described war veterans, aided and supported by state security agents and by ruling party officials. In December 2000 government created an auxiliary youth militia—officially dubbed a "National Youth Service Training" program. It deployed them the following year to strengthen ZANU-PF's capacity to destabilize the opposition and local communities across the country. The youth militia was trained by state security agents and war veterans and numbered perhaps more than twenty thousand in all. In the campaign preceding the 2002 presidential elections, they were responsible for an increasing proportion of violence committed against the MDC, its supporters, civil society activists, and others. The youth militia, established on bases around the country, also played a key role in the politicization of food and access to health and education services in the early 2000s. In many instances it attracted the ire of even government officials (Reeler 2003; Solidarity Peace Trust 2003).

President Mugabe emerged victorious from the controversial 2002 vote but remained nonconciliatory, as noted in his victory speech: "We will make them run. If they haven't run before we will make them run now. . . . We will not pander to them any longer. That's gone. It's finished. We are now entering a new chapter, and there will be firm government, very firm government."[22]

In the early 2000s, alongside new initiatives like the youth militia, several key state institutions were restructured and brought under the growing influence of the ruling party–aligned security apparatus. These included state bodies responsible for managing elections and the media. In this clampdown on procedural democratic spaces, the government accomplished one overriding priority: the electoral containment of the MDC threat. ZANU-PF achieved this through a comprehensive strategy. It orchestrated the MDC's defeat in three successive national elections in 2000, 2002, and 2005, though in highly contested circumstances punctuated by documented allegations of widespread state malfeasance.[23]

The dramatic shift in ZANU-PF's political strategy to survive a severe political challenge precipitated new and daunting challenges for the ZCTU and its civil society and MDC allies. The first involved the deepening crisis of the economy and social reproduction: since the farm invasions of 2000, Zimbabwe has had the world's fastest shrinking economy, contracting as much as 60 percent in the period between 2000 and 2006 (Tables 6.6 and 6.7). Macroeconomic indicators plummeted shockingly, including inflation and exchange.

Table 6.6 Trends in Minimum Wages, 1996–2004

Period	1996	1997	1998	1999	2000	2001	2002	2003	April 2004
Average minimum wage (Zimbabwe $)	725.57	936.18	1294.32	1969.95	3109.76	8925.96	16478.81	60000.00	177000.00
Consumer price index 1995=100)	121.4	144.3	190.1	301.3	469.6	807.5	3489.7	8757.1	32611.0
Real wage (Zim.$)	597.67	648.77	680.86	653.82	662.22	1105.38	875.09	685.16	542.76
Real wage index 1996=100	100.0	108.6	114.0	109.4	110.8	185.0	146.4	114.6	90.8
Urban PDL[1] (family of 5) (Zimbabwe $)	1415.53	1682.36	2215.66	3512.22	5474.28	9413.35	21952.42	102086.22	380165.11
Minimum wage / PDL (%)	51.3	55.6	58.4	56.1	56.8	94.8	75.1	58.8	46.6

Source: LEDRIZ 2004.
Note: PDL equals Poverty Datum Line, standard definition for sustenance level for typical urban household.

Table 6.7 Real Value of the 1990 Zimbabwe $ (in cents)

1990	1992	1994	1996	1998	2000	2002	April 2004
100	57	37	25	16	6	1	0.1

Source: LEDRIZ's own calculations, based on the Central Statistical Office's Consumer Price Index (CPI).

By 2005, annual inflation breached the 700 percent mark (up from 22.5 percent in 1995, 31.7 percent in 1998); and by 2006, it had reached 1,200 percent or more, forcing the revaluation and reissuing of the national currency.[24] Formal sector employment contracted from 1998 up to at least 2005. Budget deficits mushroomed and domestic debt exploded. Real per capita income plunged more than 70 percent in the five-year period between 1998 and 2003, punishing working and poor Zimbabweans. Minimum wage gains for formal sector workers up to 2001 were rapidly eroded by spiraling inflation. By 2004, formal sector wages had fallen from 95 percent of the poverty level (2001) to less than 50 percent; by 2006, real wages fell further, to pre-1980 levels; perhaps 80 percent of Zimbabweans lived in profound poverty.

The deepening economic chaos of the early 2000s was compounded by widespread incidents of corruption and misappropriation of public funds and property that were initially unleashed by the farm invasions and rampant political violence. That economic chaos placed further stresses on formal employment and union affiliates in the collective bargaining process. In the agricultural sector alone, one survey estimated that only about one-third (one hundred thousand) of commercial farm workers remained employed on farms in 2003, following waves of farm invasions (Sachikonye 2003).[25] The manufacturing, engineering, and mining sectors, among others, reported escalating rates of business failures and closures, leading to employment contraction. In mining, the number of unionized workers fell from nearly thirty thousand in 1990 to less than one-third that number by 2005.[26]

For the labor movement, the deteriorating situation was particularly exacerbated beginning in early 2001 by further workplace invasions by pro–ZANU-PF war veterans and youth militia. These soon led to the emergence of a new self-styled union center, the Zimbabwe Federation of Trade Unions (ZFTU), headed by militant war veteran leader Joseph Chinotimba.[27] Developed under ZANU-PF patronage, the ZFTU evolved from a chaotic process of attacks, violent extortion, and, often, summary justice meted out to workers and management by gangs of militants. For ZANU-PF, the ZFTU presented new opportunities to undermine the ZCTU from within and extract further surplus from the business sector by extra-legal means. ZFTU activists sought to violently displace ZCTU local affiliates and forcibly conscript their shop floor members. ZCTU's personnel were physically attacked, threatened, and removed from workplaces, wreaking havoc. Dozens of illegal ZFTU business invasions, and widespread attacks on ZCTU local and national structures and public sector workers, were reported in the first half of 2001 (ZCTU 2001). By May 2001 the Employers Confederation of Zimbabwe noted that more than 186 companies had been affected, resulting in nine closures and scores of severe labor disruptions. Economic decline and attacks by ZFTU and other ZANU-PF allied forces led to a fall in union membership of 17 percent to 165,000 in 2000 and to 150,000 by 2004.

Having successfully weakened the ZCTU, albeit while provoking further decline in the business sector, the ZFTU's disruptive role quickly faded under the ruling party's direction as ZANU-PF sought to renew tripartite contact with the ZCTU from a position of strength. The rapidly shifting role of the ZFTU reflected ZANU-PF's revised strategy of labor movement containment, which moved from aggressive repression to include aspects of "consultation" under conditions and agendas dominated by government. One outcome was a form of tripartism that tended to produce agreements in principle—around minimum wages, tax relief, and economic resuscitation—without significant implementation in practice. Realizing this, in 2003 ZCTU pulled out of the TNF, saying it would stay out until government engaged in meaningful consultation. Yet the prevailing conditions were inauspicious: in the three-year period since the ZCTU's withdrawal from the TNF, more than one thousand union officials and activists were arrested, detained, beaten, and harassed in the course of their duties and protests. A concerted campaign led by the Ministry of Labor and state media in conjunction with four dissident ZCTU affiliates sought the removal of the ZCTU's executive amid unproven allegations of financial impropriety (ZCTU 2005).[28] In 2004 and 2005, attacks and victimization continued, including the deportation of two visiting fact-finding delegations from the Congress of South African Trade Unions (COSATU). Deportation of international unionists continued in 2006. Yet in 2006 the ZCTU continued to insist on more effective tripartism as a way forward—partly in an effort to highlight the need for normalization of the labor relations regime, and partly to maintain communications with some state structures.

More broadly, the rapidly growing regulatory and other legal constraints placed on a range of activities affecting labor and civil society in the early 2000s undermined associational freedoms and their ability to organize. The main target was initially the MDC, but perceived supporting institutions were also deeply affected, including the ZCTU, civil society organizations, service groups, media institutions, and professionals. Controversial legislation included the Public Order and Security Act (POSA) and Access to Information and Protection of Privacy Act (AIPPA). These were rushed through parliament in advance of the 2002 presidential elections, without fear of rebuke from a Supreme Court by now rendered compliant by government's appointment of new justices sympathetic to the ruling party.[29] They provided the state with wide-ranging and extremely arbitrary powers to preempt and harshly punish most commonly accepted forms of demonstration and association (POSA). AIPPA's regulations permitted the state to control, manipulate, threaten, de-register, and prohibit unpalatable information, journalists, and entire media houses. POSA became the state's weapon of choice in preventing or disrupting public and private meetings, including a series of ZCTU organized stay-aways and demonstrations in 2002–2006 and, on occasion, sessions of the ZCTU General Council. AIPPA enabled the banning of dozens of journalists and the forced closure in September 2003 of the only independent national daily, the *Daily News*, the country's largest circulation daily and a fierce government critic.

These and other legal constraints established the conditions in which illegal, politically motivated violence and abuses of rights could be waged with effective impunity in the name of government and the ruling party. The results had severely negative impacts on the leadership and ordinary members of the MDC, the labor movement, civil society, and local communities. It was reported that by 2004 most MDC members of parliament had been illegally detained, and many of them had been beaten, threatened, dispossessed of property, and assaulted. Hundreds more party candidates and activists were similarly affected (Zimbabwe Institute 2004). A 2006 report noted more than fifteen thousand *documented* cases of gross human rights abuses, suggesting that the number of incidents was on the rise. By 2005 the nature of the abuses had shifted from murder, rape, and torture to beatings, unlawful arrests and detentions, and property destruction (Zimbabwe NGO Human Rights Forum 2006). Human Rights Watch (2006) reported that officially sanctioned illegal violence was mounting against civil society organizations and, especially, the labor movement. In 2003, for example, a year in which the ZCTU staged four stay-aways and participated in a fifth, the number of reported illegal detentions, assaults, and other abuses rose sharply over prior levels. These attacks continue. In September 2006, in response to a ZCTU national mass action protesting poverty and demanding renewed collective bargaining, the ZCTU secretary-general, president, and a vice president were arrested, beaten, tortured, and detained.[30]

This unrelenting repression in the 2000s had a severe dampening impact on various forms of public engagement and discourse that had been a hallmark of the 1995–2000 period (Raftopoulos and Phimister 2004, 367). For example, the NCA's capacity to mobilize large numbers of members and sympathizers in public

discussion and demonstrations was all but eliminated, particularly following the brutal suppression of demonstrations in 2003–2004. All significant civics reported
disruption of membership and frequent dislocation of leadership, leading to anxiety over the likely consequences of adopting and mobilizing around opposition
positions.

The corrosive impact of state attacks on civil society was sharply exacerbated in
the extraordinary actions labeled *"Operation Murambatsvina"* (*Clear Out the Rubbish*)
by the state. Launched after the 2005 elections, this frontal attack on poor urban
communities and the informal sector saw the destruction of at least two hundred
thousand homes, the eradication of most urban informal sector infrastructure, the
displacement of perhaps more than a million citizens, and the summary arrest of
more than twenty thousand (Bracking 2005; Solidarity Peace Trust 2005; UN 2005;
Zimbabwe NGO Human Rights Forum 2005). Apart from its appalling impacts on
communities affected, and despite urgent international interventions, the *Operation
Murambatsvina* affair demonstrated the relative powerlessness of Zimbabwe's civil
society organizations and communities in *locally* confronting and halting the state's
outrageous attacks.

Deeply rooted political and administrative changes in the state itself posed difficult challenges to civil society and the labor movement in the post-2000 political climate. The old ZANU-PF welfarist state of the 1980s, already weakened by ESAP in
the 1990s, was gutted by the demands of authoritarian and militarized control under
ZANU-PF during its fight for political survival. If structural adjustment in its various forms, such as privatization, failed to substantially wither the state, militarization
of the state in the 2000s was brutally more effective, with severe consequences. The
marginalization of many key state-based professionals and their replacement by, or
political subordination to, trusted partisan personnel from state security agencies and
paramilitary groups was a critical outcome of this process that involved sections of
the civil service, military, police, and public media.[31] This wave of militarization
helped ZANU-PF impose greater and more direct partisan control over the public
administration, deskilling the state's once-impressive bureaucracy. The command
chain of policy making and implementation moved further away from accessible,
professional state structures into the restructured ruling party leadership (Institute
for Security Studies 2005).

This assault on state institutions was facilitated by physical attacks and intimidation against senior and junior civil servants, public sector professionals (teachers,
doctors, and nurses), magistrates and high court judges, and defense attorneys and
public prosecutors, among others. At times, it appeared, violence was rather gratu-
itously perpetrated as a warning aimed at dissuading others from noncompliant
behavior. The Zimbabwe National Army increasingly took on domestic "policing"
roles in monitoring and suppressing legitimate political debate and organizing.
Ominously, the specter emerged in the early 2000s of a state-based economic elite, a
"securitocracy" whose continued accumulation of wealth depended on links to the
shadowy networks of the security apparatus. Its existence posed likely problems for
any successor regime to ZANU under Mugabe.

In the first post-2000 years, most debates within the MDC and civic "opposition"
failed to take full stock of the longer-term implications of the state's degradation

through militarized restructuring. The labor movement, driven by its members' social and economic demands, and experienced in negotiating with the state through tripartism, was perhaps more predisposed than the MDC to dealing with the problem of the state. Perhaps the more ideologically fluid, and sometimes rather conservatively and elitist-inclined MDC leadership, was less committed to the kind of structural renewal of the state envisioned by the ZCTU as necessary for the resuscitation of social democratic practices (Alexander 2000; Sachikonye 2002). Others argued that the MDC itself had been transformed in ways that mirrored the negative practices of the ruling party. The question was whether, if elected, the MDC's leadership would be committed to anything more than an "elite transition" from ZANU-PF government. This would leave new economic elites intact and working and poor Zimbabweans profoundly marginalized. Faction fighting within the MDC leadership in 2004–2005 led to an eventual split of the party into two separate and competing entities in 2006. This appeared to confirm the drift of the party leadership toward an elite populism reminiscent of early ZANU-PF nationalism (Raftopoulos 2006b).

The long-term implications of recent state restructuring and the dismantling of democratic institutions and practices are profound. Observers have focused on leadership change within ZANU-PF as the key for a stable Zimbabwe. Yet this view typically fails to address the altered functions of state institutions, the shift in control over economic resources, the severely undermined social economy, and the survival of popular social forces represented by the ZCTU. The question of how to confront the array of socioeconomic forces inside and outside the Zimbabwean state in an era of neoliberal globalization stands perhaps as the major enduring challenge facing the ZCTU and its civic allies in the inevitable transition to a post-Mugabe era.

Concluding Observations

In Zimbabwe, the conditions for a labor movement–led redistributive politics in the post-independence period were undermined through a historical process of market liberalization, elite class formation, state restructuring, and unrelenting pressure on civil society groups and interests representing popular quarters. Recently, the intervention of regional and international interests in promoting capital-led strategies for national development, for an "African Renaissance," compounded the challenge. It seems entirely possible that strategies for the approaching political transition in Zimbabwe will seek to ignore the labor movement as a critical social player whose interests must be accommodated. It also seems likely that other civil society interests less accountable to a mass membership than the ZCTU would be more amenable to a transition which left in place many of those responsible for the current crisis. This includes factions of the ZANU-PF leadership, elements of the state and party security apparatus, and patronized black business elites.

For the ZCTU, a critical imperative is linkage with constituencies and institutions—national and international—that may stand as durable allies in the struggle to reassert the rights and interests of workers and the poor. In reality, the building of cooperative programs with allied social interests has been a work in progress over a long period. In the 2000s, growing links with the powerful South African and southern African labor movement were important components in the ZCTU's active construction of international solidarity and support. The *success* of these processes helped explain why the ZCTU emerged as the leading national civil society organization in Zimbabwe in the 1990s, why it was attacked, and how it has managed to resist, survive, and occasionally win.

The ruling party started its term in government in 1980 with many advantages. Among them was a labor movement weakened and divided by years of colonial subjugation. By 1985 the labor center, reconstructed under ZANU-PF tutelage, was so weakened by cronyism and political division that it was unserviceable as even a corporatist instrument of the state. The liberalization of labor-state relations that followed was limited to the narrower realm of labor relations until a wider process of political opening was initiated with the settlement of the ZANU-PF/ZAPU conflict in 1987. In succeeding years, the ZCTU served as a patron, training ground, and support network of other emergent civic interests. It worked increasingly closely with them as common issue themes of poverty, rights abuses, then corruption and state accountability moved to the fore. The national labor movement stood out as a locus of institutional and political capacity with enduring credibility, an accountable leadership, and a capacity to plan and implement effective strategies. More than any other mass-based national organization apart from ZANU-PF, the ZCTU proved its capacity to operate effectively on both state and civil society terrains.

For these reasons, and despite the apparent political ascendancy of ZANU-PF in the 2000s, the national labor movement continued to represent a key obstacle for ZANU-PF's populist-authoritarian project. A continuing flow of gross human rights abuses, legal restrictions, and state-managed rhetorical assaults targeted the ZCTU. The manipulations by the state of bargaining processes and the sowing of divisions within the labor movement served to constrain the labor movement. They highlighted the importance of redressing ZANU-PF's violations of human rights and industrial relations norms. In turn, therefore, attacks on workers, their structures, and leaders revealed as much as they concealed and silenced. More broadly, the collapse of formally democratic state institutions only raised further, insistent questions over who now controls the state, by what means, and in whose interests.

Notes

1. Raftopoulos (1995) explains the new politicization of the labor movement in terms of shifting demographics associated with the industrial growth of the 1950s, by which an increasing proportion of the black workforce came to be comprised of Zimbabwean nationals with a broader critique of social and labor relations under colonial rule.

2. By 1977, more than 90 percent of African wage workers in Harare were living below the Poverty Datum Line, with an estimated 850,000 (34 percent of the labor force) unemployed, underemployed, or self-employed in the informal sector by 1979. Wood (1988, 286) analyzes the figures published in Riddell (1981, 315).

3. Wood (1987, 73) notes the slack credentials that were required for attendance, while Shadur (1994, 103–4) cites senior unionists Jeffrey Mutandare and Michael Mawere, and the Department of Research and Planning's report of 1987, in arguing that only thirty-two of the fifty-two unions voting at the congress were authentic. According to Mitchell (1987, 114), twenty of the organizations attending the inaugural congress apparently vanished

soon after the event. Tellingly, Albert Mugabe, a close relative of the new prime minister with little labor movement experience, became the ZCTU's first secretary-general.

4. In Zimbabwean parlance, "civics" are usually taken to be community-based organizations outside of the state and political parties that represent and advocate on behalf of their organizational constituency. They are distinct from nongovernmental organizations, for example, in that the latter are typically service-providing institutions with professional staff, contracted relationships with serviced clients, and so forth.

5. The "Willowgate" car scandal of 1988–89 involved the misappropriation and reselling at high profit of motor vehicles by senior members of the ruling party. The departure of senior ZANU-PF figures followed a highly publicized public commission of inquiry. University demonstrations against corruption and government heavy-handedness, which preceded and followed Willowgate, occurred in 1988, 1989, 1991, 1992, and 1993.

6. ZANU-PF's domination of the political scene was confirmed in 1990 when Edgar Tekere's short-lived Zimbabwe Unity Movement (ZUM) received less than 17 percent of the votes in national elections and 2 of 120 seats in parliament. In the 1995 elections, ZANU-PF won more than 80 percent of the vote and an even higher percentage of parliamentary constituency seats.

7. Ministry statistics included only those figures forwarded by retrenching companies. Obvious omissions in its calculations included, for example, retrenchments at one of the largest textile manufacturers in Zimbabwe, Cone Textile, where six thousand lost their jobs in the early 1990s.

8. Mutandare had resigned his ZCTU position in 1989 after pleading guilty to fraud involving ZCTU funds. Mutandare headed the powerful Associated Mineworkers of Zimbabwe, the affiliate with the largest paid-up membership and comparatively good organizational capacities. In 1990, he launched an open attack on the ZCTU secretariat, arguing the unconstitutionality of new and increased dues set for affiliates by the Congress. It was a move designed not just to unseat the national executive (unsuccessfully), but also to demonstrate the financial and organizational clout of a key ZCTU affiliate union within the national labor center.

9. The June demonstration culminated in the arrest of six participating unionists under sections of the Law and Order (Maintenance) Act, notorious legislation inherited from Rhodesia that gave the police wide-ranging powers to approve, ban, prevent, and otherwise interfere with public meetings. The ZCTU's landmark 1994 High Court ruling curtailed these powers on the basis of Zimbabwe's constitutionally guaranteed freedom of expression.

10. See Saunders 2001 for detailed discussion of these points. See also Mungoni and Vudzijena 1995 for a useful analysis of twenty-six strikes and labor actions during the period of 1990–94. Striking groups included professionals (teachers, doctors, nurses), artisans in the railways and telecommunications sector, bus drivers, clerical workers in posts and telecommunications, staff at the University of Zimbabwe, and workers in a number of industrial sectors.

11. One survey (ZCTU 1998b) of publicly documented corruption estimated that in 1996–98 alone, more than Z$12 billion in public and private funds were implicated in a wide range of corrupt activities involving ruling party and government officials, from fraud and bribe taking, to theft by conversion, and corrupt administration of contracts and privatizations.

12. This discussion is based on accounts in ZCTU 1998 and Saunders 2001.

13. National civic networks and coalitions that prominently involved ZCTU structures and officials included the Civic Alliance for Social and Economic Progress, Community Budgetary Alliance, Community Working Group on Health, Farm Community Trust,

National Constitutional Assembly, Zimbabwe Election Support Network, Zimbabwe Human Rights Organisation, and Zimbabwe United Residents Associations.

14. In 1990–95, protests included actions highlighting grievances around poverty, police brutality, land hunger, gender discrimination and violence, corruption, press freedom, and other constraints on human rights.

15. For a more detailed account of the PVO Act affair and the divisions that emerged among some civil society organizations around how to respond to the state, see Rich Dorman 2001.

16. "Service organizations" include, for example, most human and civil rights organizations, training and technical assistance bodies, and church and other private social assistance agencies.

17. Decades old and mostly consisting of rural women, the AWC had a large national membership of more than one hundred thousand and considerable assets in the form of its club network and infrastructure. In 1995, the AWC was "listed" by the minister for alleged financial mismanagement and maladministration, and he dismissed its elected executive and replaced it with one appointed by the government, also setting the new executive's remuneration scales, to be paid from AWC resources.

18. Tens of thousands rallied in Bulawayo and thirty thousand marched in Mutare. In Harare, mass demonstrations were illegally and violently broken up by police, defying court orders allowing the demonstration to go ahead.

19. In Zimbabwe, "strikes" in this period took the label and form of "stay-aways" to reduce the vulnerability of strikers and organizers to both stringent regulations defining narrow scopes for industrial action, and to minimize a violent reaction from state authorities perpetrated on strikers at workplaces and on the streets.

20. Convened on February 27–28, 1999, by the ZCTU, the national meeting brought together delegates from rural and self-help organizations, women's and human rights groups, labor activists and residents associations, and many others to discuss and collectively develop policy recommendations for a new national development strategy.

21. See the Zimbabwe NGO Human Rights Forum's monthly violence reports for this period.

22. Robert Mugabe, speech in English and Shona in Zvimba, Zimbabwe, March 31, 2002. Cited in Zimbabwe Institute 2004. One year later, Mugabe was even more graphic as follows: "Let the MDC and its leaders be warned that those who play with fire will not only be burnt, but consumed by that fire" (speech in Nyamandlovu, Zimbabwe, June 13, 2003, cited in Zimbabwe Institute 2004).

23. In parliamentary elections in 2000 and 2005 and the presidential election of 2002, documented and widespread state-orchestrated irregularities were reported by domestic, regional, and international election monitors and observers. Irregularities included lack of fair play in registration, campaigning, and voting; voter intimidation and manipulation; violence against and harassment of voters, communities, opposition parties, and election officials; and outright cheating. See for example, Zimbabwe Election Support Network 2002.

24. In August 2006, a new-looking Zimbabwe dollar, revalued at a rate of $Z1000 (old) : Z$1 (new), was introduced in a bid to contain inflation and make cash payments more manageable. Initial evidence indicated that this move perhaps accelerated the rate of inflation, rather than contained it.

25. Sachikonye found that about two-thirds of farmworkers lost access to health and education services as well as housing and food security when their farms were taken over by political agents or reallocated. The majority of the dispossessed took refugee in the expanding peri-urban informal settlements.

26. Citing statistics from the databank of the Labor and Economic Development Research Institute of Zimbabwe (LEDRIZ) from 2004.

27. The legal and operational basis of the ZFTU and its grouping of alleged affiliates was not clear, as it appeared that stipulated procedures for affiliate and labor center registration were not followed. Moreover, various leading office holders, including Chinotimba, were not known to be union activists and, indeed, in many instances were not formally employed.

28. The campaign fuelled confusion and acrimony among affiliates, forced written declarations of loyalty among the center's thirty-five affiliates, and prompted a special ZCTU General Council meeting in August 2005, which suspended four affiliates' representatives to the council for "bringing the name of the ZCTU into disrepute," undermining the work of the center and violating its established protocol and procedures in issuing statements and representing the interests of the ZCTU.

29. In early 2001, Supreme Court Chief Justice Anthony Gubbay was pressured to resign after President Mugabe refused to guarantee his safety in the face of threats from war veterans. Gubbay's court had delivered several judgments that were unfavorable to the state on cases involving rights to association, communication, land compensation, and due process in land acquisition, among others. He was replaced by a former ZANU-PF deputy minister. Several other Supreme Court and High Court judges would follow Gubbay, citing intimidation and the lack of police and administrative compliance with delivered court judgments.

30. For example, ZCTU secretary general, Wellington Chibebe, was assaulted and hospitalized with fractures and deep wounds. Union leaders were initially held without access to lawyers or medical care, and in all, more than 225 ZCTU officials, organizers, and members were arrested nationwide during the protest. The attacks prompted outcry from regional and international labor bodies.

31. Civilian agencies in which security officials were appointed to the helm included the Electoral Supervisory Commission, Grain Marketing Board, National Oil Company of Zimbabwe, and the Zimbabwe Broadcasting Corporation. Meanwhile, several ministries saw security-linked personnel moving into top administrative posts.

References

Alexander, Peter. 2000. Zimbabwean workers, the MDC and the 2000 election. *Review of African Political Economy* 85 (September): 385–406.

Astrow, Andre. 1983. *Zimbabwe: A revolution that lost its way?* London: Zed.

Berridge, Anthony. 1993. *ESAP and education for the poor. Silveira House social series no. 5.* Gweru, Zimbabwe: Mambo Press and Silveira House.

Bond, Patrick, and Richard Saunders. 2005. Labor, the state and the struggle for a democratic Zimbabwe. *Monthly Review* 57 (December): 42–55.

Bracking, Sarah. 2005. Development denied: Autocratic militarism in post-election Zimbabwe. *Review of African Political Economy* (104–5): 341–57.

Brand, Coenraad M. 1976. Race and politics in Rhodesian trade unions. *African Perspectives* (1): 55-80.

Chisvo, Munhamo, and Lauchlan Munro. 1994. *A review of social dimensions of adjustment in Zimbabwe 1990–94.* Harare, Zimbabwe: United Nations International Childrens Emergency Fund.

Cheater, A. P. 1988. Contradictions in modeling "consciousness": Zimbabwe proletarians in the making? *Journal of Southern African Studies* 14 (2): 291–303.

Davies, Rob. 1975. Leadership and unity in Rhodesian black trade unions. *South African Labor Bulletin* 1 (9): 12–28.

Gibbon, Peter. 1995. Introduction to *Structural adjustment and the working poor in Zimbabwe. Studies on labor, women informal sector workers and health*, ed. Peter Gibbon. Uppsala, Sweden: Nordiska Afrikainstitutet.

Herbst, Jeffrey. 1990. *State politics in Zimbabwe*. Harare, Zimbabwe: University of Zimbabwe Publications.

Human Rights Watch. 2006. You will be thoroughly beaten. The brutal suppression of dissent in Zimbabwe. *Human Rights Watch* 18 (November).

Institute for Security Studies. 2005. Zimbabwe: Increased securitization of the state? Pretoria, South Africa Institute for Security Studies, September 7.

Kanyenze, Godfrey. 2004. The significance of tripartism in social cohesion and the future of the Tripartite Negotiating Forum (TNF) process in Zimbabwe. Paper presented at the Institute of Development Studies (IDS) and Fredrich Ebert Stiftung (FES) seminar, Harare, Zimbabwe, April 28.

Labor and Economic Development Research Institute (LEDRIZ). 2004. Statistical Databank. Harare, Zimbabwe: LEDRIZ.

Lennock, Jean 1994. *Paying for health. Poverty and structural adjustment in Zimbabwe*. Oxford: Oxfam.

Makanya, Stella Tandai, Trust Ngirandi, and Freek Schiphorst. 1993. Trade unions and workers' committees. Second report on research findings from the 1991/92 Educational seminars: ZCTU/FNV/APADEP-ISS Workers' Participation Development Program. Mimeograph.

Mandaza, Ibbo, and Lloyd Sachikonye, eds. 1991. *The one party state and democracy. The Zimbabwe debate*. Harare, Zimbabwe: Southern Africa Political Economy Series Trust.

Mitchell, Bruce. 1987. The state and the workers movement in Zimbabwe. *South African Labor Bulletin* 12 (6–7): 104–22.

Mungoni, Tsarai, and Ashbel Vudzijena. 1995. Causes and outcomes of industrial actions in Zimbabwe (1990–1994). Paper in the ZCTU/Friedrich Ebert Stiftung Student Attachment Program. Mimeograph.

Phimister, Ian. 1988. *An economic and social history of Zimbabwe 1890–1948: Capital accumulation and class struggle*. London: Longman.

Pillay, Devan. 1991. The ZCTU's 1990 congress: Exposing the capitalist reality beneath Zimbabwe's "socialist" rhetoric. *South African Labor Bulletin* 15 (5): 75–79.

Raftopoulos, Brian. 1992. Beyond the house of hunger: Democratic struggle in Zimbabwe. *Review of African Political Economy*, no. 54 (July): 59-74.

———. 1994. The state and the labor movement in Zimbabwe. Paper for Institute of Development Studies, University of Zimbabwe, 1994.

———. 1995. Nationalism and labor in Salisbury 1953–1965. *Journal of Southern African Studies* 21 (1): 79–93.

———. 1996. Labor internationalism and problems of autonomy and democratization in the trade union movement in southern Rhodesia: 1951–1975. Paper presented at the Conference on the Historical Dimensions of Human Rights and Democracy in Zimbabwe, University of Zimbabwe, September 1996.

———. 2006a. The Zimbabwean crisis and the challenges for the left. *Journal of Southern African Studies* 32 (June): 203–19.

———. 2006b. Reflections on opposition politics in Zimbabwe: The politics of the movement for democratic change (MDC). Cape Town: Institute for Justice and Reconciliation.

Raftopoulos, Brian, and Sam Moyo. 1995. The politics of indigenization in Zimbabwe. *Eastern Africa Social Science Research Review* 11 (June): 17–33.

Raftopoulos, Brian, and Ian Phimister. 2004. Zimbabwe now: The political economy of crisis and coercion. *Historical Materialism* 12 (4): 355–82.

Ranger, Terence. 1970. *The African voice in southern Rhodesia 1898–1930*. London: Heinemann.

Reeler, A. P. 2003. The role of militia groups in maintaining ZANU-PF's political power. Unpublished paper, March.

Rich Dorman, Sarah. 2001. NGOs and state in Zimbabwe: Implications for civil society theory. In *Civil society and authoritarianism in the third world. A conference book*, ed. B. Beckman, E. Hasnsson, and A. Sjogren. Stockholm: Stockholm University Press.

Riddell, Roger C. 1981. *Report of the Commission of Inquiry into incomes, prices and conditions of service under the chairmanship of Roger C. Riddell*. Harare, Zimbabwe: Government Printer.

Sachikonye, Lloyd. 1986. State, capital and trade unions. In *Zimbabwe: The political economy of transition 1980–1986*, ed. Ibbo Mandaza, 243–73. Dakar: CODESRIA.

———. 1995a. State and social movements in Zimbabwe. In *Democracy, civil society and the state. Social movements in southern Africa*, ed. Lloyd Sachikonye, 129–61. Harare, Zimbabwe: Southern Africa Political Economy Series Trust.

———. 1995b. Industrial relations and labor relations under ESAP in Zimbabwe. In *Structural adjustment and the working poor in Zimbabwe. Studies on labor, women informal sector workers and health*, ed. Peter Gibbon, 38–131. Uppsala, Sweden: Nordiska Afrikainstitutet.

———. 2002. Whither Zimbabwe? Crisis & democratization. *Review of African Political Economy* 91:13–20.

———. 2003. The situation of commercial farm workers after land reform in Zimbabwe. Harare, Zimbabwe: Farm Community Trust of Zimbabwe, March.

Saul, John S., and Richard Saunders. 2005. Mugabe, Gramsci and Zimbabwe at 25. In *The next liberation struggle: Capitalism, socialism and democracy in southern Africa*, ed. John S. Saul. New York: Monthly Review Press; London: Merlin Press.

Saunders, Richard. 1995. Civics in Zimbabwe: Are they making a difference? *Southern Africa Report* 10 (January): 21–25.

———. 1996. Associational life and civil society in Zimbabwe. Paper for the Conference on Historical Dimensions of Democracy and Human Rights in Zimbabwe, University of Zimbabwe, September.

———. 2000. *Never the same again: Zimbabwe's growth towards democracy 1980–2000*. Harare, Zimbabwe: Edwina Spicer Productions.

———. 2001. Striking ahead: Industrial action and labor movement development in Zimbabwe. In *Striking back: The labor movement and the post-colonial state in Zimbabwe 1980–2000*, ed. Brian Raftopoulos and Lloyd Sachikonye. Harare, Zimbabwe: Weaver Press.

Saunders, R., R. Loewenson, and N. Jazdowska. 1995. Civic organizations in Zimbabwe. Unpublished report for African Network on Economic Policy, Equity and Health. Mimeograph. Harare, Zimbabwe, June.

Schiphorst, Freek. 1995. The new place of unions in Zibabwe." In *Globalization and third world trade unions*, ed. T. Henk. (London: Zed, 1995).

Shadur, Mark A. 1994. *Labor relations in a developing country. A case study on Zimbabwe*. Aldershot, UK: Avebury.

Sibanda, Gibson. 1991. Liberalization or liberation? May Day speech by the president of the Zimbabwe Congress of Trade Unions.

Solidarity Peace Trust. 2003. National youth service training. An overview of youth militia training and activities in Zimbabwe, October 2000–August 2003. Johannesburg: Solidarity Peace Trust, September 5.

———. 2004. Disturbing the peace: An overview of civilian arrests in Zimbabwe, February 2003–January 2004. Johannesburg, South Africa: Solidarity Peace Trust, January.

———. 2005. Discarding the filth: Operation Murambatsvina. Interim report on the Zimbabwean government's "urban cleansing" and forced eviction campaign, May/June 2005. Johannesburg: Solidarity Peace Trust, June.

Stoneman, Colin. 1988. The economy: Recognizing the reality. In *Zimbabwe's prospects. Issues of race, class, state, and capital in southern Africa*, ed. Colin Stoneman, 43–62. London: Macmillan.

Tsvangirai, Morgan. 1990a. Interview with Richard Saunders. Harare, Zimbabwe, January 23 and March 9.

———. 1990b. Workers' reflections on the first decade of independence. Paper presented at ZCTU/Employers Confederation of Zimbabwe/Norwegian Agency for Development Joint Conference "The Zimbabwe Development Challenge: Perspectives on the First Decade of Independence. Harare, Zimbabwe, April.

———. 1991. What we need is mass action. Interview with Patrick Bond, April. Quoted in *Southern Africa Report*, 1991.

———. 1995. Interview with Richard Saunders. Mutare, Zimbabwe, September.

United Nations Special Envoy on Human Settlements Issues in Zimbabwe. 2005. Report of the fact-finding mission to Zimbabwe to assess the scope and impact of Operation Murambatsvina by the UN special envoy on human settlements in Zimbabwe, Mrs. Anna Kajumulo Tibaijuka. New York: United Nations, July.

van Onselen, Charles. 1974. The 1912 Wankie Colliery strike. *Journal of African History* 12 (2): 275–89.

Wood, Brian. 1987. Roots of trade union weakness in post-independence Zimbabwe. *South African Labor Bulletin* 12 (6–7): 47–92.

———. 1988. Trade union-organization and the working class. In *Zimbabwe's prospects: Issues of race, class, state, and capital in southern Africa*, ed. Colin Stoneman, 284–308. Basingstoke: Macmillan.

Zimbabwe. 1981. *Growth with equity: An economic policy statement.* Harare, Zimbabwe: Government Printer.

———. 1982. *Transitional national development plan 1982/3–1984/5.* Harare, Zimbabwe: Government Printer.

———. 1984. Ministry of labor, department of research and planning. Report of the national trade union survey. Harare, Zimbabwe, 1984.

———. 1991a. *Zimbabwe: A framework for economic reform.* Harare, Zimbabwe: Government Printer.

———. 1991b. Social dimensions of adjustment: A program to mitigate the social costs of adjustment. Mimeograph.

———. 1996. Formal sector retrenchments: January 1, 1991–December 31, 1995. Ministry of the Public Service, Labor and Social Welfare. Mimeograph.

Zimbabwe Congress of Trade Unions. 1989. ZCTU on the new investment code: Its implications to [*sic*] national independence and to the position and conditions of the working people. Mimeograph.

———. 1990. Strategies for the 1990s. Zimbabwe Congress of Trade Union paper presented for discussion to 1990 National Congress.

———. 1991. *A decade of achievement. Ten years of struggle.* Harare, Zimbabwe: Zimbabwe Congress of Trade Unions.

———. 1995a. Strategies for the labor movement from 1995 to 2000 and beyond. Zimbabwe Congress of Trade Unions paper presented for discussion to 1995 National Congress.

———. 1995b. Beyond ESAP. A framework for a long term development strategy in Zimbabwe. Harare, Zimbabwe: Zimbabwe Congress of Trade Unions.

———. 1995–96. ZCTU Economics Department staff. Interviews with Richard Saunders. Harare, Zimbabwe.

———. 1996. Behind the strikes: The public service and doctors strikes of 1996. Harare, Zimbabwe: Friedrich Ebert Stiftung/Zimbabwe Congress of Trade Unions.

———. 1998a. Staying away to move forward: A report on the national stay-away. Mimeograph.

———. 1998b. Compilation of cases of fraud and corruption from public media. Mimeograph. December.

———. 2001. Factory invasions and lawlessness in Zimbabwe. Mimeograph. Harare, Zimbabwe.

———. 2005. ZCTU suspends four affiliate union leaders. Harare, Zimbabwe: Zimbabwe Congress of Trade Unions, Information Department, August 13.

Zimbabwe Election Support Network. 2002. *2002 presidential and local authority elections report.* Harare, Zimbabwe: Zimbabwe Election Support Network. April.

Zimbabwe Institute. 2004. Playing with fire. Personal accounts of human rights abuses experienced by 50 opposition members of parliament in Zimbabwe, and 28 opposition election candidates. Johannesburg: Zimbabwe Institute, March.

Zimbabwe NGO Human Rights Forum. 2005. Order out of chaos, or chaos out of order? A preliminary report on operation "Murambatsvina." Harare, Zimbabwe: NGO Human Rights Forum, June.

———. 2006. An analysis of the Zimbabwe Human Rights NGO Forum legal cases, 1998–2006. Harare, Zimbabwe: NGO Human Rights Forum, June.

Newspapers and Magazines in Zimbabwe:

The Worker
The Daily News
The Chronicle
The Herald
The Sunday Mail
The Financial Gazette
The Zimbabwe Independent
The Standard
Horizon
Moto
Parade
Ziana

CHAPTER 7

Organized Labor in the Republic of South Africa: History and Democratic Transition

William Freund

I didn't taste apartheid or feel it–until I went into Highveld. It was the first time I had come into close contact with a white man. And you could see the way they treated us—this is inhuman. There were some jobs that were only reserved for whites. They were proud, saying if you are black you cannot do this—and I wondered how can this be? Even in the toilet, there was this thing of whites only, you could not go there. That's actually where I started to get more, more, more involved in the struggle. Because I could now feel apartheid; I could taste it.

Karl von Holdt
Beyond the Apartheid Workplace
1985

In some respects, the history of the South African labor movement has a complexity and longevity that makes it quite unique on the African continent. The key feature here is, of course, the relative historic length and depth of industrialization as an economic process in South Africa. However, it also contains features that are essential to understanding the way labor movements have developed elsewhere in Africa and that enable comparisons to be usefully made. There are also obvious areas of comparison between the labor movement in South Africa and those in colonial contexts where settlers from the colonizing country and elsewhere have formed leading sectors in the working class. The particularities of South African political development—notably the form that its colonization took—has meant that the labor force has been deeply divided. The politics of trade unionism and the consciousness of workers have always been linked closely to struggles over the class and ethnic form post-colonial power would take. Thus, the goal of an all-inclusive movement representing labor has been very elusive. South Africa is a virtual laboratory for the study of the relationship between fragmented sections of the working class, divided by race, ethnicity, and gender. Labor historian Jon Lewis has shown in detail how these historic divisions always need to be understood in terms of the typical trade union issues of skill and craft, faced with the protean nature of industrial capitalism, in order to explain the organizational and structural history of South African labor (1984). Eddie Webster brings to bear additionally the complicated question of control over workplace conditions, drawing upon the influential study of Harry Braverman to explain the history of class consciousness and organization in the South African industrial arena (Webster 1985). The particularities of this labor regime created an enormous potential for labor militancy on the part of the least skilled and most downtrodden workers. In the last quarter of the twentieth century, the combination of labor oppression and national consciousness proved to be explosive in the South African workplace. A powerful and extremely effective labor movement moved from strength to strength and played a large part in the overthrow of apartheid as a political system.

Another attendant particularity consists in the relatively rich available material on South African labor. The present-day labor movement has been the subject of several full-length studies with distinct perspectives and is covered by a journal that has been operating for more than thirty years, the *South African Labour Bulletin*, which embraces the debates of activists and intellectuals. The Sociology of Work Programme at the University of the Witwatersrand in Johannesburg has been particularly important in shaping ideas about the changing face of South African labor. The contemporary labor movement itself is the source of a wide range of policy documents on many issues. In addition, many historians have taken an interest in the labor movement, and new published material and academic theses continue to appear on South African labor history. As a result, this chapter is very much a synthesis with some reinterpretation based on reading in the available material, which will repay the interested researcher or reader who wants to know more. The bibliography is far from comprehensive, especially with regard to South African labor history.

The first section of this essay tries to move quickly through the complex history of trade unions in South Africa before 1970, emphasizing major features of the labor force. The second concentrates on the main features of the modern trade union movement and how it developed through a series of remarkable struggles in the 1970s and the 1980s. The third, and briefest section, considers the main features that seem to characterize the current trade union scene since the establishment of democratic government in 1994. The two latter sections pay particular attention to the complexities of union politics in the wider national picture.

Historical Developments

South African historians are largely agreed on the importance of what is generally known as the "Mineral Revolution," a process that began with the diamond discoveries at Kimberley in 1867 and proceeded through the development of gold mining on the Witwatersrand in 1885. Before this time, the quickening of the colonial economy, based on wool and wine exports and internally orientated meat and grain production, did begin to bring forth struggles over the conditions and price of labor—on the docks, for instance. But the Mineral Revolution represented a qualitative advance in economic change with dramatic consequences—increases in the scale of investment, the application of machinery and power, urbanization and immigration, the sheer size of the labor force, and the complex multiplier effects that had an impact on every other sector of the economy.

The gold mines themselves employed an enormous labor force that combined work on the mines with continued membership in rural production units in a system of oscillating migration that was increasingly structured by capital. Despite great expense, the heavily concentrated mining capitalists found this the most reliable and predictable way to secure and control labor over the long term (Jeeves 1985). With a workforce that was approaching a hundred thousand men before the Anglo-Boer War and twice that number at the time of the South African Union in 1910, the scale of labor required had no precedent in tropical Africa. Over most of its history, the major part of the unskilled workforce was not composed of South Africans at all but of residents of other territories in the subcontinent. These virtually lacked employment opportunities, notably Portuguese East Africa (now Mozambique) and the British colonies of Basutoland (Lesotho) and Nyasaland Protectorate (Malawi). Proponents of underdevelopment theory have argued that this absence of alternatives was itself partly structured by the policies of colonial states. Black South African workers were largely drawn from reserves characterized by land hunger, the paternalistic governance of native officials, and a system of land tenure controlled by chiefs on state salaries. Few were drawn from the rapidly growing towns where better-paid and less dangerous employment was available.

However, elsewhere in South Africa, many workers were drawn into forms of employment on the harbors and other parts of the infrastructure, in other mining operations, and on the farms, which also involved state intervention in controlling the labor market. Durban, which became the great port serving the Witwatersrand from the late nineteenth century, pioneered the so-called Durban system (Swanson 1976) and the "togt" (daily task) system of controlling labor (Hemson 1979), drawing in labor from the thickly peopled reserves of Natal and Zululand particularly. Farmers historically depended for labor on relations that have been called "semi-feudal," in which family labor was traded for access to land while the most advanced agrarian sectors used migrant systems parallel to those on the mines (Beinart, Delius and Trapido 1986; Krikler 1993). In the nineteenth century, the Natal sugar industry secured a large intake of indentured labor from India, which spread to other sectors of the provincial economy increasingly. The old-established Cape wine economy, once dependent on slavery, held on to low-wage workers through the exercise of the tot system, where they were paid in alcoholic beverages (Freund 1995; Scully 1993). Within such labor systems, which could contain elements of paternalistic protection as well as the crudest sorts of exploitation, collaboration and struggle have taken place and historians of this region have pioneered its study. Systems of control that contained significant non-cash or unpaid elements characteristically dominated the lives of workers who lacked the rights of citizens. They were not readily amenable to the advent of trade unions involved in struggles over wages and other basic economic issues. Even today, domestic and farm labor is rarely organized, and mineworkers organized successfully only in an era when they had become almost totally dependent on wage labor.

By contrast, systematic labor organization came far more naturally to those workers who could lay claim to citizens' rights but understood themselves to be in a highly vulnerable position at the workplace. The mining industry attracted many immigrants from Britain and elsewhere who were already familiar with the traditions of skilled worker organization ultimately derived from European guild traditions. Many could be said to belong to an international community of footloose single men who were found wherever rich mining lodes in remote places were discovered from the late nineteenth century on. Such men, in Canada, Australia, the United States, among other countries, found themselves frequently at loggerheads with capitalists who sought to introduce much cheaper local or imported workers of color from colonized and impoverished societies. The result was bitter and, often, violent struggles that contained elements of conflict over access to skills and retention of particular skills in particular occupations, but also overtly racist elements. The intervention of mining capitalists, however, was certainly fundamental to the process through which particular jobs in the mining industry became rigidly identified with race in southern Africa (Turrell 1987).

The white South African gold miners at first enjoyed very high wages (as did black miners, at a lower level, compared to any other means of access to cash). But their expenses were high and the extraordinary death rates due to pulmonary disease gave a desperate and sinister aspect to their work underground. Only a minority of white miners possessed skills that were not fairly transmutable to new layers of workers who acquired experience of these conditions (Lewis 1984, 15). Such miners furiously resisted efforts to change mining operations at their expense and to increase the incidence of lower-cost wages. In 1907, 1913, 1914, and 1922 massive strikes, the last two general strikes over the entire Witwatersrand, took place at phases of economic strain when mine owners sought savings at the expense of men. It took military intervention and bombs in the latter two cases to suppress workers (Krikler 2005).

In the South African context, however, it was possible for the state to intervene in order to improve substantially the conditions of the white working class. David Yudelman has termed this process one of incorporation and traced the relationship between state and mining capital under which incorporation could take place (1983). Before, and especially after, the change in government in 1924, key legislation such as the Industrial Conciliation (1924), Apprenticeship (1922), and Wage (1925) acts tried to create as favorable a legislative regime as possible for protecting the rights and conditions of white workers. In the pact government of 1924–29, the white Labour Party participated as junior partner, but its electoral purchase subsequently declined. A key feature of the politics of white trade unionism was the failure of Labour as a political party to compete equally with the National and South African parties. Instead, workers became used to obtaining favors from competing political parties, and their unions were often organizationally quite weak, particularly when they could not lay claim to educational and craft qualifications. In effect, they relied on the state to defend their privileges.

In 1907 the mines began to employ significant numbers of Afrikaner men, effectively proletarianized individuals driven off the farms, to replace British and other immigrants. The presence of an "unincorporated" class of Afrikaners who did not identify with the urban middle class was a major feature of the South African scene for more than a generation. Armed and proletarianized Afrikaners played an important role not only in the "rebellie" of 1915 but also in the Rand Revolt seven years later. They were brought only with some difficulty into trade unions dominated by British traditions and prejudices. Nationalist Afrikaners tried with varying success to draw them into trade unions that were "national" in character. In practice, however, even Nationalists in government felt unable to encourage the employment of such men at high wages in the private sector. To some extent, they created a sphere of protected but quite low-wage employment for them in the state sector, notoriously, for instance, on the railways and in public works programs. In the longer run, however, the answer lay in increasing education and skills as the Afrikaner population urbanized. Gradually in the long years of economic prosperity that succeeded the Great Depression after 1933, the so-called poor white problem diminished dramatically in significance.

Even a frankly racist government in South Africa, however, was unable simply to call for a purely racial economy, eliminating that process of incorporating poorly paid black workers that gave South African economic growth its dynamism (Kaplan and Morris 1976). The trade union movement may have wanted to exclude blacks and even people of color very generally, but it was constrained by the constant and quite legitimate fear that it might price itself too high and thereby tempt capitalists to cast the net wider and look for employees elsewhere, especially in periods of labor shortage. For this reason, it is possible to see at work both racist exclusivity and more complex and subtle policies of limited inclusivity, incorporation of Coloured, Indian, and even in time African workers in such a way as to control their access to jobs somewhat and to limit their ability to undercut white competition.

Some incorporationists were themselves hostile to racism and used pragmatic arguments to favor the expansion of trade unionism along lines that did not threaten whites but created new possibilities for workers in general. The most famous example by far, which is often discussed in the literature, was that of Solly Sachs and the Garment Workers Union (GWU). This union, created in 1909, organized largely Afrikaner women on the Witwatersrand as the industry grew during and after World War I. Sachs got them to accept racially mixed membership, in the teeth of enormous hostility from Afrikaner politicians and probably despite the propensity of the women to keep on voting for Afrikaner nationalist men who were racists, in what was in fact in their own self-interest. The union succeeded in the 1930s in significantly improving wages and working conditions in this industry confined to the domestic market. The South African Trades & Labour Council, to which most of the white labor movement belonged—and even its conservative successor, the Trade Union Council of South Africa after 1955—contained some individuals eager to encourage trade union ideals and organization among workers of all colors.

The biggest problem faced by the GWU women was undercutting. Indeed, much of the clothing industry in time moved to Cape Town and Durban to avoid the union. In Cape Town, Coloured women were also unionized, but along far more conservative and proverbially quite corrupt lines, under male white leadership. Durban, where the resident working class was in large part Indian, was another story again. A trade union leadership arose as early as the 1920s concerned with finding and preserving a niche in the labor market for Indians and thus very susceptible to the patrimonial control of middle-class Indian leaders. But this tendency was essentially ousted for a period of a decade or more when the predominantly Indian unions became extremely radical (Freund 1995; Padayachee et al. 1985). I have argued elsewhere that the turn toward nonracialism and the sympathy Indian workers felt toward the Communist Party between 1935 and 1950 came from their own structural weakness, caught between the exclusionism of working-class white Durban, on the one hand, and the growing importance of cheap migrant African labor eager to carve out some place in the expanding urban economy, on the other (Freund 1995). This was a weakness with strong parallels to what had lain behind the intense radicalism of white labor consciousness and organization. But the process of incorporation of Indian workers by the state was very much more gradual and partial in coming.

African workers always worked under less favorable conditions in South Africa, and the lack of skilled workers in their ranks certainly slowed down their movement into effective labor organizations. Obviously, white racism plays an autonomous and important role here. Convictions ran deep that the future of whites in South Africa depended on excluding blacks from citizenship, from urban life, and from membership in the organized working class. The Labour Party was the first to insist on the need to confine permanent black residence to the rural locations. Trade unions that organized blacks could not receive official recognition, and black workers had no right to strike. Pass laws were supposed to regulate the movement of Africans, although women were only obliged to register as late as 1959 (Hindson 1987). At times, the state sought to oblige African work-seekers to make use of official labor bureaus.

Yet as early as the boom years of World War I, radicals from the white labor movement began to agitate among Africans, recognizing that they were going to be more and more significant in the industrial workforce. Even in that period, Africans performed the most menial labor in industry and formed a large percentage of the total payroll. Thus, the Industrial Workers of Africa was already active from 1915 in trying to propagandize socialist ideas among Africans working in Johannesburg (Johnstone 1979). With the economic downturn that followed the war, Africans, undoubtedly aware of the proclivities of the whites among whom they worked, showed considerable capacity for organization and resistance. In 1920 a huge strike involving at its peak more than seventy thousand men took place among African mineworkers on the Rand (Bonner 1979). This major event represented an impressive feat in communication, militant agitation, and grassroots organization about which relatively little is known; it never took the form of trade union organization. Even before then, the Industrial and Commercial Workers Union (ICU) had been established in Cape Town. Under the charismatic leadership of a Malawian, Clements Kadalie, the ICU remained active through the 1920s, although more as a political force than a union, and often strongest in the countryside (Bradford 1987; Wickins 1978). The figure of a hundred thousand active members is often given for the ICU at its peak. Historian Helen Bradford has written that "it was a fluid, contradictory movement more than a disciplined, uniform organization. It articulated a multiplicity of ideas about the past, present and future; it embraced a host of causes and it encompassed an extraordinary range of struggles" (1987, 246). In one utterance at the height of his fame, Kadalie claimed that strikes were "wicked, useless and obsolete" (Lewis 1984, 47). Such non-specificity, as well as the vagaries of ambitious individuals, seems characteristic of early African political and labor organizations in South Africa as it does elsewhere on the continent.

At the same time, the radical end of the white working class had left the Labour Party to form the Communist Party of South Africa. While Communists supported the white labor revolt of 1922, internal and external pressure moved them sharply toward concentrating on the organization of people of color, especially Africans. By the late 1920s, the ultra phase—calling for a "Black Republic" in South Africa, recruiting almost entirely among African workers—was in gear. Party organization almost invariably involved the construction of trade unions and helped to engender what Jon Lewis has called a "period of considerable industrial militancy amongst African workers" in the late 1920s (Lewis 1984, 63). Early trade unionism among Africans hardly survived the decade,given state repression, destructive tendencies within the CPSA, and the impact of the Great Depression after 1929. But new organizational efforts emerged in later phases: for instance, the Food and Canning Workers Union in Cape Town involved bringing together Coloured and African workers, especially women, and the Congress of Non-European Trade Unions (CNETU) in the 1940s.

In Johannesburg an important period of sympathetic state patronage via the Wage Board and the Department of Labour led to the successful creation of unions in secondary industry at the end of the 1930s. The Wage Board was empowered in some phases of its existence to consider the conditions of black workers. The CNETU unions concentrated in good part on the large number of new African entrants into the industrial working class, but their structures were often rather localized and sometimes fleeting in nature. In his study of this era, Baruch Hirson rightly emphasizes the way industrial and community issues in the broader urban context held an organic relation as Africans began to claim the right to a foothold in the urban environment (1989) Throughout the years of the second Jan Smuts government (1939–48), the government pondered legislation to legalize African trade unions, but it never promulgated legislation to that effect (Alexander 2000).

In August, 1946, the labor history of this period climaxed in a massive strike that affected between seventy and a hundred thousand African gold mine-workers. At the core of this strike sat the Communist Party, but it succeeded in winning widespread adhesion among rural migrants who felt mounting economic pressures in the countryside that were not being addressed by the low wage system (Moodie 1986; O'Meara 1975). Indeed, much of the spread of the strike owed itself to networks that were not organized in the union and had never heard of the Communists. In some ways, it harkened back to the comparable postwar strike of 1920. The unusually severe repression of this strike (by the pre-apartheid Smuts government) and the failure of CNETU to follow up on their threat of a general strike were important markers in the decline of this phase of militancy.

It is not easy to state precisely what the heritage has been of this early history. Certain unions, notably the Food and Canning Workers Union, were able to survive for long periods of time and enjoy some continuity as organizations, maintaining a political and even cultural tradition. By emphasizing the links between family and work, this union achieved considerable long-term success in organizing women and building female leadership, according to Iris Berger (1992).

In other cases, that tradition was probably limited to legendary individuals who would emerge from jail or hiding to resume activities from time to time. CNETU did inspire numerous leaders who had become accustomed to union organization. One such figure was Harry Gwala, whose roots lay in rural Natal and in the organization of a large factory operating under semirural conditions in the village of Howick, taking advantage of the power potential of a large local waterfall. The SARMCOL workers maintained more than a foothold on regional farms and in an older agrarian economy, but hard economic setbacks could make them extremely militant. Gwala's career began at SARMCOL in the 1940s, brought him into the Communist Party, and gave him an important trajectory that bound this era with the later struggles of the 1980s and beyond. Gwala then became labeled the "Communist warlord," contesting the African National Congress (ANC) for control of Pietermaritzburg with the Inkatha Freedom Party before his death in 1995. Peter Delius refers to the career of Peter Nchabeleng, a similar if less well-known Pedi activist in the Transvaal (Delius 1990). An assumption commonly made in times when struggle was difficult was that conditions could and would improve only when the political battle was fully engaged.

African trade unionism continued to have links at the same time to sympathetic figures who survived in the white-dominated labor organizations and who often provided decisive injections of skill and system. Most of the radical labor organization that was created in the generation after the economic recovery began in 1933 was united with much more conservative structures in the "fragile unity" of the South African Trades & Labour Council formed in 1930 (Lewis 1984). Industrial change and the explosive growth of the labor force in the boom years finally fractured this unity, which existed as a possibility under the aegis of the older traditions of white trade unionism. It was white unions, afraid of the tide of dilution, which began to walk out of the council from 1950 onward. This federation split in 1955, and it would be only thirty years later, under very different leadership and ideas, that the drive toward some kind of trade union unity would again resume.

The radicals, dominated by the now underground Communist Party (SACP), created the South African Congress of Trade Unions (SACTU). It has been argued that SACTU marked an important advance in shop floor organization and an effort to bring political understanding in tandem with economic demands. While adhering to nonracial principles, it focused on lower-skilled African workers in areas where they were numerous and where some of the classic trade union issues revolving around skill and internal division were not very applicable (Lewis 1984, 153). SACTU gained from the considerable development of mass industry by the time of its creation. However, the initial rapid growth of SACTU ran into the increasing political tension of the late 1950s and the growing turn of the embattled African National Congress (ANC) and the underground SACP, now in alliance, toward mobilization and adoption of the "armed struggle." The ANC, historic home of the African elite, had at times supported worker resistance and major strikes. In this period it was edging toward becoming a nationalist organization prepared to resist white rule. SACTU unions found it hard in the circumstances of the times to deliver anything to members; instead, they tended to become sources for the recruitment of activists to illegal and military activities (Friedman 1987; Lambert 1988). While it is questionable whether well-organized shop floor structures could have gained permanent recognition and operated effectively in South African conditions at this time, the history of SACTU certainly demonstrates the problems with using labor as an arm for a political movement. After 1960, SACTU began to decline as the ANC-SACP faced illegality and persecution. Although it never became illegal itself, it essentially exiled itself as an organization. By 1964 SACTU officials took an entirely pessimistic view of the possibilities of legal trade union organization in South Africa.

SACTU's rival, the Trade Union Congress of South Africa (TUSCA), soldiered on. It lurched from periods of overt racism, including the incorporation of whites-only organizations, to opener phases, partly due to the impact of foreign pressures. In general, TUCSA sponsored "parallel" unions for "non-whites," unions that gave scope for trade union organization and sometimes sponsored real advances for workers, but they were never entirely independent of the dominant unions.

The Struggle and the Unions

By the middle of the 1960s, South Africa was in the midst of unprecedented economic growth. The gold and diamond mines were not particularly profitable in this phase; mining exports grew instead through base mineral expansion. In addition, secondary industry expanded very rapidly and absorbed many workers. It often involved foreign capital keen to establish protected production outlets locally to gain tariff protection. To an unprecedented extent, African men and, on a small scale, women began to be employed as semiskilled operatives to meet demands for labor that the racial minorities could no longer fulfill. In a sense, apartheid profited from this prosperity as a source of stability. However, it also brought about considerable contradiction. As cash dependency increased, more and more Africans found rural living economically unviable. The state in the 1960s was obliged to construct large-scale family housing on the edge of many cities to accommodate the expansion of the urban African population. As this contradiction intensified, various policy instruments were devised to try to divert economic and demographic growth away from what whites saw as their heartland. These instruments evoked bitterness and hardship but failed to push aside the settled African urban population. Despite the low budget allocations for African education, mass primary education became widespread.

Without trade unions, employers often tried to recruit and organize their African workforces through some sort of works committees or through the use of quasi-traditional leadership (in Zulu, *izinduna*). Webster quotes the American anthropologist Hoyt Alverson on how this latter system worked on the mines: "'To the *induna* falls the charge of making the organization and its policies and directives intelligible to Africans who work on the line.' It was, in addition, the *induna* who actually selected the worker, introduced him to the company with a short talk and told him what to do. Backed by the white supervisor, and the system of *impimpis* (informers), the *induna* exercised, from all accounts, a system of despotic control" (1985, 124). This system, however, was becoming increasingly stretched and ineffective as the solution of work problems.

There is much to be said here for the comparative analysis made by Gay Seidman on the emergence of new unions in Brazil and South Africa. In both countries, rapid economic growth under the auspices of a reactionary government gave way to a period of growing structural problems in the economy and a certain distance developing between the state and many industrial capitalists (1994). Business began to recognize that economic growth would need to proceed on the basis of improved labor productivity, which in turn required a concept of labor different from the lavish hiring of a very low-cost, almost totally uneducated, workforce. The usual date given for the end of the period of repression and non-organization in South Africa is January 1973, when the port city of Durban erupted in a kind of rolling general strike. The strike began at a brickworks and quickly spread to the large textile firm of Frames, a business that depended on state protection and where militant Indian unionists had been removed from the scene in the 1950s and replaced with what had long seemed like more docile "tribal" Africans. By 1973 the conjuncture was less favorable for capital; expansion had ceased, while financial pressure on poorly paid Africans mounted. A remarkable aspect of the strike wave in Durban was the invisibility of obvious leadership and the relative tolerance—at least toward wage increases—on the part of many employers. Estimates are that as many as a hundred thousand workers went on strike at some point during that year (see Table 7.1). Attempts to use the Zulu king and the hierarchy of the Kwa Zulu homeland to calm workers down proved abortive. It was obvious to some that a need for new kinds of union organization was beginning to appear (McShane et al. 1984).

One grouping that understood this consisted of young white intellectuals. Stymied by the rise of "Black Consciousness" among university students, these young whites were looking for some outlet through which to express their opposition to the state constructively. They organized wage committees that began to stimulate the organization of new unions, primarily among semiskilled African workers. Another grouping was found in the existing conservative trade union federation, TUCSA. Particularly within the industrial unions, TUSCA was a seedbed for thinking through the contradictions of a racially structured workforce in dynamic economic conditions. For instance, militant Coloured trade unionists in the National Union of Motor Assembly and Rubber Workers of South Africa (NUMARWOSA) in the eastern Cape automobile industry were eager to support an organization that had more fight and more autonomy. They were tired of white paternalism, but they were equally unincorporated by, or even directly hostile to, an ANC tradition that had never spoken to them sympathetically. There were also individuals working for TUCSA who sympathized with the new currents and were prepared to offer crucial assistance to young organizers. Finally, some African organizers from previous waves of militancy reemerged and were often critical in connecting the new unions with their potential recruits through the social networks that reemerged in townships and factories.

Morris has argued that three principles were the most important in the early phase: nonracialism, worker control, and shop floor, plant-based organization (1990,

Table 7.1 Strikes, Strikers, and Days Lost in South Africa, 1972–2005*

Years	Number of strikes	Number of strikers	Work days lost ('000)
Blacks only 1972–79			
1972	71	8814	14.96
1973	370	98029	246.07
1974	384	58975	102.18
1975	276	23488	19,21
1976	248	28098	73.59
1977	90	15334	16.15+
1978	106	14153	10.70
1979	101	23064	70.54
All strikes			
1980	192	58213	168.99
1981	292	88887	232.91
1982	394	140937	419.77
1983	354	64469	133.04
1984	469	181942	431.30
1985	389	239816	678.27
1986	793	424390	1308.96
1987	1148	591421	5825.23
1988	1025	161679	914.39
1989	942	197564	1511.50
1990	885	341097	2792.84
1991	600	172096	1339.33
1992	789	137946	1727.38
1993	781	161504	836.32
1994	776	312842	2152.80
1995	315	152956	1600.00
1996	901	247202	1700.00
1997	1324	212094	656.56
1998	560	323093	3833.1
1999	n.d.	554435	2625.54
2000	n.d.	1142428	1669.97
2001	n.d.	90392	953.61
2002	n.d.	66250	615.72
2003	n.d.	83533	919.78
2004	n.d.	395301	1286.00

Sources: ILO Labor Statistics Database, http://laborsta.ilo.org/cgi-bin/brokerv8.exe; McShane et al. 1987, 20, 58; South Africa, Department of Manpower, Labor Statistics Annual(s); estimates for 1997 and 2001, Habib and Valodia, 2006; estimates for 2002, 2005, NALEDI estimates. As compiled by Jon Kraus from sources provided by William Freund. N.d.= no data available.

* For the period of the 1980s, most strikers were African blacks, while others were largely Colored, not Indian or white. Also, some of the figures appear very lower compared with the estimates of informed observers; they do not include the great "stay-aways," which are defined as political events.

150). The new unionism was immensely energetic in the 1970s despite state persecutions and the banning or imprisonment of leaders. But it was, in fact, very fragmented and slow to organize factories. While some unions moved toward a consistent industrial pattern, concentrating in specific industries, others continued to think of themselves as "general unions," with a far more direct and obvious political motivation. Attitudes varied enormously to the banned ANC-SACP, which at first was extremely suspicious of the new unions. In the context of strategies associated with SACTU (built, as they were, on boycott and denunciation of the South African regime as essentially fascist in character), the attempt by many of the new unions to look for foreign solidarity and funding challenged basic exile assumptions. Indeed, the new unions often concentrated their attentions on multinational investors with the hopes of bringing outside pressure to bear on them, not to drive them out of the country but to allow organization to develop in their operations and to improve conditions on the ground for workers.

A repression of unprecedented bloodshed put an end to the 1976 series of township uprisings that began in Soweto but rolled forward, especially through the agency of the youth. After this, forces within the South African state that were prepared to rethink basic options became stronger. They were essentially interested in saving the essence of white power in the country. The reliance on rural control structures was not abandoned but, indeed, intensified with the granting of independence to several of the amalgamated homelands, and resources were granted for propping them up. But reconsideration of urban policy was also being made. South African capitalism in the 1970s, even during good years, was no longer in a position to absorb increasing amounts of unskilled or even semiskilled labor. The diffusion of secondary education and the solidification of urban life were creating a sense of community that made older labor controls very hard to enforce. Even on the mines, where urbanization was not a factor, labor conditions were extremely turbulent.

Under these circumstances, the unthinkable began to be broached. The Wiehahn Commission suggested that under special conditions Africans ought to be allowed to form registered trade unions. (The Commission's conditions proved unsustainable—that unions could not be nonracial, or multiracial, and that migrants could be excluded.) In 1979 African trade unionism was effectively legalized and the groundwork for an industrial court system established. The Labour Relations Act of 1981 deleted all references to race as a special determining category for workers, and in 1982 disputes over "unfair labor practices" were shifted from administrative power to the realm of the new industrial courts (Friedman 1987, 314). Strikes were made legal only under very particular conditions, but the possibility for striking without police interference suddenly became much greater. And strikes rose quickly (see Table 7.1). For the new unions, this was a surprising turn of affairs. *The South African Labour Bulletin*, which had emerged as their voice, contained intense debates about whether or not to accept registration. On the one side, registration was feared as a state plot that might lead to union emasculation and which contained conditions that were unacceptable to the largely universal ideal of "nonracialism," which held so many tendencies in place. On the other, a pragmatic approach dominated. Those unions that were coming together as the Federation of South African Trade Unions (FOSATU) felt that registration must be used and that the unacceptable conditions could be fought. This latter tendency came to dominate (Maree 1987). Indeed, the FOSATU unions secured agreements to confirm organizational strength and allow advances that would have been virtually impossible before Wiehahn.

In fact, the registered unions succeeded in growing by leaps and bounds under the new legal structure that existed. Hard struggles against unfair dismissal and for minimal bargaining rights gave way to more far-ranging campaigns. The SACTU line that claimed unions could not make gains in South African conditions proved to be the reverse. Indeed, in the new climate "community based unions" that were themselves very much in the SACTU mold began to start up. New unions began to become more and more effective as well in making imaginative and critical use of the law to build up their strength and membership. Some of the key rapid growth sectors depended on the large-scale adherence, for instance, of African migrant workers living in hostels. Where hostels have been seen as institutions of total control, they began rather to be effective as social networks where organization was built. The Metalworkers Union (MAWU) expanded very fast on this basis (Morris 1990). In previous phases of union organization, the main successes had been achieved in consumer industries. Now heavy industry in the private sector was significantly affected. The core of MAWU expansion in the metal industry of the East Rand depended on the solidification of a generation of shop stewards whose political and social ideas would mark the character of this union as much as those of any organizers from outside. Such shop stewards probably knew little of any older union traditions. MAWU would later be the largest component in the creation of the National Union of Metalworkers of South Africa (NUMSA), probably the most important source of ideology and politics in the new trade union movement.

If NUMSA had a rival in this department, it would be the National Union of Mineworkers (NUM), founded in 1982. At first, Anglo-American, the most far-sighted big mining company, saw union recognition as a way of introducing some sort of control and negotiation system into an increasingly embattled workplace. This was perhaps precisely as management was becoming less able to provide the wage increases that windfall profits had made possible in the middle and late 1970s when the price of gold had dramatically shot up. However, the NUM was able to take off on its own trajectory and move far beyond the dictates of Anglo-American. Given that it had been founded within the Black Consciousness tradition of the 1970s—unsympathetic to both the ANC and to nonracialism as a platform—its adhesion to the Congress of South African Trade Unions (COSATU) was a remarkable shift of great significance. Eventually, the mine owners and NUM would face off in a month-long strike in 1987, which would test the powers of trade unions in the South African mining industry.

A striking feature of new unionism in South Africa was the doctrine of worker democracy, which itself rested on the diffusion of shop steward organization, shop steward and regional councils, and shop steward education. COSATU unions in general eschewed the closed shop as a means of discipline, given the history of its use as a means of excluding black workers historically in South African conditions. Perhaps the fundamental institution binding ordinary members to the union were"report backs." These were mass meetings during which organizers could show faith with ordinary members and make clear that negotiations would not involve compromises that workers refused to accept. This was a particular and infectious kind of democracy that built organization, maximized consensus, and made alternative views irrelevant. Baskin terms it "majoritarian hegemony" (1991, 460). Worker control became an enshrined union concept. It could be very effective and impressive at the local level, but it was harder to make real at the level of rapid decision making for very large groups (Webster 1985, 225).

May Day, long in abeyance in South Africa, was enforced as a day when unions celebrated their distinct achievements. In time, the union movement experimented with cultural activities, promoting the activities of worker poets, for example. By 1982, on the occasion of the death in detention of a Food and Canning Worker Union organizer, Neal Aggett, a coalition of unions mounted a very successful national one-day work stoppage on as large or larger a scale as any twenty years earlier. The stronger unions—especially through the agency of the "service organizations" that sprang up based on contributions from overseas—took up a wide range of worker issues that contrasted markedly to the narrow perspectives of many established unions. These would include health and safety issues and gender equality. It is more debatable whether structural changes were actually successfully entrenched by this kind of research and agitation. Baskin suggested that attempts to promote women as leaders and issues aimed at women members, whom he estimated at 36 percent of the total, were honored mostly in the breach (1991, chapter 23).

Even in 1981 and beyond, after the significant slowdown in the economy, the new unions were increasingly able to deliver not only better wages but also more respectful treatment and successful resistance to arbitrary dismissals. Friedman's impressive and lengthy study is committed to the view that the new union movement represented a qualitatively new element in South African politics rather than a resumption of an age-old struggle against apartheid or for black liberation. As such, it exemplified what was a powerful view of the early and middle 1980s in union circles (1987).

At this time, the relationship of new unionism to the ANC-SACP alliance became a more important issue. On the one hand, the new unions increasingly included supporters of the alliance; on the other, political forces within their ranks began to speak more openly of an alternative politics flowing from the trade unions themselves. The exiled ANC was reviving in strength, having moved its headquarters to Lusaka in Zambia. The white Rhodesian and Portuguese colonial regimes had been brought to an end, in large part through armed struggle. And some successful sabotage in the name of the ANC was beginning to affect South African internal morale. FOSATU's politics reached their apotheosis in a keynote address by Secretary-General Joe Foster in 1982 (McShane et al. 1987, 125). Foster, while acknowledging the international political importance of the ANC, made no reference to the SACP and emphasized it was FOSATU that would create a genuine working-class politics in South Africa (Maree 1987). "There are two crucial policies which we can never sacrifice . . . worker control and non-racialism" (Baskin 1991, 40). Distinct working-class organization and culture were reified as the most important elements in society opposed to the apartheid state. The SACP was outraged that FOSATU would dare to substitute itself for the Communists as "the political party of the working class."

Yet despite this, the success of the new union movement increasingly precluded rejection of it as an option for the ANC. SACTU polices were increasingly irrelevant and needed to be laid to rest. By this time exiled politicos understood the immense potential for organization that lay in the legal trade union movement. Its logic following the successful acceptance of registration by FOSATU and some other unions lay in merger and rationalization. Several abortive meetings finally culminated in the agreement to create the Congress of South African Trade Unions (COSATU) in Durban in November 1985, made possible in part because elements loyal to the ANC-SACP now supported the creation of a larger labor federation.

The backdrop to the creation of COSATU, moreover, was unprecedented renewal of antistate activities within urban black townships. It was unprecedented in its organizational complexity and its willingness to attack and make "ungovernable" local institutions of all sorts, but notably schools and local authorities, amid the atmosphere of violent contestation that prevailed in more and more remote corners of the country. For much of COSATU, township struggle was at first worrying; it seemed to be empowering those in the mushrooming United Democratic Front (created in 1982) who had little belief in the need for autonomous working-class organization and its preservation. In some areas, notably Port Elizabeth in the eastern Cape, relations between COSATU and other militants, some of whom had rallied behind rival labor organizations in the past, were poor to the point of violence. However, others within COSATU, even those not directly under the control of the ANC-SACP, wanted to see a disciplined struggle against the state in which COSATU and a working-class discourse took a leading or even dominant part.

Thus tension raged in COSATU between the "workerists" and the "populists." The latter were almost invariably down-the-line supporters of the ANC, although they were often eager to give the ANC a working class content or program. They tended to accept the SACP as the main political force that could deliver such a content. The workerists were divided between those who disliked the ANC—especially the SACP—and were looking for an alternative, but not necessarily revolutionary, politics, in general, and those who wanted to stay within the ANC-SACP fold but push those politics in a more classically Left direction. It could be said that this view prevailed in the end, formally. A dramatic breakthrough was achieved for the exiled alliance when Jay Naidoo, the COSATU secretary-general, met in Harare with representatives of the exiled ANC leadership and paved the way for a large gathering in March 1986. At this meeting it was agreed that the ANC headed the national liberation movement of which COSATU was "an important and integral part" (Baskin 1991, 94). Naidoo would later become an ANC cabinet member.

At this point, historically, the ANC was filled with hope that the internal insurrection, all adhering to the ANC banner, would finally make possible the overthrow of the South African state. However, renewed repression under the state of emergency put an end to this dream. Thousands of activists were rounded up for various time periods. Terror methods were applied to individuals seen as crucial to the continuation of resistance, and the state was fairly effective at restoring its authority by the end of 1986. Moreover, the "armed struggle," relying on the use of neighboring countries as potential bases for revolutionary activity within South Africa, was largely subverted. Mozambique in particular was virtually laid waste through the stoking up of an internal insurrection that crippled the FRELIMO (Frente de Libertacao de Mozambique) government. The ANC was effectively kicked out of Mozambique and unable to operate militarily from Botswana, Lesotho, or Zimbabwe. In this context, the situation of the unions was fundamental, since the state was prepared to continue to allow them to operate legally. In the worst phases of repression, COSATU militants could bring out or close down townships where the so-called civic and other pro-ANC organizations had been effectively stifled. In terms of "stay-aways" (strikes) and other mass actions, starting with May Day 1986, COSATU was often the key element that could close down a township and create the world headlines that embarrassed the government.

However, even the pursuit of political aims that seem to accord with what ultimately became the dominant tendency in COSATU was not allowed to splinter or fragment existing unions readily. The logic of building workplace organization remained as strong or stronger than any question of adhesion to a political line. The formation of COSATU opened the way to a dramatic and heady period of growth for the trade union federation and its strongest affiliates. By 1985 COSATU had organized up to half a million workers. In the following years, unions were pushed into mergers, creating such large units as NUMSA and the South African Clothing and Textile Workers Union. The state continued to harass and persecute individual unionists who were suspected of links to the ANC-SACP, but it was unable or unwilling to curb the often explosive growth of the union movement in size and capacity. Through the late 1980s, when the economy grew very slowly and only through the injection of state funds, unionized workers were typically able to make significant wage gains (Baskin 1991, 254). The last COSATU congress before the onset of political negotiations, held in 1989, represented nearly a million members, while membership reached 1.2 million a year later (Baskin 1991, 344). The total of all South African trade union membership at that time was approximately 2.7 million, almost 53 percent of wage employees outside agriculture (Macun 1993, 49).

In 1987, prodded largely by employers, the state began the attempt to initiate a new Labour Relations Act, which would build on the Wiehahn reforms but aim at restricting strike activities. A large and enthusiastic union campaign eventually put paid to this attempt. The act was amended through negotiation to a point where COSATU found the legislation acceptable. When the state refused to put this legislation forward in 1990, a stay-away (strike) was sufficiently successful to force it to back down, and in 1991 the Labour Relations Amendment (LRA) Act was passed. This proved to be a transitional measure before the framing of a new regulatory structure for labor after the 1994 elections.

COSATU attracted a wide array of gifted political strategists and intellectuals who pushed the unions into thinking about issues of social and economic transformation. An interesting facet was the emergence of the Economic Trends Research Group (of which the author was a member), established with trade union blessing but intended to consider and ultimately to strategize for wider economic planning. In the special conjuncture of the late 1980s, it was possible to posit a historically special kind of "social movement" or "political unionism" that would transcend problems that had limited the possibilities of trade unionism internationally back to the time of Marx (Seidman 1994).

Despite the obvious centrality of COSATU unions to the events of the time, mention needs to be made of the remaining sectors of the union movement. Thus, some black unionists from the new movement held themselves apart, largely due to their preference for the ANC's rivals in the Pan-Africanist Congress or the Black Consciousness Azanian People's Organization (AZAPO). These were grouped in the Council of South African Trade Unions (CUSA), established in 1980 and later evolving into the National Council of Trade Unions (NACTU). CUSA is not a negligible federation and has some important affiliates, notably the South African Chemical Workers Union, which contested—often bitterly—with the COSATU-based Chemical Workers Industrial Union. During the anti-LRA campaign of 1989, there was significant NACTU cooperation, but relations between affiliate unions were sometimes tense.

TUCSA, as a nonracial grouping that reflected older labor patterns, went into a terminal decline and dissolved in 1986. It had tried to prop up the situation of white workers while encouraging the organization of others under its aegis. What Webster termed "bureaucratized benefit societies" (1985, 222) were unable to retain their membership under the rapidly changing, politicized conditions of South Africa in the 1980s. Organization in this tradition splintered off in every direction, losing affiliates to COSATU, to right wing racist groupings, and to the Federation of Salaried Workers (FEDSAL), which was resuscitated in 1985.

The possible threat to social change in South Africa posed by white workers organized on directly racial lines across industries seemed significant through the 1980s. One instance of this was the Mineworkers Union led by Arrie Paulus. Such workers were receiving less and less effective support from the state organizationally and as a class, and they had obvious capabilities as soldiers and skilled workers to wreak havoc on the economy. Such a threat never really eventuated, however. As early as 1979, a large-scale white miners' strike aimed primarily to prevent implementation of the Wiehahn recommendations petered out, indicating the limited possibilities of this form of action. Attempts at white militancy have fizzled out in practice and diminished progressively in importance. In fact, from the early 1990s, the obvious centrality of COSATU unions to effective labor bargaining started to bring small numbers of white, Indian, and Coloured workers into COSATU affiliates. In Cape Town, Coloured workers were in fact a major force in COSATU. From time to time COSATU was also able to work on a fairly cooperative basis with FEDSAL in strike situations.

It also ought to be stressed that the union movement was not boundless in its successes. The massive 1987 strike of NUM in the gold mines ended in mass dismissals. And a process began whereby the overall number of gold miners has since fallen dramatically while management control ideas have achieved increasing purchase. Moreover, a phase of rapid economic gains, granted in good part at the expense of the minority of white miners who once earned most of the mine payroll, was followed by one of modest increases, largely within the parameters created by management. Workers went out into the streets in their numbers again and again but had not yet assaulted the citadel of capital decisively.

The Contemporary Period

This great formative union phase ended in February 1990 with the dramatic break-through whereby State President F.W. de Klerk called for an end to the banning of the ANC and SACP and for the release of Nelson Mandela. The breakthrough initiated a tense, often highly conflict-laden but never really abandoned phase of negotiations, in which COSATU was represented. This led to the April 1994 elections that brought to power the Government of National Unity in which the ANC, with more than 60 percent of the vote, became the strongest element.

After the phase of phenomenal growth and organizational advance, there seemed to be the possibility that this phase would place the COSATU aligned unions in a powerful position to shape the new South Africa. This, in effect, would create a social as well as a political democracy. While the unions continue to be an important force in society, these ambitions were not realized, and explaining the problems they encountered must dominate this last section of the chapter. The negotiations themselves exemplified this pattern. While COSATU delegations sat in on them, the questions that COSATU would have emphasized were generally sidelined (Friedman 1993). No negotiator was more effective than the NUM leader Cyril Ramaphosa, but he became entirely enmeshed within the ANC delegation and put aside his trade union background entirely. When, after 1994, he failed to secure the succession to Nelson Mandela, he entered the business world and became one of a handful of wealthy black businessmen in South Africa by the end of the century. Some twenty members of COSATU unions were nominated by those unions to run for parliament on the ANC ticket in 1994. The post-election cabinet included some of the most prominent figures from COSATU: Jay Naidoo as minister in charge of coordinating the Reconstruction and Development Plan (RDP) in the president's office; Sydney Mafumadi as minister of safety and security; and Alec Erwin as junior minister of finance. However, as with Ramaphosa, they largely covered up their union tracks in their new roles without much ado. Some observers see this loss of leadership as causing a huge decline in capacity (Buhlungu 2005, 711).

By 1992 the ANC-aligned liberation forces accepted the new structure of a Tripartite Alliance in which SACP and COSATU were essentially accepted as junior partners (Baskin, 1991, 432). SACTU, no longer exiled, negotiated its own dissolution. The ANC made use of the immense capacity of COSATU to mobilize workers on the ground for demonstrations that reinforced the urgency of political transformation to the South African administrative and economic establishment. The spectacular 1992 stay-away to force the end of a stalemate in the constitutional negotiations process brought out an astonishing 4 million people. But, in fact, the former ANC exiles did not want the unions to play any role in formulating policy beyond legislation that concerned the workplace (Buhlungu 2005). Here there was quick progress: the Labour Relations Act of 1995 created a supportive and enabling framework for organized labor to build structures and to contest management with legal strikes when necessary.

The unions responded to this new situation with a number of strategies. During the transition period itself, influential individuals tried to see if it would be possible for unions to take over the SACP as a force on the Left (Eidelberg 2000). This foundered on the unwillingness of the SACP, used to its centrist role within the ANC, to play this part. Also, it was realized that the mass of African workers in COSATU unions were totally committed to the ANC and unwilling to turn to the SACP if it posed a rival list of candidates for office and platform. At the same time, practical participation in the National Manpower Commission, the National Economic Forum, and other state-generated bodies forced COSATU to play a new kind of "responsible" political role in the transition period.

Considerable hope was also laid on the emergence of corporate institutions (Habib and Valodia 2006, 239–42; Maree 1993; Schreiner 1994). The National Manpower Commission and the National Economic Forum had been created to secure openings on the industrial front while negotiations were in progress. These then merged into the National Economic Development and Labour Council (NED-LAC) in February 1995 (Adler and Webster 2000, 9). The COSATU Left hoped that NEDLAC would become a powerful institution where basic social and economic policies were hammered out. But this quickly was reduced to a discourse of "social partnership" among the state, the organized corporate sector, and the trade unions. For COSATU, particularly with reference to its own rhetoric and its own political culture, this was a considerable comedown, although NEDLAC still exists.

In the buildup to the first elections in 1994, the unions as well as the UDF-linked civic movements and sympathetic NGOs stood behind the RDP, the document that outlined many of South Africa's social problems effectively (Buhlungu 2005; Götz 2000). The RDP was very popular with the electorate and appeared to be fundamental to the ANC's plans. In reality, it lacked prioritization and, most critically, any explanation of how the plan would be financed. Its neglected economic section was in fact very tentative and cautious.

The economic void of the RDP was replaced by the Growth, Employment, and Redistribution (GEAR) policy in May 1996 (Adler and Webster 2000, 11). Nelson Mandela made clear that the ANC was uninterested in any criticism of GEAR, a macroeconomic framework largely copied from a model developed in the de Klerk period with a strong emphasis on fiscal conservatism and debt repayment. For the South African Left, GEAR seemed to enshrine an inexplicable acceptance of neoliberal, Washington financial consensus orthodoxy that stymied any serious effort at transformation. It was the more maddening when the RDP office, centralized in the presidency, was summarily closed down.

In practice, GEAR was not exactly a Washington blueprint. In fact, the 1995 pro-union legislation, the practical hesitation to engage in much privatization, and the considerable budgetary emphasis on redistribution in taxation and welfare spending went against the Washington grain. But the willingness to reduce tariff barriers quickly, the drive to ease financial transfers, and the good relationship established with the World Trade Organisation and other allied groupings represented part of a strategy to win support from foreign investors. Defense of GEAR tends to focus on the precarious position of a black-led government in the middle of the 1990s within a world that had moved sharply to the right (Hirsch 2005).

The intellectual brain trust behind the unions had largely dissipated, some of it fading into the new ANC strategies. The Economic Trends Research Group had given way to the Macro-Economic Research Group (MERG), a larger grouping intended to provide economic strategizing for the entire alliance and that formed part of the basis of the ANC's 1994 electoral platform. MERG could be described as combining Left Keynesian thinking with the eclectic influence of new thinking about the so-called developmental states of East and Southeast Asia. However, it was essentially brushed aside and characterized as the voice of foreign leftist intellectuals. COSATU has been able to generate a small research facility—the National Labour and Development Institute (NALEDI)—established early in 1994 with foreign funding. However, it has for the most part been pushed back into more conventional trade union issues and activities, and its funding can hardly compare with the immense support the state can muster in the new era. Labor today cannot be said to have up its sleeve a clearly developed alternative pattern for South African economic development or for promoting an egalitarian society. (For a rare exception in the transport sector see von Holdt 2005b.)

Workers in regular employment have clearly benefited very significantly from the LRA and from the new political regime. In his impressive monograph on Highveld Steel, Karl von Holdt has pointed out that "NUMSA had succeeded in curbing dismissals. There were proper disciplinary and grievance procedures and reduced harassment, job reservations, and favoritism. Through stoppages and negotiation workers had won the right to shift allowances, adequate work clothes, cabins in which to shelter from cold weather in exposed workplaces, pulpits on machines, heaters and fans in cranes and other workstations, and stoves in the workplace, where shift-workers could cook lunch" (2003, 237).

These constituted big changes. However, he also insists that the racial hierarchy in the workplace has not really altered fundamentally. And there remains an illegitimacy to the way the economy operates in the understanding of many, if not most, participants, an illegitimacy that can even be directed at the unions themselves (von Holdt 2000, 2005a; Marks 2005). The trade unions have been successful only occasionally at establishing more democratic workplace situations. More commonly, dynamic management initiative has formed bonds with sectors of the workforce independent of the unions; in other cases, such as with construction and transport unions, wildcat strikes have at times had a big impact (Webster and von Holdt 2005b). The market imperative has pushed management to enforce conditions that undermine previous gains, requiring very substantial militant resistance to be restored even where international competitiveness is not directly a factor (Kenny 2005). Workplace forums were denoted in the 1995 legislation to give production workers a systematic voice in the labor arena, but they have been very ineffective when instituted at all (Adler 2000; Adler and Webster 2000).

It is not so easy, however, for labor to make this the basis for contesting ANC politics. To understand the difficulties of COSATU in challenging the ANC, apart from the strategic issues raised above, structural elements also need to be raised. At the start of the new millennium, Adler and Webster (2000, 14) emphasized the following negative factors in an early assessment:

(a) the loss of leadership to the world of politics and elsewhere
(b) the growing gap between an increasingly bureaucratized leadership and the worker rank and file

(c) the decline in "quality of services offered," particularly at the shop steward level

(d) the reconfiguration of the alliance, with the ANC now dominant and increasingly effective at wielding state patronage.

Indeed the ANC itself has been a key factor. Under the presidency of Thabo Mbeki especially, it has been centralized and hollowed out in terms of autonomous mass participation. With three successive landslide electoral victories, it has become a party-state, effectively able to appear as the only serious source of policy wisdom. It has achieved a remarkable success in stabilizing the economy and ending any real sense of crisis for South African business while enriching a new set of partners.

Moreover, despite the obvious desire of most business interests to see the new state attack COSATU and worker initiatives, it would be wrong to assume that the ANC has a commitment to undermine or destroy the trade union movement. Even the Afrikaner National Party came to the realization, typified by the Wiehahn Commission report being transmuted into law in 1979, that the complex and turbulent world of labor needed to be regulated and put on a new legal basis. The ANC's concern to institute a negotiated system of labor relations as beneficial as possible to the smooth running of the economy is all the greater. They still largely share the hope, which most African nationalists of the independence era held, of becoming the patrons of an increasingly modern and well-treated labor force. The penchant for incorporation, of substitution of the state or party-state for the trade union among workers, was typical of labor politics elsewhere in Africa. But this is tempered, if not entirely eliminated, in South Africa by the complex nature of the economy (Freund 1988). The ANC has tried to establish a regulatory labor regime based on constant consultation, state regulation, a nonracist workplace, and the construction of skills. However, its capacity to deliver these goods has been poor to uneven (2005b). Moreover, it has failed to tackle the roots of poverty in a country where half the population is beset by high levels of irregular employment and unemployment, very low skill levels, family instability, disease, and violence. It offers, instead, money transfers and the "delivery" of services for which the majority of people cannot really pay.

COSATU's period of relatively unproblematic growth came to an end in the late 1990s. There is a temptation to ascribe this to "globalisation" in some simple, straightforward way. It is certainly true that rapidly reduced tariffs encouraged massive waves of imports, which are seriously affecting the South African balance of payments and devastating workforces in certain sectors, such as the clothing and footwear industries (Mosoetsa 2005). However, the big job losses have come through rationalization and reorganization that reflect a managerial desire for efficiency based on a limited-size, core permanent employment base throughout the economy. An uncertain but significant number of jobs have been transformed into outsourcing and contract operations that are not covered under the LRA. Here the unions battle to organize workers.

The most remarkable job losses have come in agriculture and gold mining and have been particularly severe on low-skill male employment. The union movement, despite many resolutions, has never succeeded in really penetrating the poorest sectors of the workforce—farmworkers, domestic workers, and the growing so-called informal sector, which includes home manufacture under sweatshop conditions, street commerce, and many other activities, not to speak of the unemployed (Webster and von Holdt 2005b). The much-heralded Self-Employed Workers Union (SEWU), which began to organize women street sellers outside COSATU in Durban, has dissolved in the context of a lawsuit; conditions have proven more unfavorable than in India, where the model for SEWU emerged. A frequently heralded attempt to create cooperative employment amongst redundant miners and their families has struggled to meet even very small-scale success (Philip 2005). In these circumstances, the union movement understandably tended from the late 1990s to feel embattled and to become increasingly dominated by the need to defend existing jobs.

There are few union members in the poorest half of the population (Seekings 2000). Some key union supporters see the future of trade unionism as depending on its ability to reach out to these sectors. Certainly, existing legislation is not sufficiently enforceable and has enough loopholes so it cannot prevent crude exploitation of workers from springing up, especially outside traditional industrial areas. The conventional argument by pro-business circles that overly rigid labor markets characterize South Africa and block the poor from entry into the job market, or that trade unions are indifferent to the interests of the very poor, is wildly exaggerated if it has any truth at all (Standing, Sender, and Weeks 1996). The union movement has, for instance, been the main supporter of the Basic Income Grant program to offer all South Africans a small monthly guaranteed income (Seekings 2005).

By contrast, the most successful sectors of the economy take on surprisingly few workers: for instance, the automobile industry, which has grown rapidly based on international agreements with the big multinational giants. In general, employment is growing for the more educated and white-collar sector of the population and most markedly on the Witwatersrand, in Pretoria, and in Cape Town, while many small towns and cities are in a state of decline. COSATU's competitor NACTU, the federation with Black Consciousness and PAC roots and a weaker force aiming at the same labor market, has collapsed. FEDSAL—"the moderate voice of labor" with nearly three hundred thousand members—has a strong contingent of white workers and an officially apolitical stance. It has expanded and has been rewarded with attention and respect from the Mbeki presidency.

Job losses pushed the union movement into an essentially defensive mode in the last years of the twentieth century. Yet with more favorable economic conditions, decline has been stemmed, and since 2003 COSATU has begun to grow again slowly. However, its character has changed under the surface in important ways. Since the advent of democracy, a higher and higher percentage of members are government workers, notably in health and education (the COSATU teachers' union dates back only to 1990), nursing, policing, and municipal employment. In contrast, the centrality of industrial production workers and miners has fallen (Buhlungu and Webster 2006; Seekings 2005, 310). Government workers are, in a sense, tied in to state patronage far more than those in the private sector, and the range of those unionized now covers a complex set of economic conditions. COSATU is certainly no longer the army of the oppressed, homogenized, largely male, and low-skilled workers.

The so-called Tripartite Alliance continues, but it is a source of massive political tension. South Africa is one country where trade union conferences and union political announcements are invariably headline news. COSATU has engaged in massive demonstration strikes to express its contempt for GEAR economic policies in 2000 and subsequent years (Buhlungu 2005). And the Mbeki government has meddled in union politics to try to get a more cooperative leadership that will stand behind what the state bureaucracy asks for, and it has at times threatened to cut off COSATU from the alliance. As of late 2006, former deputy president Jacob Zuma, once an underground ANC intelligence official, had challenged Mbeki, courting COSATU in an increasingly open campaign for the presidency. This, despite the fact that Zuma stood trial on separate charges of rape and corruption, which his supporters vociferously protested. It was Zuma, cleared of these charges, rather than Mbeki, who addressed COSATU at its 2006 Congress in the name of the ANC and was warmly greeted. Growing enthusiasm about Zuma has certainly diminished the talk within unions about a break with the ANC and the formation of a real party of the Left. However, the rank-and-file union members are overwhelmingly loyal to the ANC that delivered them from apartheid, and their loyalty remains salient. The alliance is based on deep political loyalties, however illogical and frustrating it may seem at times to outsiders (Buhlungu 2005, 716; Webster 2001). It seems highly uncertain whether Zuma has more to offer than top posts for a few COSATU leaders who have been frozen out of power through the enmity of Mbeki over the years. Nor is it certain that another ANC leader will not succeed Mbeki in the end. However, a less cynical view would suggest, too, that COSATU is eager to assume a stronger and more visibly militant role politically in 2007 than has been possible during the first years of the new dispensation.

Thus, despite the important weakening effects of COSATU discussed above, it is certainly too soon to assume that this situation is irreversible. The union movement is far from down and out. It has enormous residual strength. The heritage of militancy, of internal democracy, and of independence of action remains a very strong one in its discourse and practice. Indeed, the apparent difficulties COSATU seems to pose for the ANC political leadership stem from the impatience and anger of members on the ground, not from the philosophy of the leadership which has several times now opposed, more or less publicly, significant strikes.

Can the unions be crucial in moving from political democracy to formulating a social democracy? Gay Seidman pinned hopes for a transformed international community of labor on the new labor movements of Brazil and South Africa a decade ago; her assumptions now seem far too optimistic (1994). Some voices in the trade union movement have seen in insurgent "social movements" a potential ally in resuming the struggle. These movements are often formed in anger at failures or delays in the state delivery of housing, electricity, water, AIDS drugs, and other services (Buhlungu 2005, 715; Buhlungu and Webster 2006). Indeed, it is interesting that a very recent assessment of the union movement chooses to *define* it as a social movement (Habib and Valodia 2006). Another view would see the problems with the ANC as being due to its subjection to plans made in the Washington institutions; opposing this would mean, of course, formulating alternative policies with some coherence as well as relevant international linkages. The continued vitality of the

South African trade union movement will require new invigoration and new strategies to suit a changing and challenging situation.

References

Adler, Glenn, ed. 2000. *Engaging the state and business: The labor movement and co-determination in contemporary South Africa*. Johannesburg: Witwatersrand University Press.

Adler, Glenn, and Eddie Webster, eds. 2000. *Trade unions and democratization in South Africa 1985–97*. Johannesburg: Witwatersrand University Press; Houndmills, UK: Macmillan.

Alexander, Peter. 2000. *Workers, war and the origins of apartheid: Labor and politics in South Africa 1939–48*. London: James Currey.

Baskin, Jeremy. 1991. *Striking back: A history of COSATU*. Johannesburg: Ravan Press.

Beinart, William, Peter Delius, and Stanley Trapido, eds. 1986. *Putting a plough to the ground: Accumulation and dispossession in rural South Africa 1950–1960*. Johannesburg: Ravan Press.

Berger, Iris. 1992. *Threads of solidarity: Women in South African industry*. Bloomington: Indiana University Press.

Bonner, P. 1979. The 1920 black mineworkers' strike: A preliminary account. In *Labour, townships and protest*, ed. Belinda Bozzoli. Johannesburg: Raven Press.

Bozzoli, Belinda, ed. 1979. *Labour, townships and protest*. Johannesburg: Ravan Press.

Bradford, Helen. 1987. *A taste of freedom: The ICU in rural South Africa 1924–30*. New Haven, CT: Yale University Press.

Buhlungu, Sakhela. 2005. Union-party alliances in the era of market regulation: The case of South Africa. *Journal of Southern African Studies* 31 (4): 701–17.

Buhlungu, Sakhela, and Eddie Webster. 2006. Work restructuring and the future of labor in South Africa. In *State of the Nation*, ed. Sakhela Buhlungu, Jessice Lutchman, John Daniel, and Roger Southall. Cape Town: HSRC Press.

Delius, Peter. 1990. Migrants, comrades and rural revolt: Sekhukhuneland 1950–87. *Transformation* 13:2–26.

Eidelberg, P. G. 2000. The tripartite alliance on the eve of a new millennium: COSATU, the ANC and the SACP. In *Trade unions and democratization in South Africa 1985–97*, ed. Adler, Glenn, and Eddie Webster, 129–58. Johannesburg: Witwatersrand University Press; Houndmills, UK: Macmillan.

Freund, Bill. 1988. *The African worker*. Cambridge: Cambridge University Press.

———. 1995. *Insiders and outsiders: The Indian working class of Durban 1910–90*. Portsmouth, NH: Heinemann.

Friedman, Steven. 1987. *Building tomorrow today: African workers in trade unions 1970–84*. Johannesburg: Ravan Press.

———. 1993. *The long journey: South Africa's quest for a negotiated settlement*. Johannesburg: Ravan Press.

Götz, Graeme. 2000. "Shoot everything that flies, claim everything that falls": Labor and the changing definition of the reconstruction and development program. In *Trade unions and democratization in South Africa 1985–97*, ed. Adler, Glenn, and Eddie Webster, 159–89. Johannesburg: Witwatersrand University Press; Houndmills, UK: Macmillan. Johannesburg: Witwatersrand University Press and Houndsmill: Macmillan.

Greenberg, Stanley. 1980. *Race and state in capitalist development: A comparative perspective*. New Haven, CT: Yale University Press.

Habib, Adam, and Imraan Valodia. 2006. Reconstructing a social movement in an era of globalization: A case study of COSATU. In *Voices of protest: Social movements in post-apartheid South Africa*, ed. Richard Ballard, Adam Habib, and Imraan Valodia, 425–55. Pietermaritzburg: University of KwaZule-Natal Press.

Hemson, David. 1979. Class consciousness and migrant workers: The dockworkers of Durban. PhD diss., University of Warwick.

Hindson, Doug. 1987. *Pass controls and the urban African proletariat*. Johannesburg: Ravan Press.

Hirsch, Alan. 2005. *Season of hope: Economic reform under Mandela and Mbeki*. Pietermaritzburg: University of KwaZulu-Natal Press; Ottawa: IDRC.

Hirson, Baruch. 1989. *Yours for the union: Class and community struggles in South Africa, 1930–47*. Johannesburg: Witwatersrand University Press.

Jeeves, Alan. 1985. *Migrant labour in South Africa's mining economy: The struggle for the gold mines' labour supply 1890–1920*. Johannesburg: Witwatersrand University Press.

Johnson, F. W. 1979. The IWA on the Rand: Socialist organizing among black workers on the Rand, 1917-18. In *Labour, Townships and Protest*, ed. Belinda Bozzoli. Johannesburg: Raven Press.

Kaplan, D., and M. Morris. 1976. Labour policies in a state corporation: A case study of the South African iron and steel corporation. *South African Labour Bulletin* 2 (6): 21–33; 2 (8): 2–21.

Kenny, Bridget. 2005. The "market hegemonic" workplace or order in food retailing. In *Beyond the apartheid workplace: Studies in transition*, ed. Eddie Webster and Karl von Holdt, 217–41. Pietermaritzburg: University of KwaZulu-Natal.

Krikler, Jeremy. 2005. *The Rand revolt: The 1922 insurrection and racial killing in South Africa*. Johannesburg: Jonathan Ball.

———. 1993. *Revolution from above, rebellion from below: The agrarian Transvaal at the turn of the century*. Oxford: Clarendon Press.

Lambert, Robert V. 1988. Political unionism in South Africa: The South African congress of trade unions 1955–65. PhD diss. Johannesburg: University of the Witwatersrand.

Lewis, Jon. 1984. *Industrialisation and trade union Organisation in South Africa, 1924–55: The rise and fall of the South African trades and labour council*. Cambridge: Cambridge University Press.

Macun, Ian. 1993. South African unions: Still growing? *South African Labour Bulletin* 17 (4): 48–53.

Maree, Johann, ed. 1987. *The independent trade unions 1974–84: Ten years of the South African Labour Bulletin*. Johannesburg: Ravan Press.

———. 1993. Trade unions and corporatism in South Africa. *Transformation* 21: 24-54.

Marks, Monique. 2005. *Transforming the robocops: Changing police in South Africa*. Scottsville: University of KwaZulu-Natal Press.

McShane, Dennis, Martin Plaut, and David Ward. 1987. *Power! Black workers, their unions and the struggle for freedom in South Africa*. London: Spokesman.

Moodie, Dunbar. 1986. The moral economy of the black miners' strike of 1946. *Journal of Southern African Studies* 13 (1): 1–35.

Morris, M. 1990. Unions and industrial councils: Why do unions' policies change? In *Political economy of South Africa*, ed. N. Nattrass and E. Ardington. Cape Town: Oxford University Press.

Mosoetsa, Sarah. 2005a. The consequences of South Africa's economic transition: The remnants of the footwear industry. In *Beyond the apartheid workplace: Studies in transition*, ed. Eddie Webster and Karl von Holdt, 317–34. Pietermaritzburg: University of KwaZulu-Natal.

Meara, Dan. 1975. The 1946 mine workers' strike in the political economy of South Africa. *Journal of Comparative and Commonwealth Politics* 12 (2): 146-73.

Padayachee, Vishnu, Paul Tichman, and Shahid Vawda. 1985. Indian workers and trade unions in Durban 1930–50. In *Research Report 20*. Durban: University of Durban-Westville, Institute for Social and Economic Research.

Philip, Kate. 2005. Rural enterprise: Work on the margins. In *Beyond the apartheid workplace: Studies in transition*, ed. Eddie Webster and Karl von Holdt, 361–86. Pietermaritzburg: University of KwaZulu-Natal.

Schreiner, Geoff. 1994. Beyond corporatism. *Transformation* 23:1–22.

Scully, Pamela. 1993. Liquor and labor in the western Cape 1870–1900. In *Liquor and labor in southern Africa*, ed. Charles Ambler and Jonathan Crush. Athens: Ohio University Press.

Seekings, Jeremy. 2005. Trade unions, social policy and class compromise in post-apartheid South Africa. *Review of African Political Economy* 100:399–412.

Seidman, Gay. 1994. *Manufacturing militance: Workers' movements in Brazil and South Africa, 1970–85*. Berkeley: University of California Press.

Simons, Jack, and Ray Simons. 1983. *Class and colour in South Africa 1850–1950*. Reprint. London: International Defense and Aid Fund.

South African Labour Bulletin 1974–.

Standing, Guy, J. Sender, and J. Weeks. 1996. *Restructuring the labour market: The South African challenge*. Geneva: International Labor Organization.

Swanson, M. W. 1976. The Durban system: Roots of urban apartheid in colonial Natal. *African Studies* 35:159–76.

Turrell, Robert V. 1987. *Capital and labour on the Kimberley diamond fields 1871–90*. Cambridge: Cambridge University Press.

von Holdt, Karl. 1991. The COSATU/ANC alliance: What does COSATU think? *South African Labor Bulletin* 15 (8): 17–29.

———. 2000. From the politics of resistance to the politics of reconstruction? The union and "ungovernability" in the workplace. In *Trade Unions and Democratization in South Africa 1985-97*, ed. Glenn Adler and Eddie Webster, 100–28. Johannesburg: Witwatersrand University Press.

———. 2003. *Transition from below: Trade unionism and workplace change in South Africa*. Pietermaritzburg:University of KwaZulu-Natal Press.

———. 2005a. Political transition and the changing workplace order in a South African steelworks. In *Beyond the apartheid workplace: Studies in transition*, ed. Karl von Holdt and Eddie Webster, 47–71. Pietermaritzburg: University of KwaZule-Natal Press.

———. 2005b. "Saving government from itself," trade union engagement with the restructuring of Spoornet. In *Beyond the apartheid workplace: Studies in transition*, ed. Eddie Webster and Karl von Holdt, 413–34. Pietermaritzburg: University of KwaZulu-Natal.

———. 1995. Workplace forums: Can they tame management? *South African Labour Bulletin* 19 (1): 31–34.

Webster, Eddie. 1981. Stayaways and the black working class: Evaluating a strategy. *Labor, Capital and Society* 14:10–38.

———. 1985. *Cast in a Racial Mould: Labour Process and Trade Unionism in the Foundaries*. Johannesburg: Ravan Press.

———. 2001. The alliance under stress: Governing in a globalizing world. In *Opposition and democracy in South Africa*, ed. Roger Southall, 255–74. London: Frank Cass.

Webster, Eddie, and Karl von Holdt, eds. 2005a. *Beyond the apartheid workplace: Studies in transition*. Pietermaritzburg: University of KwaZulu-Natal Press.

———. 2005b Work restructuring and the crisis of social reproduction: A southern perspective. *Beyond the apartheid workplace: Studies in transition*. In Eddie Webster and Karl von Holdt, 3–40. Pietermaritzburg: University of Kwazulu-Natal

Wickins, Peter. 1978. *The industrial and commercial workers union of Africa*. Cape Town: Oxford University Press.

Yudelman, David. 1983. *The emergence of modern South Africa: State, capital and the incorporation of organized labor on the South African gold fields, 1902–39*. Westport, CT: Greenwood.

Appendix 1

Union Membership Figures

Registered Trade Union Membership of All

1975	n/a
1976	632,286
1977	678,146
1978	698, 931
1979	701,758
1980	781,727
1981	1,054,405
1982	1,225,454
1983	1,288,748
1984	1,406,302
1985	1,391,423
1986	1,698,157
1987	1,879,400
1988	2,084,323
1989	2,168,567
1990	2,436,238
1991	2,718,970
1992	2,906,100
1993	2,439,703
2005	2,800,000 (Naledi estimate)

Source: S.A. Labor Statistics Annuals, Department of Manpower.

Appendix 2

Trade Union Organizations

Trade Union Groups in the Historic Period

Council for Non-European Trade Unions (CNETU): organization of industrial unions that functioned in the 1940s.

Garment Workers Union (GWU); had a long history of organizing workers of different races. Associated with the retention of Afrikaner women in nonracial unionism in the 1930s.

Industrial & Commercial Workers Union of Africa (ICU): general union that flourished amongst African workers in the 1920s.

Industrial Workers of Africa (IWA): a pioneer organisation of radicals interested in organizing black workers during World War I.

South African Congress of Trade Unions (SACTU): radical SACP aligned trade union federation of the 1950s; existed almost exclusively in exile after the early 1960s.

South African Trade & Labour Council SAT&LC: a body which between 1930 and 1955 embraced a wide spectrum of union opinion.

Trade Union Congress of South Africa (TUCSA): organised moderate unions until 1986.

Trade Union Groupings in the Post-1970 Period

COSATU (Congress of South African Trade Unions): Principal Founding Unions in 1985 (claimed memberships over 10,000 [cf. Baskin 1991, 55])

FOSATU (Federation of South African Trade Unions)
CCAWUSA (Commercial, Catering and Allied Workers Union of South Africa)
CWIU (Chemical Workers Industrial Union of South Africa)
MAWU (Metal and Allied Workers Union)
NAAWU (National Automobile and Workers Union)
NUM (National Union of Mineworkers)
NUTW (National Union of Textile Workers)
PWAWU (Paper, Wood and Allied Workers Union)
SFAWU (Sweet, Food and Allied Workers Union)
TGWU (Transport and General Workers Union)

Main COSATU Constituent Unions, 2003 (50,000 plus members [Habib and Valodia 2003])

Chemical, Energy, Paper, Printing Wood and Allied Workers Union (67,162 members)
*Democratic Nurses Organisation of South Africa (72,000 members)
Food and Allied Workers Union (85,069 members)
*National Education, Health and Allied Workers Union (234,607 members)
National Union of Mineworkers (299,509 members)
National Union of Metalworkers of South Africa (174,212 members)
*Police and Prison Civil Rights Union (75,937 members)
South African Clothing and Textile Workers Union (110,216 members)
South African Commercial, Catering and Allied Workers Union (107,533 members)
*South African Democratic Teachers Union (214,865 members)
*South African Municipal Workers Union (114,127 members)
*South African Public Servants Association (144,127 members)

South African Society of Bank Officials (58,656 members; previously in Federation of South African Labour
*South African Transport and Allied Workers Union (79,325 members)

(*state employees, entirely or partially)

Other Federations and Unions

CUSA (Council of South African Trade Unions, founded 1980; see National Council of Trade Unions
FEDSAL (Federation of South African Labour; previously of Federation of Salaried Workers
MWU (Mine Workers Union; racially exclusive)
NACTU (National Council of Trade Unions), succeeded CUSA, dissolved in 2005

CHAPTER 8

"Nothing to Lose but Their Subordination to the State"? Trade Unions in Namibia Fifteen Years after Independence

Gretchen Bauer

Introduction

In the aftermath of World War II trade unions emerged in significant numbers and strength throughout Africa. In many African colonies they joined together with nascent nationalist movements to lead the struggle for political independence. For many organized labor movements, however, independence was no boon.[1] Rather, in many instances, political independence in Africa led to the rapid demobilization of trade unions. This demobilization was accomplished in a variety of ways:

- the absorption of trade unions into ruling political parties
- the co-optation of trade union leaders into government
- the imposition of trade union unity through the creation of national labor centers
- the selection of trade union leaders by government appointment rather than rank and file election
- the implementation of restrictive labor laws and/or state of emergency regulations
- or the state-sanctioned establishment of workplace liaison committees, rather than autonomous trade union branches

In the 1980s and 1990s, however, as many African countries attempted fundamental economic and political reforms, trade unions reemerged as a significant social force. In states as diverse as Zambia, Ghana, Senegal, Zimbabwe, Malawi, Nigeria, and South Africa, trade unions figured prominently in efforts to democratize the polity. Indeed, in their work on regime transitions in Africa, Bratton and van de Walle found the number of trade unions to be positively and strongly correlated with the frequency of political protest in the prelude to a democratic opening (1997). Moreover, in the view of many, labor movements occupy a special place among the forces of a democratizing civil society. Rueschemeyer, Stephens, and Stephens, comparing Latin America and Eastern Europe, argued that the growth of a working class—developed and sustained by trade unions, working-class political parties, and similar groupings—was critical for the promotion of democracy (1992). Similarly, Collier and Collier suggested that in several Latin American countries the way in which worker protest and organized labor movements were first handled by governments and political parties had important implications for the future political trajectories of those countries (1991).

The potential roles for trade unions in the democratization process are many. Trade unions have traditionally acted as vehicles for the expression of workers' economic and political grievances, and in Africa these have usually included the demands of wider groups than just small working classes (Jeffries 1975; Marks 1989; Peace 1975). But trade unions do more than simply articulate grievances. More important is their capacity for collective action—a capacity that is enhanced by their mass base and their ability to disrupt the national economy. Indeed, for many governments, one of the most significant aspects of trade unions is their ability to confer (or not) legitimacy upon a regime. For states and political parties alike, the capacity to control a labor movement or to mobilize a labor movement's political support is a much sought after asset. In the absence of such an asset, governments run the risk of worker protest against their policies (Collier and Collier 1991; Valenzuela 1989). Attempts at simultaneous economic and political reform in Africa in the 1980s and 1990s, marked by harsh austerity measures and democratic openings, made an increased trade union role all the more likely.

In some southern African countries during this period, trade unions and labor movements took the step most feared by many governments.[2] In Malawi, Zambia, and Zimbabwe, with differing results, national labor federations formed the basis for new opposition political parties that strongly, and in some cases successfully, challenged undemocratic incumbent regimes. In Namibia and South Africa, workers and their organizations played a pivotal role in the transitions to independence and black majority rule in 1990 and 1994, respectively. But what has happened since these transitions? This chapter examines the role of organized labor during the first decades of independence in Namibia, focusing on the most significant labor center in the country, the National Union of Namibian Workers (NUNW) and its affiliated unions. In contrast to other countries in southern Africa, at this time in an independent Namibia the national labor federation and member unions show little inclination to challenge an increasingly intolerant government led by the unions' long-standing affiliate, the ruling South West African People's Organisation (SWAPO) party. At the same time, the NUNW and member unions may still hold the potential to act as a democratizing force in Namibia.

The chapter begins with an overview of the origins and evolution of the trade union movement in Namibia, as well as an analysis of the unions' role in the transition to independence, both of which are essential to understanding labor in contemporary

Namibia. Second, the chapter investigates the labor relations environment in Namibia in the first decade and a half of independence. Third, the chapter examines an issue of particular relevance to the NUNW, namely, trade union autonomy vis-à-vis the ruling party and government and the continued lack of trade union unity in the country. Fourth, the chapter explores a set of priority issues for unions in Namibia in the early 2000s. The chapter concludes by considering the potential contributions of trade unions to democratization in Namibia.

Origins of Namibian Unions and Their Role in the Transition to Independence

In marked contrast to other places in Africa, trade unions as they exist in Namibia today really only emerged in the mid-1980s.[3] While earlier attempts to organize unions were made inside and outside of Namibia, they were not successful. This is despite the fact that wage labor has long figured prominently in Namibian economy and society. Already by the early 1900s, German colonizers had established the contours of a contract labor system in Namibia, one that drew large numbers of migrant workers from north to south. Prompted by their need for labor to work lucrative mineral deposits, to expand a nascent transport infrastructure, and to build new settler farms, colonial authorities set about creating a comprehensive system of labor control and exploitation (Emmett 1999). Fundamental to this system was the designation of two-thirds of the territory—that area south of the so-called Red Line—as a police zone to which residents of the "Native Reserves" could travel only with special permits (and usually only for purposes of work). When South Africa took over the territory after World War I, two labor recruiting agencies (which later were merged into one) were created to further regulate the flow of migrant labor from north to south. The whole contract migrant labor system was codified in a series of laws meant to control the movement, employment, and place of residence of indigenous Namibians (Kane-Berman 1972). As elsewhere in southern Africa, much of the activity of the colonial state concerned assuring a cheap and steady flow of labor to industry, mines, and settler farms.

With a few short-lived but important exceptions, no organization of trade unions among Namibia's largely migrant labor force was attempted in the territory until after the general strike of 1971–72. While the first recorded strike in Namibia took place at the Gross Otavi mine in 1893, and countless other acts of labor protest and resistance were recorded for nearly every year thereafter (Gottschalk 1978), the seminal event in Namibian labor history was the general strike of 1971–72. SWAPO secondary school students initiated the strike, but it was largely carried out by migrant workers inspired by their long-standing grievances against the contract labor system.[4] An estimated thirteen to twenty thousand workers took part in the strike, bringing the economy of the territory to a standstill and, in the process, demonstrating the potential power of an organized workforce in Namibia.

Ultimately, the strike and its aftermath (including a torrent of violence unleashed in northern Namibia as striking workers returned home) were a signal to South African colonial authorities and employers that their political and labor policies would have to be amended. The general strike, then, was an important impetus for a process of reform of labor (and political) relations that unfolded in Namibia during the 1970s. For Namibian workers the general strike brought about a gradual amelioration of the worst features of the hated contract labor system, although the continuation of existing pass laws tended to mitigate the effects of these changes (Kane-Berman 1972, 1973).

Predictably, many employers—particularly those in commercial agriculture—vehemently opposed the few changes to the labor recruitment system that followed the strike. At the same time, a number of sources suggest that a rise in workers' wages did occur in the aftermath of the strike (Peltola 1995). Moreover, for the first time in South African–occupied Namibia, some employers began to acknowledge publicly the need for trade unions for black workers. While companies such as Metal Box and Walvis Bay Containers, both in the fishing industry, attempted their own internal adjustments to ward off worker discontent, the Windhoek Chamber of Commerce president made a plea in 1972 for the organization of workers into trade unions.[5] At that time, however, trade unions were not yet a legal option for black workers. While the 1952 Wage and Industrial Conciliation Ordinance provided for the organization of trade unions in the territory, it also excluded black workers from the definition of "employee" and therefore precluded their effective participation in trade unions. This only changed in 1978, when the definition of employee was expanded to include black workers.[6]

While some accounts have suggested that a general workers' union might have been involved in the organization of the 1971–72 general strike, this was not the case. Earlier, on April 24, 1970, SWAPO launched a National Union of Namibian Workers in exile (SWAPO 1984). This NUNW was run out of the SWAPO Department of Labour, with Solomon Mifima serving as SWAPO labor secretary and NUNW secretary-general until he was stripped of both posts in 1976. Mifima's successor, John Ya Otto, held both positions until 1989, when SWAPO returned to Namibia from exile.

While a NUNW apparently existed (if only on paper) in exile starting in 1970, inside Namibia the first stirrings of a general workers' union were under the guise of a Namibian Workers Union (NAWU), which quickly became known, however, as the National Union of Namibian Workers. Initial efforts to organize a general workers' union under the NAWU rubric were undertaken from about 1977 and led by the SWAPO labor secretary inside Namibia, Jason Angula, and others, such as the Lutheran pastor Gerson Max. Ultimately, however, their efforts were joined with those of workers at the Rossing Uranium Mine who began to organize workers there in 1978. The end result was the formation of a National Union of Namibian Workers. This early attempt at forming a general workers' union in Namibia also involved SWAPO in exile; in particular, Swedish trade unionists were sent into Namibia, via SWAPO and the NUNW in exile, to assist in this effort. Moreover, union organizers from Namibia met with SWAPO labor officials in Botswana in late 1979 where, interestingly, they encountered in each other starkly different notions of trade unionism.[7]

By mid-1980, however, this early attempt at organizing a black trade union in Namibia was over, with the main organizers forced out of the country, detained, or arrested. In general, the late 1970s and early 1980s were a period of particularly harsh political repression in Namibia, and the effort at trade union organization suffered the consequences. Meanwhile, in exile—where there were no workers—the NUNW continued to operate out of the SWAPO Department of Labour. John Ya Otto spent much of his time fostering contacts with national and international labor movements and solidarity organizations. But the primary activities of the NUNW in exile revolved around education and training. Dozens of future trade unionists were sent abroad for short courses and training and, eventually, in the early 1980s, a trade union school, funded from abroad, was established at one of the SWAPO resettlement centers in Angola.

Again inside Namibia during the late 1970s some employers were continuing with tentative steps toward reform. The multinational mining companies were at the forefront of this tepid reform effort, reflecting their increasingly sophisticated methods of production, a fear of the post-independence dispensation, and a concerted international campaign against them. Heavily influenced by developments in industry in South Africa, including a significant dismantling of many apartheid controls and a gradual reform of labor relations, organizations such as the Chamber of Mines began to examine the existing industrial relations system in Namibia and to contemplate changing it. A number of new organizations, for example, the Private Sector Foundation and the Namibia Institute for Economic Affairs, emerged during this same period and developed labor relations projects of their own.

But these were just initial forays on the part of employers and their organizations. In the late 1970s and early 1980s, neither workers nor their bosses were able to organize effectively in Namibia. While the law preventing the organization of black trade unions was changed in 1978, enhanced security legislation and a new prohibition on political affiliation for unions achieved much the same end.[8] While Namibian workers continued to agitate and occasionally strike, such action did not translate into concrete gains for workers, either in terms of the organization of trade unions or of significant changes to the existing labor relations framework. These changes had to wait until the mid-1980s to occur.

The final emergence of trade unions in Namibia actually grew out of the renewed efforts of workers at the two largest mines, together with the activities of community activists from the Windhoek townships and former SWAPO combatants released from Robben Island in the mid-1980s. Somewhat independently of each other, in 1984 and 1985 mineworkers began to organize at the Consolidated Diamond Mines (CDM) in Oranjemund on Namibia's southern border and, again, at the Rossing Uranium Mine in Arandis near the coast. National Union of Mineworkers organizers from South Africa initiated the efforts at CDM to organize all diamond mines in southern Africa. At Rossing, black workers still felt the kind of discrimination that had prompted strikes and other collective action in the late 1970s and the initial attempt to organize a NUNW in 1978–79. Hostile to management's offer of consultative committees for worker representation, workers opted instead for the formation of their own union.

In Windhoek's black townships, meanwhile, community activists had been handling worker grievances for some time. While the repression of the late 1970s and early 1980s had been successful for a time in stifling political activity, by the early to mid-1980s a new movement began to build at the grassroots level. A response to the crisis of daily living in Namibian townships—in housing, employment, health, education, and social welfare (exacerbated by severe drought in the country in the early 1980s)—and influenced by the groundswell of organizing and community activity in South Africa (where many Namibians attended university), community organizations were formed in growing numbers in the 1980s.[9] One of these was a Workers Action Committee established in early 1985 to address the many complaints of township workers—unfair dismissals, low wages, no leave, and inadequate housing and public transportation.

When these two developments—in the mines and in the townships— came together with a third development, the result was the launching of the industrial unions of the National Union of Namibian Workers. As mentioned previously, in 1984 and 1985 Namibians who had been incarcerated on Robben Island were released. They included former SWAPO combatant Ben Ulenga. Once back in Namibia, Ulenga and other "Islanders" quickly integrated themselves into SWAPO structures in Windhoek and took the decision in 1986 to "reactivate" the NUNW. A committee of field-workers was formed and began organizing workers around the country. Some months later, members of this committee met with members of the Workers Action Committee and the two committees merged to form the Workers Steering Committee (WOSC).

The WOSC set about its task and soon one industrial union after another was formed. In late 1986 the Namibian Food and Allied Union (NAFAU) and the Mineworkers Union of Namibia (MUN) were launched. In 1987 two more unions were established: the Metal and Allied Namibian Workers Union in May, and the Namibia Public Workers Union (NAPWU) in December. The Namibia Transport and Allied Union was formed in July 1988, the Namibia National Teachers Union (NANTU) in March 1989, and the Namibia Domestic and Allied Workers Union in April 1990. The NUNW itself was not formally constituted as a federation until a consolidation congress was held in Windhoek in June 1989.

Other unions were being organized during the 1980s as well, though ultimately not as successfully. Some, such as the Namibia Federation of Trade Unions, the Namibian Trade Union Council, a Namibia Confederation of Trade Unions, and a Namibia National Workers Union—all federations in existence in January 1985, according to *The Namibian*—never amounted to anything. Another, the Namibia Trade Union, founded in December 1985 and loosely associated with the Workers Revolutionary Party, continued to have an office in Windhoek into the 1990s, though with no perceptible impact.

A second trade union federation, however, with some significant member unions and memberships, did emerge in Namibia during this period. Known originally as the Namibian Christian Social Trade Unions (NCSTU), this federation transformed itself into the Namibian People's Social Movement (NPSM) at its first congress in October 1992. Member unions initially included: the Namibian Building Workers Union, the Namibia Wholesale and Retail Workers Union, the Public Service Union of Namibia (PSUN), the Local Authorities Union of Namibia, the South West Africa Mine Workers Union, and the Bank Workers Union of Namibia.

Some of these early alternatives to the NUNW unions received funds and other support from the second of two "interim governments" in Namibia. Indeed, encouraging the growth of "non-political" trade unions was one aspect of the piece-meal reform effort that commenced ever so slowly after the general strike of 1971–72. In 1986 two new labor laws were passed—a Conditions of Employment Act and a National Labour Council Act—neither of which, however, went very far in redressing workers grievances. In 1987 workers were finally successful in winning May Day as a public holiday. These pre-independence reforms occurred during a period of generally deteriorating labor relations in Namibia and culminated in the Wiehahn Commission reports of 1989. As in South Africa nearly a decade earlier, a Commission of Inquiry, chaired by South African professor Nic Wiehahn, was convened in 1987 to investigate and make recommendations on labor relations in Namibia.[10] Just months after the recommendations were submitted, however, Namibia achieved its independence, and within months plans for a new labor dispensation would be announced.

What role, then, did the labor movement and nascent trade unions play in the transition to independence in Namibia in March 1990—an independence finally secured after twenty-five years of war and international diplomatic struggle? As the brief narrative just elaborated indicates, the labor movement in the territory played an important mobilizational role in the years before independence, bringing pressure on the pre-independence regimes to concede limited reforms and on the South Africans, ultimately, to grant independence. In particular, during the 1980s the trade unions were at the forefront of the wave of community organizing that took advantage of the slight opening offered by the transitional government of national unity from 1985 onward. Once organized, workers began to make their presence known. There is little doubt, for example, that the appointment of the Wiehahn Commission in 1987 was motivated in part by the high incidence of strikes in 1986 and 1987 (Van Rooyen 1996). (See Table 8.1) Moreover, strikers' demands and strategies during the two-month-long strike at the Tsumeb copper mine in 1987 "showed strong resemblance with the action proposals put forward by the so-called Ai/Gams meeting in June 1986 . . . [which] proposed numerous ways of facilitating political conscientizing, mass action and general civil disobedience to promote the anti-colonial struggle" (Van Rooyen 1996, 210). While strike activity in general declined in 1988, the most significant action by organized workers that year was the call for a two-day stay-away in June 1988 in support of a national schools boycott protesting the close proximity of South African security forces to schools in northern Namibia. In 1989, strikes reached an all-time pre-independence high when, according to Van Rooyen: "developments on the political front at long last brought the hope of Namibian independence into the realm of tangible reality. The general excitement and heightened expectations found expression in an agitated labor force . . . "(1996, 207). More to the point, according to Murray and Wood, "For workers, the strikes of 1989 and 1990 can be understood as a show of strength, sending a clear message to employers that it was time for a fundamental change in the employment relationship" (1997a, 304). And with a new SWAPO government about to take power, workers were convinced that the relationship would change markedly in their favor.

The influence of the newly formed trade unions on the transition to independence was not confined to their mobilizational and strike activity, however. Some of

Table 8.1 Reported Strikes in Namibia, 1977–94

Year	Strikes reported
1977	1
1978	2
1979	4
1980	0
1981	3
1982	2
1983	2
1984	0
1985	0
1986	4
1987	22
1988	8
1989	28
1990	35
1991	9
1992	27
1993	9
1994	22

Sources: Van Rooyen 1996, 208, 256.

those trade union activists first involved in organizing the unions in the late 1980s also participated in the meetings of Namibian professionals and businesspeople with SWAPO in exile—the meetings that contributed to Namibia's "pacted" transition to independence.[11] Moreover, three key trade union leaders—Ben Ulenga of the Mineworkers Union of Namibia, Marco Hausiku of the Namibian National Teachers Union, and NUNW Secretary-General John Ya Otto—were among those SWAPO members elected to the constituent assembly in November 1989. That body drafted Namibia's constitution and became the first national assembly upon Namibia's independence in March 1990.

Labor Relations after Independence

Despite its vast land area, Namibia had a very small population of just 2 million people in the mid-2000s. According to the 2001 population and housing census, about 54 percent of the population over the age of fifteen was economically active. Further, according to the census, about 69 percent of the economically active population was employed.[12] Fifty-seven percent of employed Namibians worked in private and public services (including hotels and restaurants, transport and communications, finance, real estate and business services, and government and community service activities) in 2001; 25 percent in agriculture (including subsistence agriculture and commercial farms); 12 percent in manufacturing (including mining, electricity, water supply, and construction); and 4 percent in wholesale and retail trade (EIU 2004, 51). According to Jauch, in the early 2000s about half of all Namibian households (48 percent) relied on wages and salaries for their main source of income; the figure was even higher (76 percent) in urban areas. As Jauch observes, "These figures indicate the critical importance that wages and salaries have for the survival of Namibian households" (2004, 11).

Indeed, by the time Namibia finally achieved its independence, a significant number of trade unions had emerged in the country. Within the decade that number had increased markedly to about thirty registered trade unions (LaRRI 1998, 32). The most visible of these unions are affiliated to the National Union of Namibian Workers, which claimed a total membership of about sixty to seventy thousand in 2004, divided among its ten member unions (Jauch 2004, 26).[13] Other unions are affiliated with a second trade union federation, the Trade Union Congress of Namibia (TUCNA), formed in 2002 from a merger of the NPSM and the Namibian Federation of Trade Unions (NAFTU), which had been formed as a third federation in 1998. TUCNA had fourteen affiliated unions in early 2005, including the large public sector union, the PSUN, with twenty-five to twenty-eight thousand members, for a total membership of around forty-five thousand.[14] In 2004 it was estimated that about half of Namibia's formal sector labor force (51 percent) was unionized. The highest unionization rates were in mining and energy (83 percent), the public sector (75–80 percent), textiles (67 percent), and the food, fishing, hospitality, and wholesale and retail trade sectors (65 percent). Unionization rates are lowest among domestic workers (20 percent) and the small business sector (10 percent) (Jauch 2004, 12–13; Jauch 2006).[15] (See Table 8.2.)

Table 8.2 Estimated Unionization Rates by Sector, 2004

Sector	Approximate number of employees	Estimated unionization rate (signed-up members)
Agriculture (excluding communal farmers, and unpaid family labor)	29,200	9,000 (31%)
Manufacturing, building, and construction	28,900	10,500 (36%)
Mining and energy	4,800	4,000 (83%)
Food, fishing, wholesale, retail, and hospitality	34,000	22,000 (65%)
Textiles	9,000	6,000 (67%)
Public service, parastatals, and municipalities (excluding army, police, and teachers)	80,000	60,000 (75%)
Teachers	15,000	12,000 (80%)
Domestic work	17,900	3,500 (20%)
Banking, insurance, real estate, and business services	24,000	4,500 (19%)
Transport, communication, and security	12,000	3,000 (25%)
Other	22,700	6,000 (26%)
Total	277,500	140,700 (50.7%)

Source: Jauch 2004, 13.

Given that exploitative labor relations were inextricably linked with oppressive colonial relations in Namibia, and that so much of SWAPO's support was based among the territory's contract migrant workers, it is not surprising that one of the first priorities of the SWAPO government after independence was a new labor dispensation. This new labor dispensation was brought into being with the implementation of a comprehensive new labor law—Labour Act No. 6 of 1992—in late 1992. The new labor law was by any standard a progressive law that offered a number of significant opportunities to workers and their unions. Labour Act No. 6 introduced fairness into the labor relations context through the notion of an unfair labor practice. Employees could be dismissed only for a "valid and fair" reason and in a "procedurally fair" way. Guidelines for disciplinary action were clearly laid out, and the onus was placed on employers to show that disciplinary actions and dismissals were fair. Labor relations were decriminalized in that complaints were processed in district labor courts. Provision was made for the introduction of a minimum wage in certain sectors following the directives of a wages commission. As far as collective labor relations were concerned, unions no longer had to demonstrate "representativeness" in registering with the labor commissioner, and they could seek recourse in the Labour Court if an employer did not accept a proposed bargaining unit or reach agreement with the union. Union members were allowed access to employer premises for purposes of organizing workers. And the act provided for an extensive, though qualified, right to strike (Bauer 1992; Corbett 1993; Ford 1993).

A fundamental principle on which the new labor dispensation was based was tripartism. Jauch observes that after independence, "the new SWAPO government tried to shift labor relations towards a 'social partnership' characterized by consultations [among] government, employers and trade unions" (2000a, 1). Indeed, a number of the structures provided for in Labour Act No. 6 promoted tripartism in labor relations, or were tripartite bodies themselves. A Labour Advisory Council (LAC)—composed of four representatives each from government, employers' organizations, and trade unions—was established to advise the minister on labor-related matters. Wages commissions would also consist of a chairperson and one representative each from unions and employers' organizations. In addition, assessors in the Labour Court and district labor courts were to be appointed in equal numbers from trade unions and employers' organizations. Finally, an Office of the Labour Commissioner was established to facilitate healthy labor relations among the "social partners."

Despite the new labor law, relations between workers and their bosses have not been harmonious since independence. Not surprisingly, the legacy of apartheid endures in most workplaces and will likely do so for some time to come. Shortly after independence, the Namibia Institute for Economic Affairs felt compelled to issue a press release warning that allegations of unfair labor practices were influencing the "productivity, potential and motivation" of the Namibian workforce. The statement continued that the labor practices of Namibian employers were not conducive to the economic development so desperately needed in Namibia. Employers in future would have to play "their rightful role" in the country's economic development, which included treating the labor force as "a valuable and key resource rather than as a cost factor" (*The Namibian*, April 20, 1990).

In the early years of independence, newspapers such as *The Namibian Worker, The Namibian,* and *New Era* were rife with stories about unfair dismissals, ongoing racism and discrimination in the workplace, victimization of union members, violations of recognition agreements, inadequate worker accommodation, employer refusal to adhere to provisions of the new labor legislation, and retrenchments. Outgoing NUNW president, John Shaetonhodi, complained in May 1991 that employers were misusing national reconciliation—that after independence they had only "intensified exploitation of the worker. . . . We see it in various industries; how people are being dismissed; how they are being denied trade union freedom in the workplaces (quoted in Bauer, 1998, 121). Workers responded to these and other complaints (disputes over wages and conditions of employment, retrenchments) in the first few years of independence with a rash of strikes. Indeed, as Table 8.1 indicates, the annual incidence of strikes in the first years of independence was much greater than in the twelve years immediately prior to independence. Van Rooyen attributes the spate of strikes immediately before and after independence to workers' high expectations for the new era and continued concern about lingering inequities from the previous era (1996, 254–55). Further, in Van Rooney's view, the drop in strikes in 1993 may be attributed to the much-delayed implementation of Labour Act No. 6 in November 1992, only to be followed by another outbreak of strikes in 1994 as workers recognized that the act "did not constitute a magical panacea for all problems on the labor front" (1996, 255). One of the country's worst labor strikes occurred at the Tsumeb Copper Limited copper mine in 1996. A significant wage hike for workers was a part of the deal to resolve the strike, but when the company was placed under liquidation in 1998, about two thousand workers lost their jobs (LaRRI 2006, 20).

By the end of the 1990s the labor relations environment in the country still had not improved as significantly as expected. An annual report from the Ministry of Labour, tabled in the National Assembly in September 1999, cited the attitude of employers and organized labor as one of the main impediments to improved labor relations. "Despite several efforts to provide general guidelines and advice, these partners deal with each other in bad faith and wrong perceptions have been created towards each other" (*The Namibian,* September 15, 1999). Workers and their representatives were said to lack basic information and negotiating skills, while employers were accused of an "arrogant and counterproductive style of handling labor relations matters." In May 2000, the minister of labor accused employers in three sectors—agriculture, hospitality, and fishing—of continuing to exploit workers (*The Namibian,* May 30, 2000). In late 2005 the labor climate in Namibia was still described as "dismal, with the number of dismissals, illegal strikes and disputes soaring way above that of the previous year." More than ten thousand complaints were lodged with the labor commissioner in 2004, an increase of 20 percent over the previous year, and largely illegal "industrial action" cost the economy roughly fifty-seven workdays in 2004, up from twenty-two days in 2003.[16] At mid-decade some of the most common complaints concerned maltreatment and poor wages for Namibian workers (and a general disregard for the country's labor laws) at the hands of foreign-owned businesses and companies.[17]

A widespread perception of declining labor relations in Namibia led to the decision to replace the "loophole-riddled Labour Act" with a new one. Both the NUNW and the Namibia Employers Federation supported the plan to overhaul Labour Act No. 6, citing problems with the old law's dispute resolution mechanism and backlogs in the district labor courts, among other things (*The Namibian*, April 14, 2000). In October 2004 the National Assembly passed a new labor bill. This bill retains many of the provisions of the old one; the changes, however, include: a redrafting of the bill in language that is more accessible to ordinary workers (as compared to a legal language understandable only by lawyers), and significant improvements to the dispute resolution mechanisms contained in the original bill (Jauch 2004, 20–21). The new bill also strengthens the role of the tripartite LAC, particularly in dispute prevention and resolution (LaRRI 2006, 21–22). By late 2005 only a few sections of the new labor law had come into effect, namely, those that would enable the appointment and operation of both LAC committees—the Committee on Dispute Prevention and Resolution and the Essential Services Commission—with the full implementation of the new labor law slated for late 2006. In general, the trade union movement in Namibia has welcomed the improvements contained in the new (2004) labor act (LaRRI 2006, 20–23).

Unable to Achieve Trade Union Autonomy

While unions have struggled considerably with employers since independence, they have also struggled more than anticipated with the third partner in the tripartite relationship—the government. For the unions of the NUNW, trade union–government relations in the early years of independence were dominated by the trade union–(ruling) party relationship. During the transition to independence in 1989, NUNW energies were channeled enthusiastically toward a SWAPO victory in the November elections for a constituent assembly. Also during that year, as tens of thousands of Namibians returned home after decades in exile, a consolidation congress of the NUNW was held to launch the NUNW officially as a trade union federation. The question of the NUNW's affiliation to SWAPO, however, was not formally addressed until late March 1991, when an extraordinary congress of the NUNW was convened. At the congress, delegates reaffirmed the NUNW's formal affiliation to SWAPO as a "historically tested organization committed to the total liberation of the working people." Congress resolutions acknowledged the political nature of trade unions and noted that in affiliating to a political party, unions would be able to take part more fully in decision making, to achieve greater unity for common goals, and to obtain greater support for common objectives. Delegates pledged to reconsider affiliation to SWAPO once it had transformed itself from a liberation movement into a political party (as it did at its first congress in an independent Namibia in early December 1991) (*The Namibian Worker* May 1991, 2).

The affiliation question was revisited at the NUNW's next congress—its first ordinary congress—held in September 1993 in Katutura. At that congress three member unions—NANTU, NAFAU, and MUN—introduced a resolution calling for the disaffiliation of the NUNW from SWAPO, but they were quickly defeated. The issue did not even go to a vote, but was rejected during debate in the house (*The Namibian*, September 27, 1993). Indeed, journalists and observers who attended the congress "accused the congress of undemocratic procedures in this regard [the resolution not to disaffiliate]. The motions for disaffiliation were scantily debated and not voted on" (Melber 1993, 63; Terreblanche 1993, 7). After the congress, the newly elected leadership told the media that the congress had "resolved to continue with the historical ties to SWAPO, as it was felt that affiliation to the ruling party had caused no concrete damage." The issue was raised once again, at the NUNW's congress in 1998, and once again the union federation's affiliation to SWAPO was reaffirmed (LaRRI 1999, 34).

An affiliation accord between the NUNW and the ruling party was formally established in 1997. The accord "states that the affiliation shall be based on the independence and decision-making autonomy of both organisations. It also states that consultations will guide the relationship and that both organisations are mandated to work in the interests of their members—subject to broader principles enshrined in the SWAPO constitution" (LaRRI 1999, 34). Interestingly, the accord stipulates "that the NUNW recognizes SWAPO as the senior partner in the relationship" between the two.

In general, the NUNW defends its affiliation to SWAPO as useful for influencing decision making within the party. During the first decade of independence, the NUNW claimed to have influenced the party on a few occasions: in drafting of the first National Development Plan, amending the Export Processing Zones Act, and setting up the LAC (LaRRI 1999, 34). At the same time, leaders of NUNW member unions insisted that "their unions have always worked independently and have ensured that they are at no stage influenced by the government or ruling party" (LaRRI 1999, 35). Those who disagree with the unions' affiliation to the ruling party cite a number of potential drawbacks: for example, some employers insist that they want to negotiate with a labor union and not a political party or a union associated with a party. Moreover, some union officials worry that the unions' affiliation to the ruling party might hinder their recruitment efforts among workers who do not support the ruling party. Many of those critical of the NUNW-SWAPO affiliation, however, mute their criticisms, fearful of victimization if they voice their concerns (LaRRI 1999, 35–36).

The issue of affiliation has been one of the main factors inhibiting unity among the major trade union federations. Not surprisingly, there has been intermittent talk of the need for trade union unity in a country where dozens of unions represent a small formal sector labor force. In May 1995, trade unions from the two then-existing federations—the NUNW and the NPSM—came together for formal unity talks, issuing a document containing twenty points of agreement and six of disagreement (*The Namibian*, May 23, 1995). At the least, delegates agreed on the need for the establishment of a forum representing all Namibian unions in order to be able to discuss common socioeconomic concerns and input into national policy making. According to *The Namibian Worker* (June 1995), most of the delegates to the talks indicated their wish to form a single umbrella body for Namibian trade unions. Such a body was never formed, however. An attempt in 1994 to unite trade unions in the public sector, under the guise of a Joint Coordinating Forum (JCF), similarly came to naught. Differences among unions led to the rapid dissolution of the JCF, with the PSUN accusing the NUNW-affiliated unions of bowing to pressure from SWAPO over policy and wage issues of concern to public sector unions (Murray and

Wood 1997b, 192–93). The emergence of a third trade union federation (NAFTU) in Namibia in late 1998, and its merger with the NPSM to form TUCNA in 2002, gave the final blow to efforts to forge unity among Namibian workers. Like its predecessor, TUCNA disavows affiliation with any political party (Jauch 2004). At century's end the NUNW's political affiliation was cited as the main stumbling block to greater trade union unity in Namibia (LaRRI 1999, 38). In addition, power struggles for leadership positions were considered a potential hindrance to a merger of the country's unions.

Challenges and Future Priorities for the NUNW

Despite the NUNW's affiliation to the ruling party SWAPO, the NUNW and government have disagreed publicly on a number of issues. A notable example followed from the government's promotion of export processing zones (EPZs) in Namibia. While the unions did not object to the notion of EPZs in and of themselves, they objected strongly to the government's attempt to have Namibia's progressive labor law *not* apply in the EPZs. Throughout 1995, union and government leaders attempted to reach an agreement, with the government calling the unions' attitude "confrontational" and the "wrangling" between the two sides "unfortunate" (*New Era*, June 8–14, 1995), and the unions threatening to take the government to court over the matter. Ultimately, the parties agreed to a compromise, namely, that the 1992 labor act would apply in EPZs, but the EPZs would be considered essential service areas, so that strikes and lockouts would be prohibited. This prohibition on strikes and lockouts in the EPZs would apply for only five years, however; according to Trade and Industry Minister Hidipo Hamutenya " . . . if we discover there are no serious threats of strikes, we will relax the laws" (*The Namibian*, May 10, 1996). In the event, the clause prohibiting strikes and lockouts was not renewed, and since 2001 EPZ workers and companies have the right to strike and lockout. Indeed, the labor act now applies fully to the EPZs (Jauch 2006; Jauch and Sindondola 2003).

In the prelude to the compromise NUNW leaders openly expressed their concern. In March 1996 NUNW President Israel Kalenga described the problem of the EPZs as one of "gravity and magnitude" for Namibian workers. He warned that Namibian workers would not be sacrificed for their cheap labor power, and he challenged the government to abide by, rather than to dishonor, International Labor Organization conventions (*The Namibian*, March 14, 1996). Some trade unionists predicted disastrous consequences of the compromise, noting that workers would be forced into "wildcat, illegal strikes," thereby prompting companies to lose confidence in the government. To many in the unions, the EPZ compromise was evidence of the problem with affiliation: it "makes it almost impossible for the federation to vigorously oppose Government policies" (*The Namibian*, May 17, 1996). For some in the unions, the government's decision on the EPZs was another "betrayal of trust" and an example of its failure to consult with them. This incident had followed closely on the heels of government's "unilateral" decision (according to the unions) in late 1994 to offer public servants only a 10 percent wage increase (*The Namibian Worker*, June and August 1995); the unions also complained about a lack of consultation on the commercialization of lower-level civil service posts (*The Namibian*, May 2, 1996).

Indeed, Namibia's privatization program, begun in the mid-1990s, is another issue that has tested the NUNW-government relationship. The goals of the privatization program are to shrink the public sector, reduce government deficits, and improve efficiency and service delivery. So far the program has taken the form of commercialization and outsourcing (the privatization of service provision), with the direct sale of state entities anticipated in the future. According to Jauch, the NUNW, "realizing the danger of privatization/commercialization not only for its members but also for the delivery of affordable services to the poor," mobilized its standing committee on economics to focus on this issue (2004, 15). Indeed, in late 2001 NUNW members made a comprehensive presentation directly to President Sam Nujoma. And yet, by mid-decade the government had proceeded with its plan to implement a privatization/commercialization program, despite clear and vocal trade union opposition (Jauch 2006). The Labour Resource and Research Institute (LaRRI) director Herbert Jauch observed that although government had consulted the unions on EPZs and privatization, ultimately "government decisions tended to ignore the proposals made by labor" (2004, 32).

Another aspect of the trade union–government relationship during the first decades of independence has been the steady loss of trade union leaders to government. The first to go was the unions' capable and charismatic leader ex-Robben Islander Ben Ulenga, who played such a pivotal role in launching the unions in the mid-1980s. Together with NANTU leader Hausiku and NUNW leader Ya Otto, Ulenga was among those SWAPO members elected to the constituent assembly in 1989 and thus to the first national assembly at independence. Another ex-Robben Islander, former NAFAU Secretary-General John Pandeni, was elected to the Khomas regional council (and ultimately regional governor) during the 1992 regional elections. After the December 1994 national assembly elections, the NUNW and member unions lost three more of their top leaders—Bernhardt Esau, John Shaetonhodi, and Walter Kemba—to SWAPO seats in parliament. In addition, Petrus Ilonga, ex-Robben Islander and NAPWU secretary-general, was subsequently brought into the National Assembly to replace another SWAPO member of parliament (MP). Most of these MPs were also given cabinet positions, thereby rendering them unable to continue working with the unions. In 1999, LaRRI estimated that during the first decade of independence, more than sixty union leaders and officials had left the NUNW and member unions. Those who left cited reasons ranging from political aspirations to better conditions of employment. In response to the loss of leaders, some unions implemented leadership training programs in hope of building a pool of unionists ready to take on leadership positions when others left. But without a trade union school to serve Namibia's labor movement (as in South Africa), such programs are difficult to sustain (LaRRI 1999, 19).

More important, perhaps, is Jauch's contention that despite the presence of trade unionists in parliament, "there is little evidence that their presence has influenced policies in favor of workers. Once in parliament (or cabinet), they are accountable to the party and bound by government policy. Few have dared to publicly oppose government plans . . . "(2000b, 32). A notable exception cited by Jauch was the former NAPWU Secretary-General Iilonga who vehemently opposed the government's privatization plans in parliament in the late 1990s. Interestingly, the NUNW unions fared particularly badly in the 2004 national assembly election. At SWAPO's electoral convention none of the NUNW's six delegates was placed high enough on the party list to win a seat in the National Assembly. Veteran labor MPs were returned to parliament, but no new unionists made it into the National Assembly.[18]

Another distressing trend has been the move of trade union leaders onto the boards of companies "as part of ill-defined trade union investment deals." In addition, some trade union leaders have retained their union leadership roles even after being appointed to full-time management positions in the private and public sectors (Jauch 2006, 4). According to Jauch, such developments are indicative of a "deep-seated ideological confusion" on the part of Namibian unions and their leaders. As further evidence for this he suggests that sentiments of radical nationalism and liberation are freely mixed with an acceptance of free-market and neoliberal economic principles. Overall, Jauch finds a general lack of clarity among trade union leaders over whose interests the unions are meant to serve (2006, 4).

Conclusion: Trade Unions and Democratization in Namibia

Nearly two decades after independence in Namibia the ruling political party, SWAPO, has clearly consolidated its position, such that Namibia is now a dominant party state. SWAPO's electoral support since independence, demonstrated in nine different elections (at the local, regional, and national levels), has ranged from a low of about 57 percent to a high of 76 percent (see Table 8.3). While six opposition parties have at least one seat (each) in the fourth National Assembly, elected in 2004 (as in the first one, elected in 1989), SWAPO thoroughly dominates both houses of parliament with a better than two-thirds' representation in each and has done so since 1994. Many had anticipated a much stronger showing in the 1999 National Assembly election by the newly formed Congress of Democrats (COD), led by one-time trade union leader (and SWAPO MP) Ben Ulenga. While the COD did come in second in that election, its 9.9 percent of the vote was far behind SWAPO's 76.3 percent. In the 2004 election the COD fared worse, not better, losing two seats in the National Assembly (down to five from seven out of a total seventy-two). In marked contrast to Zambia and Zimbabwe, onetime trade union leader Ulenga has not been able to muster any significant support from Namibia's trade unions for his new party.

In light of such a situation—a trend toward single-party dominant rule—strong organizations of civil society are all the more vital. Trade unions in particular, with an organized mass base of more than a hundred thousand members, have been viewed as a potentially critical element in the democratization process in Namibia. As noted earlier, trade unions generally possess the potential to play a significant role in democratization. For neighboring South Africa, Adler and Webster note the central role that trade unions played in the transition there (as in Namibia). In 1995, Adler and Webster were optimistic about the impact the unions' strategy of radical reform could have upon the consolidation of democracy in South Africa (99–100).

At first glance, however, a number of factors seem to work against a strong trade union movement in Namibia and against a positive contribution to democratization.

Table 8.3 Election Results in Namibia by Party: 1989–2004 (in percentages)

	1989 CA	1992 LA	1992 RC	1994 NA	1998 LA	1998 RC	1999 NA	2004 LA	2004 NA	2004 RC
Voter turnout	98.05	82.33	81.07	76.05	33.75	40.01	62.00	—	84.60	53.50
SWAPO	56.90	58.02	68.76	73.89	60.35	67.92	76.30	—	76.10	79.20
DTA	28.34	33.26	27.68	20.78	23.91	23.91	9.40	—	5.10	5.60
COD	—	—	—	—	—	—	9.90	—	7.30	5.50
UDF	5.60	5.88	2.49	2.72	6.66	4.45	2.90	—	3.60	3.40
FCN	1.55	—	—	0.24	—	0.17	0.10	—	—	—
DCN NPF	—	—	—	—	—	—	—	—	—	—
CAN	5.09	0.06	0.20	0.83	0.53	—	0.30	—	—	—
SWANU (NNF)	0.79	1.49	0.72	0.53	0.23	—	0.30	—	—	—
MAG	—	—	—	0.82	—	—	0.70	—	0.9	—
Residents associations	—	—	—	—	8.22	—	—	—	—	—

Source: Bauer 2001; EIU 2005.

CA = constituent assembly; LA = local authorities; RC = regional councils; NA = national assembly

For example, there are the structural limitations of Namibia's under-industrialized economy. Even by African standards, the contribution of manufacturing in Namibia to gross domestic product (10 percent in 2002) and employment (12 percent in 2001) is low; moreover, constraints on the future development of the sector are many, including the small domestic market, close economic integration with South Africa, and the shortage of skilled workers (EIU 2004, 60, 51). Such a small manufacturing sector may prove a particular disadvantage for Namibian unions. As Seidman (1994) has shown for the South African case, a significant manufacturing sector employing large numbers of skilled workers can be crucial to the growth and strength of trade unions. While this does not discount the importance and potential for the organization of workers in strategic primary export sectors, there is little doubt that workers in key manufacturing sectors are better positioned to form powerful trade unions.

Second, the colonial legacy of repression and reform militates against a strong trade union movement in Namibia. Throughout Africa the political legacy of the colonial state has taken its toll on the postcolonial state. In Namibia, colonial strategies of repression and reform help to explain the situation of trade unions today. At first, the highly repressive nature of South African colonial rule, manifest in a carefully regulated contract labor system, restrictive security legislation, and an oppressive political environment precluded the possibility of effectively organizing black trade unions in Namibia. Later, a reform process that sought, among other things, to encourage the development of "nonpolitical" trade unions made available the space for the organization of unions, but with the result that organized labor in Namibia today is highly fragmented.

Around Africa resistance to the organization of trade unions was particularly strong in settler colonies (Damachi et al. 1979), and in this Namibia was no exception. Indeed, part of the reason for the continuing repression of trade unions was the association, first of contract workers and later of the unions, with the nationalist struggle. For employers, unions were unequivocally associated with SWAPO and the resistance to colonialism. With union activity perceived as SWAPO activity, every effort was undertaken to suppress the emerging union movement. At the same time, this association with the nationalist movement ultimately served to distract workers from organizing for an economic as well as a political end. For workers, their struggles in the workplace were subordinated to the struggle for independence from South African colonial rule. Trade unions, when they finally emerged, did so (for the most part) not from the shop floor but from within or at least alongside of the broader liberation struggle. With the independence struggle over, however, trade unions found themselves less well equipped to assert their economic rights and to make their economic demands.[19]

Third, the relationship of the NUNW, the largest trade union federation, to the ruling political party SWAPO remains a challenge to the unions. As in Namibia, labor movements throughout Africa played a significant role in the anticolonial struggle. In many places, however, once in power, former nationalist allies either "subverted or destroyed" trade unions and, according to Freund, "Namibia is only the latest in a long list of countries that exemplify this pattern" (1992, 378). Indeed, strong nationalist impulses, all socialist rhetoric aside, have strongly influenced the attitudes of the SWAPO leadership toward labor and the organization of labor within Namibia. The labor movement has been seen, by at least some within SWAPO, as a potential alternative power base for rival political parties or rival political leaders. Indeed, very different conceptions of trade unionism and trade union–government relations developed among some SWAPO leaders in exile and trade unionists inside Namibia, with the former expecting a clearly subordinate trade union role. Also in exile, as the SWAPO "spy drama" of the 1980s unfolded and hundreds of SWAPO cadres were detained by the party's security apparatus, NUNW labor activists were accused of attempting to form a party within a party. Inside Namibia in the 1980s, at least initially, the organization of labor, like other pre-independence "development" efforts, was seen as antithetical to the nationalist struggle because it threatened to divert scarce resources from the liberation effort or even to reduce the impetus to struggle. After independence, the slightest suggestion that NUNW union members might not vote for SWAPO or that the federation might run its own candidates or form its own party has brought immediate rebukes to union leaders. In the latest example of this a "purge" of the NUNW leadership took place in late December 2005, when certain union leaders dared to contradict former President Nujoma's version of events surrounding the deployment and killing of SWAPO combatants in northern Namibia during the 1989 transition to independence. More broadly, this so-called purge was seen as an attempt by those closest to the former president to take over leadership of the labor umbrella in advance of its own "watershed congress" in March 2006.[20]

Unlike many other places in Africa, trade unions in Namibia were born out of the nationalist movement and not the other way around. Moreover, they were born out of a nationalist movement that privileged national independence above all else, and that developed an essentially authoritarian political culture in exile (Leys and Saul 1995) that has been increasingly evident in an independent Namibia (Melber 2003). While many factors account for these developments, their consequences must be taken into consideration. These include the ruling party's preference to maintain the NUNW as a subordinate auxiliary organization, not as an autonomous body. Another consequence has been that union leadership is more accountable to party leaders than to the unions' own members. Moreover, union leaders are being steadily co-opted into government, in particular into positions that preclude them from continuing their trade union activities. At the same time, the benefits of a close association with the nationalist movement have so far eluded the NUNW. Still, it has been suggested that although few of the unions' demands for redistributive and other measures have been met, "the majority of NUNW affiliates still believe that a continued affiliation to SWAPO will be the best vehicle for influencing broader socioeconomic policies in favor of workers" (Jauch 2004, 28).

Finally, unions in Namibia are affected by many of the same trends facing unions throughout the world. All over the developing (and developed) world, trade unions confront increasing challenges to their organization and effectiveness resulting, in many places, in "confusion and a lack of clarity with respect to roles and possibilities . . . "(Thomas 1995, 3). As noted, in Africa, trade unions have been particularly hampered by a general lack of industrialization (and more recently an actual de-industrialization) accompanied by massive urban informal sectors, significant rural underemployment, and large-scale labor migration. With the implementation of structural adjustment programs in the 1980s and 1990s, the resulting "casualization" of work, falling wage rates, public sector retrenchments, and privatization of state-owned enterprises and consequent job losses have all greatly aggravated an already untenable situation. Moreover, as noted, unions in Africa have been weakened by authoritarian political regimes, too close an association with ruling political parties, insufficient attention to internal democratic structures, serious deficiencies in organizational and financial capacity, and an almost total male dominance of union structures (Mihyo and Schiphorst 1995, 193).

At the same time, the record of the first decade of independence offers some reason for guarded optimism for trade unionism and labor in general in Namibia. As noted above, a relatively high percentage of the economically active population is in the formal sector labor force (nearly half) and about half of those are organized into one or another union. Unions are strongest in the mining industry, a crucial revenue-generating sector, and in the public sector (especially among teachers), where they confront the largest single employer in the country, government. Moreover, in Namibia today workers confront the most favorable legal and political environment ever with the new labor law representing a dramatic gain for Namibian workers—elevating them to the status of "partners with, and not subordinates to, the state and employers" (Southall 1997, 354).

In addition, in the years since independence, unions from the largest federation, the NUNW (and presumably other unions as well), have made significant strides in building organizational, administrative, financial, and research capacity. In the early years after independence the unions of the NUNW, like many others, were preoccupied with their own transition—from the more political and mobilizational role they had played inside Namibia in the final years of the liberation struggle to a more narrow trade union role focused on building their organizations and servicing their members (*The Namibian Worker*, June 1992). Indeed, at mid-decade, the 1995–96 Labour Relations Survey[21] reported a relatively low "trade union efficacy," in other words, that survey respondents were "not wholly convinced of the performance of trade unions," in particular in terms of improving conditions of employment (Murray and Wood 1997b, 184). The survey also found that a high proportion of Namibian workers were ill informed about provisions of the new Labour Act, an issue Murray and Wood felt "should be of some concern to the unions" (1997b, 184). The Labour Relations Survey also confirmed earlier findings about weaknesses in overall union capacity in the areas mentioned above.

By the end of the decade, however, LaRRI, founded in early 1998, reported some improvements. Many of the unions of the NUNW had achieved financial self-reliance, although they still needed additional resources for capacity building programs. By 2006 it was reported that the NUNW unions had achieved a "remarkable degree of financial independence," with membership fees at about 1 percent of basic wages, and some unions setting up their own investment companies (Jauch 2006, 4). The establishment of LaRRI was an important step in addressing the unions' lack of capacity in the areas of research and input into the policy-making process. LaRRI is also expected to help the unions build their institutional capacity. Some of LaRRI's anticipated activities include building a resource center for the labor movement, conducting leadership training, strengthening local and regional union structures, and carrying out research on privatization, commercialization, export processing zones, subcontracting, and labor hiring companies (LaRRI 1998, 34).

Trade unions in Namibia can also boast a high level of internal democracy, according to findings of the Labour Relations Survey. This is reflected, according to the survey, in "the high levels of workplace representation by trade union representatives, as well [as] the strong sense of accountability which was both demanded and found to exist on the shop floor (Murray and Wood 1997b, 180). As further evidence for this, Murray and Wood report that most workplace representatives belong to a union and are elected through regular elections (1997b, 183). Moreover, there is a relatively high level of attendance at union meetings and a high demand for accountability from shop stewards. The authors note, however, at least in the case of the NUNW, that the high levels of internal democracy do not necessarily reach to the higher decision-making structures of the unions (Murray and Wood 1997b, 184). They suggest that stronger regional structures for the unions and federation would help to address this problem.

Finally, and most importantly, the potential exists for close links between trade unions and other organizations of civil society. For example, the unions joined forces with other nongovernmental organizations (NGOs) in 1994 to convene their own conference on the land question—albeit without any tangible result. The unions were somewhat more successful in 1996 when they enlisted the support of the Legal Assistance Center to combat the government's attempt to prevent the new labor law from applying in Namibia's export processing zones. On May Day 1999 the NUNW, the Namibia Nongovernmental Organization Forum, and the Namibia National Farmers Union allied to confront the land issue once again; they presented a petition to government demanding a faster and more effective land redistribution program (Jauch 2000b, 33). While the NGO sector suffers from many of the same organizational and capacity weaknesses as do the unions, observers have also identified a number of strengths of the Namibian NGO sector.[22] Together, the unions and other organizations of civil society in Namibia could be important advocates on behalf of the economically and socially disadvantaged (LaRRI 1998, 33). For this to happen, however, the unions must revive past strategic alliances with different sectors of civil society. In the view of those who work closely with them, the unions must continue their focus on workplace issues, but they must also articulate workers' interests (and those of other marginalized and unorganized groups) on broader socioeconomic issues. They must redefine their role as "struggle organizations" with a specific base and strategic agenda and in so doing "play a central role in the fight for socioeconomic justice" (Jauch 2004, 35). At the same time, they will have to reassert their political independence, revive their internal structures, and regain their accountability to their membership (Jauch 2006). In this and other ways, trade unions could make their own small contribution to the consolidation of democracy in Namibia.

Notes

1. See Hodgkin (1957), Freund (1988), Orr (1966), and Woddis (1961) for discussions of union roles in nationalist movements. See Berg and Butler (1966) and Davies (1966) on the fate of unions after independence.

2. As Chazan noted in 1992 (295): "Regimes have tended to view broadly based trade, student, professional, and civil rights associations as the greatest threats to their authority because these organizations have historically formed the launching pad for new political parties."

3. This section draws heavily on my 1998 book, *Labor and Democracy in Namibia, 1971–1996*. See also Bauer (1997).

4. For more on the general strike and its aftermath see Bauer (1998), chapter two. SWAPO had been formed out of the Ovamboland People's Organization in early 1960; it was one of the first black political organizations in Namibia and ultimately led the liberation struggle against South Africa. SWAPO was the only nationalist organization to take up arms against the South Africans and by the mid 1970s was deemed the 'sole and authentic representative of the Namibian people' by the international community (in particular the United Nations). Tens of thousands of Namibians lived for decades in SWAPO exile bases in Zambia and Angola and in training and study around the world.

5. *Windhoek Advertiser*, June 20, 1972. At the trial of workers involved in the general strike, the magistrate said that after the strike most employers realized that they had been underpaying their workers. At the same trial, the advocate for the defense noted that it was because the workers had no trade unions that they had been forced to strike. *Windhoek Advertiser*, June 6, 1972.

6. ILO (1977, 71–73). The ordinance did not prohibit black workers from forming trade unions as such; however, black trade unions could not be registered nor could they apply for the establishment of a conciliation board or participate in any other dispute resolution

mechanisms. In addition, black workers were effectively prohibited from engaging in strikes.

7. See Bauer (1998), chapter three. In exile a notion of trade unionism in service of the nationalist movement was predominant. A labor activist inside Namibia in the late 1970s, Arthur Pickering, felt that the union leader in exile, John Ya Otto, "was more concerned about us having t-shirts and NUNW having SWAPO colors and so on. He had ideas of trade unions that were very East European . . . " Efforts to organize workers inside Namibia at the time, by contrast, revolved around very real worker grievances, though the organizers were usually SWAPO members.

8. In the early 1980s the only unions that existed were those 'white' unions or staff associations attempting to become multiracial. The South West African Municipal Association (SWAMSA) was founded in 1969 and the Government Service Staff Association (GSSA) in 1981; SWAMSA became multiracial in 1978, in part because of the increasing numbers of 'non-white' staff in the municipalities (anyone working for the municipalities had to join SWAMSA); from its inception the GSSA also accepted 'non-white' members. In 1983 only five trade unions were registered with the Department of Civic Affairs and Manpower, with only two described as "functioning unions." Streek (1984, 14).

9. By 1986 one publication listed 18 community based organizations in Katutura, including trade unions, a community newspaper, a primary school, women's organizations, a social research unit and health and residents' committees. By 1987 the number had grown to 28, including unions and workers' organizations (Strauss 1986, 37–39; 1987, 193–95).

10. In late 1989 Commission Chair Wiehahn described Namibia's system of industrial relations as "underdeveloped and unsophisticated" and lagging behind even that of South Africa; ultimately, the Commission recommended that the labor relations system in Namibia be "de-South Africanized and the new one antagonized as far as possible," that the new system should "in the greatest degree" conform to international labor standards, and that the new system should be flexible and allow for maximum future growth. Wiehahn (1989, 62); South West Africa (1989, ii).

11. The transition in Namibia had a significant international component in that independence was part of a regional peace accord that affected neighboring Angola and South Africa as well. Indeed, the actual yearlong transition to independence was supervised by United Nations peacekeeping troops. In addition, the peace settlement that enabled the transition, while part of a regional accord, was facilitated by an elite level transitional pact between opposing sides, a pact that set out some of the central tenets of the new constitution and the contours of some of the post-independence institutions to be established (Forrest 1998, 42). See also Erasmus 2000.

12. According to the EIU (2004, 51): " . . . in its 2003 annual report, the central bank states that the 2001 census results should be treated with caution as the enumerators did not always filter out those not actively seeking employment."

13. In addition to those NUNW unions formed before 1990, the Namibia Farmworkers Union was established in 1994, the Namibia Financial Institutions Union in 2000, and the Namibia Music Industry Union in 2002 (Jauch 2004, 26).

14. Jauch 2004, 30; Herbert Jauch, personal email communication, February 18, 2005.

15. Murray and Wood (1997b, 176) reported a trade union density in Namibia of about 52 percent in the mid 1990s. They attributed the much higher rate in the public sector (80 percent) than in the private sector (38 percent) to anti-union sentiments among management structures in Namibia.

16. Lindsay Detlinger, 'Labour Harmony Eludes Namibia.' *The Namibian*, September 23, 2005.

17. See Jata Kazondu, 'Unions, Chinese Go Head to Head on Labour Relations.' *The Namibian*, August 24, 2006; see also Denver Isaacs, 'Government, NUNW Meet Over Ramatex Issue.' *The Namibian*, August 18, 2006.
18. Tangeni Amupadhi. 'Unions Fail to Make Swapo Cut.' *The Namibian*. October 6, 2004.
19. Jauch (2004, 31) suggests that the TUCNA and non-affiliated unions are more narrowly focused on the workplace and are less active than the NUNW unions in the broader policy arena.
20. Christof Maletsky, 'NUNW In-fighting Takes New Turn.' *The Namibian*, January 4, 2006. Christof Maletsky, 'Union "Purge" Claims Casualties.' *The Namibian*, December 16, 2005.
21. The 1995/96 Labour Relations Survey was conducted by Gilton Klerck, Andrew Murray, Martin Sycholt and a team of student researchers from the University of Namibia. Their findings form the basis of the book by Klerck, Murray and Sycholt, eds. (1997).
22. These include: providing services not offered by government, providing important leadership skills, raising public awareness of significant social issues, providing skills to target groups, a commitment to transparent working styles and internal democracy, and capable leaders and staff. LaRRI (1998, 9).

References

Adler, Glenn, and Eddie Webster. 1995. Challenging transition theory: The labor movement, radical reform, and the transition to democracy in South Africa. *Politics and Society* 23 (1): 75–106.
Bauer, Gretchen. 1992. The new labour act: Best compromise achievable. *Namibia Review* 1 (6): 18–24.
———. 1997. Labour relations in occupied Namibia. In *Continuity and change: Labour relations in independent Namibia*, ed. Gilton Klerck, Andrew Murray, and Martin Sycholt. Windhoek, Namibia: Gamsberg Macmillan.
———. 1998. *Labor and democracy in Namibia, 1971–1996*. Athens: Ohio University Press; Oxford: James Currey.
———. 2001. Namibia in the first decade of independence: How democratic? *Journal of Southern African Studies* 27 (1): 33–55.
Berg, Elliot, and Jeffrey Butler. 1966. Trade unions. In *Political parties and national integrations in tropical Africa*, ed. James Coleman and Carl Rosberg. Berkeley: University of California Press.
Bratton, Michael, and Nicolas van de Walle. 1997. *Democratic experiments in Africa: Regime transitions in comparative perspective*. Cambridge: Cambridge University Press.
Chazan, Naomi. 1992. The new politics of participation in tropical Africa. *Comparative Politics* 14 (2): 169–89.
Cliffe, Lionel, Ray Bush, Jenny Lindsay, Brian Mokopakgosi, Donna Pankhurst, and Balefi Tsie. 1993. *The transition to independence in Namibia*. Boulder, CO: Lynne Rienner.
Collier, Ruth Berins, and David Collier. 1991. *Shaping the political arena: Critical junctures, the labor movement and regime dynamics in Latin America*. Princeton, NJ: Princeton University Press.
Corbett, Andrew. 1993. Capital, labour and government. *Namibia Yearbook 1992–1993* 3:52–55.
Damachi, Ukandi, Dieter Seibel, and Lester Trachtman, eds. 1979. *Industrial relations in Africa*. London: Macmillan.
Davies, Ioan. 1966. *African trade unions*. Harmondsworth, UK: Penguin.

Economist Intelligence Unit (EIU). 2004. *Namibia country profile 2004*. London: Economist Intelligence Unit.

———. 2005. *Namibia country profile 2005*. London: Economist Intelligence Unit.

Emmett, Anthony. 1999. *Popular resistance and the roots of nationalism in Namibia, 1915–1966*. Basel: P. Schlettwein.

Erasmus, Gerhard. 2000. The constitution: Its impact on Namibian statehood and politics. In *State, society and democracy: A reader in Namibian politics*, ed. Christiaan Keulder. Windhoek, Namibia: Gamsberg Macmillan.

Ford, John. 1993. The labour act—how it affects your business. *Namibia Business Journal* 3 (1): 1–9.

Forrest, Joshua. 1998. *Namibia's post-apartheid regional institutions: The founding year*. Rochester, NY: University of Rochester Press.

Freund, Bill. 1992. The unions of South Africa. *Dissent* 39 (3): 378–85.

———. 1988. *The African worker*. Cambridge: Cambridge University Press.

Hodgkin, Thomas. 1957. *Nationalism in colonial Africa*. New York: New York University Press.

International Labour Organization. 1977. *Labour and discrimination in Namibia*. Geneva: International Labour Organization.

Jauch, Herbert. 2000a. Labour relations at 10: Moving towards "social partnership"? Windhoek, Namibia: Labour Resource and Research Institute.

———. 2000b. Tough choices: Trade unions and swapo. *Southern African Report* (Toronto) 15 (4): 31–33.

———. 2004. *Trade unions in Namibia: Defining a new role?* Windhoek, Namibia: Labour Resource and Research Institute.

———. 2006. The Namibian labour movement at the crossroads. Public lecture delivered at the University of Namibia, Windhoek, August 2.

Jauch, Herbert, and Hilma Sindondola. 2003. *Ramatex: On the other side of the fence*. Windhoek, Namibia: Labour Resource and Research Institute.

Jeffries, Richard. 1975. The labour aristocracy? Ghana case study. *Review of African Political Economy* 3:59–70.

Kane-Berman, John. 1972. Contract labour in south west Africa. Johannesburg: South African Institute of Race Relations.

———. 1973. The labour situation in south west Africa. Johannesburg: South African Institute of Race Relations.

Klerck, Gilton, Andrew Murray, and Martin Sycholt, eds. 1997. *Continuity and change: Labour relations in independent Namibia*. Windhoek: Namibia: Gamsberg Macmillan.

Kraus, Jon. 1976. African trade unions: Progress or poverty? *African Studies Review* 19 (3): 95–108.

Labour Resource and Research Institute (LaRRI). 1998. *Still fighting for social justice: A survey of trade unions, women's organisations, communal farmers' and service organisations in Namibia*. Windhoek, Namibia: Labour Resource and Research Institute.

———. 1999. *Understanding the past and present—mapping the future: The national union of Namibian workers (NUNW) facing the 21st century*. Windhoek, Namibia: Labour Resource and Research Institute.

———. 2006. *The struggle for workers' rights in Namibia*. Windhoek, Namibia: Labour Resource and Research Institute.

Leys, Colin, and John Saul. 1995. Introduction to *Namibia's liberation struggle: The two-edged sword*, ed. Colin Leys and John Saul. London: James Currey.

Marks, Gary. 1989. *Unions in politics: Britain, Germany and the United States in the nineteenth and early twentieth centuries*. Princeton, NJ: Princeton University Press.

Melber, Henning. 1993. Trade unions in Namibia: Which way and where to? *Southern African Political and Economic Weekly* (Harare) 7 (1): 63–64.

———. 2003. Limits to liberation: An introduction to Namibia's postcolonial political culture. In *Re-examining liberation in Namibia: Political culture since independence*, ed. Henning Melber. Uppsala, Sweden: Nordiska Afrikainstitutet.

Mihyo, Paschal, and Freek Schiphorst. 1995. A context of sharp economic decline. In *Globalization and third world unions: The challenge of rapid economic change*, ed. Henk Thomas. London: Zed.

Murray, Andrew, and Geoffrey Wood. 1997a. Industrial action: Conflict and accommodation. In *Continuity and Change: Labour Relations in Independent Namibia*, ed. Gilton Klerck, Andrew Murray, and Martin Sycholt. Windhoek, Namibia: Gamberg Macmillan.

———. 1997b. The Namibian trade union movement: Trends, practices, and shop floor perception.' In *Continuity and Change: Labour Relations in Independent Namibia*, ed. Gilton Klerck, Andrew Murray, and Martin Sycholt. Windhoek, Namibia: Gamberg Macmillan.

New labour bill draws praise and criticism—A gender analysis. 2004. *LAC News* 14 (March): 16–17. Windhoek: Legal Assistance Center.

Orr, Charles. 1966. Trade unionism in colonial Africa. *Journal of Modern African Studies* 4:65–81.

Peace, Adrian. 1975. The Lagos proletariat: Labour aristocrats or populist militants? In *The development of an African working class*, ed. Richard Sandbrook and Robin Cohen. London: Longman.

Peltola, Pekka. 1995. *The lost May Day: Namibian workers struggle for independence.* Helsinki: University of Helsinki Press.

Rueschemeyer, Dietrich, Evelyne Huber Stephens, and John Stephens. 1992. *Capitalist development and democracy.* Chicago: University of Chicago Press.

Seidman, Gay. 1994. *Manufacturing militance: workers' movements in Brazil and South Africa, 1970–1985.* Berkeley: University of California Press.

South West Africa. 1989. *Report of the commission of inquiry into labour matters in Namibia.* [Wiehahn Report]. Windhoek, Namibia: Office of the Administrator General.

SWAPO. 1984. *The struggle for trade union rights in Namibia.* Luanda, Angola: Swapo Department of Labour.

Southall, Roger. 1997. Labour relations challenges in the sub-continent. In *Continuity and Change: Labour Relations in Independent Namibia*, ed. Gilton Klerck,Andrew Murray, Martin Sycholt. Windhoek, Namibia: Gamsberg Macmillan.

Strauss, Andre. 1986. Community based organisations (CBOs) in Katutura. In *Katutura revisited: essays on a black Namibian suburb*, ed. Christine Van Garnier. Windhoek, Namibia: Roman Catholic Church.

———. 1987. Community organisations in Namibia. In *Namibia in perspective*, ed. Gerhard Toetemeyer, Vezera Kandetu, and Wolfgang Werner. Windhoek, Namibia: Council of Churches of Namibia.

Streek, Barry. 1984. Unions in Namibia. *South African Labour Bulletin* 9:14–16.

Terreblanche, Christelle. 1993. Namibian trade unions in tatters. *South* (Johannesburg) October 29–November 2.

Thomas, Henk. ed. 1995. *Globalization and third world unions: The challenge of rapid economic change.* London: Zed.

———. 1995. The erosion of trade unions. In *Globalization and third world unions*, ed.Henk Thomas. London: Zed.

Valenzuela, Samuel. 1989. Labor movements in transitions to democracy: A framework for analysis. *Comparative Politics* 21 (4): 445–72.

Van Rooyen, Johann. 1996. *Portfolio of partnership: An analysis of labour relations in a transitional society—Namibia*. Windhoek, Namibia: Gamsberg Macmillan.

Wiehan, Nic. 1989. Industrial relations in Namibia.' *Optima* 37:57–63.

Weiland, Heribert, and Matthew Braham, eds. 1994. *The Namibian peace process: Implications and lessons for the future*. Freiburg, Germany: Arnold-Bergstraesser-Institut.

Woddis, Jack. 1961. *Africa: The lion awakes*. London: Lawrence and Wishart.

CHAPTER 9

Conclusion: Trade Unions and Democratization in Africa

Jon Kraus

Democracy is not an isolated phenomenon. Political democracy, economic democracy, social democracy, and industrial democracy are not necessarily separate. . . . They complement one another and contribute to the overall development of democracy in our society. Those who seek to destroy the trade union movement must take their cue from history, that the workers' movement can never be destroyed in modern history. We can only experience setbacks.

L. K. K. Ocloo
General Secretary, Industrial and Commercial Workers Union
1987

Trade unions in many African countries played a muscular and seminal role in the late 1980s and early 1990s in mobilizing the mass protests and strikes that led to the overthrow of old authoritarian regimes and ushered in democratic transitions. In some other countries the unions' intermittent strike movements and protests were critical in creating, over time, political "space" in which other social and political groups could mount protests and political coalitions. These crystallized in political liberalization and democratization. Moreover, in the post-transition period, trade unions have often continued to play leading roles in public and political life in ways crucial to the vitality of democracy in these countries. These democratic unions are responsive to their members who have generally not been beneficiaries of the market-oriented policies of the successor governments. These have invariably been in thrall and bondage to the zealous market advocacies and resource blackmails of the International Monetary Fund (IMF), the World Bank, and foreign donor countries. Consequently, labor protests and strikes have often continued, being called by workers whose living standards and organizing rights have suffered under the democratic regimes they were crucial in creating.

These finding are fundamental because the existing literature on the causes of democratization in Africa and assessments of democratic life under the new regimes tend to ignore entirely the significance of trade unions and other collective actors. As argued in the introduction, scholars have tended to focus on their statistical studies of election outcomes, levels of political liberties, and whether voting was "free and fair" as the key determinants of the state of democracy in Africa—that is, the procedural elements of democracy. Obviously, these are crucial, but the existence of gross inequalities in socioeconomic and political power in African societies conditions how and for whom these procedures and political rights work in practice. It is as important to examine the responsiveness of governments to claims upon public resources and access to rule-making institutions by various groups, institutional interests, and collective actors in society. When newly ensconced leaders can seize with impunity vast public resources in terms of salaries, offices, and contracts—as in democratic Kenya, Nigeria, and South Africa—democracy becomes a mirage for the majority excluded from access. The measure of democracy includes the relative responsiveness of government to claims upon public resources and access to rule-making institutions by various groups, interests, and collective actors in society. It is important to question whether politics is merely a struggle among dominant elites or involves and engages representative groups and the popular classes. The real significance of trade unions for democratic life in Africa is that they are virtually the only group representing the popular classes that has continuing organizational influence at the national level and poses challenging questions about rights of mass access to public resources.

This study set out to respond to some major questions. First, did trade unions play a significant or crucial role in the struggles that launched the renewal of democracy in the seven African countries studied? Have continuing high levels of strikes or protests endangered the democratic transition in any countries? Second, what major factors animated trade union and worker protests? Were they major political or economic conditions? Or were union protests more likely to occur because of qualities of the union movement itself, for example, relative or absolute size or autonomy? Third, what have been the roles of the trade unions in the newly democratized polities—if democratic life survived? Are unions active only in addressing key public issues or more directly involved in political life through parties or mobilizing demands and protests? Have trade unions been able to retain their autonomy and sufficient resources in practice to fight in the broader political economy? Also, in this era of neoliberal global dominance, have trade unions and workers been—or thought themselves to be—beneficiaries or victims of the democratic era? To what extent has the answer to that question affected union support for democracy?

Significance of Trade Unions in Initiating Democratization

This study was initiated in the recognition that union strikes and other worker protests seemed to be extremely important in directly leading the struggles that unmoored old autocrats and opened the way for political liberalization and democratic changes—or helped create the political space for these. In the seven cases in this book, union strikes and mobilization directly prompted political liberalization in four cases (Niger, South Africa, Zambia, and Zimbabwe), or by a pattern of struggles created the "political space" that induced political liberalization (Ghana and Senegal). Or, labor strikes and protests contributed importantly to resistance to white minority rule, which helped the democratic struggle, as in Namibia. Trade unions also continued to play crucial roles in political life after the transition in countries where unions were relatively large (South Africa, Ghana, Zambia, and Zimbabwe, where a transition has not yet occurred). Table 9.1 lists countries where worker/union protests and demonstrations were either significant or not, in the broader universe of forty-three African countries, by types of regime up to 1989 (seven were excluded; see Table 9.1 note). The countries in which the high level of worker/union protests were crucial in democratization are indicated in bold; countries where worker/union protests occurred, but were not as influential, are italicized.

Several points regarding the role of unions in democratization stand out. One can see that worker protests were important in both of the countries with white minority regimes in 1990, which were illegitimate on a nationalist basis. Large protests/strikes were important in only two of the five countries that were relatively democratic (that is, they had regular elections and some degree of free speech, association, and press). And this was in the two countries, Senegal and Zimbabwe, where one-party dominant regimes existed despite the levels of political liberties; the other three in this category were more democratic. There is also a category of countries that intermittently had democratic regimes, or key features of democracy, and hence where it was probable that trade unions had been independent (or still were), and ideas of political liberties had become widespread. In half of the eight countries, worker protests were either significant in democratization (Benin and Zambia) or in forcefully creating space for the renewal of political liberties by contesting the regimes (Ghana and Nigeria [ouster of Babangida government in 1993]). In all types of authoritarian regimes a far smaller percentage of countries (seven of twenty-eight, or 25 percent) experienced forceful worker protests: this occurred in four of seventeen countries, or 23.5 percent, with one-party personalist regimes; in three of eight countries, or 37 percent, with military regimes, some of which had become personalist regimes with parties; and in no cases in Afro-Marxist regimes (three countries) where, ironically, unions were either incredibly weakened (Ethiopia) or virtually non-existent.

One can draw several conclusions from Table 9.1. First, prior or existing democratic experience greatly increased the probability of a strong union role in democratization. Second, strong worker protests or other union resistance that created political space that led to the removal of an authoritarian regimes and renewal of political liberties occurred in about fifteen of the forty-three countries (35 percent), a not insignificant number. In addition, there were major union strikes or protests in at least seven other African states (italicized in table), which did not directly lead to the removal of the regime in power but in which partial political liberalization occurred. Third, drawing upon our cases primarily but noting some others, one can see that there were a wide variety of ways in which trade union movements could play a crucial role in, first, the collapse of authoritarian regimes and, second, the transitions to democracy. This also occurred in a wide variety of regime types.

Table 9.1 Trade Unions in Democratic Struggles (in bold) by Types of Prior Regimes and Trade Union Autonomy up to 1989[a]

Types of political regimes (43)	*Trade union movements by autonomy & strength*					
	Largely autonomous		*Intermittently autonomous*		*No autonomy*	
	Strong	*Weak*	*Strong*	*Weak*		
White minority regimes (2)	**South Africa**			**Namibia**		
Relatively democratic systems (5)	Mauritius **Zimbabwe** (from mid-1980s)	Gambia		**Senegal** Botswana		
Countries that intermittently had democracies (8)	**Ghana** (since 1966) **Nigeria** **Dahomey/Benin** (pre-1972) **Zambia** (pre-1971 & mid-1980s on) Burkina Faso (to about mid-1980s)	Morocco		Sudan *Sierra Leone*		
Authoritarian regimes						
One-party personalist (17)	Tunisia (to mid-1980s)			**Algeria** (1962–65, 1977–80) **Congo Republic** (1960s) *Madagascar* *Swaziland*	**Côte d'Ivoire** **Malawi** *Gabon* Tanzania Kenya Liberia Uganda	*Cameroon* Libya Egypt Lesotho
Military regimes (8)				Zaire	**Mali** **Central African Republic** *Mauritania* Chad	**Niger** *Togo* Somalia

Table 9.1 Trade Unions in Democratic Struggles (in bold) by Types of Prior Regimes and Trade Union Autonomy up to 1989 (continued)

Afro-Marxist (3)	Angola Mozambique Ethiopia (since 1975)

[a] **Countries in bold had protests/strikes that led to democratization.** *Countries in italics had strikes/protests, but these did not lead to overthrow of regimes.* Autonomy is used to indicate a union organization relatively free from external interventions to choose leaders and policies, but union behavior may be restrained by the state. 'Relative strength' refers to a union's level and extensiveness of activities, ability to organize members, and persistence over time. **The dates** beside countries refer to the known time period of autonomy and strength.

[b] Countries were included in the most democratic category in which they fit. Zimbabwe could also have been put under white minority regimes, but unions did not play a key role in the anti-colonial struggle. Zambia was relatively democratic in the 1960s, but because a personalist one-party regime until 1990, it is included in the intermittently democratic category. Excluded countries (7) were those on which there was little information up to 1989–90 on unions, which were minor or non-existent: Rwanda, Burundi, Guinea-Bissau, Djibouti, Eritrea, Cape Verde, and Equatorial Guinea.

One can differentiate between our cases in terms of a number of distinguishing factors:

(a) the nature of the existing regimes and antecedent regimes (those with no democratic experiences and those with some);
(b) the extensiveness of the trade union/worker protests and strikes, in terms of length of strikes/protests or levels of violence or deaths (about which data are very incomplete);
(c) whether trade unions acted in isolation or in concert with other groups or parties (in South Africa, Namibia, and Senegal, for instance); or
(d) the nature of the transition.

It is useful to draw conclusions from our cases and others about the nature of the transition, since the latter also tends to be affected by the extensiveness of protests and the roles of trade unions in later stages.

One can differentiate three major patterns of democratic transition. First is the category *"authoritarian collapse–new regime,"* which involves cases of the collapse of the authoritarian order in the face of sustained strikes and protests. The old leaders experience a complete loss of power because of the total erosion of regime legitimacy and of armed force to sustain the old regime. New institutions are created by opposition leaders immediately after the collapse. This is illustrated by the case of Niger and also by Benin, Congo Republic, Mali, and perhaps also CAR—all in 1989–91.

Second is the pattern *"regime weakening–negotiated transitions."* There was a long, sustained resistance in strikes and protests to the old order, which understood that it could not keep itself in power indefinitely. It then opened up the system gradually to democratic changes, legalizing political opposition while keeping control of state institutions of violence. But the opposition forces posed sufficient threat to be recognized as partners in setting the terms of the transition, so it emerged in a negotiated "pact," for example, in the case of South Africa, Zambia, and Namibia (much less sustained resistance). The case of Namibia was strongly influenced by decisions taken in South Africa, and it was the armed rebellion of the South West African People's Organisation (SWAPO), rather than mass or union protests, that wore down the Namibian authorities. In South Africa and Zambia, trade union movements and opposition leaders were directly or indirectly involved in the transition process: working out transition arrangements and rules, decisions about the modalities of democracy (e.g., constitution-making), the elections, and new governments.

Third are the cases I call *"resistance–regime-controlled transition,"* where the protests were either less intense or less widespread than in the others, or even where protest was intense (intermittently in Senegal) and where the existing regimes opened the system up sufficiently while retaining control over security forces. But the regimes were able to insist on writing the rules of the transition to a greater or lesser extent. In some cases the transition then occurred by stages over time, as in Senegal, with its gradual democratization, or relatively quickly, for example, in Ghana. Or else the authorities resisted a genuine transition despite the levels of union/worker protests, for example, in Algeria (Chikhi), Nigeria, where presidential elections were aborted, and Zimbabwe, where elections have been held but under conditions of violence and intimidation, so that democratic space has shrunk since 2000. The general strike by the Nigerian Labor Congress (NLC) in July/August 1993 forced the regime of General I. B. Babangida to resign. But, despite later strikes by the NLC and the petroleum union, a new military coup ousted the interim regime (Beckman 1995; Beckman 2000; Ihonvbere 1997).

We will discuss our cases in terms of these patterns of transition. First are the *authoritarian collapse–new regime* cases. Robert Charlick analyzes the collapse of an authoritarian regime in Niger, where a previously regime-controlled *Union des syndicats des travailleurs du Niger* (USTN) was deeply aggrieved by arrears in pay and the negative effects on labor of structural adjustment programs (SAPs). In 1989 this very small union movement demanded elections and multipartyism. It and other unions aligned themselves in early 1990 with the cause of secondary and university students, who were killed in protests against the effects of SAPs in education. In mid-1990 key unions organized a Committee to Coordinate the Democratic Struggle in order to launch protests and strikes. The regime was widely regarded as illegitimate. In November a five-day general strike paralyzed Niger's formal economic sector. Unable to repress the unions, President Ali Saïbou accepted multipartyism. In Niger, as elsewhere in many Francophone African countries, the groups involved in the protests— unions, students, teachers, opposition party leaders—seized the advantage. Amazingly, they declared that they would establish a sovereign National Conference in order to create a new constitution and democratic national institutions. The old regime and its armed forces were too weak to stop this process.

Charlick theorizes that this could occur in Niger—and also be reversed—because of the relatively low levels of capabilities of both the state and the civil society actors. When the power and resources of both are low, relatively slight changes in the capacity of either can greatly alter the balance of power between state and modern social groups and permit dramatic political changes. The old regime's capabilities, including repressive ones, were undermined by overwhelming budget austerities, the different leadership style of President Saibou, and the growth of the anti-SAP coalition led by trade unions, students, and young ethnic leaders and technocrats.

In Niger, the trade unions also played a disproportionately large role in the transitional National Conference that created the new institutions, as unions had done in Benin and Mali. But they lost their relative power when elections were held, and ethnic/regional forces played a much larger role in political parties than did unions. Neither unions nor the new government had political/economic resources to counter the power of the IMF and the World Bank, which demanded drastic budget cuts and reductions in government services and employment. The new government was without funds. Hence, it had to be more responsive to the IMF and the World Bank than to union demands. These measures alienated the unions in increasing stages, as wage arrears persisted. As unions again mounted strikes and protests, the balance of legitimacy shifted against the unions, and the military intervened again. Nevertheless, sporadic but persistent union and other protests in Niger helped to force a return to democratic government in 1999. The trade unions, however fragmented and relatively small in size within the society, have proved sufficiently resilient to be independent actors in Niger as well as in Benin and Mali, where democratic life has persisted (Heilbrun 1993; Villalon and Idrissa 2005). But, argues Charlick, in the democratic era since 1999 the fragmented unions in Niger have had a declining ability to mobilize protests and have had little effective power regarding public policies.

Cases of *regime weakening–negotiated transition* include South Africa, Namibia, and Zambia. In South Africa, as William Freund observes, there was a long history of African wage labor and early unionization that did not survive apartheid repression. New industrial and other unions were organized in the late 1970s and early 1980s following strikes and new labor laws that legalized African unionization. The new unions were democratic, independent, and strongly responsive to worker, not political, goals. A new labor federation, the highly independent Congress of South African Trade Unions (COSATU), was created after several mergers in 1985. Other, smaller labor federations also developed (Table 9.2).

In the mid-1980s there was an explosion of African protests against apartheid rule, organized in the absence of the banned African National Congress (ANC) by many politicized student and neighborhood groups under the umbrella of the United Democratic Front (UDF). As Freund notes, the initially wary unions in COSATU were drawn into this conflict. The African townships ringing South Africa's cities were the sites of virtual insurrections. After a massive government crackdown, the persistence of resistance came to rest on the backs of the union movement, whose leadership had greater depth and organization. After ANC-COSATU negotiations, it became the third, but independent, leg of the Tripartite Alliance, together with the ANC and the Communist Party (SACP). During 1986–90 and also 1990–93, when the transition to an ANC/Nationalists unity government occurred, the trade union movement experienced massive losses of its leaders: many were arrested or killed by police or management thugs (ICFTU 1991–94).

COSATU's resistance was important in the National Party's historic decision to remove the ban on the ANC and the SACP and to begin negotiations for majority rule. COSATU's organizational power was equally crucial in the transition to majority rule. By 1990 COSATU's unions had 1.2 million members, and COSATU leaders insisted upon a role in a negotiation forum, which assured union interests in the constitution. When constitutional talks were deadlocked, COSATU's spectacular "stay-away"—a general strike, involving 4 million workers—forced the National Party to compromise its positions. COSATU's continued militance contradicts the thesis that argues that high levels of trade union protests and demonstrations are likely to throw the democratization process off track (Adler and Webster 1995). COSATU played a major role in the transition institutions, with its strong base providing organizing and electoral support for the ANC: COSATU leaders were offered twenty parliamentary ANC seats, while others were given positions in the cabinet, elective regional councils, and the state bureaucracy. COSATU unions helped develop the major economic program on which the ANC successfully ran in the 1994 election. Eventually, however, COSATU and its unions were changed by the loss of their leadership to political life, and COSATU's militance was diluted by its participation in a political alliance and in political processes.

The development of unions within Namibia in the 1980s, after years of illegality, and their support of SWAPO helped to persuade South Africa to agree to negotiate Namibia's independence. As Gretchen Bauer notes, however, unlike in South Africa, the major disruptive and violent threat to the quasi-colonial political order in Namibia was the military threat from SWAPO.

In the early 1970s in Zambia, the nationalist United National Independence Party (UNIP) government had forced the merger of independent unions into a single union federation, the Zambia Congress of Trade Unions (ZCTU). It was aligned with the one-party UNIP government, inaugurated in 1973. However, independent, strong unions—in particular the Mineworkers Union of Zambia (MUZ)—had developed during the colonial era. As Emmanuel Akwetey and Jon Kraus note, the UNIP government economic expansion program experienced severe crises starting in the 1970s. It was compelled to adopt SAPs to get loans from the IMF and foreign aid donors. Though formally aligned with UNIP, ZCTU started a series of strikes and protests in the 1980s to combat austerity measures, six stabilization and SAP programs, and losses of income and jobs. The union had the financial resources to develop a strong organization and the support of most workers, especially mineworkers in Zambia's copper companies. ZCTU became the most vocal opponent of key government economic policies. The total ZCTU-UNIP break came with the government's attempts in 1988 and 1990 to unilaterally break up the ZCTU or else to proscribe it. The ZCTU moved to opposition and launched demands for democracy. The strength of ZCTU strikes and protests had created the political space for ZCTU to mobilize support for an opposition party, Movement for Multiparty Democracy (MMD). ZCTU provided the mass base, organizational linkages, and leadership for MMD. It was joined by students, businessmen, church leaders, and disaffected UNIP ministers. Forced by massive protests to restore political liberties, the UNIP government agreed to MMD demands for legalization of opposition parties, electoral register revision, and an election date. MMD won the election in a landslide in October 1991.

The *resistance–regime-controlled transitions* are shown in the cases of Senegal, Ghana, and the ongoing struggle in Zimbabwe. Regarding Senegal, Geoffrey Bergen argues persuasively how unions, though weak organizations, have "indisputably . . . been key arbiters of political change" and democratization. This happened over a twenty-year period as the dominant *Parti socialiste* (PS) of Léopold Senghor opened single-party rule in stages to increased political liberties and political competition by the PS's desire to avoid labor challenges and upheavals. It acted because of the small opposition parties' efforts to build labor support and alliances and by struggles of the small unions to unify their strikes in order to increase their autonomy and to stave off declining living standards and constant threatened layoffs posed by SAPs. There were small autonomous unions, linked in federations, whose leaders were involved in small leftist parties, as well as a pro-*PS* dominant labor group, the *Confédération nationale des travailleurs du Sénégal* (CNTS). *CNTS* unions intermittently joined other unions in major strikes in order to retain their members' loyalties. The transition occurred in three periods when the fissiparous trade union movement was able to unify its efforts.

The first occasion occurred in 1968–69, when major student outbreaks occurred, which were joined by the dominant union and others, plus urban elements, in massive protests and strikes. This prompted repression and creation of a one-party state

Table 9.2 African Trade Unions and Union Membership

Country	Union movements	Membership ('000) 1976	1988	1990	1994	Number of union centers	Number of unions
South Africa	Union workers, all races	632.3	2,084	2,700	2,439	5	
	Cong. of S.African Tr. Unions (COSATU)		500 (1985)	1,200	1,317		15
	Nat'l Council of Tr Unions (NACTU)				334.7		18
	Federation of South African Labor (FEDSAL)				257.3		16
	Federation of Inde. Trade Unions (FITU)				236.0		24
	S. Af. Confederation of Labor (SACOL)				54.3		4
Nigeria	Nigerian Labor Congress (NLC)	1974		1990 / Est 600	2004 / Est 2,000	2	
	Trade Union Congress of Nigeria (TUCN)				n.d.		
	Congress of Free Trade Unions (GFTU)				n.d.		
Ghana	Trade Union Congress of Ghana (TUC)	1988/89 / 345.0			2004 / 283.1	2	18
	Gh. Federation of Labor (GFL)				6.0		5–6
	Gh. Nat'l Association of Teachers (GNAT)				Est. 100		
Zimbabwe	Zimbabwe Congress of Trade Unions (ZCTU)	162.8		1992 / 200.7	150.0	1	32
Zambia	Zambia Congress of Trade Unions (ZCTU)	352.9			240.0 (2001)		18
	Fed. of Free Trade Unions of Zambia (FFTUZ)				n.d.		n.d.
Senegal	Confédération national des travailleurs du Sénégal (CNTS)			1990 / 50.0		2	

Table 9.2 African Trade Unions and Union Membership (continued)

Country	Union movements	1976	Membership ('000) 1988	1990	1994	Number of union centers	Number of unions
Senegal (continued)	Confédération des syndicats autonomes (CSA)			20.0 (the CSA and UNSAS together)			
	Union des syndicats autonomes du Sénégal (UNSAS)				2004	2	
Namibia	National Union of Namibian Workers (NUNW)				60.0		10
	Trade Union Congress of Namibia (TUCN)				45.0		14
Niger	Union des syndicats des travailleurs du Niger (USTN)				48.0		5

Sources: country chapters; African Labor Research Network, Trade Unions in Africa (December 2003); Webster and Glenn, 2001, p. 125; The Times of Zambia, 12/2/2004. Est. = estimate of membership.

and a single PS-controlled labor federation. But, Bergen argues, it was Senghor's fear of the discontent of state *fonctionaires* in independent unions that led Senghor to reopen the political system by allowing a limited number of political parties in 1973–74. Senghor specifically disavowed trade union pluralism or legalizing the small radical leftist parties. But the illegal status of the leftist parties drove them to cooperate in supporting labor unity and to launch the major teachers' strike in 1980. This led to widening public and private sector strikes, popular support for teachers, school closures, and, finally, Senghor's resignation from office in 1980. President Abdoul Diouf, Senghor's successor, escaped this dilemma by legalizing many political parties, thus enhancing democratic possibilities, and also legalizing multiple unions. The third occasion was when, despairing of cracking PS dominance, the opposition parties created a united front in 1989 in order to also generate labor unity and rally these forces against the Diouf government. Political mobilization quickened; independent unions in alliance led a series of threatening strikes in 1990. Fearing a multi-sector strike, Diouf offered cabinet seats to the opposition parties in a national unity government in March 1991, the opposition's first access to government power since independence. New attempts to build labor unity led to a general strike in 1999. The opposition victory in the 2000 presidential election and the 2001 legislative elections marked a major democratic transition.

In Ghana, the Trade Union Congress (TUC) has fought since 1966 to maintain its autonomy and power to struggle for worker interests in union and public arenas. Despite strong democratic norms, the TUC commitment to democracy was undermined by efforts of the 1969–72 democratic government to split the unions and then dissolve the TUC and weaken its seventeen national unions. Under the successor military regime (1972–78) it regained its organizational strength and had large membership increases with state help. But the TUC leaders were deeply sympathetic to, and supported, democratic government during its brief renewal in 1979–81. In 1982–83 the Provisional National Defense Committee (PNDC) government of Jerry Rawlings frontally attacked the trade unions, expelled and arrested top union leaders, installed interim leaders, created Workers Defense Committees (WDCs) to replace unions as worker representatives, and tried to curtail union negotiating powers.

During 1982–90 union members and leaders fought the PNDC on an ongoing basis, in order to democratically elect leaders in the unions and TUC, which occurred in 1983. They resisted repeatedly the harsh SAP policies. The initially radical populist PNDC cowed or jailed leaders of other associational groups and parties. So the TUC stood practically alone in the 1983–89 period in resisting the PNDC, insisting on its own democratic rights, and by 1986–87 demanding a return to democratic rule. The resistance took the form of strikes, protests, threatened protests, and public challenges to policies. There were no massive strikes, but the often successful resistance created an important democratic "space" and opened the way for a renewal of protests by other groups by 1989–90. Despite PNDC intimidation, militant pressures from below and from some unions maintained the resistance. By 1989–91 politicians, religious leaders, student groups, and others had mounted renewed pressures for political liberties and democracy. In 1991 Rawlings reluctantly dropped political restrictions and started a transition, which he managed with cleverness, threats, and effective political organization. Although Rawlings won the 1992 presidential election, the presence of a new constitution, political liberties, and a reinvigorated Supreme Court in 1993 animated a genuine political transition. The TUC became a major critical public voice in the absence of a parliamentary opposition between 1993 and 1996. The opposition won both parliamentary and presidential elections in 2000.

In Zimbabwe there were substantial political liberties for some years in the 1980s after independence, though more for interest groups that developed under white colonial rule than for the opposition party. It was treated harshly. The Zimbabwe African National Union-Patriotic Front (ZANU-PF), which later incorporated the opposition party, had led military resistance in Rhodesia and established a dominant party regime after independence. Previously existing unions, some with traditions of autonomy, were incorporated into a new pro-ZANU Zimbabwe Congress of Trade Unions (ZCTU). As Richard Saunders argues, growing ZCTU corruption and eroding economic conditions in the late 1980s led to the emergence and election of new ZCTU leaders from within the constituent unions, which had become well organized and asserted their independence. They protested vigorously ZANU's adoption of economic "reforms" under SAP, advocating instead populist-nationalist policies. This resistance led quickly to attempts by the ZANU-PF government to delegitimate and to de-register ZCTU. Despite the one-party dominance, ZCTU used existing political liberties to attack ZANU-PF's monopoly and to demand the need for democratic accountability to go with economic reforms. Throughout the 1990s ZCTU unions waged strikes and protests both to oppose provisions of the SAPs and to maintain legal labor rights. To broaden support, ZCTU leaders increasingly aligned themselves with other interest groups who protested the drastic decline in living standards and participatory rights. ZCTU played a leading role in the organization of a "National Constitutional Assembly" of civic groups and others who wanted a more democratic constitution. In 1999, with strong ZCTU organizational backing, the Movement for Democratic Change (MDC) was organized as an opposition party. Its elected leaders were the secretary-general and president of ZCTU. MDC has challenged ZANU-PF in elections in 2000 and after, in a highly repressive environment, keeping democratic processes alive even as democratic space shrank rapidly.

In conclusion, in three of the seven cases (South Africa, Niger, and Zambia), the trade unions and union leaders played major roles not only in the first stage of democratization (overthrow of the old regime) but also in the second stage, the transition and setting up of new democratic institutions. This was particularly true in Zambia, where the trade unions organized and led the opposition political party. In Namibia the union role was smaller. Where the regime controlled the transition, as in Ghana and Senegal (and Nigeria), unions tended not to play a large rule in the transition process itself, except to keep it going.

It is argued by some that high levels of strikes and labor protests can retard democratization by seeming to mount radical challenges, hence threatening property and capitalist relationships (see introduction; Valenzuela 1989). This allegedly leads moderates in authoritarian governments who favor political liberalization to lose ground to hardliners who abort democratic transitions. In general, major cases in Latin America (Brazil, Argentina, Peru), Asia, and southern Europe (Spain, Portugal) fail to support this idea (Bermeo 1997; Collier and Mahoney 1997). In Africa it was more likely that political liberalization initiated by mass-based protests would lead to democratic transitions than ruling incumbent-initiated political reforms (Bratton and van de Walle 1997, 185). In these, autocrats simply restored some political liberties but found ways to manipulate the system and hang on to power indefinitely, for example, in Gabon, Zaire, and Togo. However, the persistence of huge strikes in South Africa was crucial in breaking a constitutional deadlock and facilitating a complete democratization. In Zimbabwe, with the desperate efforts of Robert Mugabe to stay in power, the continuation of major strikes and protests did increase repression of labor and other democratic forces. As the MDC, the ZCTU-supported party, contested ZANU-PF power politically, there were repeated attacks upon union, MDC, and civic group leaders and organizations. But ZCTU strikes/protests persisted because of the failure to democratize, not because of a radical program. In Senegal, Bergen notes that the state was clearly apprehensive that major strikes could paralyze the public sector and delegitimate the regime; the response repeatedly was to widen the field of political liberties and democratic competition.

Why Did Trade Union Strikes and Protests Occur?

Our second major interest has been the factors that animated these trade union and worker protests. Some analysts add: why at this time, 1989–90, believing that the major sources of democratic change were the collapse of communist regimes in Eastern Europe. But, in fact, crucial strike and protest movements varied in time and often preceded 1989–90: in South Africa throughout the late 1980s; Namibia in the late 1980s; Zambia from 1987–88 onward; Zimbabwe also from the late 1988 period to the 2000s; Senegal at three major time periods during the 1960s through the 1990s; and Ghana during 1984–88. Those that occurred in 1989–91 were largely in Francophone Africa, starting in Benin and occurring in Niger, Mali, Côte d'Ivoire, and Congo Republic, and they did influence each other. The cases of South Africa and Namibia were distinct in the sense that they targeted white minority regimes with little or no legitimacy to black Africans.

Our case studies demonstrate that major strikes and protests tended to originate in the workers' consciousness of falling wages and living standards, and that initial protests tended to be treated in highly repressive ways. State repressive activities and actual or threatened punitive legislation to reduce trade union rights raised challenges to unions regarding their independence and right to act as representatives of worker interests. These repressive activities compelled union leaders, despite real hesitations and divisions, to demand forcefully their own political liberties, such as the rights to oppose and protest, and, in the face of sustained state hostility, to demand the renewal of democratic institutions. In almost all countries they reached out to other social and political forces—such as student, teacher, legal, and religious groups—to strengthen their demands. And in Zambia and Zimbabwe, they took the leadership role in wide popular mobilization, organizing and leading new opposition political parties. *So, in all these countries, economic and political struggle were inextricably intertwined. The longer the struggle had been going on, the more conscious union leaders were that they needed democratization to ensure their own rights and ability to pursue their representative interests.* This was true in Ghana, Senegal, Nigeria, Zambia, and Zimbabwe, where the struggle has persisted for some time. In Niger and

Mali, previously non-independent union movements made the linkage between economic and political struggles only during the conflict in 1989–91. Despite legislation in South Africa and Namibia permitting unions, unions were engaged in harsh union recognition struggles against white employers in racist regimes and understood their political vulnerability.

It has to be added that there were often hesitations and divisions among union leaders in challenging the state. The stakes were high for union leaders and for union survival itself. Governments freely used their coercive power to try to intimidate or arrest union leaders and strikers, to dismiss workers, and to shoot or beat demonstrators. Such divisions and hesitations certainly occurred in Nigeria, Ghana, Senegal, and Zimbabwe, where ZCTU, despite repeated conflicts, hesitated for years to break entirely with the ZANU-PF government and organize an opposition party. It persisted in seeking tripartite negotiations even in periods of political and electoral conflict in order to retain access to government. In Côte d'Ivoire and Algeria the major protests and strikes may have used union organization at the base level, but they occurred without leadership support. The NLC and constituent unions in Nigeria had their leaders summarily dismissed and union organizations taken over by the state in 1988 and 1994–98 after national strikes, leading to major inter-union conflicts over tactics. The NLC was threatened with legal dissolution in 2004–2006 because of protests and strikes against gas prices.

In many countries protests against economic conditions and government policies had increased greatly in the late 1980s. African economies in general declined economically in the 1980s (-2.4 percent GDP per capita) vs. the 1970s (-0.2 percent) and the 1960s (+1.4 percent) (Kraus 1995, A61). Strikes and protests occurred in five of the seven countries, with the lowest growth rates in the 1986–90 period (+1 percent-negative: Algeria, Benin, Zambia, Côte d'Ivoire, and Gabon). In only three of twelve states with moderate growth (1-3 percent) were there significant protests (Congo Republic, CAR, and Niger). Of seventeen states with more than 3 percent growth, only three (Mali, Nigeria, and Senegal) had substantial protests and strikes (Kraus 1995, A61). But the breadth of protests in Africa is explained by the fact that even in those states that did experience gains in economic growth in 1986–90—such as Ghana, Mali, and Nigeria—workers and the urban population were experiencing the same grave economic difficulties and sharply falling living standards as those in the lowest growth states. This greatly weakened regime legitimacy, as did sharp pay cuts in some states and constant and lengthy delays in paying the already diminished wages. *The imposition of SAPs in many of these countries forced states to adopt macro- and microeconomic policies that led to public and private sector layoffs, rising unemployment, disruptions in collective bargaining, rising food prices, and sharply falling or stagnant real wages. As the cases of Senegal (Bergen), Niger (Charlick), Ghana (Kraus), Zimbabwe (Saunders), and Zambia (Akwetey/Kraus) emphasize, governments' implementation of SAPs provoked major populist protests and strikes.* This was also true in other states where there were successful protests that led to democratization or movement toward transitions, as in Nigeria (1987–88), Algeria, Côte d'Ivoire, Benin, Congo Republic, and Mali.

Moreover, these strikes and protests had a high tendency to move into generalized protests against the political system for several reasons. First, SAPs invariably had, initially at least, distinctly negative impacts on living standards, especially in urban areas: among the impacts were reduced public expenditures and services; market liberalization, which raised food, transport, and utility costs; and layoffs of public and private sector workers. Second, unionists did not see the impacts of SAPs as flowing from market forces but from the specific decisions of governments. Perhaps the most sensitive, apart from ending food subsidies, was currency devaluations, which immediately raised the price of all imports, transport (imported oil), and, hence, local foods staples. SAPs were politicized further because governments tended to crack down harshly on the labor movements in order to undermine opposition to SAP policies, which was invariably led by unions. In addition, the decision of governments in Zambia and Ghana to embrace neoliberal IMF reform programs followed the governments' prior support for more redistributive or populist policies, which was a shock for the unions. Similarly, COSATU leaders were angry when the ANC abandoned the redistributive economic program on which it ran for office in 1994 for a more neoliberal one. Bratton and van de Walle confirm that the number of SAPs correlated highly with politically destabilizing protests (1997, 149–51).

In conclusion, the origins of union protests and strikes flowed from economic deprivation, the specific anger about the pain inflicted by SAPs, and from opposition to authoritarian political regimes that inflicted such measures and sought to crush labor's representative rights.

Apart from economic and political conditions, do our case studies suggest that the trade union protests were more likely to happen as a consequence of (a) qualities of the trade union movement itself, (b) the type of political regime or regime antecedents, or (c) colonial heritage? Important qualities of a trade union movement that can potentially affect its capacity to launch protests and strikes include: its relative autonomy or independence or history of being independent; the size of the union movement, absolute size or size relative to the total labor force; and its strategic position in the economy (Kraus 1988). Looking at Table 9.1, one can see that the countries where trade union movements played significant roles in generating democratization (in bold) tend overwhelmingly to be from countries, as of 1989, that were (a) white minority ruled (and where there was some tradition of associational group freedoms, even if restricted to whites); (b) relatively democratic systems (some degree of political competition and elections); or (c) countries that had previously had some period of democratic rule. In these countries during democratic periods the trade union movements had developed substantial independence and had engaged in strike and protest behavior. In all eight cases where protests/strikes were important within these three categories of countries, union movements had some or substantial autonomy in practice, while some were relatively strong and others weak (in activities, organization, persistence over time—see Table 9.1 note). In those countries which had authoritarian regimes of one kind or another largely since independence, in only 25 percent of cases (seven of twenty-eight) did major strikes and protests lead to a transition to democracy (whether aborted or not): Algeria, Malawi, Congo Republic, Mali, Niger, Central African Republic, and Côte d'Ivoire. In only two of these countries had there been any periods of trade union autonomy. The last five countries noted were all relatively small Francophone countries, with small wage labor forces. Thus, ten of the fifteen cases (67 percent) where trade union protests played a large role in democratization involved countries where there was trade union autonomy or periods of such autonomy. If one excludes Nigeria and Algeria, where the democratization process was aborted, in 62 percent of the cases (eight of thirteen) the trade unions, or working classes whose protests were key to democratization, involved unions with either long-term or intermittent autonomy.

Hence, a history of union autonomy appears important in determining in which countries powerful strikes and protests to support democracy would occur. Trade union autonomy seems more important than simply the *number* of unions, which Bratton and van de Walle found highly correlated with the outbreak of protests (1997, 148–51).

Still, it seems significant that substantial union/worker protests broke out in countries that were authoritarian and where union movements had previously been tightly controlled, as in Niger, Mali, CAR, and Malawi, for instance. In the first three, Francophone countries, secondary schoolteacher unions and technical unions with more educated civil servants, which had grown since independence, often led the way (Bergen and Charlick chapters). And in all four cases, the political liberalization has permitted the union movements to maintain the independence they acquired in 1990–92, though in some cases—most notably, Central African Republic—only in the face of sustained government hostility and violence (ICFTU, 1995–2005). In Algeria (Chikhi, 1991) and Côte d'Ivoire major worker protests occurred without, and sometimes against, trade union leadership, and they were important in sparking a democratic transition. But in neither of these cases were the major unions able to acquire union independence, though a small union federation in Côte d'Ivoire, *Dignite*, has tried to develop its autonomy.

Relative or absolute trade union size was not directly related to a major strike/protest role in democratization, as one can see in Table 9.2. Our cases include union movements with the largest and smallest size in Africa: South Africa with more than 2.5 million union members and five union federations; Ghana with roughly 300,000 members (with a lot more in 1990); Zambia with 240,000 to 300,000; Zimbabwe with about 150,000 to 200,000 in the 1990–2004 period; and smaller union movements in Senegal, Namibia, and Niger—all of which also had much smaller populations. In the Anglophone countries, teachers were organized in associations, not unions, with about 100,000 in Ghana and 43,000 in Zambia. Major protest strikes also occurred in Nigeria, with about 2 million members in 1994, which challenged military rule successfully in 1993, but no democratic transition occurred until later. On solely economic issues the unions plus student protests in 1987–88 were able to bring Nigeria to a halt, though unionized workers are a small percentage of the labor force (Beckman 1995, 2000; Fashoyin 1990; Ihonvbere 1997). Large worker strikes and protests also occurred in other countries with relatively small unionized labor forces: Côte d'Ivoire, Mali, Central African Republic, and Malawi. In these cases, as well as those in Senegal and Niger, however, it was often crucial that urban labor segments were engaged in strikes and protests: the strongly organized teachers' unions and important skilled segments of the public sector labor force (Bergen and Charlick chapters).

The degree of democracy and of a democratic ethos within unions is probably related to a readiness to strike and protest, to hold union leaders accountable, and to induce union leaders to pursue worker interests strongly. And this tends to drive union center leaders to demand the right to participate in the making of the crucial economic decisions that structure workers' lives and fortunes. Regularly elected rather than bureaucratic authoritarian or imposed leaders are undoubtedly more responsive to worker grievances and infringements of union rights. We have insufficient information on democracy within unions in our cases and in Africa generally. Still, there is evidence that democratically elected leadership and unions with a strong democratic ethos probably correlate with those unions that have fought to remain independent of state power. As noted, autonomous unions tend to occur in countries that are, or have been intermittently, democratic. Also, the movement toward autonomy in many countries has come from below, from workers angry with SAP policies and attempts to choke off protests, as in Zambia, Zimbabwe, Ghana, Senegal, and Nigeria, all of which have had some autonomy (see Table 9.1 for others). These unions elected and supported leaders in national unions and in federations who were responsive to worker demands and strikes from below. Democratic union practices and traditions are noted in the chapters on South Africa, Ghana, Zimbabwe, Zambia, and Senegal (in small unions) and are also found in Nigeria. It is the upward transmission of protests to which democratic leaders must be responsive in order to keep their positions, which offsets the downward pressures of force and co-optation by political leaders (Kraus 1979; Sandbrook 1981).

The nature of the regime does not *seem* a significant differentiator for where trade union actions fostered democratization, since almost by definition virtually all the regimes were authoritarian. However, as noted earlier, 62 percent of the cases in which trade union strikes and protests helped animate democratic transitions involved countries in which there had developed in the current or past regimes significant qualities of associational group freedoms and democratic processes (see Table 9.1). Despite their clear authoritarianism, many of the other countries (Congo Republic, Côte d'Ivoire, Mali, Niger) had regular (if pro forma) elections in the one-party systems, and several had developed competitive elections within the party for legislative seats (e.g., Côte d'Ivoire). Bratton and van de Walle also found that the number of prior elections was one of the most important factors associated with political protest (1997, 151).

There is no obvious distinction between countries of different colonial heritages in terms of where trade union protests were critical. Of the fifteen countries listed in Table 9.1, seven had British-rooted colonial antecedents, and eight had French colonial backgrounds. However, other things being equal, one would expect that the trade union movements in Anglophone countries would be stronger and maintain greater independence. The British trade union practices and norms involve central roles for local and national unions in collective bargaining and grassroots activities. Labor legislation and union rules recognize this. They also have participatory and democratic norms. Bergen notes that in Senegal, as in much of Francophone Africa, the factory or organization-level activities of unions are insignificant; in practice, there is virtually no institutionalization of collective bargaining with private sector firms or the national government. This removes from the grassroots level a major activity around which mobilization occurs. In Francophone Africa national governments have tended to set the wages for the most important sectors of the labor force that private sector firms often follow. While this does tend to politicize wage discussions, it also tends to make the union grass roots atrophy. This makes state repression and the manipulation of national union leaders easier.

Trade Unions in Post-Transition Democratic Life

Our third major interest in this volume has been what the roles of trade unions have been in the newly democratized polities where they have survived. First, in all the cases in this volume and in Nigeria, democratic life has persisted, with a serious interruption in Niger where the military overthrew a deadlocked government in 1996 and remained in power tenuously until new elections in 1999 restored democratic rule. In Ghana and Senegal former ruling parties and their leadership were removed in elections widely regarded as fair, and multiple parties still contest for power (see Table 9.3). In South Africa, Namibia, Zambia, and Nigeria, there have been repeated free elections and a change in the leadership of the party in power, but no change in the party holding power since the democratic transition. In Nigeria the 2007 elections, whose outcome has been highly disputed, involved change in at least the president. And elections are seriously undermined by fraud. In Zimbabwe democratic competition is alive but kept under desperate siege by Mugabe's militarized government. The labor-organized opposition party and the unions have suffered massive arrests and intimidation in organizing. There has been no democratic transition.

Has there been a throttling of trade union activities and protests in the new democracies? In Table 9.4 we have summarized some of the crucial qualities of union-state interactions in the countries studied. In most of the eight countries, trade unions have maintained a substantial autonomy of organization and action, with a few exceptions. In Namibia, the main union federation (National Union of Namibian Workers [NUNW]) remains linked to SWAPO, with efforts to break this linkage effectively crushed at the federation's conventions (Bauer chapter). NUNW leaders are still represented on major SWAPO political committees, which probably serve as a SWAPO influence on NUNW rather than the other way around. In South Africa COSATU is clearly constrained by its alliance with the ANC, but COSATU has substantial leverage to oppose strongly and publicly the ANC, and it does. In Senegal the small trade unions remain autonomous, while the CNTS remains strongly linked to the previously dominant party, now in opposition. But it seems to have more freedom of action now that the PS is no longer the government. In Nigeria the often militant Nigerian Labor Congress (NLC) has a high level of autonomy. But military governments have in the past eradicated this autonomy by decree, taking over union assets, offices, and resources while dismissing the elected leaders, who reemerge with the next elections. The NLC is again under attack by the democratic Nigerian government for its powerful opposition to increased fuel prices. It faced intense state intimidation in 2004–2005. The state introduced to the National Assembly legislation to de-register the NLC and affiliate unions and to abolish automatic check-off, that is, to cripple the movement. And the Nigerian government has periodically detained and beaten its major leaders, without deterring union protests. In five of the countries there is no violence or intimidation visited by the state upon the trade unions, despite their strikes and protests. But in Zimbabwe, where the ZCTU also organized the main opposition party, major violence and intimidation have been inflicted upon ZCTU's leadership, especially during 2000–2006. In Niger this was also true up to 1999, when democracy was restored.

In many other African countries where democratization movements increased the level of political freedoms, trade unions have confronted major levels of intimidation, violence, and intolerance as they have sought to exercise their rights. This is true in CAR, Guinea, Nigeria, Swaziland, Tanzania, Rwanda, and Tunisia, which had until the mid-1980s one of Africa's strongest union movements (ICFTU 1995–2005; Zeghidi 1995).

In all the country cases, governments have moved from previous attempts at primarily *corporatist labor control strategies* to *liberal market control strategies*. The corporatist design includes some form of alliance between government/party and unions, or state incorporation of unions, as a means of providing labor with some stake while controlling it through co-optation of leaders and coercion. The liberal market control strategy is where there are no formal controls, but supportive labor legislation and policies are reduced. Labor markets as well as others are "liberalized," making dismissals easier and reducing support for collective bargaining and union organizing. The state uses divide and rule strategies, tough legislation, and some coercion to weaken labor. The *corporatist labor control strategy* was previously the model in Namibia, Zambia, Zimbabwe (before 1988–89), Senegal, and Niger. In South Africa the alliance and "corporatism" were initially consensual: there were major efforts to develop co-determination types of structures in labor policy. In Ghana the PNDC regime during 1982–92 tried to incorporate a resistant union movement and quickly resorted to exclusion and coercion with labor market liberalization. And the modest corporatist components of Nigerian labor strategies (establishing the NLC and

Table 9.3 Persistence of Democracy in Selected African Countries

Countries	Multiple parties?	Change in parties in power?	Change in leaders?	Relatively free elections and participation?
South Africa*	Yes	No, after 1st coalition gov't.	Yes	Yes
Namibia	Yes	No	Yes	Yes
Zambia	Yes	No	Yes	Yes
Zimbabwe	Yes	No	No	No, high intimidation, fraud
Ghana	Yes	Yes	Yes	Yes
Senegal	Yes	Yes	Yes	Yes
Niger*	Yes	Yes	Yes	Yes
Nigeria	Yes	No	Yes	Qualified yes; corrupt

*Niger had a president from one party in 1993, a military government 1996-99, and a different president from another party elected in 1999. In South Africa, the first government representing all South Africans was a unity government of the ANC and Nationalist Party (former ruling party) formed after the 1993 elections. After 1999 elections, the ANC ruled alone.

Table 9.4 Union Participation in Democratic Life in the Post-Transition Era, Early 1990s Forward

Country	Union autonomy		Violence & intimidation against unions*	Unions engaged w/ public issues high–medium–low	Union links w/ political parties	Unions organized parties
	Full	Partial				
South Africa	Yes		No	Yes, high	Yes	No, but key in party organization
Namibia		Some, w/ SWAPO leaders	No	Not clear	Yes, SWAPO	No
Zambia	Yes		Yes, attacks against critical union leaders, arrests, deregistration of unions, union election interference	Yes, medium high	Yes, in early 1990s, not now	Yes
Zimbabwe	Yes		Yes, by government; constant harassment, threats, & violence	Yes, high	Yes, with the major opposition party	Yes
Ghana	Yes		No, not after 1991	Yes, medium high	No	No
Senegal	Small unions	Main federation	No	Low	Yes: small unions, only via leaders; main federation affiliated to ruling party 1968–2000	No
Niger	Yes		Occasional	Yes, low	No	No
Nigeria	Yes, but intermittently banned by government		Yes, dismissals, intimidation, & arrests to deter strikes & protests	Yes, high	No, but briefly in early 1990s in political transition	No

*Does not refer to police violence coincident to industrial protests. For levels of violence and intimidation, see ICFTU, *Annual survey(s) of Violations of Trade Union Rights*, annual reports, 1991–2005.

check-off) are offset by banning union activity intermittently. In all the democracies now, the states pursue liberal market strategies; this includes South Africa, despite the corporatist qualities of the ANC-COSATU alliance and cooperative structures. The neoliberal market policies make regime alliances with labor very difficult, since most policies are unfavorable to trade unions.

In virtually all these countries the unions have remained vitally involved in addressing major public policy issues, especially those in education, employment, and the economy. The governments have been involved in implementing SAPs and neoliberal economic policies, reducing state economic roles, and liberalizing labor markets. This has drawn the constant opposition of the trade unions. This union attention to public policies, roughly judged, seems to occur at a high level in South Africa, Zimbabwe, Zambia, and Nigeria, at a little lower level in Ghana, and at a much lower level in Niger and Senegal (perhaps partly because of lack of resources to assess economic policies). Where unions are directly linked to political parties, some of this policy contestation occurs within the party. But much of its takes place in the public domain as well as at party and union conferences. In South Africa and Namibia the union movements are linked to a party in power, though the role of COSATU is a much larger one than NUNW's because of its past role in the ANC, its autonomy, its size, and its mobilizing capacities. In Senegal and Zimbabwe trade unions are allied with parties that are not in power. While the ZCTU gave birth to the MMD in Zambia in 1990, once the MMD became the governing party, it broke from its ZCTU base. Indeed, the MMD worked to divide and weaken the union movement, with some success, because of pressures to implement tough SAP policies (Akwetey/Kraus chapter). The ZCTU has distanced itself from MMD and tended to support opposition parties in the 2006 elections. In Ghana, Niger, Nigeria, and currently in Zambia, the unions are purposely not linked with any political parties. Partisan linkages would and do divide the unions.

Critics of trade unions have argued that while they might mobilize disorderly strikes and protests to weaken authoritarian regimes, they failed to contribute to the democratization process after this. Barchiesi criticizes the inability of unions to lead political transformations. When mass mobilization "had to be translated into programs and institutional arrangements, labor turned out to be the missing link. It generally proved unable to overcome entrenched social divides and to shape alternative political coalitions" (1996, 352). African trade unions have not been revolutionary instruments of social change. Its members often have only a populist political consciousness (Sandbrook 1981). However, economic, political, and organizational conditions have tended to radicalize workers and unions at critical times and push them into demanding radical changes, such as highly participatory labor roles, greater access to political power, and a strong voice in determining crucial public policies, such as in Zambia, Zimbabwe, Ghana, and South Africa. As such, they have indeed been able "to shape alternative political coalitions," as the leading roles of the unions in Zambia (before and after democratization), Zimbabwe, and South Africa clearly show (Akwetey/Kraus, Saunders, and Freund chapters, respectively). In doing so, unions and their members displayed a determined political consciousness to pursue not only union concerns but also broader social and economic interests shared with the popular classes.

Drawing upon examples from the South Africa, Ghana, and Zimbabwe chapters, we discuss the evidence of more modest union contributions to post-democratization political processes in certain domains:

(a) elections;
(b) political party activities and organization;
(c) participation in interest and civic group coalitions to create alternative public policies;
(d) interest group advocacy in existing institutions (e.g., parliaments);
(e) institutional representation in government; and
(f) protest activity to effect changes in key government policies.

But these activities have to be seen within the overarching structure of the democratized systems. That structure is, in most instances, one where the new governments are ruling in implicit coalition with the IMF-World Bank-foreign donors as major partners who help to develop a liberal capitalist pattern of development in which the range of policies and the roles of unions are tightly circumscribed. This contradiction is the source of the recurring conflicts in policies and vision between unions and the new democratizing states regarding what the government should be doing. Some of these policies may indeed be increasing productive capacities and the range of goods available, but the beneficiaries are overwhelmingly located in a narrow stratum at the top of the class structure.

In South Africa, COSATU and its affiliates continued to play a huge role in the ANC during the elections of the 1990s and after. Union leaders and members were heavily involved in ANC organization in the 1994 and 1999 elections. As many as sixty COSATU union leaders won ANC seats in parliament and in regional councils. Union organization was drawn into election activities, with individual unions releasing a full-time official and shop stewards to campaign (Freund chapter; Ginsburg et al. 1995). As part of the Triple Alliance with the ANC and the Communist Party of South Africa (SACP), COSATU and its affiliate unions had initially been able to help craft an alternative Reconstruction and Development Program (RDP); to push for its adoption by the ANC; to have the COSATU secretary-general (Jay Naidoo) appointed as a minister to coordinate it; and to get a National Economic Development and Labor Council (NEDLAC) established, with COSATU representation. NEDLAC presents possibilities for COSATU to participate in crucial policy decisions with the corporate sector and within and across different sectors of the ANC government. NEDLAC attainments have been limited thus far, partly by state policy prerogatives, but there is no equivalent institutional role for labor in Africa (Adler 2000; Desai and Habib 1997).

But, as Freund observes, by 1996–97, the Triple Alliance had effectively been dissolved. COSATU alliance with the ANC choked off its more radical aspirations as the ANC leadership negotiated a transition conducive to retaining the existing structures of capitalist power, in the belief that this assured economic growth and jobs. Clearly, the state had acquired the upper hand and has scolded or castigated its constant critics in COSATU during 1996–2006 (Freund chapter in present volume; McKinley 2004; Webster and Adler 2001). However, COSATU aligns itself on various issues with the SACP and has reached out to civic groups to support alternative policies to those of the ANC. It supported land reform favoring rural workers. It continues, with varying vigor, to articulate COSATU interests and preferences in parliament and in government forums. Intra-ANC struggles, as occurred in 2006–07 over future ANC leadership, increases COSATU's influence. But there are criticisms that COSATU unions compromise the interests of labor.

Ghana's TUC has refused to align with any party. But key union leaders in 1979–81 made efforts to try to preserve democracy. Union leaders were joyous at the return to democratic rule in 1993 and knew its incredible value to unions. They had regained access to the media and could organize and demonstrate without fear of jail threats and harassment. In the absence of any parliamentary opposition in 1993–96, the TUC believed that it had to represent alternative views to the public, and it did so in the press and through lobbying. And in 1996–2000 most union leaders were sympathetic to the efforts of the opposition New Patriotic Party (NPP) to defeat the incumbent NDC government, which in its authoritarian days (1982–92) had so attacked the TUC. Its advocacy of democracy induced the unions to work closely with civic groups in major efforts to monitor elections to ensure their fairness in 1992–2004. In 2004 the TUC invited presidential candidates to its conference to bid for labor votes. Unions reached out to align themselves with, or support, other civic groups on a range of issues, such as to oppose for years (with some success) the privatization of the urban water supply and to protest rising education charges, utility rate hikes, and the passage of a VAT tax. The TUC organized large conferences in 1993 and 1996 on the costs of SAPs. When President Jerry Rawlings attacked some major Ghanaian entrepreneurs, the TUC quickly organized with the Association of Ghanaian Industries a "buy Ghana and save our jobs" campaign. A senior TUC official monitored activities in the National Assembly, and the TUC appeared before its committees to testify and lobby on legislation, trade, tax, and wage issues. It broadened the labor front by bringing the teachers, civil servant, and nurses associations into tripartite meetings with government and business. It also took the initiative to organize retreats with business and government representatives to hammer out areas of agreement on a new labor code and minimum wage guidelines (Kraus chapter).

Probably the ZCTU in Zimbabwe has developed more extensive ties with civic groups than in most African countries, as from the early 1990s on it sought broad support for its protests against the ZANU-PF government's implementation of SAP policies (Saunders chapter). As it found itself under consistent attack, it reached out to student, church, business, retail market women, and many other types of associations and civics to protest to the government the horrendous impact of SAP on standards of living. By the late 1990s it needed even more strongly to develop support, extending into the rural areas to build the base for the new opposition party, MDC, which the ZCTU successfully organized (Saunders). In Zambia, too, where the labor-organized party ruled in a democratic Zambia, the unions and workers as well as most Zambians fared poorly under new SAP policies, with massive declines in living standards during 1990–2002. Gradually the ZCTU, with new leadership, reestablished its autonomy and survived myriad attempts to weaken it. It worked again in 1998–2006 with many civic and associational groups to pose alternative policies and to organize against the government's policies (Akwetey/Kraus chapter).

Unions in many other countries have shown a capacity to engage in democratic public arenas in behalf of their interests, including those in Nigeria, Namibia, Niger, and Senegal. But, as noted below, union efforts have frequently foundered against the shoals of IMF-World Bank-foreign donor influence with Africa's governments.

The Multiple Impacts of Structural Adjustment on Trade Unions and Democracy

There has been a long, unresolved debate on the relative nature and impact of SAP policies on African economies and various sectors and social classes. No doubt, African countries had to reform their economies under the incredibly bad economic conditions of the 1980s, to reduce state expenditures that could not be sustained, and to permit market signals to govern some major allocations. But the evidence is overwhelming that SAPs have often been unsuccessful, have been applied as rigid formulas, and have had very damaging effects upon many economies and on the incomes of formal sector workers (Broad 1988; Gibbon 1993, 1995; Helleiner 1990; Killick 1995; Kraus 1991; Sachs 1998; Stiglitz 2002, chapters 2 and 3). SAP policies, including currency devaluations, have had some positive impacts. But probably a greater positive impact has stemmed simply from the larger inflows of foreign aid that were conditioned on implementation of SAPs and neoliberal policies. But these policies have increased economic and social inequality in Africa, as elsewhere, including in industrialized countries. They have also undermined national bases of industrial capacity, which, in their weakened state, cannot compete with efficiently produced imports. The insistence of IMF, the World Bank, and foreign donors that only a liberal economy in a globalized world constitutes a viable path to development is pursued religiously, despite evidence that there are multiple paths to development and that globalization costs are profound (Baker et al. 1998; Berger and Dore 1996; Greider 1997; Haggard 1990; Sklair 1994; Stiglitz 2002; Wade 1990, 1998). Some argue that it is government agreement, not IMF/World Bank/foreign donor economic coercion, that led to implementation of SAP reforms (Hanson and Hentz 1999). Clearly, some governments have agreed with *some* reforms. But economic coercion in the form of cutting off loans and aid is frequently imposed for failures to implement individual policies. As Zambia's finance minister noted in 2003, "We are running the country, but the budget is controlled by donors" (Larmer 2005, 42).

Many criticisms of SAPs and their impact on standards of living by African governments, economists, and even some donor governments led to slight changes in the nature of these programs in the 1990s. The huge unpopularity of SAPs among civil society groups, and findings that there had been declines in health and educational standards partly because of SAP-imposed budgetary spending limits and "user fees," helped to propel this change. Strong pressures also arose for a reduction in the unsustainable debt burdens of African countries, which led to an initiative by donors for Highly Indebted Poor Countries. Countries could get their debt reduced greatly if they, in (often perfunctory) consultation with civil society groups in their countries, designed a Poverty Reduction Strategy Paper (PRSP), which then required the approval of the boards of the World Bank and IMF. Under PSRPs, governments still had to pursue the same structural adjustment programs as before. But if they achieved certain performance levels—such as reducing budget deficits and government staff, privatizing the major state industries, etc.—the IMF, the World Bank, and major donor countries would cut their debt by a large percentage. The funds formerly destined for debt repayments, plus new aid, would be targeted at poverty reduction in the areas of health, education, and social services (see Akwetey/Kraus chapter for how this played out).

The impact of SAPs and their close cousins, PRSPs, on workers and trade unions and exposure to the new international division of labor have been multiple. They affect levels of formal sector wage employment, ease of dismissals, union membership, and the resources that unions possess in order to carry out their activities. There are few accurate statistics on formal sector employment, though Anglophone state labor departments used to collect them. The total indifference of the IMF and the World Bank to generating employment, in contrast to labor market liberalization (World Bank 1995), means that of all the many statistics African governments have been compelled to develop, none involves the changing size of the wage/salary labor force. South Africa does collect data but did not have IMF-imposed SAPs during 1993–2006. It had real growth in jobs in the 1996–2002 period, but unemployment increased annually, rising from 20 percent to 30.5 percent (strictly defined) during 1994–2002, or 28.6 percent to 41.8 percent (Altman 2005, 425–30). We can estimate roughly the effects of SAPs on the size of the wage/salary labor force by two measures: changes in the state sector and changes in trade union membership. As contributors note, state sector employment has shrunk sharply through layoffs in all African states except, perhaps, South Africa, which had its post-independence expansion only after 1994. Increases in state salary budgets were used, at the World Bank's direction, to expand wage differentials in order to provide greater incentives for high-level manpower. Our chapters detail the job losses in state and private sectors. Labor regulations were eased, or ignored, to permit the state to downsize, a source of many strikes.

Table 9.2 has some data on trade union membership drawn from the chapters, though it is inadequate for across-time comparisons. South Africa's union membership rose sharply in the late 1980s and early 1990s, but there seems to have been some reduction in 2000–2005. Nigeria's union membership has declined greatly since the 1994 figure of 2 million, as continuous budgetary crises have led to a shedding of state workers, the largest percentage of unionized workers. Ghana's union membership grew until the mid-1980s. The figure for 2004 shows a drop of more than 50 percent of members from 1990, largely from state layoffs, though prior membership was exaggerated. In Zimbabwe, Saunders's chapter documents the loss of jobs under SAP, which was also felt in union membership (see Table 9.2). In Zambia the wide-scale dismissal of state workers, especially mineworkers, had debilitating effects upon the unions and union morale (Akwetey/Kraus chapter). This is reflected in the 32 percent drop in union members during 1989–2001. We have only single time counts of union members in Namibia, Senegal, and Niger, but the chapters on the latter two relate that the crises with labor reflected both major state downsizing and also endless arrears in wage/salary payments (Charlick and Bergen chapters, respectively).

The major layoffs of state sector workers as a result of SAP policies requiring budget reductions and closure or sale of state corporations have greatly increased the growth of casual labor, the informal sector, and unemployment. For some years African economies have been unable to absorb even the secondary school and college educated into the formal sector labor force, a process accelerated by hiring freezes and layoffs. The salaried middle class has shrunk (Packer 2006, 69). With regulations changed to facilitate state layoffs, the formal private sector also quickly shed workers in many countries. This reflects the ability of both sectors to employ workers on a casual, hence cheaper, basis from among the huge pool of unemployed, including the educated. The layoffs have led to a growing rise in casual labor: that is, workers are hired for a specific job, for example, in construction, or on a daily or short-term contract basis, unprotected by state regulations or unions. This has been accelerated by the creation of Export Processing Zones (EPZs) in many African countries, where unions are forcefully discouraged when not prohibited from operating. Industrial and other firms there are dismissing permanent employees in favor of contract workers (ICFTU 2005, 2006). In turn, the informal sector, not bound by labor regulations, has expanded, for example, in construction and commerce at every level, where job security is zero, pay is low, and benefits are nonexistent. These layoffs have led to a huge decline in union size in many countries (see Table 9.3). Despite twenty years of economic growth in Ghana, formal sector employment has fallen and union membership has contracted sharply in *all areas* (Kraus chapter), as it has elsewhere in Africa (see Table 9.2). The labor market is thus sharply segmented in wages and benefits between formal sector workers and casual and informal sector workers.

The sharp decline in union membership has led directly to a fall in union revenues and resources. This has eroded the ability of unions to retain organizers to work with unions. A shrinkage in such union activities as meetings, educational seminars, and delegates congresses has occurred, as has the need for union movements to develop mergers among smaller unions. But the merger of diverse workers into a single union can reduce the rank and file's sense of solidarity with their unions. South African, Ghanaian, and Nigerian unions have recently moved toward merging unions. Falling union membership and resources can also generate conservative behavior among leaders and rank and file, making them less likely to assert their rights or contest management. Still, union shrinkages have not reduced strikes and protests in Ghana, South Africa, Zambia, Nigeria, and Zimbabwe.

SAPs have also significantly increased the cost of living to people in urban economies who formerly received certain services, such as pipe-borne water, electricity, education, mail, and transport. The solution to the need to increase revenues to pay for these services has led to "cost recovery" service charges. These greatly increased the cost of living for the urban populace and often made these services unavailable to those who once had them (McDonald and Pape 2002).

Conclusion

Trade unions in Africa have clearly contributed powerfully, and at different stages, to the democratization process in Africa. In the chapters and this conclusion we have detailed the case for the significance of trade unions in democratization and its vitality. But we are aware of the weaknesses of trade unions: their problems in organizing under current economic conditions; the extent of the state's ability, even in democracies, to manipulate and harass union movements; declining union membership; and problems of internal union democracy. The relatively low levels of economic growth and of wage labor in African societies, the deregulation of labor markets, and the pressures on governments from donors to depress wages all create profound problems for union organizing and representation. Moreover, the economic crises that helped to propel the overthrow of authoritarian regimes because of the pain of SAP economic reforms have persisted, as have the harsh policy measures. Where economic growth has led to evident general improvements, for example, in Ghana and South Africa, economic inequalities have demonstrably increased. Astute observers of the historical role of unions in democracy have noted that in this current era of democratization there has developed a growing tendency toward inequality rather than the egalitarian tendencies of earlier democratic periods (Huber, Rueschemeyer, and Stephens 1997). This is related to the dynamics of globalization and the capitalist international division of labor in this era (Southall 1988a, 1988b).

Still, trade unions in many African states have persisted, have become more powerful public, collective actors, and have a major public voice in those countries with moderate-sized wage labor forces. This includes South Africa, Ghana, Zimbabwe, Zambia, and Nigeria (Andrae and Beckman 1998). These larger trade union movements are more likely to be able to sustain their independence, organization, and ability to project their views publicly than smaller unions. Some now have continuous histories of forty to sixty years of struggle and representation. They embody in their several generations of leaders at different union levels their recent histories of social and political struggles, organizational skills, strategic lessons learned, and a democratic dynamic that keeps leaders responsive. Unions in countries with smaller wage labor and union forces—as in Senegal, Niger, and Namibia—may well be intermittently significant because of their strategic location and the qualities listed above that they share with larger union movements. For example, despite the high levels of authoritarianism in Guinea and long-term repression of union activities, the labor center started to demand major changes with a two-day general strike in November 2005. Facing continued stagnation in living standards and a nonresponsive government, Guinea's labor center launched an unlimited general strike in January 2007. Despite many deaths and arrests, it persisted for eighteen days and closed schools, government, and commercial life through much of the country until the ailing president promised to nominate a prime minister acceptable to key constituencies. When the president appointed a crony, the unions renewed the general strike and their demand for democratic responsiveness, forcing the appointment of a new prime minister (*Africa Focus Bulletin*, January 31, 2007).

Trade unions are also the largest, and sometimes only, significant organizational force that represents the interests of *the popular classes, the nonelite*. Some have argued that the demands of relatively highly paid civil servants and teachers (usually a small percent of labor) for higher wages are inegalitarian in the context of African political economies, many of which remain largely rural. However, most wage workers are not highly paid and have suffered real wage losses for years. In elite-dominated polities,

African unions represent the interests of the popular classes in key senses. Many union efforts have focused on raising minimum wages to offset inflation or on creating a national minimum. Unions often represent the popular classes on key public policies where they share interests and protests with urban residents, including taxes, keeping governments accountable, and obtaining broader access to affordable public education, health clinics, transportation, and public utilities.

Will trade unions continue to support democratic paths and institutions if they find that they are suffering economically and are unheard by those in power? Neoliberal "development" is, sadly, one where actual increases in productive and human capabilities and well-being often fail to occur despite some economic growth. Actual development appears to be entirely elusive to ordinary Africans and unionists. Despite worker protests, union leaders in many countries have accepted the need for some painful SAP reforms, such as closing or privatizing nonproductive state firms. But unionists find it difficult to discern positive state activity to stimulate *national* production and employment—goals that the World Bank championed in the 1970s. African countries cannot begin to absorb productively the new job seekers in the modern or informal labor sectors. Political leaders in many of these countries ardently seek foreign capital as their political and economic salvation, but little arrives that is not in the mining/oil sectors. Union members in most countries hear and read about blatant self-enrichment and corruption among the new democratic leaders, particularly in Zambia, South Africa, and Nigeria. Driven by rank-and-file-anger, the explosions of labor protest of 1988–91 and after can easily reoccur if the nascent democracies cannot give workers and unions some palpable sense that some improvements and jobs are part of their life chances. If democracies cannot provide workers with this, the next time that military leaders claim power, with mantras to end corruption, re-create order, and nationalize foreign capital, unions may hear in this the promise of progress as they have before.

References

Adler, Glenn, 2000. Engaging the state and business. In *Engaging the state and business*, ed. Glenn Adler, 1–32. Johannesburg, South Africa:Witwatersrand University Press.

Adler, Glenn, and Eddie Webster. 1995. Challenging transition theory: The labor movement, radical reform, and transition to democracy in South Africa. *Politics and Society* 23 (March): 75–106.

Africa Focus Bulletin. 2007. January 31. http://www.africafocus.org/country/guinea_news.php.

Altman, Miriam. 2005. The state of employment. In *State of the nation: South Africa 2004-2005*, ed. J. Daniel, R. Southall, and J. Lutchman, 423–54. Cape Town: HSRC Press.

Andrae, Gunilla, and Bjorn Beckman. 1998. *Union power in the Nigerian textile industry.* Uppsala, Sweden: Nordiska Afrikainstitutet.

Baker, Dean, Gerald Epstein, and Robert Pollin, eds. 1998. *Globalization and Progressive Economic Policy.* New York: Cambridge University Press.

Bangura, Yusuf. 1987. The recession and workers' struggles in the vehicle assembly plants: Streyr-Nigeria. *Review of African Political Economy* 39 (September): 4–22.

Barchiesi, Franco. 1996. The social construction of labor in the struggle for democracy: The case of post-independence Nigeria. *Review of African Political Economy* 23 (September): 349–69.

Beckman, Bjorn, 1995. The politics of labor and adjustment: The experience of the Nigeria Labor Congress. In *Between liberalization and oppression*, ed. Thandika Mkandawire and Adebayo Olukoshi, 281–323. Dakar: CODESRIA.

———. 2000. Resistance and collaboration: The Nigerian labor congress under military rule. Unpublished draft chapter.

Beckman, Bjorn, and Lloyd Sachikonye. 2001. Labor regimes and liberalization in Africa: An introduction. In *Labor regimes and liberalization*, ed. Bjorn Beckman and Lloyd Sachikonye, 10–21. Harare, Zimbabwe: University of Zimbabwe Publications.

Bergen, Geoffrey. 1994. Unions in Senegal. 2 vols. PhD diss., University of Michigan.

Berger, Suzanne and Ronald Dore, eds. 1996. *National Diversity and Global Capitalism*. Ithaca, NY: Cornell University Press.

Bermeo, Nancy. 1997. Myths of moderation: Confrontation and conflict during democratic transitions. *Comparative Politics* 29 (April): 305–21.

Bratton, Michael, and Nicholas van de Walle. 1997. *Democratic Experiments in Africa*. New York: Cambridge University Press.

Broad, Robin. 1988. *Unequal alliance: The World Bank, IMF and Philippines*. Berkeley: University of California Press.

Chikhi, Said. 1991. *Algeria: from mass rebellion in October 1988 to workers' social protest*. Current African Issues Series, no. 13. Uppsala, Sweden: Nordiska Afrikainstitutet.

Collier, Ruth Berins, and James Mahoney. 1997. Adding collective actors to collective outcomes: Labor and recent democratization in South America and southern Europe. *Comparative Politics* 29 (April): 285–303.

Cornia, Andrea and Rolph van der Hoeber, eds. 1992. *Africa's recovery in the 1990's*. New York: St. Martin's Press.

Deyo, Frederic. 1989. *Beneath the miracle: Labor subordination in the new Asian industrialism*. Berkeley: University of California Press.

Desai, Ashwin, and Adam Habib. 1997. Labor relations in transition: The rise of corporatism in South Africa's automobile industry. *Journal of Modern African Studies* 35 (September): 495–518.

Diamond, Larry. 1995. Nigeria: The uncivic society and the descent into praetorianism. In *Politics in developing countries*, ed. Larry Diamond, Juan Linz, and S. M. Lipset, 417–91. 2nd ed. Boulder, CO: Lynne Rienner.

Fashoyin, Tayo. 1990. Nigerian labor and the military: Towards exclusion? *Labour, Capital and Society* 23 (April): 12–37.

Gibbon, Peter, ed. 1993. *Social change and economic reform in Africa*. Uppsala, Sweden: Nordiska Afrikainstitutet.

———, ed. 1995. *Structural adjustment and the working poor in Zimbabwe*. Uppsala, Sweden: Nordiska Afrikainstitutet.

Ginsburg, David, Eddie Webster, Roger Southall, Geoff Wood, Sakhela Buhlungu, Johann Maree, Janet Cherry, Richard Haines, and Gilton Klerck. 1995. *Taking democracy seriously: Worker expectations and parliamentary democracy in South Africa*. Durban, South Africa: Indicator Press.

Greider, William. 1997. *One world, ready or not: The manic logic of global capitalism*. New York: Simon and Schuster.

Grimaud, Nicole. 1978. Les relations de travail en Algerie: Le Cinquieme Congres de L'UGTA. *Maghreb-Machrek* 80 (April–June): 57–62.

Haggard, Stephen. 1990. *Pathways from the Periphery*. Ithaca, NY: Cornell University Press.

Hansen, Margaret, and James Hentz. 1999. Neocolonialism and neoliberalism in South Africa and Zambia. *Political Science Quarterly* 114 (Fall): 479–502.

Heilbron, John. 1993. Social origins of national conferences in Benin and Togo. *Journal of Modern African Studies* 31 (June): 277–300.

Helleiner, G. K. 1990. Conventional foolishness and overall ignorance. *Canadian Journal of Development Studies* 10 (1): 107–20.

Huber, Evelyne, Dietrich Rueschemeyer, and John Stephens. 1997. The paradoxes of contemporary democracy. *Comparative Politics* 29 (April): 323–41.

International Confederation of Free Trade Unions. 1992–2006. *Annual survey(s) of violations of trade union rights*. Brussels, Belgium: International Confederation of Free Trade Unions.

Ihonvbere, Julius O. 1997. Organized labor and the struggle for democracy in Nigeria. *African Studies Review* 40 (December): 77–110.

Killick, Tony. 1995. *IMF programmes in developing countries: Design and impact*. London: Routledge.

Kraus, Jon. 1979. Strikes and labor power in Ghana. *Development and Change* 10 (April): 259–86.

———. 1988. The political economy of trade union-state relations in radical and populist regimes in Africa. In *Labor and trade unions in Asia and Africa*, ed. Roger Southall, 171–210. New York: St. Martin's Press.

———. 1991. The political economy of stabilization and structural adjustment in Ghana. In *Ghana: The political economy of reform*, ed. Donald Rothchild, 119–55. Boulder, CO: Lynne Rienner Publishers.

———. 1995. Trade unions and democratization in Africa. In *Africa contemporary record, 1989-1990*, ed. Marion Doro and Colin Legum, A53–A72. New York: Africana.

Larmer, Miles. 2005. Reaction and resistance to neo-liberalism in Zambia. *Review Of African Political Economy* 32, 103 (March): 29–45

Mahon, James. 1999. Economic crisis in Latin America: Global contagion, local pain. *Current History* 98 (March): 105–10.

McAdam, Douglas, Sidney Tarrow, and Charles Tilly. 2001. *Dynamics of contention*. Cambridge University Press.

McDonald, David, and John Pape. 2002. *Cost recovery and the crisis of service delivery in South Africa*. Cape Town: Human Science Research Council Press.

McKinley, Dale. 2004. Cosatu and the triple alliance since 1994. http://spip.red.m2014.net.

Muase, Charles K. 1989. *Syndicalisme et democratie en Afrique noire: L'experience du Burkina Faso (1936–1988)*. Paris: Editions Karthala.

Packer, George. 2006. The megacity: Decoding the chaos of Lagos. *New Yorker*, November 13, pp. 61–75.

Reuschmeyer, D. E., H. Stephens, J. D. Stephens. 1992. *Capitalist development and democracy*. Chicago: University of Chicago Press.

Sachs, Jeffrey. 1998. The IMF and the Asian flu. *American Prospect* (March–April): 16–21.

Sandbrook, Richard. 1981. Worker consciousness and populist protest in tropical Africa. In *Research in the sociology of work, I*, ed. Richard Simpson and I. H. Simpson, 1–36. Greenwich, CT: Jai Press.

Sklair, Leslie, ed. 1994. *Capitalism & development*. New York: Routledge.

Southall, Roger. 1988a. Introduction to *Labour and unions in Asia And Africa*, ed. Roger Southall, 1–31. London: St. Martin's Press.

———. 1988b. Introduction: At issue: Third world trade unions in the changing international division of Labor. In *Trade unions and the new industrialization of the third world*, ed. Roger Southall, 1–34. Pittsburgh: University of Pittsburgh Press.

Stiglitz, Joseph. 2002. *Globalization and its discontents*. New York: W. W. Norton.

Valenzuela, J. Samuel. 1989. Labor movements in transitions to democracy. *Comparative Politics* 21 (July): 445–71.

Villalon, Leonardo, and A. Idrissa. 2005. The tribulations of a successful transition. In *The fate of Africa's democratic experiments*, ed. Leonardo Villalon and Peter Von Doepp, 49–73. Bloomington: University of Indiana Press.

Wade, Robert. 1990. *Governing the market*. Princeton, NJ: Princeton University Press.

———. 1998. The gathering world slump and the battle over capital controls. *New Left Review* (September–October): 13–42.

Webster, Eddie, and Glenn Adler. 2001. Exodus without a map? The labor movement in a liberalizing South Africa. In *Labor regimes and liberalization*, ed. Bjorn Beckman and L.M. Sachikonye, 120–46. Harare, Zimbabwe: Zimbabwe University Press.

World Bank. 1995. *World development report 1995: Workers in an integrating world*. Washington, DC: World Bank.

Zeghidi, Salah. 1995. Tunisian trade unionism: A central pole of social and democratic challenge. In *African studies in social movements and democracy*, ed. Mahmood Mamdani and Ernest Wamba-dia-Wamba, 337–68. Dakar: CODESIRA.

Contributors

Jon Kraus, professor emeritus and former chair, Political Science Department, State University of New York (SUNY)/Fredonia until 2003, now lives in New York City. His research fields include African political economy, democratization in Africa, trade unions, and U.S. foreign policy. Since 1964 he has conducted field research regularly in West Africa, especially in Ghana and Nigeria, and in the Middle East. Dr. Kraus is coauthor/editor of *Transformed by Crisis: The Presidency of George W. Bush* (Palgrave/Macmillan, 2004), contributing a critique of the Bush government's foreign policy. Dr. Kraus has contributed to some twenty books, including *When Parties Fail, Labor and Unions in Asia and Africa, Ghana: Political Economy of Reform, Soldier and State in Africa, Socialism in the Third World, Industrial Relations in Africa, Africa's Agrarian Crisis, Coping with Africa's Food Crisis, Privatization and Investment in Sub-Saharan Africa, African Development Perspectives Yearbook 4, Ghana and the Ivory Coast, Political Economy of Foreign Policy in Ecowas States,* and *Africa Contemporary Survey, 1989-90.* He is also the author of twenty-plus articles that have been published in the *Journal of Modern African Studies, African Studies Review, Development and Change, Current History, Africa Report,* and *Labor, Capital and Society.* He has served as a consultant to the U.S. Department of State and on AID & USIA contracts on civil society and democratization in Ghana and Nigeria. Dr. Kraus is also a former associate editor/board member of the *Canadian Journal of African Studies.*

Emmanuel Akwetey is the executive director of the Institute of Democratic Governance, a think-tank in Accra, Ghana, through which he maintains regular links with civil society groups and research institutes in Africa to develop governance capabilities. He received his PhD in 1994 from the University of Stockholm with completion of his thesis, *Trade Unions and Democratization: Comparative Study of Zambia and Ghana.* Dr. Akwetey is the author of "Democratic Transition and Post-Colonial Labor Regimes in Zambia and Ghana," in Bjorn Beckman & L. M. Sachikonye, eds., *Labor Regimes and Liberalization* (2001). In Ghana Dr. Akwetey has worked as a research coordinator and public policy analyst on projects for major state and non-state organizations. He has also served as a consultant to the government of Ghana and several international development partners, including the UNDP, the World Bank, the Canadian International Development Agency, and Danida.

Gretchen Bauer is an associate professor in the Department of Political Science and International Relations at the University of Delaware. She is currently serving as associate dean for the Social Sciences and History in the College of Arts and

Sciences. She is the author of *Labor and Democracy in Namibia, 1971–1996* (1998); *Politics in Southern Africa: State and Society in Transition* (2005), with Scott D. Taylor; and *Women in African Parliaments* (2006), edited with Hannah E. Britton. She has also published in the *Journal of Southern African Studies* and the *Journal of Modern African Studies*. Dr. Bauer began her work and study in Africa as a Peace Corps volunteer in Kenya from1982 to 1983 and was a Ford Foundation intern in Nairobi in the summer of 1989. From 1991 to 1993 she was a visiting research fellow at the Namibia Institute for Social and Economic Research, and during 2002 she was a visiting researcher at the Institute for Public Policy Research in Windhoek, Namibia. Her current research focuses on women in national legislatures in east and southern Africa.

Geoffrey Bergen is currently country program coordinator for Kenya, Eritrea, and Somalia at the World Bank. Since joining that agency in 1993, he has held positions as head of development communications, country manager for Niger, and speechwriter to the president. Dr. Bergen earned his PhD in political science from UCLA in 1994. His dissertation was titled *Unions in Senegal: A Perspective on National Development in Africa*. Dr. Bergen also holds an MA in international relations from the Johns Hopkins School of Advanced International Studies (1985), and a BA in English from the University of California–Berkeley (1977). He was a Peace Corps volunteer in Niger (1977–79) and has worked for the U.S. Department of Labor.

Robert Charlick is a professor of political science and international relations at Cleveland State University. From 1991 to 1994 he was senior governance advisor to the African Bureau of the United States Agency for International Development (USAID). His areas of research specialty are the development of "civil society" as a political force, local organization and democratic development, particularly in West Africa, and conflict prevention and management. Dr. Charlick has participated in and directed studies on these subjects in more than twenty countries, and he has written extensively about rural development, cooperatives, unions, and student organizations in Africa, Asia, and the Caribbean. He is the author of *Niger: Personal Rule and Survival in the Sahel* (1991) and contributor to *The Political Economy of Foreign Policy in Ecowas, Democratie et developpement: Mirage ou espoir raisonable?* and *Transitions in Africa* (forthcoming). He also has published articles in such scholarly journals as *African Studies Review, Public Administration and Development, African Review, Corruption and Reform, Rural Africana*, and *Sociology of Education*. Most recently, Dr. Charlick has been working on the nature of Islamism in Africa and its relationship to global economic and political forces.

William Freund has recently retired as professor of economic history at the University of KwaZulu-Natal in South Africa, where he continues to teach part-time. A recent Festschrift in his honor, published by the journal *African Studies* (Johannesburg), outlines his career in the field. His PhD dissertation at Yale University concerned the last phase of Dutch rule at the Cape of South Africa at the start of the nineteenth century. His more recent interests include African political economy, development issues, labor, and urban history. He is the author of, among other titles, *The Making of Contemporary Africa* and *The African Worker*. Dr. Freund is the coeditor of *(D)urban Vortex: South African City in Transition*. His newest book, *The African City: A History*, was released in 2007 by Cambridge University Press. His 1984 article "Labor and Labor History in African Studies," in *African Studies Review* is a seminal survey of the field. Apart from his South African experience, he has taught in the past in Nigeria and Tanzania, and at Kirkland College and Harvard University in the United States. He is currently on the experts panel for Corus 2, the development-funding arm of the French foreign ministry.

Richard Saunders is an associate professor in the Department of Political Science at York University, Toronto. From 1986 to 2002 he lived and worked in Zimbabwe as a journalist and civil society researcher and strategist. He has worked closely with the Zimbabwe Congress of Trade Unions and other community-based organizations and civic networks active in the area of social and economic rights. His research and writing focus includes social unionism in southern Africa, media policy, democratization, and regional responses to post-apartheid South African capital flows into neighboring countries. Dr. Saunders is the author of *Dancing Out of Tune: A History of the Media in Zimbabwe* (1999) and *Never the Same Again: Zimbabwe's Growth Towards Democracy, 1980–2000* (2000). His forthcoming book (2007) is *Mediating Zimbabwe: The Press, Politics and Power*.

Index

other union federations, 215; strikes and
stay-aways, 209; Triple Alliance, 213,
219–21; union membership, 211–14,
225–27; unions since 1970s, 210–13
Convention démocratique et sociale (CDS) (Niger),
64, 65, 71, 72
Convention People's Party, 1949–66 (CPP), 89,
91, 97
Côte d'Ivoire, 2, 3, 19, 20, 66, 258, 268–72

De Klerk, F. W., 216, 217
Democratic Turnhalle Alliance, 245
democratization: causes, 9–10, 13–20; critique of
theory, 4–26; postdemocratic transition,
273–79; socioeconomic factors, 268–73;
stages 14–15; theory, union, 3–5, 10–16,
20–26, 85–88, 256–63, 266–68; theory,
working class, 16–18; trade union roles,
255–68
Diop, Cheikh Anta, 56
Diop, Madia, 47, 49, 51, 52, 55, 56
Diori, Hamani, 66
Diouf, Abdou, 35, 45–49, 52–56
District Councils of Labor (DCLs) (Ghana),
106–9, 112, 113, 115

Economic Structural Adjustment Program
(ESAP), 170–72, 174–78, 188
elite analysis/theory, 12–14, 15–18, 20, 21, 25,
26, 62, 85, 86, 189, 256
Employers Confederation of Zimbabwe, 186
Export Processing Zones, 241, 242, 248, 249,
281

Fall, Mamadou "Puritain," 43
Federation of Free Trade Unions of Zambia
(FFTUZ), 135, 140, 141, 143–51, 153, 265
Federation of South African Trade Unions (FOS-
ATU), 210–13, 226

General Transport, Petroleum, and Chemical
Workers Union (GTPCWU), viii, 90, 111
Ghana, 2, 3, 9, 15, 17, 19–21, 23–25, 28–29,
83–121, 257, 258, 260, 263–78, 280–82;
CDRs, 109, 110, 115; early union development, 88, 89; labor force, 89; union autonomy, 2, 84, 86–88, 94, 95, 104, 117; union
resistance to PNDC, 101–13; unions in 4th
Republic, 113–17; unions and CPP, 89–92;
unions and NLC, 92–94; unions and
PNDC, 93–113; unions and PNP, 97–99;
unions and PP, 94–95; unions and SMC and
SMCII, 95–97; WDCs, 87, 88, 99–104,
106–7
Ghana National Association of Teachers, 99, 109,
113, 265

Growth, Employment, and Redistribution
(GEAR) policy, 217

Highly Indebted Poor Countries (HIPC), 147,
148
Hikaumba, Leonard, 141, 144–45, 147–51
Human Development Index, 142

Industrial and Commercial Workers Union
(ICU) (Ghana), vii, 90, 98, 102–4, 107, 108,
110, 111, 115
Industrial and Commercial Workers Union
(ICU) (South Africa), 204, 226
Industrial Relations Act (Ghana), 91–92
Industrial Relations Act (Zambia), 127, 128
informal sector, 181, 188, 220, 247, 281, 283
Interim Management Committees, 101–4
International Confederation of Free Trade Union
(ICFTU), 9, 101, 134, 160, 262
International Labor Organization (ILO), 28, 88,
101, 102, 134
International Monetary Fund (IMF), 6–8, 12,
19, 67, 68, 75, 79, 89, 94, 95, 97, 98, 100,
103, 106–9, 111, 112, 114, 115, 129–31,
133, 136, 140–42, 144–47, 149, 153, 170,
255, 261, 263, 270, 277, 279, 280
Interprofessional Collective Bargaining
Agreement, 47
iron law of oligarchy, 24
Issifu, I. M., 96, 97, 100
Issoufou, Mahamadou, 69, 71, 72, 79

Jamela, Reuben, 159

Kalenga, Israel, 242
Kaunda, Kenneth, 1, 2, 15, 21, 129, 133–35,
148
Kemba, Walter, 243
Kountche, Seyni, 63, 64, 66–68, 75
Kueme Preko, 115
Kwame Nkrumah Revolutionary Guards
(KNRG), 109, 110, 112
Kwei, Amartey, 98, 100, 102

labor control strategies, 22, 26–28, 87, 88,
274–76
labor department (Ghana), 102, 106
Labor Relations Act (LRA) (Zimbabwe), 163–65,
175, 177, 214, 215, 218, 219
Laouali, Moutari, 70
Liato, Austin, 144, 145, 148
liberalization, 1–5, 7, 10–12, 14–16, 18, 22, 25,
26, 83–86, 129, 132–34, 136, 141, 142,
150, 153, 168, 170, 174, 255–57, 267, 271
Ligue démocratique, 43, 45, 46, 48–50, 52,
54–56